POLICING AND PRISONS IN THE MIDDLE EAST

Policing and Prisons in the Middle East

Formations of Coercion

Edited by
Laleh Khalili
and Jillian Schwedler

HURST & COMPANY, LONDON

First published in the United Kingdom in 2010 by
C. Hurst & Co. (Publishers) Ltd.,
41 Great Russell Street, London, WC1B 3PL

Printed in India

A Cataloguing-in-Publication data record for this book is available from the British Library.

ISBN: 978-1-84904-057-0 hardback
978-1-84904-058-7 paperback

This book is printed using paper from registered sustainable and managed sources.

www.hurstpub.co.uk

For Our Parents,
Khadijeh Tamaddon and Hedayat Khalili
and Marvin and Diana Schwedler

CONTENTS

ACKNOWLEDGEMENTS

First and foremost, we would like to thank our contributors, all of whom have been extraordinary intellectual interlocutors, and whose punctuality, patience, and hard work has made the job of editing this book a pleasure.

This volume emerged out of a series of conferences, and we are grateful to the Middle East Studies Association of the United States for holding the first of them. We also especially thank the Robert Schuman Centre for Advanced Studies at the European University Institute for generously holding our panel as part of their Eighth Mediterranean Research Meeting. Paul Amar, John Collins, Katharina Lenner, Esmail Nashif, Kent Schull, and Özge Serin presented their excellent research at the panels at MESA or the Mediterranean Meeting, but their contributions, for one reason or another, were regretfully not included here. We also would like to extend a special thanks to Dan Neep who went far beyond the call of duty at the Mediterranean Meeting and translated from French for us.

Lori Allen, Paul Amar, Jill Crystal, Khaled Fahmy, Adrienne LeBas, and Yezid Sayigh have read the Introduction, and given cogent suggestions and encouragement. We thank them, and apologise if some of their suggestions were not fully incorporated. We are also grateful to our very perceptive and generous anonymous referee whose suggestions were excellent and we have done our best to address them.

Laleh is grateful to John Chalcraft whose companionship, support, humour and saintly fortitude has carried her all these years, and is pleased that working on the grim stories of prisons and prisoners seems not to have affected the joyous laughter of her lovely daughter May or the serene and sunny disposition of her son Pablo whom she carried through the latter stages of working on this volume. Laleh also thanks her co-editor Jillian whose lively wit, intelligence and joie-de-vivre makes any joint project a pleasure. Jillian Schwedler wishes to thank Joel Sherman for his endless patience and support, and her beautiful little gentlemen, Jake and Nick Ronin, who have made her life richer and more joyous. Sam Fayyaz provided remarkable research assistance throughout this project. Jillian would also like to thank Laleh for a wonderful collaborative experience.

CONTRIBUTORS

Banu Bargu is Assistant Professor of Political Science at the New School for Social Research and the author of *Human Weapons: Sovereignty and Sacrifice in the Death Fast Movement of Turkey* (forthcoming). Her research focuses on how contemporary forms of political self-sacrifice, such as hunger strikes, suicide attacks, and self-immolation, shed light on theories of sovereignty, order/disorder, agency, and violence. She is currently working on her second manuscript on Machiavelli.

Biriz Berksoy is an Acting Assistant Professor of Political Science at the Department of International Relations, Istanbul University. She has publications in Turkish on the re-structuring and militarization of the police organization in Turkey, its altering tactics and sub-culture. She focuses mainly on the relation of these processes with the modifying state strategies devised for the reconstruction of the social order. Her areas of interest include penal policies (concerning particularly the police organizations), sociology of neo-liberalism, Marxist theory and contemporary social theory, politics of Turkey.

Sam Fayyaz is a doctoral candidate in the Department of Political Science at the University of Massachusetts Amherst. He is currently writing his dissertation, "Competing Governmentalities: The Subject and Power in Post-Revolutionary Iran."

Ilana Feldman is Assistant Professor of Anthropology and International Affairs at George Washington University. She is a cultural and historical anthropologist who works in the Middle East. Her primary research has been on Gaza during the periods of the British Mandate and Egyptian Administration, examining practices of government, humanitarianism, policing, and citizenship. Her book *Governing Gaza:*

Bureaucracy, Authority and the Work of Rule (1917–67) was published in 2008 by Duke University Press. She is currently engaged in research tracing the Palestinian experience in humanitarianism since 1948, exploring both how this dynamic has shaped Palestinian social and political life and how the Palestinian experience has influenced the broader post-war humanitarian regime.

Anthony Gorman has taught at universities in Australia, Egypt, at the School of Oriental and African Studies, University of London and is currently a Lecturer in Modern Middle Eastern History at the University of Edinburgh. He is the author of *Historians, State and Politics in Twentieth Century Egypt: Contesting the Nation* (Routledge Curzon, 2003), as well as a number of articles dealing with aspects of radical secular politics in Egypt. He is currently working on a monograph of the history of the Middle Eastern prison during the colonial period.

Sune Haugbolle is Assistant Professor in Arabic and Middle East Studies at the Department of Cross-cultural and Regional Studies, University of Copenhagen, author of *War and Memory in Lebanon* (Cambridge University Press, 2010), and editor of *The Politics of Violence, Truth and Reconciliation in the Arab Middle East* (Routledge, 2009).

Laleh Khalili is Senior Lecturer in Middle East Politics at the School of Oriental and African Studies, the author of *Heroes and Martyrs of Palestine; the Politics of National Commemoration* (Cambridge, 2007) and the editor of *Politics of the Modern Arab World* (Routledge, 2008). She is currently working on a genealogy of detention and incarceration practices in colonial counterinsurgencies.

Roberta Micallef is Visiting Assistant Professor in Modern Languages and Comparative Literature at Boston University. She is currently working on Muslim women's travel narratives. Her recent publications include: "Cultural Encounters in Turkish Children's Literature" in Stefan Helgesson (ed.), *Literary Interactions in the Modern World* (De Gruyter Press, 2006), "Turkish Women Write War" in Annika Rabo and Bo Utas (eds.), *The Role of the State in West Asian Cultures and Societies* (I.B. Tauris, 2005) and "Hatay Joins the Motherland" in Inga Brandell (ed.), *Borders Boundaries and Transgressions* (I.B. Tauris, 2005).

Daniel Neep is Lecturer in International and Middle East Studies in the Department of Politics, University of Exeter. His doctoral work, undertaken at the School of Oriental and African Studies, looks at space, insurgency and colonial state formation in Syria. His current research interests centre on militarism and authoritarian governmentality in Syria under the Ba'th. Publications include "The Limits of Discipline: The Government of Military Training in Syria from the French Mandate to Bashar al-Asad" in Yezid Sayigh (ed.), *The Military and the State in the Middle East: A New Problématique* (forthcoming).

Arzoo Osanloo is an anthropologist and Associate Professor of the Law, Societies, and Justice Program at the University of Washington, Seattle, Washington. Formerly an immigration and asylum/refugee attorney, she conducts research and teaches courses focusing on the intersection of law and culture, including human rights, refugee rights and identity, and women's rights in Muslim societies. Her geographical focus is on the Middle East, especially Iran. She has published in various journals, including American Ethnologist, Cultural Anthropology and Iranian Studies. Her book, *The Politics of Women's Rights in Iran* (2009), is published by Princeton University Press.

Nigel Parsons is a senior lecturer in Politics at Massey University in New Zealand, and the author of *The Politics of the Palestinian Authority: From Oslo to al-Aqsa* (Routledge, 2005). He specialises in Palestinian institutions. He is currently researching Israeli biopolitics through the policies of closure, colonisation and military violence in the West Bank and Gaza Strip, as well as associated institutional change within the PA and Fatah.

Sayres Rudy writes on social science, political philosophy, and conceptual analysis in the study of collective action. His publications on the statist rather than global causes of diverse Islamist ideologies and strategies include "Subjectivity, Political Evaluation, and Islamist Trajectories" in Birgit Schaebler and Leif Stenberg (eds.), *Globalization and the Muslim World* (Syracuse 2004) and "Pros and Cons: Americanism against Islamism in the 'War on Terror'" in *Muslim World* 97:1 (Jan 2007). Rudy has researched in Algeria, Egypt, Jordan, Palestine, Syria, Lebanon, and elsewhere. He has taught social theory, political philosophy and comparative politics at, principally, Harvard University and Amherst College.

Jillian Schwedler is Associate Professor in the Department of Political Science at the University of Massachusetts Amherst and Chair of the

Board of Directors of the Middle East Research and Information Project (MERIP), publishers of the quarterly Middle East Report. She is the author of *Faith in Moderation: Islamist Parties in Jordan and Yemen* (Cambridge, 2006), along with three edited volumes and numerous articles. Her current book project examines the political geography of protest in Jordan.

Staci Strobl is Assistant Professor in the Department of Law, Police Science and Criminal Justice Administration at John Jay College of Criminal Justice. Her areas of specialization are women in policing in the Arabian Gulf, comic book portrayals of crime in the United States and alternative dispute resolution. She was the recipient of a Fulbright grant to Bahrain where she completed an ethnographic study of policewomen. Earlier in her career, she worked as a U.S. Probation Officer and a crime journalist. Dr. Strobl completed her doctorate in Criminal Justice at the City University of New York's Graduate Center, received her MA in Criminal Justice at John Jay and her BA in Near Eastern Studies at Cornell University.

Ayşen Uysal is Associate Professor in Political Science at the Dokuz Eylül University in Turkey. She completed her doctorate in Paris I Panthéon-Sorbonne University in 2005. Her publications include "Organisation du maintien de l'ordre et répression policière en Turquie" in Donatella Della Porta & Olivier Fillieule (eds.), *Police et Manifestants: Maintien de l'ordre et gestion des conflits* (Presses de Sciences Po, 2006), "Maintien de l'ordre et risques liés aux manifestations de rue" in Gilles Dorronsoro (ed.), *La Turquie conteste. Etat sécuritaire et mobilisations politiques en Turquie* (CNRS Editions, 2005), and "Cosmopolites et enracinés" with Boris Gobille, in Isabelle Sommier and Eric Agrikoliansky (eds.), *Radiographie du mouvement altermondialiste* (la Dispute/SNEDIT, 2005). Uysal is currently working on political party networks.

INTRODUCTION

Laleh Khalili and *Jillian Schwedler*

The emergence of the modern nation-state in the Middle East—as elsewhere—has been accompanied by a concentration of coercive power within the body of the state and the bureaucratisation of instruments of governance. In many instances, these transformations have entailed the establishment of government agencies monitoring, governing, and reporting on various spheres of social and political life, codification of large bodies of laws and sometimes the bifurcation of secular and religious juridical system (with the latter becoming weakened), introduction of "modern" methods of education, an attempt at standardisation and bureaucratisation of many spheres of social interaction, and the constant process of production and reproduction of systems of discipline, surveillance, and intricate techniques of governmentality.

The making and maintenance of centralised state power has "required" the expansion and centralisation of coercive apparatuses of the state: the military, various police agencies, and internal security and surveillance forces. But these coercive apparatuses have also functioned as vehicles aimed at producing uniform subjects (and sometimes citizens) of the state, and as mechanisms for the construction and reproduction of internal and asymmetrical hierarchies of power. Although much has been written about the role of militaries in the making of the state (Tilly 1992 is only one of the most prominent and articulate in a vast body of literature), scholarship on policing has primarily occurred in the field of criminology, with focus on the technical aspects of this state function, and to a lesser extent in social movement theory, where studies analyze the dynamics of police-protester interactions. As for prisons, Foucault's seminal work (1977) has been as much a metaphorical diagnostic of modern power as it has a (much-critiqued) historical account of the emergence of modern prisons. His work has been extremely influential in scholarship on internal coercion, extending beyond the study of prisons to include all manner of security, surveillance, and state power. Some of the more deterministic narratives, inspired by Foucault and viewing the expanded and centralised coercive state apparatuses as the inevitable outcome of modernity, are at odds with the Gramscian perspective that posits the process of centralisation of state coercion as incomplete and a site of contention over the articulation of hegemony. Tensions between these two views animate much of the literature on prisons and policing in particular, and state power in general.

In the context of the modern Middle East (and perhaps beyond), the emergence of modern policing and prisons and their continued predominance in the politics of the region provides a useful lens through which the complexity of state power and the contours of popular contentious politics can be read. The continued impact of the colonial origins of much policing in many countries of the Middle East (such as in Egypt) and the post-independence emergence of policing in a number of others (e.g. in Jordan), the centrality of criminalisation of dissident politics there, the micro-practices of policing and incarceration, and the ambiguous boundaries between police and military are all topics which still require urgent investigation, and which this volume begins to approach. As important, existing literature on the prison as university, the makings of crime and criminality as social categories, and the strategies of contention and resistance in the face of police and prisons needs further bolstering by new research over different periods and across state boundaries in the region.

This volume is only an early step in exploring this rich field. As such, it neither attempts at comprehensiveness nor representativeness. Indeed, the varieties in the histories of policing and prisons and the diversity of the current politico-sociology of prisons and policing in the Middle East does not easily lend itself to a comprehensive or unified approach. However, we have hoped to address some of the critical and enduring themes in debates about the role of internal state coercion in the shaping of state power and its relationship with the public in the Middle East.

Theoretical Discussion of Prisons and Policing

A growing body of literature in disciplines as diverse as anthropology, criminology, sociology, psychology, political science, history, and cultural studies, to name just a few, interrogates the diverse technologies of state repression as exercised through penal discipline, punishment, political prisons, and policing dissent. Topics once relegated to separate literatures or disciplines—even within the field of criminology, the study of prisons was distinct from the study of policing—have in recent decades given way to integrative approaches (Feldman 1991; the journal *Punishment and Society*, established in 1999, engages the interrelations between crime, punishment, and socio-political power). Many of these new studies view policing, prisons, and other disciplinary techniques as part of a complex of state power that also includes the judiciary, schools, banking systems, and other sites where the ideal citizen is articulated and produced. Frequently historical and ethnographic in approach, much of the more recent scholarship also emphasizes the productive capacity of state repressive powers, with the conventional notion of policing and prisons as primarily reactive and corrective giving way to close examination of their roles in producing particular kinds of social and political order—indeed, producing particular kinds of citizens and subjectivities.

The literature on policing and prisons produced in the twentieth century has been overwhelmingly Western-centric in approach, at least within the mainstream literatures from criminology. This focus is beginning to change, however, as like studies of security and repression, scholars of prisons and policing alike must increasingly attend to the impact of the international security economy on domestic security practices in western as well as non-western contexts. States have long relied on the expertise of foreign firms and consultants in the construction of prisons and police forces. Colonial powers, for example, created repressive apparatuses in the colony based on the prison and policing systems at home, bringing experts to the colonies as well as training local peoples in the logics and rationales of the carceral system. Newly independent states likewise frequently rely on foreign expertise; the foreign aid packages granted by powerful industrialized states to smaller states often include the expertise as well as the material resources that make policing, surveillance, and incarceration possible. The United States, Great Britain, and Israel, for example, are among the states that frequently provide training to foreign policing agencies. And as policing and military forces have become increasingly privatized, the distinctions between domestic and foreign security agencies have become blurred (Kinsey 2007; Singer 2007).

Studies of Policing

Studies of the police are nearly as old as the first police units themselves. The first police force that would be recognizable to police units today was established in 1667 by King Louis XIV in France. The institution did not become common until nineteenth century, however, with the formation of the Glasgow Police, the London Marine Police, and the Prefecture of Police in Paris under Napoleon. The first policing agency to explicitly view the prevention of crime as part of its mandate was the London Metropolitan Police, which was established in 1829 ostensibly to deal with the bane of middle class citizenry, "crime and debauchery", but as part of a broader process of capitalist modernity and the order it required. The emergence of police was—in some senses—an outgrowth not only of the centralisation of state and the production of modern individualised "subjects", but also a result of activism by social reformers who saw a more lawfully institutionalised criminal justice system as bulwarks against arbitrary punishment and spectacles of torture and brutality. Early police studies emphasized the police's role in establishing and maintaining government power, and even included critiques that were to virtually disappear from the literature as police studies were subsumed under the larger rubric of criminology and other studies of crime and punishment.

Along with broader critiques of the power of the state, the literature on policing has evolved dramatically over recent decades (McCormick and Visano 1992). Until recently, most studies of policing were produced in the field of criminology, which views policing as a mechanism aimed at preventing, stopping, or apprehending criminals (Walker 1977). Mainstream criminology defines the primary job of the police as looking for and recognizing crimes, the definition of which is primarily established by legislative bodies and initially concentrated around property rights. In practice, of course, what constitutes a crime is always a moving target, subject to interpretation by policing agencies, lawyers, and judges, as well as public political debate. The orthodox stream within the field of criminology still continues to treat crime as an unproblematic category, and assumes that crimes can be explained primarily by differences among individuals. This approach is based on the underlying proposition that human behaviour is the product of the free choice of individuals, and thus understanding individual motivations is the means to understanding (and thus preventing) criminal activities. Reflecting the particular ideological discourses of their times, the now defunct biological criminology (which based the prediction of crime on "racial sciences") and the still prevalent ecological criminology (which saw specific locales such as slums or "Oriental alleyways" as the "breeding ground" for crime) have underwritten this liberal understanding of crime and policing. Behavioural forensics, which focuses on the minds and habits of "criminals," is the most dominant thread in criminology today.

Against this mainstream, the subfield of critical criminology emerged in the 1970s and drew on the insights of Marxist thought concerning structural factors and the exploitation of the powerless by capitalism. Critical criminology seeks to understand the connections between social, economic, and cultural structures, and particularly how socially constructed notions of race, class, and gender within those structures become central to the understanding of criminal practices and the various practices of justice and social control deployed (Lynch and Michalowski 2000; Garland 1993; 2002). Studies of the social construction of crime attend to the ways in which social inequality is a central dimension of how "crime" is defined and how punishment is exercised (Bayley 1969; 1985; Chevigny 1997; Katzenstein 1996; Ungar 2002). Police are viewed critically to the extent that they are seen to reproduce some of these categories through the ways in which they seek to maintain "order" and prevent "crimes" (Barkin 2008). Explicitly normative, critical criminology has strongly advocated police accountability and the abolition of prisons.

The study of American and European crime and punishment continues to be a burgeoning field, where a range of different debates attest to the depth and breadth of the study of policing and punishment (Pisciotta 1994; Rhodes 1998; Spierenburg 1991). These studies also transcend orthodox criminological concerns and increasingly investigate the historical and social context of emergence of the state's coercive bodies. They sometimes interrogate the field itself, critically examining its assumptions and conclusions, and attempt to contextualize it within larger social and political narratives (for the latter see especially the work of Loïc Wacquant).

Policing has also been a key object of study in the literatures on conflict and social movements. The field of conflict studies, for example, has tended to examine the role of the police in terms of whether or not police units act impartially in the midst of conflict situations, whether they exacerbate or deflate conflict over time, and their relations to various parties to a conflict. Studies of policing in Northern Ireland are exemplary in this respect: they focus on tactics and strategies, the legalities of movements, the role of police in exacerbating identity conflicts, community policing bodies, armed non-state militias, and various state actors (McEvoy and Newburn 2003; Heiberg, O'Leary, and Tirman 2008).

In the field of social movement theory, the study of policing has largely focused on the police's engagements with protesters as a component of interactions between state and non-state actors (Della Porta and Reiter 1998). In democracies, police are seen to not only protect property and otherwise prevent crimes, but to also insure the civil rights of protesters themselves (Meyer and Tarrow 1997; Earl and Soule 2006). But policing agencies in democracies and non-democracies alike also use a variety of police instruments to repress individuals and groups who, for reasons determined by state institutions and frequently in secret, are deemed too threatening to state power or public order (Earl 2003, Davenport 2007).

Like the study of prisons, recent critical work on policing has sought to shift the focus from spectacular instances of police engagement with non-state actors—e.g. the police beating protestors around the globe in 1968—to examinations of state power and the micro-techniques of its exercise. As Neocleous notes, the term "policing" that has found wide currency in Foucauldian studies of state power has seldom referred to actual police units and, in fact, is frequently left undefined (2000). "Policing" becomes almost a synonym for "disciplinary" practices, while the micro-practices of policing units themselves have received less direct attention. But Foucault-inspired studies have succeeded in refocusing studies about the exercise of state power from, for example, the ways the police maintain order and prevent crimes, to the productive capacity of power to fabricate order in part by defining and categorizing the population. Ever new surveillance techniques and apparatuses—marketed globally through invitation-only "security expositions"—allow for a population to be systematically searched for its "criminal" elements. In this sense, the police are a crucial means for the state to intervene in everyday life out of concern for the safety and well-being of the citizenry (Manning 1997; Neocleous 2000).

The Study of Prisons

Some form of prisons have existed for thousands of years, many of which were used not as a form of punishment but as a place to hold prisoners until physical punishment could be carried out. Modern prisons emerged in the nineteenth century, replacing dungeons during the same period that spectacular public punishments—e.g. beheadings and hangings, but also whipping, tarring, quartering, and various gruesome forms of corporal punishment—were beginning to disappear. The ideas of Jeremy Bentham came to fruition first in London, where his modern penitentiary sought to deprive inmates of certain personal rights as central to their punishment and to produce a particular conscience in the prisoner through meaningless, repetitive labour (Semple 1993). Like the scholarship on policing, the literature on prisons is vast and diverse, but the largest concentration of scholarship is still produced in the field of criminology, with its concentration on crime and punishment, law and order. Key debates focus on technologies: the best means of rehabilitation, the structure and organization of prisons, and how to administer the largest number of prisoners most efficiently—meaning by the fewest prison officers and with the least amount of violence. Prison growth has been enormous, with nearly ten million individuals imprisoned worldwide, a quarter of them in the United States. Indeed, the "prison industry" is a multi–billion dollar business that depends not only upon prison growth but on ever new technologies for administering prisons and surveilling and restraining prisoners (Dyer 2000).

Many scholars have deconstructed the orthodox criminology perspectives on prisons and its emphasis on the technological administration of prisons and the effectiveness of prisons in preventing future crimes. In parallel with its critique of orthodox views of policing, critical criminology argues that individualist understandings of criminal activity cannot explain why three-fourths of prisoners in the United States are people of colour (Currie 1998) or why the incarceration rate for African-Americans has increased while their crime rates have remained almost constant (Tonry 1995). Political policies such as the War on Drugs and three-strikes have increased incarceration rates and lengthened sentences without producing the promised reduction in crime in the United States. Undeniably, racism is reproduced through the narrative of law-abiding citizens threatened by the "reality" of black crime as evidence by incarceration statistics (Davis 2003; Marez 2004; Parenti 1999). In addition to racism, the crowdedness of prisons contributes directly to the idea of the "enemy within" (Duguid 2000), a frightening image that maps easily onto stereotypes of blacks and other people of colour, and, since the 11 September attacks, onto Arabs and Muslims (Gilmore 2007; Simon 2007). Indeed, both within and beyond the borders of the United States, the examination of political incarceration has become increasingly more urgent: the US "war on terror" has resulted in carceral practices that contravene international treaties and norms (Danner 2004; Hooks 2005; McClintock 2004), notably including rendition, the construction of prisons outside US borders, or outsourcing the torture of US detainees.

Theoretical examinations of incarceration always have to contend with Michel Foucault's *Discipline and Punish* (1978), which argues that with the advent of modernity, sovereign power, with its need for spectacular punishments, has given way to disciplinary power, which works through the routinisation of control over quotidian manners, bodies, and behaviours. What Foucault's work does uniquely well is to establish the relationship between state power and forms of incarceration, and elucidate the mechanisms through which a particular variety of state power results in the emergence of specific punitive measures in prisons. However, the fact that modernity has not necessarily put an end to spectacular punishments and torture brings Foucault's conclusions into question. European colonies, for example, relied heavily on spectacular punishments even as modern technologies of incarceration were exported there. Furthermore, Foucault's earlier works have a deterministic quality, attributing a final and irreversible concentration of coercive power in the body of the state, a conclusion that a more Gramscian dialectic challenges.

Alongside Foucault's works, other scholars have examined the ways in which the architecture of prisons, the modes of managements of inmates, and punitive technologies therein—e.g. solitary confinement—come to affect the prisoners' inner lives (Rothman 1990 [1971]; Ignatieff 1978). Prisons are viewed as a political response to hysteria about social disorder (Rothman 1971, 2002), where loneliness and silence are part and parcel of the punishment of being removed from normal social relations (Ignatieff 1978).

The study of torture in prisons has given rise to a separate but related body of literature (Maran 1989; Rejali 1994; 2008; Scarry 1984; Huggins et al 2002; Lazreg 2008). The varieties of discourses—focusing on "reform", "justice" or "punishment"—used to justify carceral power have been subjected to examination and critique (Ignatieff 1978; Howe 1994). The influence of prisons on the identities and sense of selfhood of inmates have been interrogated in texts examining prison memoirs, and in ethnographies and oral histories of prisoner resistance (Abrahamian 1999; Feldman 1991; Buntman 2003). A bibliography of memoirs and literary treatments of the experience of political prisoners would easily run to tens of pages and would include such illustrious names as Nelson Mandela, Malcolm X, Martin Luther King, Fyodor Dostoyevsky, Vaclav Havel, Franz Kafka, Alexander Solzhenitsyn, Nawwal al-Saadawi, Tahar ben Jalloun and Breyten Breytenbach just to name a few (see Davies 1990 and Harlow 1992 for a critical reading of prison writings). Critiques have also been generated from within the prison by current prisoners, originally through the circulation of prison newsletters, but increasingly also through internet sites. *Prison Legal News*, for example, reports on prison conditions and legal actions, with a web site that links to numerous other sites. Prisoner rights groups are also common in industrialized countries, though their activities, reports, and campaigns address prison conditions globally, and their work is often a source of primary materials for researchers.

Policing in the Middle East

When deployed by its military, the Middle Eastern states' monopoly over the use of political violence has been extensively analysed (e.g. Abdel-Malek 1968; Barnett 1992; Batatu 1981; Ben-Eliezer 1998; Fahmy 1997; Gongora 1997; Hale 1994; Heydemann 2000; Khuri 1982; Picard 1993a; Torrey 1963; Vatikiotis 1961; 1967; Zabih 1988). But although the region has encompassed numerous "*mukhabarat* [secret police] states", extensive and varied policing and carceral regimes, and widespread use of torture and spectacular punishments, and although the region's prisons and policing practices are regularly highlighted and criticised by human rights organisations, the literature systematically examining the emergence of *internal* coercive institutions within the Middle East has been surprisingly sparse.

As regards policing, with very few exceptions (Crystal 2001; 2005; Fahmy 1999a; 1999b; Strobl 2008; Tollefson 1999), most scholarly works are technical discussions of police organisation, rather than a contextualisation of the police and policing within broader political or sociological discussions. The same is more or less true of prisons, where most socio-political analyses are very recent (Gorman 2007; Peters 2002; 2004) or tend to be focused on political prisoners and torture (Abrahamian 1999; Harlow 1992; Nashif 2008; Rejali 1994).

In the Middle East, the centralisation of policing in the offices of the state, and its professionalization, are both relatively recent phenomena. Although both incarceration and some form of punitive "policing" (for example, to prevent theft and brigandage, or to ensure honesty in weighing and measurement in markets) have long existed in the Middle East, the modern police as a subsidiary institution in the Interior Ministry, with its reformative *as well as* punitive functions and its formal separation from military functions, primarily emerged in the nineteenth century (although in a number of the counties, these institutions did not appear until after independence in the post-Second World War period).

In pre-modern times, the *shurta* (the police) was charged with "enforcing proper conduct in public places, dispensing criminal justice, ... riot control in the cities, protection of villages against brigandage, checking the quality of the work of artisans and support for tax enforcement," as well as acting as nightwatchmen and bodyguards for the rulers (Nielsen and Marin 2005). By the time the Mamluks rose to power, the gradual decentralization of authority, and the "local urban quarters developing their local forms of collective defence and social discipline", the role of the *shurta* was much reduced (Nielsen and Marin 2005).

In both the Ottoman Empire and Persia under Safavid and Qajar rule, military and internally coercive institutions were inseparable at least until the early modern times. While in the former, janissary officers took on the task of ensuring order in Ottoman cities, in the latter (and especially under the Safavids), the *darugha* was a military officer whose duties included the management of nightwatchmen, as well as preventing "misdeeds, tyranny, brawls, and actions contrary to the *shari'a*, such as prostitution, drinking, and gambling" (Lambton 2005). Their mandate expanded in the eighteenth and nineteenth century to regulation of market prices and weighing and measurement standards, as well as the maintenance of order in public places.

With the establishment of the Constitutional regime in Iran in the early twentieth century, the *darugha*'s duties were assumed by the municipalities and the modern bureaucracies. The hiring of European consultants to aid the establishment of Iran's modern police forces began with the Austrian Count de Montfort who took over the administration of Tehran police under Nasir al-Din Shah in the mid-nineteenth century. The first nation-wide police force, the gendarmerie, was founded in 1911 under the umbrella of the Ministry of Interior, and Swedish officers were hired to manage it. It had a counterpart in the American Morgan Shuster's Treasury, which was primarily tasked with collecting taxes (Abrahamian 2008). The gendarmerie was intended to patrol the highways and roads and maintain order in the cities (Cronin 1996). The Swedish advisers also established a police college, a police hospital, and the first secret police in Iran (Rejali 1994: 57).

In 1922, the Swedish officers were in turn dismissed by Reza Shah, who folded the gendarmerie and the Cossack Brigades (which since the Soviet Revolution of 1917 had been controlled by the British) into the new army, had the Interior Ministry take charge of policing and appointed an Iranian to become the first chief of the state police (Aqeli N.D.; Abrahmian 2008: 63–71). French, and later German, officers acted as advisors on these major transformations, which established specific ministries and which created professionalised and specialist branches for the police, including "a national police; a rural gendarmerie; a railroad police; a customs police; the Amniyya, or 'Road Guard'; and the Red Lion and Sun Society, a mobile medical service attached to the Ministry of War," while the secret police changed its name to "the Intelligence Agency" (Rejali 1994: 57).

Until the first half of the nineteenth century, in the cities and towns of the Ottoman Empire, order-maintenance functions—along with firefighting and public security–were performed by janissary officers, whose duties were transferred to the *Ser'askar*, or the War Department in 1826 (Lewis N.D.). With the *Tanzimat* reforms, police duty was taken away from the *Ser'askar* in 1845, and French police regulations were translated and adapted for use by the new police institution in the Ottoman Metropole (Aydin 1997: 77). The ad hoc Ottoman Gendarmerie (*asakir-i–zabtiye*), first established in the 1840s, was institutionalised in 1879, becoming "the empire's principal internal security organization" (Özbek 2008). After the founding of the Ministries of Police and Justice in 1870 and 1879 respectively, the task of policing had become significantly bureaucratised and this process was completed in 1909, when the police was attached to the Ministry of Interior and its domain of control was expanded to the hinterland as well (Ergut 2000; Kırlı 2005; Kuran 2005; Özbek 2008). This transformation was a significant part of the modernization of the system of Ottoman rule and the emergence of a bureaucratic elite (Ahmad et al. 2005). The Ottoman system of policing was in effect not only in the metropole, but also in the Arab cities. For example, in late eighteenth and early nineteenth century Ottoman Algiers, the much praised Algiers police force maintained order in the marketplace and residential neighbourhoods (Hoexter N.D.).

In the provinces of the Ottoman Empire, the policing of rural areas, however, was not as centralised and organised an affair as the policing of cities had become. In the Arab *Mashriq*, the rural police force consisted of ragtag irregular militias of locals and other Ottoman subjects, sometimes hired out to the Sublime Porte by local mercenaries, who themselves had dubious relationships with the gangs and brigands they were supposed to police (Swanson 1972: 253–4). This force was fully reorganised under the French in 1929, and used extensively to repress popular dissent against the Mandatory powers (Ghazi 1999: 216–7). The lack of a centralised rural police force throughout the Ottoman Empire was perhaps most apparent in the Arabian Peninsula, where for example, the local tribal leaders maintained control of the hinterland, and this diffusion of power continued (especially in North Yemen), and has persisted up to the present, where state institutions have only the sparsest presence in the Yemeni hinterland (Nasr et al 2004: 6; Wedeen 2008: *passim*).

In those provinces of Ottoman Empire, however, where centralised politics was already well-formed, the situation of policing, and its eventual bureaucratisation is quite distinct. For example, in early nineteenth century Egypt, Muhammad Ali, established a police force which reported to a governor or commissioner, and whose area of operation—via commanding officers–reached beyond Cairo to different parts of Egypt (Ahmad et al. 2005). Khaled Fahmy has argued that via "the attempt to found a state 'of law and order' in Egypt", Muhammad Ali hoped to "entice Europe to support his bid for independence from the Ottoman Empire" (Fahmy 1999: 346). As such, the creation of modern bureaucratic and coercive apparatuses was intended to signal political readiness for rule. Another characteristic of this modern police force was the expansion of an elaborate web of surveillance and monitoring via state agents who included spies, sentries, and uniformed police soldiers (Fahmy 1999: 351).

To better underline the isomorphism of these institutions with their European counterparts, the subsequent Egyptian civil and criminal penal codes promulgated under Khedive Ismail in the latter half of the nineteenth century were modelled on European law. The ubiquitous presence of European advisors meant that both the founding regulatory documents and the practices of policing were influenced by the unequal relations between Egypt and its European rivals.

With the advent of British colonial rule, the character of Egyptian police and security forces were even further transformed to fit the model of colonial policing advocated throughout the British Empire (Anderson and Killingray 1991; 1992). This model gave the police a more militarised—rather than civilianised and locally-controlled–function and often developed its use as an instrument of control of political dissent far more than a "crime-fighting" institution. The British, as in many other colonial contexts, aimed to lower the cost of governance, while concurrently centralising state power. This, in effect, meant that the British colonial administration in Egypt favoured a militarised police, minimally trained and uniformed, over the more expensive professionalised civilian police force (Tollefson 1999). Furthermore, European officers were crucial to the operation, training and command of local police forces in Egypt. For example, in 1886, some 354 Europeans (primarily Italian, Austrian and British military officers) served in the Egyptian police, gendarmerie and prison administration (Ibid.: 41).

As in Egypt, though at a later period (1920s and 1930s), the British were instrumental in creating a semi–militarised police or internal security force in Iraq, Aden, the Persian Gulf emirates, and what later became Jordan. In Iraq, the emergence of the modern police was concurrent with the consolidation of a modern Iraqi army after "independence" but under the Anglo-Iraqi treaty. In Aden, the British founded the Aden Police in 1937, which was joined by "the Armed

Police, the Riot and Security Police and the Rural Police" in 1967, and developed at this later date with the aid of German advisors (Nasr et al 2004: 6).

The origins of the Jordanian police, on the other hand, lay in the Arab Legion, created by the British in 1921, "initially as a paramilitary force tasked primarily with internal order and protecting the regime" (Nasr et al 2004: 17). The police and the army were initially separated in 1956, and this separation was consolidated two years later. The underlying public security "concerns" which were transferred from the head of the army to the Interior Ministry were primarily the supervision of the Bedouins and the tribal courts. In a scathing evaluation of this transformation, Joseph Massad (2001: 58) writes, "It was thus that from 1958 until 1976, the Bedouins were no longer living under martial law with the army running their lives; rather they were now living under the constant surveillance of the police..."

In the early twentieth century, most Gulf rulers relied on mercenary forces drawn from slave or Bedouin populations who were bolstered by urban levy and allied tribal forces in times of crisis (Crystal 2005: 160). The consolidation of British power in the Gulf brought with it the establishment of a series of modern police forces drawn according to a single template. Despite the basic uniformity of this template, however, as Jill Crystal points out, the specific geopolitical/imperial concerns of the British dictated the shape and intensity of the public order apparatus. "Bahrain, for instance, developed a larger and more forceful police than its neighbours, in part because it played a more central administrative role for Britain. Kuwait, more peripheral and peaceful, required less direct policing. Qatar lay in between" (Crystal 2005: 159). Given their small indigenous populations and peculiar socioeconomic structures, the Gulf nations have had continued trouble recruiting local men to police service, which partially accounts for some of the Gulf emirates allowing women to join the police force, while others have relied on the *bidun* (or paper-less) populations for their police forces (Ayubi 1995: 286).

The importance of the predecessor colonial models is just as apparent in those Middle Eastern nations which had formed the colonial/mandatory domains of the French Empire. Morocco's police force, for example, is still based on the French model, and in its early years after the Moroccan independence, it included a substantial number of former colonial policemen. Its division into a Surete National (which polices urban areas) and a Royal Gendarmerie (in charge of the rural hinterland) is familiar from the French model (Nasr et al. 2004: 9–10). This same structure was followed in both Lebanon and Syria as well (Ibid.: 20–24), although in Ottoman Syria, prior to the Mandate, a police force, intertwined with the army as a singular *jund wa shurta* (army and police), had already been established in 1878 and further consolidated by 1888. Further, in Lebanon, order maintenance in Beirut was distinct from other cities (where the gendarmerie had control). In Syria circa 1906, even specialist police academies were established there (Ghazi 1999: 125–7), and while some policemen were trained in the police school, others were sent to Europe for training in forensic technology (Ghazi 1999: 129).

Both French and British colonial regimes, then, depended on a rural gendarmerie bolstered occasionally by irregular forces recruited locally (and as such central to the co-optation and monitoring of rural populations), an urban police force that dealt with both crime and urban protest, and a military whose frequent involvement in politics (even, perhaps especially, in the post-independence period) spoke of its "significant domestic policing responsibilities" (Crystal 2001: 471).

Perhaps the most striking progeny of the British colonial policing has been the Israeli police apparatus, modelled after the (in)famous Palestine Police, an oft-cited archetypical representative of all imperial policing. The Palestine Police—drawn largely from demobilised soldiers and the Royal Irish Constabulary and including a number of the notorious Black and Tan men—was to become a model of imperial policing and a source of British colonial officers in counterinsurgencies in Malaya, Kenya, Cyprus, or Aden in subsequent decades. In the 1930s, and especially with the advent of the Arab Revolt, the Palestine Police—which originally employed both Jews and Arabs—came to rely increasingly on Jewish recruits.

During the Arab Revolt (1936–1939), the Palestine Police also enlisted the help of Sir Charles Tegart of the British Imperial Police in Bengal, whose policing innovations in Palestine included the use of Doberman Pinscher dogs imported from South Africa in searches, wall-and-watch-tower complexes intended (mostly unsuccessfully) to prevent the movement of insurgents, collective punishment of entire villages and towns for the perceived transgression of one resident, and the establishment of Arab Investigation Centres "at which 'selected' police officers were to be trained in the gentle art of 'third degree', for use on Arabs until they 'spilled the beans', as it is termed in criminal circles" (Keith-Roach 1994: 191). These new methods were added to an already existing repressive repertoire of such methods as large-scale search-and-seizure operations which cordoned off entire villages or even cities, house destructions as punishment for a family member joining the rebels, and the use of civilian hostages as human shields (Duff 1953; Keith-Roach 1994; Pimlott 1988; Samuel 1957; Segev 1999; Tegart N.D.).

As a sympathetic proponent of the new Israeli state wrote, "the structure and methods of the police in Israel are those of the former Palestine Police, almost unchanged" (Samuel 1957: 32). Not only were these counterinsurgency techniques incorporated into the methods of the later Israeli security forces, but also the internal police organisation followed the colonial model by having distinct police forces—along a broad spectrum from community-based and civilian to repressive and militarised—for the Jewish and Palestinian peoples under the control of the Israeli state (Hovav and Amir 1979: 6), and more mundanely, even the Israeli police uniforms were, at least in their early years, "almost identical with the uniform of the British section of the Palestine Police and with those of the former Tel Aviv Divisional Police" (Samuel 1957: 33).

Most important among the continuities between the British colonial police force and Israeli policing of the Palestinians under its control (whether inside its borders before 1966 or in the Occupied Territories since 1967), however, have been the Israeli Administrative Detention Laws which were adopted wholesale from a predecessor colonial law enacted by the British during the Arab Revolt in 1937 (Rudolph 1994: 61). Indeed, wherever such colonial "emergency" laws existed, they were incorporated in the post-independence legal codes of the states (Harding and Hatchard 1993).

The travelling of the law and juridical structures from one place to the next is the other noteworthy characteristic of the system of crime and punishment in the Middle East. For example, the Qatari *'adliyya* (justice) system of courts "was clearly modelled after the Kuwaiti (in turn modelled on the Egyptian), with separate civil and criminal sections and an [sic] unified appeal court" (Brown 1997: 152), while Jordan's 1959 criminal code was adopted from the Syrian and Lebanese models, themselves borrowed from the French (Nasr et al 2004: 17). Egypt's 1901 prison law, passed under the aegis of the British, "retained much previous legislation, itself a mixture of the French and local penal codes" (Gorman 2007: 104). Today, in a number of other countries of the Middle East, a dual legal code (sometimes called legal pluralism) exists, some combination of statute law, constitution, and criminal code on the one hand, and broadly varying *Shari'a* law on the hand. While Saudi Arabia's legal system and criminal procedures are almost wholly *Shari'a*-based and secular law is only supplemental, in almost all other Middle Eastern countries, where the two might coexist, secular law prevails (Peters 2005: *passim*). Where law is codified, the residues of past processes of codification can often be found.

This borrowing and layering of codes, processes, and structures, and the continued influence of European and American powers on modes of policing—more recently, for example, on the founding of riot-control police in full protective gear–has resulted in broad similarities between different police forces of the Middle East. The police in most of the Middle East are engaged in the same sorts of activities as elsewhere—"drug control, vice/prostitution/shop regulation, gang conflicts, land/eviction/tax disputes, extortion from businesses, traffic, internal and external migration control, and, crucially, the production of informants for banal peri–legal social control and protection racket-functions."[1] However, the history of authoritarian control and occasional military rule (in most Arab nations as well as Iran) and occupation (in the case of Israel) has meant that the police forces of all Middle Eastern nations have had prominently repressive characters, and this repressive character has been the predominant subject of most studies (Aydin 1997; Crystal 2001; 2005; Hovav and Amir 1979; Nasr et al 2004; Picard 1993b; Rejali 1994). The *political* importance attached to policing as a counterinsurgency (or counter-terrorist, or anticommunist, and now anti–Islamist) force during the Cold War and since has meant that this repressive character has been only fortified from outside. Furthermore, the continued role of European and North American advisors and funding in the training of police forces in the Middle East (for example, most recently, of the Lebanese Internal Security Forces or of the Palestinian Authority's various police divisions) has contributed to the institutional isomorphism of the police. This isomorphism exists even when there is less direct training and funding, perhaps because of the emergence of global modes and norms

[1] From personal correspondence from Paul Amar, dated 13 February 2009. See also Amar 2010 forthcoming.

of policing, especially in the context of "counter-terrorism" and the perpetuation of internal order and "security" regimes.

Punishment and Prisons in the Middle East

In the nineteenth century, in most Middle Eastern countries where indigenous police institutions (rather than imported colonial ones) existed, the police were also in charge of the maintenance of prisons (e.g. Tollefson 1999: 85). Prisons, however, were not intended as reform institutions until late nineteenth century at the earliest.

In pre-modern times, although prisons were used for debtors, pre-trial detention, apostasy, and some political crimes, classical punishments for crimes were flogging, admonishment and banishment. In many places, citadels were used as prisons, which is why a number of older prisons throughout the Middle East are called "fort" or "palace" prisons (Eftekharzadeh 1998: 18–19).[2]

The governments of the time "could send to prison proven or alleged heretics, religious fanatics, charlatans and all those guilty of violating public order. Officials who failed to carry out their order were imprisoned. Judges who were not willing to serve could be put in jail" (Schneider 2005). Enemies of the ruler could be put in chains and condemned to hard labour (Schneider 2005; also see Peters 2005). In nineteenth century Iran, the punishments meted out for crimes included being placed in public stocks, or detained—for highly placed prisoners, at the houses of administrators or *ulama* (clerics); for more ordinary prisoners in dungeons—in anticipation of more common forms of punishment, corporal or exilic. At the time, Lord Curzon wrote of Iran that "there is no such thing as penal servitude for life, or even a term of years; hard labour is unknown as a sentence, and confinement for any period is rare" (quoted in Rejali 1994: 54). Indeed, spectacular public punishments were slowly set aside towards the end of the nineteenth century, and through the efforts of judicial reformers, by the late 1920s, a penal code modelled after Italy and Switzerland, and modern judicial structures and prisons had taken the place of public hangings and executions in Iran (Abrahamian 1999).

[2] See for example the al-Jalali Fort in Muscat, Fort Morbut Prison in Aden, or the Cairo Citadel which held prisoners until the 1960s. For this latter point, I am grateful to Charles Tripp.

By contrast, in late nineteenth-century Egypt (as in the rest of the Ottoman Empire), corporal punishment (flogging, for example) for petty crimes had given way to detention, while capital punishment, rare by the end of the century, was predominantly used in homicide cases (Peters 2002: 35; Peters 2005: 108–9). What is fascinating, however, is the extent to which the management and operation of prisons in Egypt at that time were haphazard and dictated by a wide range of interest and institutions. As Rudolph Peters shows, a prisoner could be transferred from the fortifications of Qanatir al-Khayriyya (for hard labour) to the Alexandria Dockyard prison, be conscripted into the military from the prison, or transferred to the Department of Industry, or the Alexandria Prison, for forced labour (Peters 2002: 34), while a penal colony in the Khargeh Oasis in the Western desert would receive detainees who had violated their terms of police supervision (Tollefson 1999: 146).

The conditions of these prisons were often terrible. One of the largest was the Liman (or arsenal) of Alexandria, built during the reign of Muhammad Ali, which housed "a variety of people who were banished from their habitual locales. At one point the Arsenal had between five and six thousand people... At one time an investigation had to be undertaken to determine why a large number of the prisoners were dying. Those interned at Liman, moreover, had little control over their bodies and the authorities could use them for whatever purpose they saw fit" including medical experiments with the plague in 1843 (Fahmy 1997: 136). Of the prison in Alexandretta was said that "if a prisoner was not liberated in 110 days death would liberate him", while the Mosul prison was described as "wretched, and filthy beyond conception" where "vermin of every description abounds" (quoted in Gorman 2007: 98). The prisoners in Tehran's Central Jail dreaded the cell blocks of the ground floor "because it was damp and dark", while Iran's provincial prisons "lacked such amenities as beds, showers, and proper toilets" (Abrahmian 1999: 25).[3]

Anthony Gorman's excellent survey of the emergence of prisons in the Egypt and Algeria (2007) shows the centrality of British and French colonial regimes in shaping the prison services of the countries

[3] Although as Yezid Sayigh has pointed out, given the exigencies of the time, the condition of military barracks or other state institutions would not be much different than those of the prisons (personal comments; 16 February 2009).

under their control in late nineteenth century. Those countries not colonised, Gorman shows, also borrowed and adapted regimes of prison management and construction from European nations in early twentieth century. The same impulses for reform which seemed to have driven the prison and policing movements in Europe also appear in the Middle Eastern context, with the diminishment in corporal punishment being one of the most apparent manifestations of this reformism. For example, the extensive and well-funded prison reform movement that emerged in the Ottoman Empire in the early decades of the twentieth century, not only took account of better hygiene and living conditions, but justified the reform in terms of "laws of civilisation" (Schull 2007). These reforms could be seen as experiments in nation-building performed in the laboratories of Ottoman prisons.

The first prison in the Middle East built along the European lines was the Lambese prison in Algeria, built in 1852 by the French colonial government; and its huge size allowed for the prison authorities to racially segregate the European and "native" prisoners. Indeed, a two-tiered legal system allowed for the detention of the native Algerians without trial, individually or collectively; and this was justified by claiming that the Muslim population had not yet reached the requisite level of civilization. Such segregation, however, was difficult to uphold in smaller prisons, or in women's prisons in Algeria (Gorman 2007: 116–118).

At the turn of the twentieth century, the Egyptian prison system consisted of the punitive convict prisons, holding those sentenced to penal servitude and hard labour for crimes such as murder, rape, or robbery; of central prisons found in regional centres and holding the majority of the prison population, including women and elderly men; and of local prisons which were used as pre-trial detention centres. Until the early years of twentieth century, the prisoners were obligated to feed themselves, at which point these tasks were transferred to the prison officials, and the cost of the prison-provided food was paid for by the forced labour of the prisoners (Gorman 2007: 105–7).

Penal labour existed in both Egypt and Algeria, in both places for extraction of economic value from the prisoners and generation of revenue. In Egypt, prisoners convicted of minor offences could reduce their sentences by performing *corveé* labour, and in fact, in its first year of operation in 1898, some forty thousand prisoners did so (Gorman 2007: 121). The Palestine Police also used political detainees arrested during the Arab Revolt for such forced labour.[4] The nascent Israeli state followed this tradition by forcing prisoners of war to build war trenches and fortifications (Sayigh 2007: 25).

In the 1920s, the governments of Reza Shah and Kemal Ataturk in Iran and Turkey began building "model" prisons, based on European models, many of which were completed decades later (Abrahamian 1999: 27; Gorman 2007: 123). In Kuwait of 1930s, "the Police were the criminal justice system: they investigated, convicted and sanctioned... *Shari'ah* corporal punishments were rarely imposed, although a secular beating often was. Prison was rarely used for either dissidents or deviants. Until the 1938 Majlis Movement, Kuwait had no formal prison, only a place in the palace that rarely held more than one prisoner. The preferred sanction was a fine" (Crystal 2005: 160–1). This was the case in much of the Arabian Peninsula, although historical research in this area is quite sparse.

We know for example that prison conditions were the subject of political organisation by Beiruti women (Thompson 2000: 97) or that the population of Damascus stormed the citadel on 20 July 1920 hoping to free a popular political reader and other political prisoners interned there by the Amir Faysal (Gelvin 1998: 2) but we have very little knowledge about the prisons themselves. We know about the writings of Palestinian prisoners (Harlow 1992), or their status in society after their release (Rosenfeld 2004), but less so about the huge transformations that the mass imprisonment of Palestinians (Cook et al 2004) since 1948, and especially since 1967 has wrought in the political process, structures, and struggles of Palestinians (Hajjar 2005 and a handful of others are exceptions). We know very little of the making and transformation of most prison systems in the Middle East, and the role they play in shaping the polity. Novels about prison experiences and prison memoirs are so abundant in both Arabic and Persian as to command their own particular literary genre, yet they are only rarely drawn on for historical, sociological or political or ethnographic studies.

We know much more about contemporary prison conditions because of the extent to which human rights groups such as Amnesty International or Human Rights Watch, and international NGOs and research think tanks have made it their business to collect witness statements,

[4] See for example, UK National Archives, CO 859/71/16.

and images of and statistics about these prisons. Often, the reports produced by these organisations become quite problematic when trying to reconcile international human rights laws with local interpretations of *Shari'a* law, all too frequently against a background of US or European military intervention cloaked in the discourse of human rights (An-Na'im 1990; 2008). Even when such military intervention is not preeminent, North-South inequalities of access to power and resources, and the prevalence of a neoliberal discourse of agency in the North, mean that the human rights discourse surrounding state coercion tends to place the onus for change on Northern INGOs and minimise the possibility or impact of oppositional popular mobilisation in the South (An-Na'im 2001). The strategies chosen by these INGOs and human rights organisations include "naming and shaming" and the production of reports and advocacy, and are themselves controversial and largely ineffective when their locus of operation is European or US metropoles, and their means of interaction are more about hectoring than creation of local constituencies for such human rights measures (Modirzadeh 2006).

No matter how incomplete they may be, the data collated by these INGOs show a surprising picture of the state of imprisonment in the Middle East. The statistics about imprisonment collected by the International Centre of Prison Studies at King's College London (see Table 1) shows that Israel has the largest prison population rate in the Middle East (326 per 100,000 of population), followed by Tunisia (263), United Arab Emirates (238) and Iran (222). Neither however matches the US, which imprisons some 756 persons per 100,000 of its population. The statistics, however startling, do not tell us about the particular socioeconomic condition, legal contexts, and political processes that result in the extent of incarceration in those countries. Most likely, Palestinians held prisoner for struggling against the occupation make up the bulk of Israeli prisoners, while the fact that some 92 per cent of prisoners in the Emirates are foreign (and presumably migrant labourers), might indicate the racialisation of the juridical system and the inscription of ethnic hierarchies in law, where a significant segment of the population is criminalised on the basis of their inability to cloak themselves in the mantle of citizenship. Given the authoritarian nature of Tunisia and Iran, it is much more difficult to gauge whether the prisoners there are political or criminal.

Indeed, drawing a clear boundary between political and criminal prisoners is itself problematic. Criminalising armed struggle in a counterinsurgency, for example, would increase the number of "criminal" prisoners, where in fact, those prisoners would consider themselves political. Beyond such conceptual confusions, "crime" itself is a political category, over-determined by the constantly changing mores and norms (for example, in post-Revolutionary Iran, bearing certain physical markers such as women's "Westernised" clothing or men's long hair-styles can land a person in prison), by the particular socioeconomic conditions (such as imprisonment for debts, now abolished in most of the world), and by the definition of politics of itself (e.g. where the boundaries of "private" and "public" are drawn).

A future agenda of research on policing and prisons in the Middle East will have to include a more substantial examination of the colonial role of military and police; the making of "crime" as a social and political category; the birth and transformation of modern prisons and policing; the role of spectacular punishments; the seeming inseparability of police and military in the Middle East; the process by which the police became professionalised, bureaucratised and standardised; the transmission of penal codes and practices across national boundaries; the mutual constitution of this apparatus of coercion and the body of the state itself; and the deep and abiding legacies of colonial policing and prisons. Much more can be written about the politics of prisons and policing in the Middle East, and this edited volume hopes to be an opening gesture, an invitation to researching this difficult and important subject.

Outline of the Book

We have organized the contributions to this volume into three sections that aim to draw out themes that interrelate in the study of policing and prisons, rather than divide the chapters according to whether they deal with policing or with prisons. Most of the chapters could have fit easily into more than one of the thematic sections, so their placement reflects our intention not to compartmentalize and classify the chapters but to place them into explicit dialogue with one another.

In all these articles, Foucault is a ghostly presence, not only in his articulation of carcerality, but also in the ways in which he envisioned the modern transformations of power from sovereign ("power over life and death") to disciplinary and biopolitical. Whether or not he is invoked explicitly, his arguments hover over the authors' understanding of policing and prisons, even if to be challenged by the richly theoretical and innovatively grounded and concrete understandings of how power and resistance are made in the moment of encounter between the police or carceral systems and the public.

The contributions to Part I, "Coercion from Colonialism to Neoliberalism", draw attention to the variety of coercive practices that have marked the region from the early twentieth century to the present and engage and critique—perhaps most directly–Foucault's aforementioned teleology of transformation of power. In his account of how the French mandatory powers policed the desert and transformed the Syrian Bedouin population, Dan Neep argues that the analytic dichotomy between consent and coercion too often elides the fact that consent in colonial instances can be acquired by force, rather than through acquiescence. In this, Neep also challenges Foucault's contention that modern states only use disciplinary powers by showing that the very same states that used these techniques of governmentality in the metropole, deployed naked coercion in their colonial holdings. However, Neep also incorporates Foucault's insight that power can be productive by showing the ways in which the social engineering of the French Mandatory powers made desert spaces into "territories" and Bedouin into the subjects of the state.

Nigel Parsons' examination of the regime of coercion and control in the settler colonial configuration of the Israeli state similarly shows the difficulty of bracketing disciplinary power from violence and coercion. He shows how biopolitical means—techniques intended to create and control populations *in toto*—are deployed by the Israeli state, and the manner in which it easily deploys violence and sovereign power (defined in the Foucauldian sense as the power over life and death) when its proxies in the Palestinian Authority do not fulfil their obligation to Israel to discipline and control Palestinian dissent in the Occupied Territories.

This use of proxies is the thread that connects Parsons' account to Khalili's. Khalili is concerned about the ways in which the United States deploys proxies—in this instance, private firms—in its operation of Abu Ghraib prison. In her argument, the state is not bound and autonomous, but inevitably overlapping with market firms, allowing for this parastatal complex's deployment of coercion to be more diffuse, and therefore difficult to counter through targeted resistance. In a sense then, even without Foucault being invoked, Khalili shows the diffuseness of power, even when this power is so coercive as to not easily fit the disciplinary model.

In writing about the continuities between the colonial French regime in Algeria and the neoliberal market-state in the 1990s Algeria, Sayres Rudy shows the porosity of both temporal and conceptual boundaries of the neoliberal state and the manner in which carcerality, deployed through spectacular internment camps, has become a technique of coercion intended to suppress dissent against both colonial economic exploitation and neoliberal inequalities. In Rudy's account, Foucault is then critiqued for his much too deterministic account of progression of power.

Whereas sovereign power over life and death shapes the relationships of the French with Syrians and Algerians, the US with Iraqis, and Israelis with Palestinians, Bahrain's police shows the suppleness and resilience of disciplinary power when deployed by a colonial state. In this instance, through a reading of the history of policewomen in Bahrain, Staci Strobl shows that British colonial powers put into place policewomen in order to reinforce local "custom" in so far as it bolstered their rule. These same policewomen are ironically considered relevant by post-Independence Islamists who see them as possible guardian of an "authentic" tradition, and of Bahraini "custom." In this sense, the continuity between colonial and postcolonial regimes is maintained in the particular forms of policing, even if legitimating narratives have been transformed.

The suppleness of the modern state is also on display in Biriz Berksoy's article on the Turkish police and their construction of "citizens" and "enemies." In her study of the re-structuring of the police organization in Turkey following the 1980 military coup, Berksoy shows the productive power of policing in creating political subjects—again, an implicit engagement with Foucault's notions of productivity of state power. Berksoy looks at the routinization of the police even as it becomes more militarized. In a sense, rather than *maintaining* order, the Turkish police are now engaged in projects of *creating* order through such techniques as dramatically increased surveillance capacity, including the installation of electronic cameras on the streets. The neoliberal regimes of coercion both Berksoy and Strobl write about, then, resonate with echoes of colonial techniques of rule, while showing the particular ruptures that have occurred in more recent times.

The second section of the volume, "Constituting States and Citizens," is concerned with the manner in which prisons and policing are both reflections of the dynamic power of the state in its encounter with the citizens as well as a constitutive part of the state imaginary itself and a maker of citizens and subjectivities.

Anthony Gorman's chapter, for example, examines the various techniques of coercion used by the Egyptian state before 1952, arguing that as state capacity in Egypt increased, so did its coercive capabilities. Borrowing from the colonial state and innovating carceral forms, the indigenous elite criminalised political dissent, expanding prisons and bolstering the apparatuses of confinement. Gorman, however, also shows the unintended consequences of the broad carceral powers of the state. Throughout the political prisons and camps, political subjectivities evolved and expanded, ironically producing an outcome antithetical to the objectives of political incarceration.

Like Gorman, Feldman is interested with the coercive capabilities of the Egyptian state, but in Gaza between 1948 and 1967. Feldman, invoking Foucault, shows the productive power of policing instantiated through fine-grained bureaucratic practice. Feldman shows that the production of often-mundane, seemingly "useless" daily reports by the police in fact worked to create hegemonic state narratives and political subjecthoods. Challenging Foucault, however, Feldman also shows that the biopolitical power of the Egyptian state here did not necessarily operate on the basis of precise measurement, categorization, and statistical accuracy, but quite the opposite. By espousing a policy of vagueness, the Egyptian state in Gaza shored up its power through ambiguity, arbitrariness, and uncertainty.

The articles by Ayşen Usyal and Roberta Micallef—both about Turkey, the former on the process of police training and socialisation in dealing with dissent, the latter about the discourses of gender channelled through women prisoners' memoirs—also show the technologies of power deployed in state coercion which at once aim to control and "make" citizens and dissidents. Usyal shows in great detail how the training of the Turkish police adopts a coercive sociology which imagines dissent as a kind of mob deviance, meant to be tamed, controlled, and in the last instance, quashed. Micallef reflects on the gendering of dissident bodies, and the use of women-specific forms of repression which produce certain kinds of gendered political subjects. Ironically, Micallef also shows that oppositional discourses deployed by male dissidents do not trouble the state's gendered hierarchies. In both instances, a kind of biopolitical technology is in operation, where bodies are construed as deviant, or as devalued, and as such made more vulnerable to control and domination.

The final section of the volume focuses on the "Refusals, Resistances, and Protests" that emerge in carceral and policed spaces and which challenge or are co-opted by the coercive apparatus of the state. Here, our contributors examine a broad spectrum of forms of resistance, whether it is hunger strikes, refusal of recognition of the authority of the state, prison protests, or resistance to interrogations.

Sune Haugbolle draws on prison literature by prisoners of the Syrian regime respectively, to examine the implications of incarceration for the subjectivity of the prisoners. Haugbolle shows the paradoxical effects of prison dissent: the heroic figure of the prisoner comes to be articulated as an individual liberal self counterposed against collectivist tropes of Arab nationhood. These heroic figures who would not necessarily consider themselves to be harbingers of a Eurocentric subjectivity, nevertheless reproduce its central characteristics of liberal bounded individuality. Banu Bargu's moving ethnography of the Turkish death fast movement also challenges Foucault. If for Foucault, power was so diffuse that all resistance was already always embedded therein, Bargu shows that in fact a pin-pointed targeted resistance against the new carceral disciplinarity of a Turkish regime is not only possible but also already happening in Turkish prisons. The Communist prisoners who were engaged in hunger strikes to the death were in fact not only challenging the panopticon-like systems of prison surveillance (implemented through EU-compliant H-block-like prison architecture), but also, by framing their resistance as class war, struggling against neoliberalism.

Like the hunger strikers in Turkish prisons, the Iranian dissidents Arzoo Osanloo writes about also seek a pure martyrdom as a way of challenging sovereign regimes. In this instance, two dissident intellectuals condemned to death refuse to seek mercy from the state. Osanloo shows that the state's demand that the condemned ask for mercy is in a sense the means by which the state mandates that its legitimacy be recognised. Refusing to plea for mercy is how the prisoners disrupt the state's sovereign power by refusing to recognise its power over their life and death. Interestingly, Osanloo also draws a parallel between the Iranian plea for mercy and the pardons requested by and granted to prisoners in the United States and shows that although some performative elements of the Iranian plea for mercy may seem unfamiliar or

Other, the practice itself is nevertheless analogous to other instances where juridical pardon reinscribes the state's sovereign authority.

Finally, Jillian Schwedler and Sam Fayyaz examine protests in Jordan in opposition to the invasion by Israeli troops of Palestinian cities and towns. The chapter recounts two forms of protest: popular demonstrations organised from below, and "peaceful" protests managed by the state and attended and led by the Queen herself. This cooptation of popular protest speaks of the profound suppleness of modern liberal states in which protests are absorbed and formalized in law and thus stripped of their disruptive capability.

Ultimately, the contributions in this volume engage in an empirically grounded and theoretically innovative manner with the broader interdisciplinary scholarship on prisons and policing. Like Foucault in *Discipline and Punish*, their articles not only examine policing and prisons *qua* specific technologies of state coercion, but also as a more expansive diagnostics of power, all the while challenging an implicit teleology which sees sovereign power replaced by disciplinary power. Like Gramsci they view the transformation of state power into disciplinary modes of control as incomplete and with great sympathy and analytic rigour show how in resisting state coercion, citizen and dissident selves are forged.

Bibliography

Abdel-Malek, Anouar. 1968. *Egypt, Military Society: The Army Regime, the Left, and Social Change Under Nasser*. Trans. Charles Lam Markmann. New York: Random House.

Abrahamian, Ervand. 1999. *Tortured Confessions: Prisons and Public Recantations in Iran*. Berkeley: University of California Press.

Ahmad, F. et al. 2005. "Hukūma" in Peri J. Bearman et al (eds.) *Encyclopaedia of Islam, Second Edition*. Leiden: Brill.

Al Shaali, Khalifa Rashid and Neil Kibble. 2000. "Policing and Police Accountability in the UAE: The Case for Reform" in *Arab Law Quarterly* 15(3): 272–303.

Alshahrani, Mohammed A. 2005. *Police Powers, Legal Rights and Pre-trial Procedures in Saudi Arabia: A Comparison With England and Wales*. Hull: University of Hull.

Amin, S.H. 1985. *Middle East Legal Systems*. Glasgow: Royston limited.

Amar, Paul. Forthcoming. *The Security Archipelago: Police Militarization, Urban Sexual Outlaws, and the End of Neoliberalism*. Durham: Duke University Press.

Amin, S.H. 1991. *The Legal System of Kuwait*. Glasgow: Royston limited.
Anderson, David M. and David Killingray (eds.) 1991. *Policing the Empire: Government, Authority and Control 1830–1940*. Manchester: Manchester University Press.
Anderson, David M. and David Killingray (ed.). 1992. *Policing and Decolonisation: Politics, Nationalism and the Police, 1917–65*. Manchester: Manchester University Press.
Aqeli, Baqer. N.D. "Daraghi, Mohammad" in Ehsan Yarshater et al (eds.) *Encyclopaedia Iranica*. New York: Routldge and Kegan Paul. http://www.iranica.com.
Asad, Talal. 1997. "On Torture, or Cruel, Inhuman, and Degrading Treatment" in Arthur Kleinman et al (eds.), *Social Suffering*. Berkeley: University of California Press.
Aydin, Ahmet H. 1997. *Police Organisation and Legitimacy: Case Studies of England, Wales and Turkey*. Aldershot: Avebury.
Ayubi, Nazih N. 1995. *Over-stating the Arab State: Politics and Society in the Middle East*. London: I.B. Tauris.
Barkin, Steven. 2008. *Criminology: A Sociological Understanding*, fourth ed. New York: Prentice Hall.
Barnett, Michael N. 1992. *Confronting the Costs of War: Military Power, State, and Society in Egypt and Israel*. Princeton: Princeton University Press.
Batatu, Hanna. 1981. "Some Observations on the Social Roots of Syria's Ruling, Military Group and the Causes for Its Dominance" in *Middle East Journal* 35(3): 331–344.
Bayley, David. 1969. *The Police and Political Development in India*. Princeton: Princeton University Press.
Bayley, David. 1985. *Patterns of Policing*. New Brunswick, N.J.: Rutgers University Press.
Bell, Jeannine. 2004. "The Police and Policing" in Austin Sarat (ed.) *The Blackwell Companion to Law and Society*. Oxford: Blackwell Publishers; 131–145.
Ben-Eliezer, Uri. 1998. *The Making of Israeli Militarism*. Bloomington: Indiana University Press.
Bornstein, Avram. 2001. "Ethnography and the Politics of Prisoners in Palestine-Israel" in *Journal of Contemporary Ethnography* 30(5): 546–575.
Brown, Nathan. 1997. *The Rule of Law in the Arab World: Courts in Egypt and the Gulf*. Cambridge: Cambridge University Press.
Buck, Marilyn. 2000. "Prisons, social control, and political prisoners" in *Social Justice* 27(3): 25–9.
Buntman, Fran Lisa. 2003. *Robben Island and Prisoner Resistance to Apartheid*. Cambridge: Cambridge University Press.
Chevigny, Paul. 1997. *Edge of the Knife: Police Violence in the Americas*. New York: New Press.
Cook, Catherine, Adam Hanieh, and Adah Kay. 2004. *Stolen Youth: The Politics of Israel's Detention of Palestinian Children*. London: Pluto Press.

Cooper, Frederick. 2005. *Colonialism in Question: Theory, Knowledge, History*. Berkeley: University of California Press.

Crelinsten, Ronald D. and Alex P. Schmid. 1995. *The Politics of Pain: Torturers and Their Masters*. Boulder, Colorado: Westview Press.

Cronin, Stephanie. 1996. "An Experiment in Military Modernization: Constitutionalism, Political Reform and the Iranian Gendarmerie, 1910–21" in *Middle Eastern Studies* 32(3): 106–138.

Crystal, Jill. 2001. "Criminal Justice in the Middle East" in *Journal of Criminal Justice* 29: 469–482.

Crystal, Jill. 2002. "The Saudi Legal System" in Herbert Kritzer (ed.) *Legal Systems of the World: a Political, Social, and Cultural Encyclopedia*. Santa Barbara: ABC-CLIO.

Crystal, Jill. 2005. "Public Order and Authority: Policing Kuwait" in James Piscatori and Paul Dresch (eds.) *Monarchies and Nations: Globalisation and Identity in the Arab States of the Gulf*. London: I.B. Tauris; 158–181.

Currie, Elliott. 1998. *Crime and Punishment in America: Why the Solutions to America's Most Stubborn Social Crisis Have Not Worked and What Will*. New York: Henry Holt.

Danner, Mark. 2004. *Torture and Truth: America, Abu Ghraib, and the War on Terror*. New York: New York Review of Books.

Davenport, Christian. 2007. *State Repression and the Domestic Democratic Peace*. New York: Cambridge University Press.

Davies, Ioan. 1990. *Writers in Prison*. New York: Blackwell.

Davis, Angela. 2003. *Are Prisons Obsolete?* New York: Seven Stories Press.

Della Porta, Donatella, and Herbert Reiter, eds. 1998. *Policing Protest: The Control of Mass Demonstrations in Western Democracies*. Minneapolis: University of Minnesota Press.

Duff, Douglas V. 1953. *Bailing with a Teaspoon*. London: John Long Ltd.

Dyer, Joel. 2000. *Perpetual Prisoner Machine: How America Profits from Prisons*. New York: Basic Books.

Earl, Jennifer and Sarah A. Soule. 2006. "Seeing Blue: A Police-Centered Explanation of Protest Policing" in *Mobilization* 11(2): 145–164.

Earl, Jennifer. 2003. "Tanks, Tear Gas and Taxes: Toward a Theory of Movement Repression" in *Sociological Theory* 21: 44–68.

Eftekharzadeh, Yahya. 1998. *Nazmiyyeh dar dawreh Pahlavi*. Tehran: Ashkan Publishers.

Ergut, Ferdan. 2000. *State and Social Control: The Police in the Late Ottoman Empire and the Early Republican Turkey, 1839–1939*. New School for Social Research: PhD dissertation.

Ettehadieh, Mansoureh. 2008. "Crime, Security, and Insecurity: Socio-Political Conditions of Iran, 1875–1924" in Roxane Farmanfarmaian (ed.) *War and Peace in Qajar Persia: Implications Past and Present*. London: Routledge.

Fahmy, Khaled. 1997. *All the Pasha's Men: Mehmed Ali, his army and the making of modern Egypt*. Cambridge: Cambridge University Press.

Fahmy, Khaled. 1999a. "The Anatomy of Justice: Forensic Medicine and Criminal Law in Nineteenth-Century Egypt" in *Islamic Law and Society* 6(2): 224–271.

Fahmy, Khaled. 1999b. "The Police and the People in Nineteenth-Century Egypt" in *Die Welt des Islams* 39 (3): 340–377.

Fahmy, Khalid and Rudolph Peters. 1999. "The Legal History of Ottoman Egypt: Introduction" in *Islamic Law and Society* 6(2): 129–135.

Feldman, Allen. 1991. *Formations of Violence: The Narrative of the Body and Political Terror in Northern Ireland.* Chicago: University of Chicago Press.

Finzsch, Norbert and Robert Jutte (eds.). 1996. *Institutions of Confinement: Hospitals, Asylums, and Prisons in Western Europe and North America, 1500–1950.* Cambridge: Cambridge University Press. Foucault, Michel. 1977. *Discipline and Punish: The Birth of the Prison.* Trans. Alan Sheridan. New York: Vintage Books.

Fitzgerald, Mike Gregor McLennon and Jennie Pawson (eds.). 1981. *Crime and Society: Readings in History and Theory.* London: Routledge & Kegan Paul in association with Open University Press.

Garland, David. 1993. *Punishment and Modern Society: A Study in Social Theory.* Chicago: University of Chicago Press.

Garland, David. 2002. *The Culture of Control: Crime and Social Order in Contemporary Society.* Oxford: Oxford University Press.

Gelvin, James L. 1998. *Divided Loyalties: Nationalism and Mass Politics in Syria at the Close of Empire.* Berkeley: University of California Press.

Ghazi, Ibrahim. 1999. *Nash'at al Shurta wa Tarikhuha fi Suriya.* Damascus: Dar al-Ilm al-Hadith.

Gilmore, Ruth. 2007. *Golden Gulag: Prisons, Surplus, Crisis, and Opposition in Globalizing California.* Berkeley: University of California Press.

Gongora, Thierry. 1997. "War-making and State Power in the Contemporary Middle East" in the *International Journal of Middle East Studies* 29(3): 323–340.

Gorman, Anthony. 2007. "Regulation, Reform and Resistance in the Middle Eastern Prison" in Frank Dikötter and Ian Brown (eds.) *Cultures of Confinement: A History of the Prison in Africa, Asia and Latin America.* London: Hurst & Co.; 95–146.

Haas, Kenneth and Geoffrey Alpert (eds.). 1995. *The Dilemmas of Corrections: Contemporary Readings.* Prospect Heights, IL: Waveland Press, 1995.

Hajjar, Lisa. 2005. *Courting Conflict: The Israeli Military Court System in the West Bank and Gaza.* Berkeley: University of California Press.

Hale, William M. 1994. *Turkish politics and the military.* London: Routledge.

Harding, Andrew and John Hatchard (eds.). 1993. *Preventive Detention and Security Law: A Comparative Survey.* Dordrech: Martinus Nijhoff Publishers.

Harlow, Barbara. 1992. *Barred: Women, Writing, and Political Detention.* Hanover: Wesleyan University Press.

Heiberg, Marianne, Brendan O'Leary, and John Tirman, (eds.) 2008. *Terror, Insurgency, and the State: Ending Protracted Conflict*. Philadelphia: University of Pennsylvania Press.

Heyd, Uriel. 1973. *Studies in Old Ottoman Criminal Law*. Oxford: Clarendon Press.

Heydemann, Steven (ed.). 2000. *War, Institutions, and Social Change in the Middle East*. Berkeley: University of California Press.

Hindess, Barry. 1996. *Discourses of Power: from Hobbes to Foucault*. Oxford: Blackwell Publishers.

Hoexter, M. N.D. "Algiers" in Gudrun Krämer et al. (eds.). *Encyclopaedia of Islam, THREE*. Leiden: Brill. http://www.brillonline.nl

Hooks, Gregory. 2005. "Outrages Against Personal Dignity: Rationalizing Abuse and Torture in the War on Terror" in *Social Forces* 83(4): 1627–1645.

Hovav, Meir and Menachem Amir. 1979. "Israel Police: History and Analysis" in *Police Studies* 2(2): 5–31.

Howe, Adrian. 1990. *Punish and Critique: Towards a Feminist Analysis of Penality*. London: Routledge.

Huggins, Martha K., Mika Haritos-Fatouros, and Philip G. Zimbardo. 2002. *Violence Workers: Police Torturers and Murderers Reconstruct Brazilian Atrocities*. Berkeley: University of California Press.

Ignatieff, Michael. 1978. *A Just Measure of Pain: The Penitentiary in the Industrial Revolution 1750–1850*. London: Macmillan.

Jacobs, James B. 1978. *Stateville: The Penitentiary in Mass Society*. Chicago: University of Chicago Press.

Katzenstein, Peter J. 1996. *Cultural Norms and National Security: Police and Military in Postwar Japan*. Ithaca: Cornell University Press.

Keenan, Brian. 1993. *An Evil Cradling*. New York: Vintage.

Keith-Roach, Edward. 1994. *Pasha of Jerusalem: Memoirs of a District Commissioner under the British Mandate*. London: The Radcliffe Press.

Khuri, Fuad. 1982. "The Study of Civil-Military Relations in Modernizing Societies in the Middle East: A Critical Assessment" in R Kolkowitz and A Kobronski (eds.), *Soldiers, Peasants and Bureaucrats: Civil-Military Relations in Communist and Modernizing Societies*. London: Allen and Unwin; 9–27.

Kinsey, Christop. 2007. *Corporate Soldiers: The Rise of Private Military Companies*. New York: Routledge.

Kirli, Cengiz. 2005. *The Struggle Over Space: Coffehouses of Ottoman Istanbul*. Binghamton University: PhD dissertation.

Kuran, E. 2005. "Karakol" in Peri J. Bearman et al (eds.) *Encyclopaedia of Islam, Second Edition*. Leiden: Brill.

Lababidi, Salah. 1970. *Mudhakkirat Mudi Bulis*. Beirut: N.P.

Lambton, Anne K.S. 2005. "Darugha" in Peri J. Bearman et al (eds.) *Encyclopaedia of Islam, Second Edition*. Leiden: Brill.

Lazreg, Marnia. 2008. *Torture and the Twilight of Empire: From Algiers to Baghdad*. Princeton: Princeton University Press.

Lewis, Bernard. 2005. "Dabtiyya" in Peri J. Bearman et al (eds.). *Encyclopaedia of Islam, Second Edition.* Leiden: Brill.

Lia, Brynjar. 2006. *A Police Force without a State: A History of the Palestinian Security Forces in the West Bank and Gaza.* Reading: Ithaca Press.

Liebesny, Herbert J. 1975. *The Law of the Near and Middle East: Readings, Cases, and Materials.* Albany: State University of New York Press.

Liebesny, Herbert J. 1983. "Judicial Systems in the Near and Middle East: Evolutionary Development and Islamic Revival" in *Middle East Journal* 37(2): 202–217.

Lippman, Matthew, Sean McConville and Mordechai Yerushalmi. 1988. *Islamic Criminal Law and Procedure: An Introduction.* New York: Praeger.

Lynch, Michael J., and Raymond J. Michalowski. 2000. *The New Primer on Radical Criminology: Critical Perspectives on Crime, Power, and Identity.* Monsey, NY: Criminal Justice Press.

Manning, Peter K. 1997. *Police Work: The Social Organization of Policing.* Illinois: Waveland Press.

Maran, Rita. 1989. *Torture: The Role of Ideology in the French-Algerian Civil War.* New York: Praeger.

Marenin, Otwin (ed.). 1996. *Policing Change, Changing Police: International Perspectives.* New York: Garland.

Marez, Curtis. 2004. *Drug Wars: The Political Economy of Narcotics.* Minneapolis: University of Minnesota Press.

Markaz Buhuth al-Shurtah. 1982. *Al-Shurtah wa al-Nidal al-Watani, 1881–1981.* Cairo: Interior Ministry; The Police Academy.

Massad, Joseph A. 2001. *Colonial Effects: The Making of National Identity in Jordan.* New York: Columbia University Press.

McClintock, Scott. 2004. "The Penal Colony: the Inscription of the Subject in Literature and Law and Detainees as Legal Non-Persons at Camp X-Ray" in *Comparative Literature Studies* 41(1): 153–167.

McCormick, Kevin, and Livy Visano. 1992. *Understanding Policing.* Toronto: Canadian Scholars Press.

McEvoy, Kieran, and Tim Newburn, (eds.) 2003. *Criminology, Conflict Resolution, and Restorative Justice.* London: Palgrave Macmillan.

Meyer, David S., and Sidney Tarrow, (eds.) 1997. *The Social Movement Society: Contentious Politics for a New Century.* New York: Roman and Littlefeld.

Modirzadeh, Naz. 2006. "Taking Islamic Law Seriously: INGOs and the Battle for Muslim Hearts and Minds" in *Harvard Human Rights Journal* 19: 191–233.

Mosallem, Elsayed Abo. 1980. "The Police Academy, Cairo, Egypt" in *Police Studies* 3(1): 3–9.

An-Na'im, Abdullahi Ahmed. 1990. *Toward an Islamic Reformation: Civil Liberties, Human Rights and International Law.* Syracuse: Syracuse University Press.

An-Na'im, Abdullahi Ahmed. 2001. "Human Rights in the Arab World: A Regional Perspective" in *Human Rights Quarterly* 23: 701–732.

An-Na'im, Abdullahi Ahmed. 2008. *Islam and the Secular State: Negotiating the Future of Shari'a*. Cambridge, Mass: Harvard University Press.

Nashif, Esmail. 2008. *Palestinian Political Prisoners: Identity and Community*. London: Routledge.

Nasr, Hesham, Jill Crystal, and Nathan J. Brown. 2004. "Criminal Justice and Prosecution in the Arab World: A Study Prepared for the United Nations Development Program; Program on Governance in the Arab Region" at www.pogar.org/publications/judiciary/criminaljustice-brown-e.pdf accessed on 4 November 2008.

Neocleous, Mark. 2000. *Fabrication of social order: A critical theory of police power*. Sterling: Pluto Press.

Newman, Graeme. 1982. "Khomeini and Criminal Justice: Notes on Crime and Culture" in *The Journal of Criminal Law and Criminology* 73(2): 561–581.

Nielsen, J.S. and Marín, Manuela. 2005. "Shurta" in Peri J. Bearman et al (eds.) *Encyclopaedia of Islam, Second Edition*. Leiden: Brill.

Özbek, Nadir. 2008. "Policing the Countryside: Gendarmes of the Late 19th Century Ottoman Empire (1876–1908)" in *International Journal of Middle East Studies* 40: 47–67.

Pakes, Francis J. 2004. *Comparative Criminal Justice*. Cullompton: Willan Publishing.

Parenti, Christian. 2008. *Lockdown America: Police and Prisons in the Age of Crisis*, revised and expanded ed. New York: Verso.

Peteet, Julie. 1994 "Male Gender and Rituals of Resistance in the Palestinian Intifada: A Cultural Politics of Violence" in *American Ethnologist* 21(1): 31–49.

Peters, Rudolph. 1999a. "'For His Correction and as a Deterrent Example for Others': Mehmed Ali's First Criminal Legislation (1829–1830)" in *Islamic Law and Society* 6(2): 164–192.

Peters, Rudolph. 1999b. "Administrators and Magistrates: The Development of a Secular Judiciary in Egypt, 1842–1871" in *Die Welt des Islams* 39(3): 378–397.

Peters, Rudolph. 1999c. "State, Law and Society in Nineteenth-Century Egypt: Introduction" in *Die Welt des Islams* 39(3): 267–272.

Peters, Rudolph. 2002. "Prisons and Marginalisation in Nineteenth Century Egypt" in Eugene Rogan (ed.) *Outside In: On the Margins of the Modern Middle East*. London: I.B. Tauris; 31–52.

Peters, Rudolph. 2004. "Controlled Suffering: Mortality and Living Conditions in 19th-Century Egyptian Prisons" in the *International Journal of Middle East Studies* 36: 387–407.

Peters, Rudolph. 2005. *Crime and Punishment in Islamic Law: Theory and Practice from the Sixteenth to the Twenty-first Century*. Cambridge: Cambridge University Press.

Picard, Elizabeth. 1993a. "Arab Military In Politics: From Revolutionary Plot To Authoritarian State" in Albert Hourani, Philip S. Khoury and Mary C. Wilson (eds.). *The Modern Middle East: a Reader*. London: I.B. Tauris.

Picard, Elizabeth. 1993b. "State and Society in the Arab World: Towards a New Role for the Security Services" in Bahgat Korany, Paul Noble and Rex Brynen (eds.). *The Many Faces of National Security in the Arab World*. London: Palgrave Macmillan.

Pimlott, John. 1988. "The British Experience" in Ian Beckett (ed.) *The Roots of Counter-Insurgency: Armies and Guerrilla Warfare 1900–1945*. London: Blandford Press.

Pisciotta, Alexander. 1994. *Benevolent Repression: Social Control and the American Reformatory-Prison Movement*. New York: New York University Press.

Rejali, Darius M. 1994. *Torture and Modernity: Self, Society and State in Modern Iran*. Boulder, CO: Westview Press.

Rejali, Darius. 2008. *Torture and Democracy*. Princeton: Princeton University Press.

Rhodes, Lorna. 1998. "Panoptical Intimacies" in *Public Culture* 10(2): 285–311.

Rhodes, Lorna. 2001. "Toward an Anthropology of Prisons" in *Annual Review of Anthropology* 30: 65–83.

Ron, James. 2003. *Frontiers and Ghettos: State Violence in Serbia and Israel*. Berkeley: University of California Press.

Rosenfeld, Maya. 2004. *Confronting the Occupation: Work, Education, and Political Activism of Palestinian Families in a Refugee Camp*. Palo Alto: Stanford University Press.

Ross, Jeffrey Ian. 1996. "Policing Change in the Gulf States: The Effect of the Gulf Conflict" in Otwin Marenin (ed.) *Policing Change, Changing Police: International Perspectives*. New York: Garland Publishing, Inc.; 79–105.

Rothman, David. 1990 [1971]. *The Discovery of the Asylum: Social Order and Disorder in the New Republic*. (Revised edition). Boston: Little, Brown and Co.

Rothman, David. 2002. *Conscience and Convenience: The Asylum and its Alternatives in Progressive America*, revised ed. Hawthorne, New York: Aldine Gruyter.

Rudolph, Harold. 1994. *Security, Terrorism, Torture: Detainee's Rights in South African and Israel; a Comparative Study*. Cape Town: Juta & Co, LTD.

Samuel, Edwin. 1957. *British Traditions in the Administration of Israel*. With a foreword by HE the Israeli Ambassador. London: Valentine, Mitchell for the Anglo-Israel Association.

Sayigh, Yusif. 2007. "Prisoner of War: 1948–1949, as told to Rosemary Sayigh" in *Jerusalem Quarterly File* 29: 13–32.

Scarry, Elaine. 1984. *The Body in Pain: The Making and Unmaking of the World*. Oxford University Press.

Scheffler, Judith. 1986. *Wall Tappings: An Anthology of Writings By Women Political Prisoners*. New York: Feminist Press.

Schneider, Irene. 1995. "Imprisonment in pre-classical and classical Islamic law" in *Islamic Law and Society* 2(2): 157–173.

Schneider, Irene. 2005. "Sidjn" in Peri J. Bearman et al (eds.) *Encyclopaedia of Islam, Second Edition*. Leiden: Brill. http://www.brillonline.nl.

Schull, Kent F. 2007. "Penal Institutions, Nation-State Construction, and Modernity in the Late Ottoman Empire 1908–1919." Los Angeles: Unpublished UCLA Doctoral thesis.

Segev, Tom. 1999. *One Palestine Complete: Jews and Arabs under the British Mandate*. Trans. Haim Watzman. New York: Henry Holt and Company.

Semple, Janet. 1993. *Bentham's Prison: A Study of Panopticon Penitentiary*. New York: Oxford University Press.

Siegfried, Nikolaus A. 2000. "Legislation and Legitimation in Oman: The Basic Law" in *Islamic Law and Society* 7(3): 359–397.

Simon, Jonathan. 2000. "The 'Society of Captives' in the Era of Hyper-Incarceration" in *Theoretical Criminology* 4(3): 285–308.

Simon, Jonathan. 2007. *Governing through Crime: How the War on Crime Transformed American Democracy and Created a Culture of Fear*. Oxford: Oxford University Press.

Singer, Peter W. 2007. *Corporate Warriors: The Rise of the Privatized Military Industry*. Ithaca, NY: Cornell University Press.

Solaim, Soliman A. 1971. "Saudi Arabia's Judicial System" in *Middle East Journal* 25(3): 403–407.

Spierenburg, Pieter. 1991. *The Prison Experience: Disciplinary Institutions and Their Inmates in Early Modern Europe*. New Brunswick: Rutgers University Press.

Strobl, Staci. 2008. "The Women's Police Directorate in Bahrain: An Ethnographic Exploration of Gender Segregation and the Likelihood of Future Integration" in *International Criminal Justice Review* 18(1): 39–58.

Swanson, Glen W. 1972. "The Ottoman Police" in *Journal of Contemporary History* 7(1/2): 243–260.

Sykes, Gresham M. 1971. *The Society of Captives: A Study of a Maximum Security Prison*. Princeton: Princeton University Press.

Tegart, K.F. N.D. *Charles Tegart: Memoir of an Indian Police Officer*. London: British Library; India Office Records; Unpublished manuscript (MSS Eur c.235).

Thompson, Elizabeth. 2000. *Colonial Citizens: Republican Rights, Paternal Privilege, and Gender in French Syria and Lebanon*. New York: Columbia University Press.

Tilly, Charles. 1992. *Coercion, Capital, and European States, AD 990–1990*. Oxford: Blackwell Publishing.

Tollefson, Harold. 1999. *Policing Islam: The British Occupation of Egypt and the Anglo-Egyptian Struggle over Control of the Police, 1882–1914*. Westport, CT: Greenwood Press.

Tonry, Michael. 1995. *Malign Neglect: Race, Crime and Punishment in America*. New York: Oxford University Press.

Torrey, Gordon H. 1963. *Syrian politics and the military, 1945–1958*. Columbus: Ohio State University Press.

Ungar, Mark. 2002. *Elusive Reform: Democracy and the Rule of Law in Latin America*. Boulder: Lynne Rienner Publishers.

Vatikiotis, Panayiotis J. 1961. *The Egyptian Army in politics: Pattern for new nations?* Bloomington: Indiana University Press 1961.

Vatikiotis, Panayiotis J. 1967. *Politics and the Military in Jordan: A Study of the Arab Legion, 1921–1957*. London: Frank Cass Publishers.

Vogler, Richard. 2005. *A World View of Criminal Justice*. Aldershot: Ashgate.

Voglis, Polymeris. 2003. *Becoming a Subject: Political Prisoners During the Greek Civil War*. New York: Berghahn.

Wacquant, Loïc. 2001. "Deadly Symbiosis: When Ghetto and Prison Meet and Mesh." in *Punishment and Society* 3(1): 95–134.

Wacquant, Loïc. 2002. "From Slavery to Mass Incarceration," in *New Left Review* 13: 41–60.

Wacquant, Loïc. 2009. *Punishing the Poor: The Neoliberal Government of Social Insecurity*. Durham: Duke University Press.

Walker, Samuel. 1977. *A Critical History of Police Reform: The Emergence of Professionalism*. Lanham, MD: Lexington Books.

Wedeen, Lisa. 2008. *Peripheral Visions: Publics, Power, and Performance in Yemen*. Chicago: University of Chicago Press.

Zabih, Sepehr. 1988. *The Iranian Military in Revolution and War*. London: Routledge.

Zamani, Amir. 1989. "Law Enforcement in the Islamic Republic of Iran and the Socialist Peoples' Libyan Arab Jamahiriya" in *Police Studies* 12(2): 39–50.

Zinoman, Peter. 2001. *The Colonial Bastille: A History of Imprisonment in Vietnam, 1862–1940*. Berkeley: University of California Press.

Table 1: Prison populations in the Middle East, contrasted with the USA, England and Wales, and Sweden. Notes: the number in parentheses is the year for which data were last to be collected. The Israeli prison data *does* include most Palestinians held in administrative detention, because since the end of 2006, Palestinian detainees are held by the Israeli Prison Services. A much smaller number of Palestinian detainees—not recorded in this data—are held by the Israeli military, and their numbers are tracked by Israeli and Palestinian human rights organisations.

Country	*Prison population total (including pre-trial detainees/ remand prisoners)*	*Prison population rate (per 100,000 of national population)*	*Pre-trial detainees/ remand prisoners (percentage of prison population)*	*Female prisoners (percentage of prison population)*	*Foreign prisoners (percentage of prison population)*	*Number of establishments/ institutions*	*Official capacity of prison system*	*Occupancy level (percentage based on official capacity)*
Algeria	54,000 (2007)	158 (2007)	11.3 (2007)	1.1 (2006)	1.0 (2006)	127 (2007)	31,500 (2006)	171.8 (2006)
Bahrain	701 (2004)	95 (2004)	16 (2004)	18.5 (2004)	N/A	1 (2006)	816 (2006)	91 (2004)
Egypt	64,378 (2006)	85 (2006)	9.9 (2006)	3.7 (2006)	1.0 (2002)	44 (2006)	N/A	N/A
Iran	158,351 (2007)	222 (2007)	24.8 (1993)	3.7 (2007)	N/A	184 (2001)	65,000 (2001)	243.1 (2001)
Iraq	27,336 (2008) Not including over 23,000 detainees held by the US and the UK.	93 (2008)	N/A	2.5 (2005)	N/A	Over 1000 facilities not including unofficial US detention centres (2007)	14,698 (2005)	59.7 (2005)
Israel	22,788 (2008)	326 (2008)	36.5 (2007)	2.3 (2007)	6.6 (2007)	28 (2007)	23,796 (2007)	92.2 (2007)

Jordan	c. 7,500 (2008)	c. 123 (2008)	46.1 (2006)	3.1 (2006)	9.6 (2006)	10 (2008)	6,802 (2002)	82.2 (2002)
Kuwait	c. 3,500 (2005)	130 (2005)	18.6 (2002)	14.9 (2003)	13.5 (2003)	6 (1994)	2,886 (2002)	102.8 (2002)
Lebanon	5,870 (2008)	159 (2007)	62.5 (2007)	3.8 (2006)	38 (2006)	30 (2005)	4,940 (2005)	120.9 (2005)
Libya	12,748 (2007)	209 (2007)	50.1 (2007)	2.7 (2007)	30.5 (2007)	36 (2007)	9,000 (2007)	141.6 (2007)
Morocco	53,580 (2006)	167 (2006)	46.5 (2006)	2.7 (2006)	2.2 (2006)	59 (2006)	27,113 (2006)	197.6 (2006)
Oman	2,020 (2000)	81 (2000)	N/A	5 (2000)	20.3 (2000)	3 (2000)	N/A	N/A
Qatar	465 (2004)	55 (2004)	1.9 (2004)	1.1 (2004)	59.7 (2004)	1 (2004)	N/A	N/A
Saudi Arabia	28,612 (2002)	132 (2002)	58.7 (2002)	5.7 (2002)	46.9 (2002)	30 (2002)	N/A	N/A
Syria	10,599 (2004)	58 (2004)	50.5 (2004)	7.4 (2004)	7.3 (2004)	35 (2004)	16,161 (2004)	65.6 (2004)
Tunisia	c. 26,000 (2004)	c. 263 (2004)	22.7 (1996)	N/A	N/A	36 (2004)	N/A	N/A
Turkey	101,100 (2008)	142 (2008)	60.9 (2007)	3.4 (2008)	1.4 (2007)	458 (2007)	90,558 (2008)	105.5 (2008)
UAE	11,193 (2006)	238 (2006)	45.9 (2006)	11.2 (2006)	92.2 (2006)	21 (2006)	7,045 (2006)	158.9 (2006)
Yemen	14,000 (1998)	83 (1998)	N/A	N/A	N/A	N/A	N/A	N/A

See overleaf for contrasting cases.

Country	Prison population total (including pre-trial detainees/ remand prisoners)	Prison population rate (per 100,000 of national population)	Pre-trial detainees/ remand prisoners (percentage of prison population)	Female prisoners (percentage of prison population)	Foreign prisoners (percentage of prison population)	Number of establishments/ institutions	Official capacity of prison system	Occupancy level (percentage based on official capacity)
Contrasting Cases								
England and Wales	82,918 (2008)	152 (2008)	16.3 (2008)	5.3 (2008)	13.4 (2008)	140 (2008)	74,270 (2008)	112.3 (2008)
Sweden	6,770 (2007)	74 (2007)	22.2 (2006)	4.1 (2006)	27.5 (2006)	55 (2006)	6,752 (2006)	106.3 (2006)
USA	2,293,157 (2007)	756 (2007)	21 (2007)	9.1 (2007)	5.8 (2007)	5069 (2007)	c. 2,096,645 (2007)	c. 108 (2007)

Source: *World Prison Brief*, International Centre for Prison Studies, King's College London.

PART I

COERCION FROM COLONIALISM TO NEOLIBERALISM

1

POLICING THE DESERT

COERCION, CONSENT AND THE COLONIAL ORDER[1]

Daniel Neep

Historians of colonialism typically note that the law enforcement agencies of Empire had a decidedly coercive character in comparison to their metropolitan counterparts. The refusal of indigenous populations to accept European claims of sovereignty over their lands meant that colonial administrations were obliged to depend on the use of force to maintain political and social order (Thomas 2006: 700). As a result, the literature suggests, colonial police tended to assume explicitly military characteristics (Anderson and Killingray 1991: 4–5). Ideas of serving the community and policing by consent made little headway in colonial contexts (Arnold 1986: 232–234): the transition to consensual policing which developed during the twentieth century in Europe was not replicated in colonial cities, where labour disputes and rising nationalist activities led the police to increase their role in maintaining internal security, rather than reduce it (Killingray and Anderson 1992:

[1] This chapter is drawn from PhD fieldwork supported by a Doctoral Award from the Arts & Humanities Research Council (AHRC). I would like to thank Charles Tripp and the participants in the Eighth Mediterranean Research Meeting hosted by the EUI in March 2007 for their helpful comments on earlier incarnations of this paper.

5–10). In colonial peripheries, such as the frontier or "savage" territories, policing retained its coercive character even when a less overtly violent mode of operations had been introduced in more developed areas (Johnston 1991; Killingray 1991). In general, the literature on colonial policing has tended to adopt uncritically the common conceptualization of coercion and consent as opposed and mutually exclusive techniques of generating and maintaining power, techniques which operate on the physical and the mental level respectively.

This chapter seeks to explore the binary opposition between consent and coercion to obtain a fuller understanding of how the authorities of the French Mandate imposed order upon the Syrian steppe in the 1920s and 1930s. I focus on two problematic areas of the neat division between coercion and consent. At the most elementary level of analysis, this conceptual dualism disguises the extent to which consensus was less freely given than forcefully imposed in colonial contexts. The framework of the League of Nations Mandate for Syria and Lebanon obliged the French authorities to implement the transition from military to civilian rule and to administer the territories in an increasingly indirect manner, but even these apparently more consensual techniques fundamentally relied upon the threat of violent sanctions. I demonstrate this point by examining the institutional framework established to control the Syrian *badiya* and the political rationalities which shaped French Bedouin policy.[2] A specialist officer corps, the Contrôle Bédouin (Bedouin Inspectorate), was created to police the desert, supported by the army's camel-mounted Méhariste Companies. While conflict between the two bodies has usually been explained by their contradictory sensitivities to the use of coercion, I argue that these tensions were motivated by institutional rivalries rather than varying normative preferences and that Contrôle Bédouin (CB) and Méhariste officers shared a similar vision of colonial power as fundamentally dependent upon the use of force.

Secondly, the understanding of power which informs the dyad of coercion and consent must be examined more critically. Both sides of this equation envisage power as a force exerted upon political actors in order to ensure their compliance with the demands of an external will (Mitchell 1990). The conceptualisation of power as a force which

[2] *Badiya* is the Arabic term for steppe/desert; the Syrian steppe is known as *Badiyat al-Sham*. In my text I use "Bedu" as a collective noun and "Bedouin" when referring to a particular number of individuals.

operates upon free-willed, autonomous subjects is deeply rooted in Western social theory (Hindess 1996), but more recent work sees power as an equally *productive* phenomenon, capable of defining the boundaries of the potential fields of personal, social and political existence into which subjectivities emerge (Foucault 1980). While studies have explored how policing in Europe worked to shape the social order in such a way as to render it docile, malleable and susceptible to control (Fitzgerald, McLennon and Pawson 1981), the more ready recourse to the use of force in colonial policing has been used to suggest that the more subtle workings of Foucauldian notions of power are irrelevant to colonial rule (Cooper 2005: 142–143). In the second part of the chapter, I explore how "coercive" technologies were used to create new, "consensual" modes of social being. The French authorities conceptualised the Bedu's potential for violence in terms of speed and movement; their nomadic peregrinations across the steppe posed an intrinsic challenge to the calm, controlled and measured notions of spatialized political order which the French sought to impose on Syria. The colonial authorities responded to this challenge by transforming the spatial practices of the Bedu. Coercive techniques of policing movement were here an important mechanism for the production of modern notions of spatialised social order within one of the sections of Syrian society that had been least affected by European influence.

Political Rationalities of Coercion and Control

The much-vaunted success story of French dealings with the Bedouin in Morocco provided the initial model for *la politique bédouine* in Syria; Mandatory officials believed they could subcontract security functions to Bedouin chiefs in the Levant as they had in North Africa. In 1920, agreements were signed with the Amir of the Ruwala, Nuri Sha'lan, and the Amir of the Fad'an, Mujhim bn Muhayd; they were given financial subsidies and military equipment in order to secure their loyalty (Velud 1995).[3] The French believed that these two chiefs would be capable of rallying behind them all the Bedu tribes of the steppe: the Bedu's traditional disdain of Syrian townspeople would

[3] Centre des archives diplomatiques à Nantes, France, Fonds Beyrouth-Mandat, 1er versement (henceforth CADN) 1536, "Note au sujet de la question bédouine dans les Etats sous Mandats français," [c.1930].

mean the Mandate could pay them to police the desert without fearing that they might side with any urban opposition to colonial rule in the future. Although inspired by French success in Morocco (Burke 1973: 175–186; Khoury 1987: 55–57; Thomas 2003: 57), that model was inappropriate for the specificities of Syrian society. Much to the disgust of colonial officers who had served in Morocco, the Syrian Bedu were found to have little in common with their Maghribi counterparts. It was frequently opined that the Syrians lacked the nobility, honor and martial skill of the tribesmen of North Africa (Muller 1931: 178). As one French official complained: "[O]ur Bedouin chiefs have nothing of Morocco's *grands caïds*, [who are] warchiefs and thoroughbred aristocrats. In general—and without exception—they are vulgar sellers of sheep and camels, whose mentalities they share."[4] With the influence of many Bedouin chiefs barely extending throughout their own tribes, much less across the steppe as a whole, the idea of self-policing tribal zones died a rapid death in Mandatory Syria.

With direct military rule impossible under the terms of the League of Nations Mandate, the colonial power preferred to rely on the small, highly specialized officer corps of the Contrôle Bédouin (CB) to police the desert. Established in 1921, the organization was charged with five key functions: intelligence collection; ensuring security in migration and pasturing zones; the collection of information on the tribes to facilitate possible military operations; the implementation of financial and legal measures decided by the High Commission; and the composition of specialist studies about the Bedouin tribes for the benefit of the Mandatory authorities.[5] Much as their counterparts in the Service des Renseignements gathered information and intelligence about Syrian society in towns and villages (Neep 2006), CB officers built up a sizeable corpus of knowledge about the numbers, customs, leadership and genealogies of the inhabitants of the steppe. They maintained files on tribal leaders and their likely successors, detailed recent disputes or longstanding feuds between different tribes, and carefully monitored any contacts between the tribes and undesirable elements, such as urban nationalists in Damascus or Aleppo. The expertise of CB officers in the affairs of the Bedu was seen as unparalleled and was held to form an essential element of their success in maintaining security in the

[4] CADN 552, "Note au sujet de la Politique Bédouine," 3 April 1925.
[5] CADN 552, "Instruction no. 1556/K/I", Beirut, 3 December 1924.

desert; the "personal action" of the expert CB officer was repeatedly credited with the successful creation of order in the steppe.[6]

CB officers relied upon Méhariste companies to back up their words with the threat of force in the desert, though they were not authorised to command these units themselves. Modelled on the camel units of North Africa, these locally-recruited companies failed to impress CB officers with their skills, personal qualities or commitment. "Let us not draw comparison with the Méhariste companies of Sauoara, Touat, Mauritania, Sudan or Chad," grumbled Captain Raynaud about the company based at Palmyra, "we shall be cruelly disillusioned." According to French officers, Méharistes were recruited without any knowledge of their background or character, some had little aptitude for desert life but were simply attracted by the prestige of the Méhariste corps and most lacked any sense of patriotic duty—or even the warrior instinct that characterised other colonial peoples.

The cultural and institutional distinctions between the Contrôle Bédouin and the Méhariste companies have encouraged the perception that each one embodied a particular approach to maintaining order among the Bedu. Despite their shortcomings and their relatively low numbers, the Méhariste companies were the instrument of coercion most easily available to the CB officer in the *badiya* and, as such, played a key role in enforcing the personal actions of those officers in policing the desert. Reproducing the binary opposition between coercion and consent that characterises the literature on colonial policing, some historians see CB expertise and personal contacts as replacing a more explicitly martial *politique bédouine*. For example, Thomas points out that "Tribal control defied easy categorization or *force majeure* solutions. [...] [T]he prevention of bedouin dissent was less a matter of repressive policing than of penetrating nomad society to ensure the cooperation of clan leaders. [...] Tribal control was less about colonial mastery than the transformation of clan loyalties, preferably by persuasion and example rather than force" (Thomas 2003: 542, 546).

However, while CB officers prided themselves on their intricate knowledge of the tribes, they never lost sight of the importance of coercive techniques in ensuring the compliance of the Bedu. Indeed, CB officers typically used their claims of cultural expertise not to avoid

[6] CADN 987, Directeur du Service des Renseignements to Chargé du Contrôle Bédouin de la Mouvance d'Alep, Beirut, 4 January 1928.

force, but to justify it. Lt. Deleuze ridiculed the idea that force might not be the best way to deal with the "simple-minded" Bedouin, who "cannot conceive that someone might give orders and be obeyed without the means of being strong."[7] Deleuze recounts an anecdote involving the Saba' tribe during the migrations of 1922 as evidence of this self-evident truth:

A complete ignorance of Bedouin psychology has encouraged the idea that if we seek to impose our will on the Sbaa [Saba'] then we risk troubling security. This is utter nonsense. [...] The whole Bedouin mentality, characterised by its submission to force and its respect for powerful government, is illustrated by an incident in early August. During a patrol which might have been very productive, the Faure detachment settled in for the night near to a Sbaa camp. The interpreter was sent to the Sbaa to buy five sheep. Convinced that the detachment had come to collect the *ouédi* [tax], the Sbaa refused to make the sale. So Commandant Faure sent a corporal and four men to obtain the sheep. The chief of the Bedouin camp gathered twenty men and said to the corporal: "I have 20 guns, you have five. I am stronger, so you shall not have any sheep." Cdt. Faure sent back a whole squad of men, to which the Bedouin chief replied: "You are stronger, take the sheep." It would not have proven much more difficult for the Faure detachment to collect the whole of the *ouédi* instead of the five sheep—they only needed to ask.[8]

As well as being used to justify the day-to-day use of force in dealings with the tribesmen at the grassroots level, the Bedu's supposed respect for strength and violence was also used as evidence in high-level discussions about *la politique bédouine*. The Delegate of the High Commissioner in Damascus explained that the respect for force demonstrated that the various tribes of the steppe were a socially and ethnically homogenous social formation, different to the inhabitants of Syria's towns and villages. Tribes such as the Ruwala and the Fad'an were "primitives who disdain following administrative regulations and only submit to authority when it is backed up with force."[9] As such, the Mandatory power was justified in seeking to isolate these tribes from Syria's city-dwellers and keeping them under a separate administrative regime.

Despite the broad consensus on the need for the use of force by French colonial forces, CB officers and the Méhariste companies

[7] CADN 986, "Rapport sur l'estivage des Tribus Nomades dans le Sandjak de Hama, été 1922," Hama, 22 October 1922.

[8] CADN 986, ibid.

[9] CADN 986, Lt. Col. Catroux, Délégué du Haut-Commissaire à Damas, to General Gouraud, Haut-Commissaire, Damascus 7 November 1922.

repeatedly found themselves at loggerheads over a number of incidents where their interpretations of these norms apparently varied. This conflict was for the most part a consequence of institutional rivalry and CB officer claims that their expert knowledge of the Bedu—not the physical force of the Méharistes—was most crucial in ensuring the security of the desert:

> It must be remarked that the influence of the CB officer, a specialist in his field, is necessarily based upon his awareness of [tribal] customs. What value would it serve to replace him with Méhariste officers whose time is partly taken up with other tasks (e.g. administration, training) and whose authority might [therefore] be delegated to junior French officers, who would have to arbitrate Bedouin cases without prior preparation, and the Méharistes themselves (a large number of whom are foreigners from the Nejd) and who might be tempted to apply customary law spuriously, to further their own interests?[10]

Conversely, military officials unsympathetic to the apparent need for expertise in Bedouin affairs would criticise the CB for going native and compromising their objectivity. General Jacquot, commander of the Troupes du Levant in the Euphrates region, angrily complained to the Delegate of the High Commissioner in Damascus of intelligence reports which detailed the "intellectual deformation frequently encountered by those in too intimate contact with the Bedouin," whereby the nomads were inevitably seen as innocent victims of villagers' complaints and administrative authority errors. He accused the local CB officer of collecting any manner of rumour which reflected well on the Bedu but badly on the sedentary population, and of filing it in his reports as if it were objective truth without verifying its accuracy.[11]

Tension between the two services and the different approaches they represented came to a head in the Qaryatayn incident of 1933. On 18 July three members of the Ruwala tribe led by Nuri Sha'lan were allegedly beaten by an officer of the 1st Méhariste Company of Palmyra and six of his men when they were arrested for their suspected involvment in a raid on the Umur Khursan tribe in the region of al-Sha'ar.[12] Hashash

[10] CADN 552, "Note sur la réorganisation du contrôle bédouin," Beirut, 18 January 1935.

[11] CADN 413, General Jacquot, commandant les Troupes du Territoire de l'Euphrate et Délégué-Adjoint du Haut-Commissaire to Délégué du Haut-Commissaire à Damas, Secteur Postal 613, n.d. [probably May 1936].

[12] CADN 552, Translation of letter from Nuri Sha'lan to Inspecteur du Contrôle Bédouin de la Mouvance de Damas-Palmyre, 22 July 1933.

ibn Btayha, a *mukhtar* of the Ja'ja' fraction of the Ruwala tribe, claimed that he lost the hearing in his right ear as a result of the incident; Doujan ibn Ghushm, also a *mukhtar* of the Ja'ja', displayed scars on his right leg.[13] An initial inquiry into the affair by a military officer concluded that the men probably had been "mistreated" by the Méharistes.[14] Higher ranking military officers came out in support of the Méharistes accused of wrong-doing,[15] but the report by CB officer Commandant Tringa sympathetically attributed blame for the incident on the Méharistes' lack of cultural expertise. He pointed out that the Méharistes were often drawn into Bedouin affairs which they lacked the training or ability to resolve: their greater numbers meant they were more accessible to the Bedu than CB officers and the tribesmen themselves would often ask for Mhariste intervention. Tringa noted that many difficult incidents had not been reported by CB officers in the past:

> Out of military comradeship and mutual esteem—and in order not to be accused of bad camaraderie—we close our eyes, thereby skipping over a pile of minor incidents, until the day when the interest of our service obliges us to bring an end to this far too invasive meddling [in Bedouin affairs] [...] one has only to travel among the tribes or to leaf through a few dossiers to appreciate the lack of esteem in which some tribal fractions hold the men of these units and the infractions they have committed since their creation (physical abuse, harassment, arbitrary arrest, illegal camp searches on the most spurious of accusations, etc).[16]

Tringa's solution to the problem was simple: the infractions would only end when the Méhariste units were transformed from military companies into administrative formations and placed under the full command of the officers of the Contrôle Bédouin, whose expert knowledge would ensure they were used in the best interests of the desert police.

[13] CADN 552, Inspecteur Général des Mouvances to Conseiller du Haut Commissionaire, Damascus, 10 October 1933.

[14] CADN 552, Chef de Bataillon Duminy to Général Commandant les Troupes des Territoires de Damas, du Djebel Druse et du Hauran, Damascus, 23 August 1933.

[15] CADN 552, Général Garchery, Commandant les Troupes des Territoires de Damas, du Djebel Druse et du Hauran to Général Commandant Supérieur, n.d. August 1933.

[16] CADN 552, Inspecteur Général des Mouvances to Conseiller du Haut Commissionaire and Delegate of the High Commissioner for Syria, Damascus, 10 October 1933.

The conflict between the two institutions continued well into the mid-1930s. On the one hand, the officers of the Contrôle Bédouin were an elite corps of specialists in Bedouin affairs whose authority rested on their knowledge of tribal customs and their ability to inveigle, flatter and threaten tribal chiefs into doing their bidding; on the other, the Méhariste companies espoused a more direct, heavy-handed approach as they sought to apprehend members of raiding parties and return stolen booty to its rightful owners. Yet it would be incorrect to situate these differing approaches within the framework of coercion versus consent which shapes much of the literature on colonial policing. As the Qaryatayn incident demonstrated, CB officers resented not so much the existence of military units in the desert as the fact that they did not command them: it was the authority which controlled the use of violence to which they objected, not the perpetration of violence itself.

Desert Space: Movement and Modernity

The French authorities spent an immense amount of time and energy worrying about the threat of the Bedu and devising strategies to contain them. Officials were clear on the need to prioritize the stability of the desert zones, as the tribes of the steppe were home to some 18,000 warriors armed with German or Turkish "Mauser" rifles left over from the First World War. The presence among the Bedu of former army officers, who might provide their vast numbers with a modicum of organization, also gave rise to concern.[17] The Mandatory authority thus needed to pay the Bedu more attention and respect than Ottoman rulers were accustomed to.[18] Even so, the Bedu proved surprisingly sedate throughout most of the 1920s and the 1930s, directing their belligerent intentions against one another, in the time-honored tradition of the inter-tribal raid (the *rezzou*, as the French rendered the Arabic *ghazu*), rather than the foreign occupiers. With the exception of the Mawali tribe's assistance to the Hama Revolt of October 1925 (which was marginal given the widespread participation of local residents), the Bedu played almost no role in opposing the Mandatory Power. While Syrian historians have typically attributed this docility to

[17] CADN 1536, "Notes au sujet de la question bédouine dans les Etats sous Mandat français" [c. 1930].

[18] CADN 552 "Note au sujet de la Politique Bédouine," 3 April 1925.

an underdeveloped nationalist sentiment, the question remains as to why the French authorities would invest so much concern in policing the security of the desert, when other parts of the country provided much more fertile breeding grounds for rebellion.

The origins of the Bedouin threat lie less in their Mausers than the way in which French colonial rule conceptualised the spaces of Syrian society coupled with the new sense of political order which it sought to impose on the Levant—and the intrinsic challenge to these notions embodied by the Bedu. As Campbell has highlighted, threats are socially constructed phenomena, not objective assessments of danger (Campbell 1997). The expansion of French authority in Syria was from the outset seen as a process of penetration and subsequent territorial control; the Mandatory power understood the nature of its military control to be intimately associated with retaining privileged access to movement through the territory over which it had claimed authority. As such, the unfettered movement of the tribes across the steppe represented not just a military threat, but a threat to the Mandate's very idea of what control should be.

Lefebvre has argued that space is neither simply an empty expanse nor an arithmetical abstraction, but a socially-produced phenomenon which plays an active instrumental and operational role in maintaining and reproducing the power of the dominant social force (Lefebvre 1991: 1–11). By organising, categorising and employing space in a particular way, on the basis of a particular logic, and with the deployment of particular technologies and forms of expertise, hegemonic forces *use* space to support their dominant position. Lefebvre's idea of space as a sociopolitical product captures an important element of the Mandatory Power's efforts to bring order to the Syrian desert by bringing a certain kind of spatial order to the movements of its Bedouin inhabitants.

The seasonal movements of the Bedu were seen as vectors for all manner of danger by the French. Their contact with the inhabitants of the Najd made them a likely channel for the transmission of radical Wahhabism to the states of the Levant;[19] even worse, movements to Iraq and Transjordan brought them into contact with British propaganda which might encourage them to "defect" to the neighbouring

[19] CADN 987, Chef du Service des Renseignements de l'État de Syrie to l'Envoyé extraordinaire auprès des Etats de Syrie et du Djebel Druse, Damascus, 15 March 1926.

country—a potential economic blow for Syria, which was massively dependent upon the nomads' animal husbandry. Bedouin migrations were also seen as potential vectors of infection for disease (Cadi 1936). Migration movements within Syria were also coded as threatening, though the precise constitution of who represented a threat to whom changed as time progressed. In the early 1920s, the Bedouin were seen as rapacious figures whose disrespect for property rights meant they would steal from the sedentary population and allow their animals to damage crops prior to harvest.[20] Yet it was not long before the Bedu came to be seen as the hapless victims of Syrian townsfolk: local administrators were seeking to exploit the tribes, the French maintained, and unfairly charge them for water, pasture and the damage caused by their herds.[21] The tribes also might be "infected" by notions of nationalism which were sweeping Syrian towns in the 1920s.[22] It was therefore for their own good that the French sought to keep the Bedu far away from Syrian functionaries. Finally, the Bedu were also under assault from the modern pace of life, which introduced automobiles and trucks in place of the camel and threatened the survival of tribal traditions. With its continuing interest in isolating the tribes from contemporary civilization, the French military provided an important role in facilitating ethnographic studies of the Bedu in the 1930s which sought to preserve their pristine primitivism in preference to improving their standard of living (Blecher 2004: 255–263).

The most challenging season for the Mandatory power's control over Syria's non-urban spaces was the bi–annual migration of the Bedu from the steppe into the more settled regions of the country and back again, as pasture grew scarce and was later replenished in the *badiya*. The periods of summer and winter migration became a natural focus for policing activity, which sought not simply to prevent the outbreak of conflict but to introduce a new, more modern notion of spatial organisation to the tribes. The French authorities sought to accomplish this task in two ways: firstly, by the more rigorous definition of the border between *ma'mura* and *badiya*, settled lands and the steppe; and

[20] CADN 986, "Renseignements sur les Tribu,"13 October 1923.

[21] CADN 552, "Note au sujet de la Politique Bédouine," 2 April 1925.

[22] CADN 552, "Directives sur la politique à suivre dans les tribus nomades pendant la période d'estivage 1926,"17 May 1926; CADN 987, "Instructions à suivre à l'égard des nomades: Directif no. 1821/K3," Beirut, 15 March 1927.

secondly, by rationalising and regulating the supposedly traditional migration routes of the tribe.

In stark contrast with Mandatory practice, under Ottoman rule the *ma'mura-badiya* line was not clearly delineated and would shift eastwards or westwards according to the natural population growth of settled local communities or desert tribes, the expansion or retreat of the steppe and—closely linked—the state of the local economies. "The desert was not necessarily arid and uncultivable, but rather the area in which the nomads wandered and which was devastated by their flocks and herds. When, as a result of neglect and feebleness on the part of the government, the tribes invaded the cultivated area, population and cultivation disappeared, weeds filled the fields and the desert advanced." (Lewis 1987: 24). The "desert line", as Lewis calls the border between the cultivated area and the steppe, was less a geographical than an economic feature: it had an elusive, fluid quality that changed from year to year and so proved impossible to fix or demarcate.

The Mandatory officials exchanged this fluidity for a rigid, static border between *ma'mura* and *badiya*, which they painstakingly plotted with rulers and maps in the early 1920s. In 1922, the line was drawn beginning at al-Hamra', then moving on to Jubleh, Furklus, Qaryatayn, Jarud, 'Utaybah, Hijaneh and ending at Mismiyeh. Not only was this fixed demarcation a novelty for the Syrian Bedu, but crossing the border was accompanied by a whole host of alien formalities: they were obliged to obtain permission from an officer of the Contrôle Bédouin before crossing into the *ma'mura*; they were allocated zones in which they were allowed to make camp and find pasture; reparations from disputes with local inhabitants were to be decided by a Special Commission comprised of a Syrian government representative, a local notable, a Bedouin shaykh and a French CB officer.[23] Although there were no attempts to disarm the Bedu as they crossed into the *ma'mura* in 1922, they were forbidden from carrying arms in the settled zone. It was not long before disarmament became part of the crossing formalities: the arms were stored in a French depot until the tribes crossed back into the steppe, when they were returned to them. The Bedu undoubtedly wondered how crossing an imaginary line could suddenly have become so complicated.

The second technique of spatial policing implemented by the Contrôle Bédouin was the "rationalisation" of the migration routes taken

[23] CADN 552, "Arrêté no. 323," 21 January 1922.

by the tribes as they crossed from one zone to the other. Rationalization is here used not as a descriptive term, but as characteristic of a certain vision of order associated with the early stages of state formation. French officers studied the traditional migration routes of the tribes and carefully plotted their trajectories on large maps which can still be consulted in the archives in Nantes, marking the paths taken by the Ruwala, Fad'an, Saba' and other tribes on their bi–annual quest for better pasture. They took particular care to ensure that these routes did not bring into close contact the *ma'mura* tribes between which there were ancient feuds or more recent enmities. The conflict between the Mawali and the Hadidiyin was considered to be the most explosive in the 1920s and even into the 1930s. French scholars pointed out that the cause was not so much the blood feud between the two tribes as it was their constant competition for scarce resources, the implication being that the technocratic management of migration patterns could resolve the problem (Boucheman 1934). The Contrôle Bédouin were only too pleased to help, carving the spaces of Syria with straight lines and directional arrows on a map, then seeking to ensure the tribes adhered to these trajectories through operations of *canalisation* (channelling), supported by Méhariste units or squads of gendarmes.

The impetus to impose regular patterns of straight lines, fixed borders and neat categorizations of different zones was not unique to the Contrôle Bédouin as it sought to expand the French Mandate's authority across the wild and trackless spaces of Syria. Scott has explained that the development of early modern European state power was directed towards similar aims: "to rationalizing and standardizing what was a social hieroglyph into a legible and administratively more convenient format" (Scott 1998: 3). States initially suffered from what Scott describes as partial blindness vis-à-vis their subjects; unaware of their identities, possessions and potential, the state's control of its population and intervention into their lives was at best minimal. Gradually, a variety of standardising processes—from the cadastral survey of land to the population census, from the unification of measurement systems to the rationalization of urban planning—succeeded in replacing the complex irregularities of pre-existing social practices with a single, universal format by which the state could observe and record them.

From this perspective, the regularisation of Bedouin migration routes was part of a more general tendency to simplify complex and "messy" social arrangements for the benefit of the far-from-omnipotent but increasingly perceptive and increasingly intrusive eyes of the state. Unfortunately, the historical record does tell us much about how this reorganisation of the spaces in which they lived their lives affected the Syrian Bedu. Suggestions may be drawn from work carried out on neighbouring tribal societies in the region which underwent a similar process of standardisation as the twentieth century progressed. At the beginning of that century, Bocco and Tell explain, the Bedu of what later became eastern Jordan expressed notions of territoriality by the word *dira*. The term encompassed the migratory space of the tribes, but there was no sense of ownership of this territory or its monopoly: "the extent to which a tribal territory was exclusive to them was thus a function of the need to assure the tribe's own access to the routes of other tribes in case of drought"(Bocco and Tell 1995: 33). As such, the limits of the Bedouin *dira* were fluid and would ebb and flow from year to year; the tribal maps drawn by European travellers are simply snapshots of a particular set of inter-tribal arrangements rather than an eternal truth about ancestral grazing lands (Bocco 1987). A 1936 map of the tribes of the Levant and Northern Arabia which takes into account the yearly variations in pasturage usage and the political relations between the tribes, superimposes one territorial body over another in a manner antithetical to the neatly delineated lines drawn by Mandatory officials in their desire to keep warring tribes separated (Bocco and Tell 1995: 35).

Conclusion

The effects of desert policing in French Mandate Syria have hitherto been rendered invisible by ill-formed notions of the contradictory relationship between strategies of consent and techniques of coercion. Colonial rationalities of violence, shared by both the Contrôle Bédouin and the Méharistes, show no clear differentiation between "consensual" and "coercive" practices: the distinction between the two is illusory, the by-product of our own conventional understandings of what practices of power should look like. A more fruitful area of inquiry is to ask how policing worked to produce new understandings of social order. In Mandatory Syria, the new spatial practices which the Contrôle Bédouin sought to impose on the Bedouin were not implemented for purely instrumental purposes, but entailed a certain notion of how political order was best conceptualized, categorized and controlled. Colonial violence was far from symptomatic of a primitive and unsophisticated form of power; here, it acted as a key technology in the transmission of modern, regulated notions of social space to the Syrian Bedu. Rather than dismiss contemporary theories of power as irrelevant in colonial contexts, rethinking violence can open up a space for new understandings of the intricacies of colonial rule.

Bibliography

Anderson, David M. and David Killingray (eds.) 1992. *Policing and Decolonisation: Politics, Nationalism and the Police, 1917–1965*. Manchester: Manchester University Press.

Anderson, David M. and David Killingray, (eds.) 1991b. "Consent, Coercion and Colonial Control: Policing the Empire, 1830–1940" in Anderson and Killingray (eds.) *Policing the Empire: Government, Authority and Control: 1830–1940*. Manchester: University of Manchester Press.

Anderson, David M. and David Killingray, (eds.) 1991a. *Policing the Empire: Government, Authority and Control: 1830–1940*. Manchester: University of Manchester Press.

Arnold, David. 1986. *Police Power and Colonial Rule: Madras, 1859–1947*. Delhi: Oxford University Press.

Blecher, Robert. 2004. "Desert Medicine, Ethnography, and the Colonial Encounter in Mandatory Syria" in Nadine Méouchy and Peter Sluglett (eds.). *The British and French Mandates in Comparative Perspective*. London: Brill.

Bocco, Ricardo and Tariq Tell. 1995. "Frontières, tribus et Etat(s) en Jordanie orientale à l'époque du Mandat" in *Monde Arabe/Maghreb-Mashrek* 147: 26–47.

Bocco, Ricardo. 1987. "La notion de *Dirah* chez les tribus bédouines en Jordanie: le cas des Bani Sakhr" in Byron D. Cannon (ed.). *Terroirs et sociétés au Maghreb et au Moyen Orient*, Lyon: Maison de l'Orient.

Boucheman, Albert de. 1934. *Note sur la rivalité de deux tribus moutonnières de Syrie, les* Mawali *et les* Hadidiyn. Paris: Librairie Orientaliste Paul Geuthner.

Burke II, Edmund. 1973. "A Comparative View of French Native Policy in Morocco and Syria, 1912–1925" in *Middle Eastern Studies* 9(2): 175–186.

Cadi, Capt Médecin. 1936. "Assistance médicale aux Bédouins" in *Revue des Troupes du Levant* 2: 35–44.

Campbell, David. 1998. *Writing Security: United States Foreign Policy and the Politics of Identity*. Revised ed. Manchester: University of Manchester Press.

Cooper, Frederick. 2005. *Colonialism in Question: Theory, Knowledge, History*. Berkeley: University of California Press.

Fitzgerald, Mike Gregor McLennon and Jennie Pawson (eds.). 1981. *Crime and Society: Readings in History and Theory*. London: Routledge & Kegan Paul in association with Open University Press.

Foucault, Michel. 1980. *Power-Knowledge: Selected Interviews and Other Writings, 1972–1977*. Brighton: Harvester Press.

Hindess, Barry. 1996. *Discourses of Power: from Hobbes to Foucault*. Oxford: Blackwell Publishers.

Johnston, Douglas H. 1991. "From Military Police to Tribal Police: Policing the Upper Nile Province of the Sudan" in Anderson and Killingray (eds.). *Policing the Empire: Government, Authority and Control: 1830–1940*. Manchester: University of Manchester Press.

Khoury, Philip. 1987. *Syria and the French Mandate: the Politics of Arab Nationalism 1920–1945*. London: IB Tauris.

Killingray, David. 1991. "Guarding the Extending Frontier: Policing the Gold Coast, 1865–1913" in Anderson and Killingray (eds.) *Policing the Empire: Government, Authority and Control: 1830–1940*. Manchester: University of Manchester Press.

Killingray, David and David M. Anderson. 1992. "An Orderly Retreat? Policing the End of Empire" in Anderson and Killingray (eds.). *Policing and Decolonisation: Politics, Nationalism and the Police, 1917–1965*. Manchester: Manchester University Press.

Lefebvre, Henri. 1991. *The Production of Space*. Trans. Donald Nicholson-Smith. Oxford: Blackwell.

Lewis, Norman. 1987. *Nomads and Settlers in Syria and Jordan, 1800–1980* Cambridge: Cambridge University Press.

Mitchell, Timothy. 1990. "Everyday Metaphors of Power" in *Theory and Society* 19(5): 545–577.

Muller, Cdt Victor. 1931. *En Syrie avec les Bédouins: les Tribus du désert*. Paris: Librairie Ernest Leroux.

Neep, Daniel. 2006. "Violence and Velocity: Constructing the State in Syria". Paper presented to the British International Studies Association Annual Conference, 18–20 December, in Cork, Ireland.

Scott, James C. 1998. *Seeing Like a State: How Certain Schemes to Improve the Human Condition Have Failed*. New Haven: Yale University Press.

Thomas, Martin. 2003. "Bedouin Tribes and the Imperial Intelligence Services in Syria, Iraq and Transjordan in the 1920s" in *Journal of Contemporary History* 38(4): 539–561.

Thomas, Martin. 2006. "Crisis Management in Colonial States: Intelligence and Counter-Insurgency in Morocco and Syria after the First World War" in *Intelligence and National Security* 21(5): 697–716.

Velud, Christian. 1995. "Syrie: tribus, mouvement national et Etat mandataire (1920–1936)" in *Monde arabe: Maghreb/Mashrek* 147: 48–71.

2

ISRAELI BIOPOLITICS, PALESTINIAN POLICING

ORDER AND RESISTANCE IN THE OCCUPIED PALESTINIAN TERRITORIES

Nigel Parsons

All my books ... are little tool boxes ... if people want to open them, use this sentence or that idea as a screwdriver or spanner to short-circuit, discredit or smash systems of power ... so much the better.

Michel Foucault, 1975.

I prefer the Palestinians to cope with the problem of enforcing order in the Gaza Strip. The Palestinians will be better at it than we were because they will allow no appeals to the Supreme Court and will prevent the Israeli Association of Civil Rights from criticizing the conditions there by denying it access to the area. They will rule by their own methods, freeing, and this is most important, the Israeli army soldiers from having to do what they will do.

Yitzhaq Rabin, 1993.

This chapter proposes the notion of Israeli biopolitics as a framework for the study of policing and incarceration in the Occupied Palestinian Territories (OPT).[1] The Gaza Strip is enclosed, and the West

[1] I would like to thank Mark Salter for an introduction to the concept of biopolitics, and Saed Mashal and Rana Halaseh for help with research in the OPT.

Bank enclosed and overlaid, by colonial infrastructure that expedites racialized biopolitical regulation. Negotiating this imposed physical and bureaucratic landscape, subject to the jurisdictional constraints of the Oslo framework and the contingencies of military occupation, agents of the Palestinian Authority (PA) work through a discrete, under-resourced local infrastructure to formulate and deliver law and order.

This chapter is organized into five parts. First, I define the Foucauldian concept of biopolitics and relate it to the OPT; the Zionist state, ethnocentric by design and projected eastward by occupation, is seen to regulate a dual policy to the detriment of the Palestinian population. Second, I present an analysis of Oslo's canon and the Palestinian security force structure, remit and jurisdiction, which points to the existence of an indigenous disciplinarity conceptualized within a racialized biopolitical schema. Third, I show how PA surveillance and correction of Palestinians are undertaken through a dependent carceral regime mandated to police the consequences of accelerated Zionist colonization; the failure of this regime to provide adequate disciplinary power by proxy drew sanctions and the spectacle of military action. Fourth, I examine how the politics of reform and contingent shifts in service capacity and remit point to indigenous coercive systems, realigned with colonial biopolitical imperatives. Fifth, I find evidence of resistance in counter-espionage, martyrdom, contestation of criminality and inter-factional tension, culminating in the de facto separation of Gaza from the West Bank.

Israeli Biopolitics

For Foucault, biopolitics mark the culmination of a swing in the purpose of government; sovereign juridical power over territory, negative and manifest in rules of prohibition, gives way to positive power exercised through the anatomo-politics of individual discipline and the biopolitics of population regulation. Population denotes something specific:

> It does not simply mean to say a numerous group of humans, but living beings, traversed, commanded, ruled by processes and biological laws. A population has a birth rate, a rate of mortality, a population has an age curve, a generation pyramid, a life-expectancy, a state of health, a population can perish or, on the contrary, grow (Foucault 2007: 161).

Biopolitics is a "technology of power" distinguished by three features: a set of processes, the phenomena under consideration, and mechanisms of control. Processes are demographic and statistical:

> the ratio of births to deaths, the rate of reproduction, the fertility of a population ... It is these processes—the birth rate, the mortality rate, longevity and so on—together with a whole series of related economic and political problems ... which ... become biopolitics' first objects of knowledge and the targets it seeks to control.

The phenomena driving biopolitics are relevant only on a mass scale and only over time. Regulatory mechanisms are dependent on demographic instruments:

> forecasts, statistical estimates, and overall measures. And their purpose is ... to intervene at the level at which these general phenomena are determined ... to establish an equilibrium, maintain an average, establish a sort of homeostasis, and compensate for variations within this general population and its aleatory field (Foucault 2003: 243–246).

If demographics allow the state to know its population through statistics, biopolitics see the state act through its population on the basis of statistical knowledge. Zionist ethnocentrism, reflected most prominently in the Law of Return and aspects of the Basic Laws,[2] compel the Israeli state to regulate the Jewish-Zionist population to maximise productivity and demographic heft. But how to deal with subjects outside of that project, who must, by definition, include the non-Jewish population of the OPT? In common with the 'improving' colonizers discussed by Dean, neglect and dispossession, repression and misrepresentation, are likely (Dean 2002: 48–49).[3]

[2] Ethnocentrism is implicit in the 1948 Declaration of the Establishment of the State of Israel as a "Jewish state", textual guarantees of non-discrimination on the basis of ethnicity or religion notwithstanding. To encourage Jewish immigration, the June 1950 Law of Return granted Jews worldwide the right to apply for citizenship in the new state. Citizenship was specified two years later, retroactive to independence and to immigrant advantage. To cope with immigration and expedite colonization, in December 1948 the Custodian of Absentee Property was charged with disposing of Palestinian assets. The Absentees' Property Law followed in 1950. Still lacking a formal constitution, Israel today is governed by a series of Basic Laws; including, in the case of territory, the Israel Lands law of 1960.

[3] For a fuller application of Dean to Israel/Palestine, see Parsons and Salter 2008.

Constructing PA Security: Force Structure, Remit, and Jurisdiction

Between 1993 and 1999, the Oslo framework negotiated between Israel and the Palestine Liberation Organization (PLO) granted the PA limited responsibility for policing and incarceration in the OPT.[4] The Interim Agreement (1995) stipulated six security branches under the generic title of Public Security.[5] Textual limits on force composition and strength would be exceeded for complex reasons, but official evolution was largely confined to this template. At least 40,000 personnel were employed in the new indigenous disciplinary mechanisms (Friedrich 2004: 48–50). The least politicised branches were National Security, Civil Defence and the Civil Police, concerned respectively with defence, emergency services and civilian law enforcement. The remaining branches were afforded remits which were conceptually distinct, but which in practice overlapped and were essentially political. General Intelligence managed counter-espionage. Presidential Security worked to ensure the safety of top PA officials and visiting foreign dignitaries. Preventive Security dealt specifically with political opposition to Oslo and the PA (Parsons 2005: 153; Riley et al 2005: 38–39).

The remits issued by Oslo speak little of mundane crime; rather, they are overwhelmingly political. Framing the canon are letters of mutual recognition in which Israel is assured that: "In light of the new era marked by the Declaration of Principles [the DoP, signed 13 September, 1993], the PLO encourages and calls upon the Palestinian people in the West Bank and Gaza Strip to take part in steps leading to the normalization of life, rejecting violence and terrorism, contributing to peace and stability and participating actively in shaping reconstruction, economic development and co-operation."[6] Palestin-

[4] Structural details of the nascent coercive apparatus first appeared in the Agreement on the Gaza Strip and the Jericho Area of 4 May 1994. Article IX called for the establishment of "The Palestinian Directorate of Police Force." Annex I, Article III (3.a) specified arrangements in detail.

[5] Annex I, "The Protocol Concerning Redeployment and Security Arrangements." The six branches set out in the Interim Agreement were: Public Security, Intelligence, Emergency Services and Rescue, the Civil Police, Preventive Security and al-Amn al-Ri'asah [sic], Presidential Security.

[6] PLO chairman Arafat's letter to Norwegian foreign minister Hölst, 9 September 1993.

ians might look to local officers for the provision of law and order, but the restoration of Palestinian policing would come at a price. For all of its military might, Israel had never "been able to 'normalize' its power relations with those under occupation" (Peteet 1994: 35): the Oslo framework required PLO acceptance of an end to anti–colonial resistance, and then issued a remit for the enforcement of "normalization" by proxy.

To that effect, PA are to provide the only legitimate Palestinian armed force in the territories. The Gaza-Jericho Agreement provided for the first IDF redeployment, the return of Yasir Arafat to Palestine on 1 July 1994, and indigenous assumption of "responsibility for public order and internal security of Palestinians." Aside from the PA and the IDF "no other organization or individual" is to "manufacture, sell, acquire, possess, import or otherwise introduce ... any firearms, ammunition, weapons, explosives, gunpowder or any related equipment."[7] The PA is required to advise immediately of "a terrorist action of any kind and from any source" and to "prosecute individuals who are suspected of perpetrating acts of violence and terror."[8] This is not confined to operations in Israel proper; Palestinian officers are required to "take all measures necessary to prevent ... hostile acts directed against the Settlements, the infrastructure serving them and the Military Installation Area."[9] Insofar as a person residing in the OPT may be "suspected of, charged with or convicted of an offence that falls within Israeli criminal jurisdiction ... Israel may request the Palestinian Authority to arrest and transfer the individual to Israel"[10] A Joint IDF-PA Security Committee and a series of District Coordination Offices (DCO) expedite cooperation in practice. The tensions inherent in the arrangements are reflected in the late-Oslo Wye River Memorandum. Foreshadowing post-9/11 rhetoric, it asserts that:

> The struggle against terror and violence must be comprehensive in that it deals with terrorists, the terror support structure, and the environment conducive to the support of terror. It must be continuous and constant over a long-term, in that there can be no pauses in the work against terrorists and their structure.[11]

[7] Articles II.6 and IX.2–3.

[8] Annex I, Article II, *Security Policy for the Prevention of Terrorism and Violence*.

[9] Article XVIII, *The Prevention of Hostile Acts*.

[10] Annex III, Article II.7(b), *Protocol Concerning Legal Matters*.

[11] Article II.

To this effect, the PA's security forces are to be bolstered by support from the CIA.[12] The message is consistent in Oslo's final component, the Sharm al-Sheikh Memorandum (1999); the PA is again called upon to collect "illegal weapons" and apprehend "suspects". To encourage implementation, a "list of Palestinian policemen" is to be forwarded "to the Israeli side" for vetting.[13]

Limits on jurisdiction excluded Israeli–defined territories, and Israeli bodies in Palestinian territories, from the authority of the PA. The DoP made Palestinians subject to the new "strong police force" but ensured that Israel would continue "to carry responsibility for defending against external threats, as well as the responsibility for overall security of the Israelis to protect their internal security and public order."[14] The Gaza-Jericho arrangements echoed this contingent authority: Palestinians gained "control" of roads within Jericho city, but patrolled them in tandem with Israeli vehicles. In the meantime, "Israeli authorities" retain "overriding responsibility and powers for security."[15] In Gaza, the PA secured some 62 per cent of the Strip, a proportion that remained constant until disengagement in 2005.[16] In the West Bank, the Interim Agreement saw PA police deploy outwards to the urban centres of Jenin, Tulkarm, Nablus, Qalqiliyya, Ramallah and Bethlehem. But it also divided the territory into three distinct zones: Area A (major urban centres with PA security and civil responsibility), Area B (PA civil responsibility with policing but ultimate IDF control), and Area C (full IDF control). The Hebron Protocol (1997) divided the city in two: a Palestinian zone H-1, governed by the PA, and an Israeli zone H-2, managed by the IDF. At the height of the PA's territorial reach,[17] Area A constituted 18.2 per cent of the West Bank, Area B 21.8 per cent,

[12] Article II.A.1.c stipulates that: "In addition to the bilateral Israeli–Palestinian security cooperation, a US-Palestinian committee will meet bi–weekly to review the steps being taken to eliminate terrorist cells and the support structure that plans, finances, supplies and abets terror."

[13] Article 8.(b).

[14] Article VIII.

[15] The Cairo Agreement, section on The Gaza Strip, item 1, 9 February 1994.

[16] The Israel State Attorney's Office has contended that post-disengagement the state carries no legal responsibility for residents of the Gaza Strip. However, human rights lawyers have argued that under the laws of occupation, derived from the Hague Convention (1907) and the Fourth Geneva Convention (1949), Israel remains in "effective control" of the Strip and remains the occupying power (B'Tselem 2007a).

[17] From March 2000 until the reinvasions of the al-Aqsa intifada.

and Area C 60 per cent.[18] The latter encompassed IDF installations, settlements and zones designated for settlement expansion. East Jerusalem remained subject to the exclusive jurisdiction of the Israeli Border Guard. Defending the cantons, but bereft of responsibility for international borders, National Security patrolled the limits of Area A (Friedrich 2004: 38). Politicized and cantonized, PA policing amounted to what we might term indigenized disciplinarity, a proxy mechanism for containing resistance to Zionist colonization as it re-engineered the demographics of occupied Palestinian space.

Policing Palestine's "Carceral Archipelago"

Indigenized disciplinarity in Palestine marked what Foucault termed a new "political economy of the power to punish". The gains for Israel were threefold: first, lower "economic and political cost" to occupation; second, better carceral results by enhancing "effectiveness and by multiplying its circuits"; and third, a reduction in "the return effects of punishment on the punishing authority" (Foucault 1977: 89–91). The PA would constitute the most immediate of multiple, concentric "carceral circles" impinging on Palestinian bodies. Beyond them, the cantonization scheme would carve a literal "carceral archipelago" into the OPT, as Palestinian society en masse became subject to "extra-penal incarceration" (Foucault 1977: 297–298).

RAND identified three phases in PA policing: first, from formation in 1994 up to the West Bank redeployment of late 1995; second, from 1996 through expansion across the West Bank and up until reinvasion in 2000; and a third, beginning with the al-Aqsa intifada (Riley et al 2005: 36). The first two constitute a continuum in the reconfiguration of Israeli–Palestinian power and violence. The third marks the breach. Upon arrival in Gaza, the PA absorbed thousands of returnee Palestinian National Liberation Army (PNLA) fighters and many local refugees; salaries would co-opt local cadres, especially the *tanzim*, the informal network of Fatah members forged in Israeli jails. Resources would then percolate downward to wider constituents, and sheer bulk render coercion feasible. Opposition was little tolerated by senior PNLA officers such as Nasir Yusif, aided by *tanzim* graduates such as Muhammad Dahlan, founding head of Preventive Security in Gaza

[18] Kjorlien, Michele L. 2000. "Chronology" in *Journal of Palestine Studies* 29(4): 175.

(and the most prominent political casualty of its loss to Hamas). The death of thirteen demonstrators outside the Palestine mosque in 1994 illustrated that the PA could and would use lethal force. The same dynamics informed West Bank deployment beyond Jericho, with additional support from Gaza: like troops from the Delta deployed in Upper Egypt, they were unknown, less amenable to pressure, their families not easily targeted for revenge. In this second phase, Palestinian disciplinary mechanisms assumed their fullest form, funded by international aid and customs revenues collected by Israel.

Carceral circuits changed hands at the same time. The greater part of the Palestinian prison infrastructure was built during the British Mandate before passing through Jordanian, Egyptian, and Israeli administration. It includes six central prisons (Reform and Rehabilitation Centers, *Markaz al-Islah wa al-Taghiyyr*), four correlating with Area A (Jenin, Nablus, Ramallah, Jericho), one with H-1 (Hebron), and one in Gaza (*al-Saraya*). In Area B, the Interim Agreement granted the PA authority for twenty-five police stations or posts, some with their own cells. Prison officers are drawn from the Civil Police and generally trained at the central academy in Jericho as well as in Jordan and Egypt. Prisoners are channelled through multiple, decentralized detention centres before trial and arrival at central prison. Criminal and political prisoners share a compound but are housed separately. Prior to Israeli attack during the Al-Aqsa intifada, which extensively damaged facilities, modest efforts were made to reform and rehabilitate those incarcerated: criminal prisoners, typically convicted of robbery, disorderly conduct, drug dealing, trading in expired goods or non-political violence, were taught trades such as tailoring. Inmates were sometimes allowed to attend lectures at nearby universities. In total, some 720 criminal prisoners were thought to be in custody toward the end of 2007. The central prison in Ramallah held 181 inmates, thirty-one of them deemed political. Data from other West Bank facilities points to a ratio of roughly four/one in favor of criminal prisoners.

The branches most heavily involved in political detention are General Intelligence and Preventive Security. Following Fatah's loss of Gaza in June 2007, a sweep across the West Bank netted some 430 known or suspected Hamas activists whose whereabouts were for some time known only to captors (International Crisis Group [ICG] 2007: 16). The immediate violence of arrest or interrogation might be ameliorated by the deployment of family members in uniform as a measure of reassurance (Parsons 2005: 163). Perhaps more mindful of procedure, the practice was officially frowned upon by the Civil Police (Zayd 2006). Human rights workers were granted limited access to security services, less readily than with police or prison officers (Mujahid 2006). Founding Preventive Security chief Jibril Rajub, by no means a gentle soul, allowed al-Haq into his Jericho facility. However, most cases of torture and death did occur in security service detention. The Palestinian Human Rights Monitoring Group (PHRMG) recorded thirty-one deaths in PA custody up to mid-2007. Eleven prisoners died with General Intelligence, nine with Preventive Security. This compared with four at the hands of the Civil Police (PHRMG 2007). The statistics are probably reflective of a greater openness to human rights training from centres such as al-Haq and al-Mizan.[19] Trainer Rafif Mujahid remembered:

> We learned that prisoners had been asked to work for some officers, to clean their cars and do other personal tasks. It wasn't torture, but it wasn't legal either. They responded positively to the extent that they asked for more training. Of all of the branches, the Civil Police were the most responsive (Mujahid 2006).

Enhanced carceral efficacy derived from local knowledge and circuit multiplication. Steeped in Palestine's culture of rebellion, officers knew how to look for recalcitrant, newly criminalized agents of resistance. Granted a remit, organized into multiple branches and equipped with a freshly-transferred prison infrastructure, they greatly augmented carceral capacity. The drive for legitimacy and control encouraged cooption and coercion. The new Palestinian "carceral circles" were the most intimate, but least technically adept. One detainee reflected bitterly:

> The Israelis ... were experts who mainly used psychological pressure and isolation to interrogate him, and when they began beating or choking, they had army doctors checking to make sure he was not dying. Under Palestinian detention and interrogation ... there was no method; there were no doctors and no International Red Cross. He feared that the Palestinian interrogators would kill him by accident (Bornstein 2001: 563).

Indicative of formative experience, officers were known to use Hebrew in interrogation; having learned it in Israeli jails, "they continued to relate to it as the language of power and intimidation" (Parsons 2005: 162). Considered by year, a high of nine deaths in custody in

[19] Courses for police officers (*shurta*), prison inspectors (*muraqib al-sujun*) and investigators (*muhaqiq*) draw on a manual, published by al-Haq in Arabic: 'International Principles and Foundations of Law Enforcement' (*al-Mubadi wa al-Quwa'id al-Dawliyya lil-Mukalifiyyn bi–Infadh al-Qanun*).

1995 reflected an early combination of zeal, inexperience and lack of training. Preventive Security officer Ibrahim Ramadan acknowledged both problems and progress:

> It is very difficult, the transition from a revolution to a state, and we made a lot of mistakes. For the first two years, we were dangerous people. But in the third year, 1997, everything got better; we learned to respect the human being, including the criminal (Ramadan 2006).

Deaths in custody actually fell to three in 1996, despite the fact of deployment across the West Bank. Doubling in 1997, it did drop thereafter. Two deaths in 2002, one in 2003 and none again until 2007, point, at least in part, to the degradation of infrastructure prompted by the second intifada (PHRMG 2007): the new arrangements had failed; the vast majority of political prisoners were back in Israeli custody.

Framed by Israeli biopolitics, Palestinian sovereign power over law and punishment reveals similar traits to its disciplinary cousin.[20] First, sovereign power does not extend to the Israeli population of the territories: biopolitical imperatives require that Israeli citizens be free to flow eastward in pursuit of demographic rebalance. Second, legal variegation attests to a complex colonial past and present: the PA draws on three separate penal codes, one for the West Bank, one for Gaza, plus the PLO's Revolutionary Penal Code of 1979, still relevant in the absence of statehood. Third, punishment is deeply politicized, highly sensitive to popular legitimacy, and unevenly applied. The West Bank penal code allows the death penalty for seventeen offences and the Gazan equivalent fifteen, both mediated by the ordinary courts. The PLO code allows the death penalty for forty-two offences "and is applied by ... military courts and state security courts. These special courts are responsible for the vast majority of death sentences imposed by the Palestinian Authority." Of sixty-three death sentences passed by the PA between 1995 and 2007, thirteen had been carried out. Capital criminal offences were often sexual; political crimes typically involved collaboration (B'Tselem 2005); the two were often related, the occupying power being highly adept at exploiting human weakness for intelligence. Tried *in camera* by State Security Courts,[21] alleged collaborators

[20] The tripartite distinction between sovereign, disciplinary and biopolitical power is drawn by Foucault (2007), discussed in Parsons and Salter (2008).

[21] State Security Courts were established by Presidential Decree 49 in 1995. They were officially abolished in 2003 (Amnesty 2004).

could be executed with astonishing speed. Tenuous legitimacy reinforces sensitivity to local pressure and widespread fear of the enemy within (Human Rights Watch 2001: 39–43). The breakdown in law and order that followed destruction of the carceral system saw a predictable return to vigilantism and summary justice, particularly for cases of alleged collaboration.

The third phase of PA policing opened with a crack in cognitive dissonance: unable to square their remit with accelerated Zionist colonization, and lacking direction or will, many officers joined the rebellion. And as the PA failed to function, colonial carceral circuits reactivated to spectacular effect. PA installations were subject to air raids, artillery and naval bombardment, reinvasion, looting and demolition. Resistance leaders were targeted for assassination. Population movement was paralysed and mass detention reintroduced. The occupier had much to draw upon: a "matrix of control" with physical and bureaucratic as well as meta-level politico-military dimensions (Halper 2001). In orthodox carceral terms, it had already expedited what the PLO points to as "the highest rate of incarceration in the world—approximately 20 per cent of the Palestinian population of the Occupied Palestinian Territories has, at one point, been arbitrarily detained or imprisoned by Israel" (PLO 2004). In terms of physical infrastructure, there were eight prisons behind the Green Line run by the Israeli General Prisons Administration, in addition to the military detention center in Megiddo and the spartan Ansar III (Ketziot) camp in the Negev, reopened for the al-Aqsa intifada. These facilities "were augmented by seven interrogation centers, three in Israel and four in the West Bank, and the cells of countless police stations. The settlement infrastructure lent support in the form of military courts located in Ariel, Beit El, and the Ofer detention center" (Parsons 2005: 313). For most of 2007, the number of Palestinians in the system stood somewhere in excess of nine thousand, dropping a little in the second half of the year as Israel released a few hundred, mostly Fatah, captives, to bolster the PA in the West Bank. The proportion held by the IDF was reduced very sharply as the military transferred Ofer, Megiddo and Ansar III to the prison service (B'Tselem 2007).[22] The change of hands suggests a significant

[22] B'Tselem records that in August 2007 there were 8,537 Palestinians in prison service custody compared to 79 held by the IDF. For the same period 2006 it was 8,085/1,078; 2005 4,588/2,714; 2004 3,290/3,997; 2003 2,194/3,256; 2002 1,176/2,644; 2001 773/896.

expansion in routine, as opposed to emergency, carceral capacity in Israel. The Israeli system now held roughly ten times as many Palestinian prisoners as did the PA. In the meantime, Ramallah transformed from a garrison town into a virtual security vacuum, the police forbidden to wear uniform, carry weapons or cross checkpoints, and their patrol cars prohibited from passing within observable distance of IDF roadblocks. Institutional law and order ground to a halt, and customary law (*hal 'asha'iri*) assumed a greater role. In a cantonized, disempowered Palestine, all policing became local.

The Politics of Security Reform

Dysfunction gave rise to demands for reform, most immediately from Palestinians, but also from major donors the EU, as well as Israel and the United States. They held widely divergent agendas.[23] Most Palestinians, in common with the EU, aspired to an accountable, respectful and efficient security apparatus that upheld the rule of law and protected Palestinians. In contrast, subsequent to demolition, Israel and the US aspired to what Roland Friedrich has termed a 'restructurist' agenda, with three main goals: the weakening or replacement of Arafat; "installation of a political leadership that will re-enter into security cooperation with Israel"; and "a Palestinian regime that will accept a final status scenario on Israeli terms" (Friedrich 2004: 15–16). Reformed along a "three-tiered Egyptian model of police, intelligence and army" (Friedrich 2004: 17), Public Security took on a new form.

The Civil Police, Preventive Security and Civil Defence now answered to the Interior Ministry, responsible in turn to the Prime Minister as head of the Cabinet. This was intended to rationalize command and better contain resistance. Concordant with responsibilities set out in the PA's Basic Law, the president retained control of the remaining two branches, General Intelligence and National Security, the latter including Military Intelligence and the re-branded Special Presidential Guard

[23] The EU contributed to judicial and security reform through the European Union Co-ordinating Office for Palestinian Police Support (EUCOPPS), "a long standing commitment of support to the transformation of the Palestinian police ... to create a more effective police service and to improve coordination of donor activities in this field" (Commission of the European Communities 2005: 6). It was superseded from January 2006 by the European Union Police Mission for the Palestinian Territories (EUPOL-COPPS) (EU Council Secretariat 2006).

(SPG). The constraints of the Oslo framework precluded an official army and hence a Ministry of Defence to which they might otherwise have reported (Riley et al. 2005: 55).

In his critical analysis of PA reform, Mushtaq Khan blames high profile governance problems on Oslo's meta-level architecture (Khan 2004: 8–10), arguing that the mainstream good governance agenda is predicated on a theoretical reversal of development causality: it requires of Palestinians a quality of governance that is rightly a function of the very economic, social and political development precluded by Oslo. Centralized executive power compensated for meta-level constraint, providing for social cohesion through the distribution of politically expedient rent (Khan 2005: 44; Friedrich 2004: 70). The same logic holds true for the security apparatus: there was indeed the formation of parallel commands and branches"; like their civilian counterparts, the security sector was:

> ... involved in tax collection, and in the turbulence of the times often spent these taxes locally without remitting them ... There were occasional bitter struggles between various security services and alliances not only over the patronage allocations from the central government, but also over the taxation of local resources (Amundsen and Ezbidi 2004: 161).

The point is that these phenomena derived from limits on the PA's jurisdiction, limits that required the PA to work in disaggregated pockets as the Zionist state projected its citizens eastward around them. Friedrich concurs with Khan that in this context, even well-intentioned security sector reform could "very well be confusing means with ends" (Friedrich 2004: 71). The 'restructurist' agenda aspired to render the PA a better disciplinary mechanism for regulating the colonized as the colonial power expedited demographic rebalance in favour of Zionism.

Resisting Israeli Biopolitics

Palestinian disciplinary and carceral mechanisms evidence bureaucratic and military resistance to their Israeli biopolitical remit. The former includes counter-intelligence, technical non-compliance with the Oslo framework, prevention of private land sales to colonial agents, and 'unauthorised' prisoner releases. In counter-intelligence, Preventive Security enjoyed real success in turning collaborators, thousands of whom had been on the pre-Oslo Israeli payroll (Usher 1996: 25); a discernable drop in Israeli intelligence reversed at least one flow of knowledge and power in the OPT. The technical requirement that the PA transfer wanted suspects to Israel was managed through prolonged obfuscation. Regime legitimacy precluded transfer of security prisoners, but did eventually allow for the handover of a suspected homicidal pedophile. It was indicative of the narrowness of the point at which Palestinian and Israeli conceptions of criminality converged.[24] Requirements that the PA crack down on the theft of Israeli vehicles, extensively recycled in refugee camp workshops, generated brief intervention; riots underlined deep tensions in Palestinian society, and studied procrastination ensued (Wahdan 2000). Land sales to Israel, especially around East Jerusalem, were fiercely discouraged by means that may have extended to extra-judicial killing. Denied a visible presence by Oslo, the PA maintained non-uniformed officers in the capital, especially amongst the growing refugee camp population at Shu'fat. Dealing with Islamist opposition, the PA was adept at publicly bringing in suspects for questioning before expediting a quick and discreet release. The phenomenon drove Israel to distraction but tactically underpinned social cohesion. The assassination of Israeli minister Rehavam Ze'evi prompted innovation to keep the prisoners in Palestinian hands: US and UK supervision in Jericho functioned for several years until Israel stormed the facility in March 2006. The operation captured wider carceral realities.

PA military resistance, decentralized and sporadic, encompassed logistical support for guerrillas, direct confrontation with the IDF and individual martyrdom. *Tanzim* and other cadres were well placed to channel equipment and intelligence to various factions during the al-Aqsa intifada; some officers resigned their commission to rejoin the fray, others fought out of uniform. Confrontation between uniformed officers and the IDF had already occurred: in September 1996, nationwide protest at the opening of Israel's Hashmonean tunnel saw police return IDF fire and overrun a military post near Nablus. In each case, the fighting reflected Israel's colonial cartography, mostly occurring around the settlement infrastructure, and officers reacted as the occupier exacted a high toll in civilian casualties (Mansur 2001: 85; Parsons 2005: 269–272). The IDF continued targeting officers long after the second uprising wound down. The attrition rate became apparent in the frequency with which security personnel were celebrated as mar-

[24] Hisham Najm from Nablus was arrested by Palestinian police and handed over to Israeli custody in January 2000 (Peace Monitor 2000: 117).

tyrs; posters circulated in public spaces and police stations routinely recorded the rank and security branch of the martyr.[25] Contemplating the post-intifada wreckage, Arafat successor Mahmud 'Abbas found the West Bank security apparatus had largely ceased to exist, the Gazan facilities run down to 30 per cent (Haaretz 2003).

Islamist resistance entered the PA through local and legislative elections. By January 2006, Hamas held the right to run the security forces previously wrested from presidential hands: the Civil Police, Preventive Security and Civil Defence. The Hamas-Fatah national unity government, brokered in Mecca the following year, appointed 'independent' Islamist Hani al-Qawasma to head the Interior Ministry. Pragmatic and flexible in practice, Hamas sought to govern through a graduated ceasefire but without agreeing to formal recognition of Israel, to abide by the Oslo canon, or to declare an official end to the armed struggle. In this respect, under Hamas the PA *became* the resistance. It was consequently outlawed. Israel launched sanctions and military action with US support and EU complicity.[26] Heedless of democratic mandate, the occupier incarcerated 46 of 132 Palestinian legislators, forty-one of them Hamas, precluding a quorum (ICG 2007: 2 & 17). Unpaid salaries encouraged recalcitrant Fatah officers to rebel. Meanwhile, the US Congress passed a multi–million dollar package in support of forces loyal to the post-Arafat presidency; the SPG and National Security were rearmed in the months preceding the June 2007 showdown with Hamas,[27] and troops were deployed independently of ministerial

[25] A sample of security service martyrs from the central West Bank were said by local sources to include Samir al-Shamala (Civil Police), Mahir Sharif 'Abd Rabbu (General Intelligence), 'Amr 'Ayydaya (National Security), and Ahmad al-'Amari (Preventive Security).

[26] The party ostensibly responsible for progress in Palestinian-Israeli negotiations is the 'Quartet', composed of the US, UN, EU and Russia. Both US and EU had previously classified Hamas as a terrorist organization and encountered legal (if far from insurmountable) obstacles to a dialogue. The US was highly pro-active in preventing all parties from breaking the impasse. For a stinging critique of Israeli–US policies during this time, see the End of Mission Report by outgoing UN Under-Secretary General, UN Special Coordinator for the Middle East Peace Process and Personal Representative of the Secretary-General to the PLO and the PA, Envoy to the Quartet Alvaro De Soto (De Soto 2007).

[27] In January 2007 the US Congress approved an "$86.3 million aid and assistance package focused on security forces under the PA president's authority,

instruction. Gaining no more traction than his predecessor, Qawasma resigned. Hamas nemesis Dahlan returned as security advisor to the presidency (ICG 2007: 7–9).[28] External pressure induced fresh crisis in Palestine's coercion-resistance dialectic.

Institutional tension over policing and security took concrete territorial form as swift but bloody action left Hamas in possession of the Gaza Strip. The 'Izz al-Din al-Qassam Brigades, and their post-election spin-off, the Executive Force, defeated and disbanded the politicized branches of the PA security apparatus. Preventive Security chiefs Yusif 'Isa and Rashid Abu Shbak joined others now exiled from Gaza. Of General Intelligence, only the building remained. Contemplating the SPG, Hamas security advisor Ahmad Yusif remarked:

> There's no need for the Presidential Guard. Why do you need 4,000 men to protect one man? Some will take early retirement; some may choose to retire at the end of the year. The rest much switch to the economic arena. But the question is how to restructure the security forces and the intelligence sector when we have documents that reveal some were serving foreign entities (ICG 2007: 18).

The PA in Ramallah issued orders for salaried officers and civil servants in Gaza to stay away from work.[29] Fatah personnel in Gaza were advised that they might rejoin the Civil Police, but not at command level. Reformed West Bank carceral circuits were afforded modest support: Israel authorized a shipment of a thousand M16 rifles from Jordan for presidential disposal, limited IDF-PA cooperation resumed under *tanzim* cadre Husayn al-Shaykh, and modest numbers of Fatah cadres were released from Israeli custody (Haaretz 2007). In the meantime, Hamas members were rounded up. The United States proffered diplomatic cover through a summit in Annapolis, and Zionist colonization progressed apace.

Conclusions

Foucault asks that we "rid ourselves of the illusion that penality is above all (if not exclusively) a means of reducing crime" (Foucault

---

in particular the National Security Forces and Presidential Guard" (ICG 2007: 9).

[28] The resignation was submitted on 14 May 2007.

[29] According to ICG: "Out of a total police force of 13,500, Hamas claimed that 400 were back at work after a fortnight" (ICG 2007: 15).

1977: 24). In Palestine, we may rid ourselves of a similar illusion in the OPT's carceral archipelago. Some indigenous carceral circles do have a mundane criminal function. The Civil Police seek to uphold the law, and the majority of prison inmates are criminal. But the Oslo framework explicitly criminalized resistance to occupation and granted the PA a remit to enforce the new order. Quantified and cantonized, Palestinians were then policed amidst a dynamic occupation that demarcated space and projected citizens eastward—at an accelerated rate—into a privileged and expanding settlement infrastructure. Palestinian disciplinary and carceral mechanisms regulated the indigenous population within this racialized biopolitical binary. Subject to enormous pressures, these mechanisms variously slipped gear and failed. In failure, they were chastised; in rebellion, demolished. The reform agenda of hegemonic powers then aspired to render indigenized disciplinarity more effective. In the late Arafat-era, a prime minister and empowered interior ministry took charge of Preventive Security. Post-Arafat, as electoral success put Hamas in notional charge, forces commanded by the presidency—especially National Security and the SPG, along with General Intelligence—were bolstered.

From the PA's inception, the concentration of coercive power continued to inhere in the colonial state. Israeli carceral circles do buttress Palestinian containment of local resistance; the tensions inherent in Oslo's arrangements were such that they could not be dispensed with. But supporting disciplinary action is only one way in which Israeli forces circumscribe Palestinian society and expedite colonization. Proximate to Palestinian circles, the IDF maintains a regime of checkpoints, patrols, planners and engineers, mass detention, and if need be, remains capable of reinvasion. In Gaza under Hamas refusal to subscribe to this biopolitical schema prompted full-spectrum containment; if carceral mechanisms would not realign, predictable sanctions applied. Institutional crisis and territorial division in the OPT reflect the biopolitical design within which Palestinian policing and incarceration unfold.

Bibliography

Al-Haq. 2004. *Al-mubadi wa al-quwa'id al-dawliyya lil-mukalifiyyn bi–infadh al-qanun*. Ramallah: al-Haq.

Amnesty International. 2004. *Report 2004: Palestinian Authority*. http://web.amnesty.org/report2004/pse-summary-eng accessed 14 November 2007.

Amundsen, Inge and Basem Ezbidi. 2004. "PNA political institutions and the future of state formation" in Mushtaq Husain Khan with George Giacaman and Inge Amundsen (eds.) *State formation in Palestine: Viability and governance during a social transformation*. London: RoutledgeCurzon: 141–167.

Bornstein, Avram. 2001. "Ethnography and the politics of prisoners in Palestine-Israel" in *Journal of Contemporary Ethnography* 30(5): 546–574.

B'Tselem: The Israeli Information Center for Human Rights in the Occupied Territories. 2005. *Death penalty in the Palestinian Authority*. http://www.btselem.org/English/PNA/Index.asp accessed 20 September 2007.

B'Tselem. 2006. *The Gaza Strip: Israel's obligations under international law*. http://www.btselem.org/English/Gaza_Strip/Israels_Obligations.asp accessed 20 September 2007.

B'Tselem. 2007. *Statistics on Palestinians in the custody of the Israeli security forces*. http://www.btselem.org/English/Statistics/Detainees_and_Prisoners.asp accessed 20 September 2007.

Commission of the European Communities. 2005. *Communication from the Commission to the Council and the European Parliament: EU-Palestinian cooperation beyond disengagement—towards a two-state solution COM(2005) 458 final. 5* October. http://eurlex.europa.eu/LexUriServ/site/en/com/2005/com2005_0458en01.pdf accessed 22 October 2007.

Dean, Mitchell. 2002. "Liberal government and authoritarianism" in *Economy and Society* 31: 37–61.

De Soto, Alvaro. 2007. *End of Mission Report. May*. http://image.guardian.co.uk/sys-files/Guardian/documents/2007/06/12/DeSotoReport.pdf accessed 15 June 2007.

EU Council Secretariat. 2006. *Factsheet. European Union Police Mission for the Palestinian Territories (EUPOL-COPPS) (EUPOL-COPPS/02). 9 February*. http://consilium.europa.eu/uedocs/cmsUpload/051222–EUPOL-COPPS.pdf accessed 14 November 2007.

Foucault, Michel. 1975. "Interview with Roger-Pol Droit" in *Le Monde* 21 February. Cited by Paul Patton. 1979, "Of Power and Prisons" in Meaghan Morris and Paul Patton (eds.). *Michel Foucault: power, truth, strategy*. Sydney: Feral Publications.

Foucault, Michel. 1977. *Discipline and punish: The birth of the prison*. Trans. Alan Sheridan. New York: Vintage.

Foucault, Michel. 2003. *Society must be defended: Lectures at the Collège de France, 1975–76*. Mauro Bertani and Alessandro Fontana (eds.). New York: Picador.

Foucault, Michel. 2007. "The meshes of power" in Jeremy W. Crampton and Stuart Elden (eds.) *Space, knowledge and power: Foucault and geography*. Aldershot: Ashgate: 153–162.

Foucault, Michel. 2007. *Security, territory, population: Lectures at the College De France, 1977–78*. Michael Senellart ed. Trans. Graham Burchill. New York: Palgrave Macmillan.

Friedrich, Roland. 2004. *Security sector reform in the Occupied Palestinian Territories*. Jerusalem: Palestinian Academic Society for the Study of International Affairs.

Ha'aretz. 2003. 28 May.

Ha'aretz. 2007. 26 July.

Halper, Jeff. 2001. *The Matrix of Control*. http://www.mediamonitors.net/halper1.html accessed 9 November 2007.

Human Rights Watch. 2001. *Justice undermined: Balancing security and human rights in the Palestinian justice system. November*. http://www.hrw.org/reports/2001/pa/ accessed 1 October 2007.

International Crisis Group. 2007. *After Gaza. Middle East Report 68. ICG, August 2*. http://www.crisisgroup.org/home/index.cfm?id=4975&l=1 accessed 20 September 2007.

Israel-PLO agreements of the Oslo process:

Letters of Mutual Recognition. 9 September 1993.

Declaration of Principles on Interim Self-Government Arrangements. 13 September 1993.

Israeli–Palestinian Cairo Agreement. 9 February 1994.

Agreement on the Gaza Strip and the Jericho Area. 4 May 1994.

Interim Agreement on the West Bank and Gaza Strip. 28 September 1995.

Protocol Concerning the Redeployment in Hebron. 15 January 1997.

Wye River Memorandum. 23 October 1998.

Sharm al-Sheikh Memorandum. 4 September 1999.

Khan, Mushtaq Husain. 2004. "Introduction: State formation in Palestine" in Mushtaq Husain Khan with George Giacaman and Inge Amundsen (eds.). *State formation in Palestine: Viability and governance during a social transformation*. London and New York: RoutledgeCurzon: 1–12

Khan, Mushtaq Husain. 2004. "Evaluating the emerging Palestinian state: 'Good governance versus "transformation potential"'" in Mushtaq Husain Khan with George Giacaman and Inge Amundsen (eds.) *State formation in Palestine: Viability and governance during a social transformation*. London: RoutledgeCurzon: 13–63.

Mansour, Camille. 2001. "Israel's colonial impasse" in *Journal of Palestine Studies* 30(4): 83–88.

Mills, Sarah. 1997. *Discourse*. London: Routledge.

Mujahid, Rafif. Al-Haq. 2006. Interview, Ramallah 22 June.

Palestine Liberation Organization Negotiations Support Unit. *Palestinian Political Prisoners*. http://www.nad-plo.org/faq1p.php accessed 20 February 2004.

Palestinian Human Rights Monitoring Group. *List of death in the Palestinian custody*. http://www.phrmg.org/phrmg%20documents/Death%20in%20Custody/Tables/death%20in%20custody%20english.htm accessed 19 September 2007.

Parsons, Nigel. 2005. *The politics of the Palestinian Authority: From Oslo to al-Aqsa*. London: Routledge.

Parsons, Nigel and Mark B. Salter. 2008. "Israeli Biopolitics: Closure, Territorialization and Governmentality in the Occupied Palestinian Territories" in *Geopolitics* 13(4): 701–723.

Peace Monitor. 2000. *Journal of Palestine Studies* 29(3): 114–129.

Peteet, Julie. 1994. "Male gender and rituals of resistance in the Palestinian intifada: a cultural politics of violence" in *American Ethnologist* 21: 31–49.

Ramadan, Ibrahim. Preventive Security officer. 2006. Interview. Dhaysha refugee camp. 20 June.

Riley, Kevin Jack, Seth G. Jones, Steven N. Simon and David Brannan with Anga R. Timilsina; 2005. "Internal Security" in The RAND Palestinian State Study Team. *Building a Successful Palestinian State*. Santa Monica CA: RAND Corp. pp. 33–71.

Rabin, Yitzhaq. 1993. *Yedioth Ahronoth*. 7 September. Cited by Graham Usher. 1995. *Palestine in crisis: The struggle for peace and political independence after Oslo*. London: Pluto Press: 71–72.

Salter, Mark B. and Nigel Parsons. 2005. "Israeli biopolitics and the documentation of Palestinian closure." Paper presented at Border Regions in Transition VII, 9 January, in West Jerusalem.

Usher, Graham. 1996. "The politics of internal security: The PA's new intelligence services" in *Journal of Palestine Studies* 25(2): 21–34.

Wahdan, Hadeel. 2000. "Refugee Robin Hood" in *Palestine Report* 7(6). 26 July.

Zayd, Tariq. Deputy Commissioner of Police for the West Bank (Northern Governorate). 2006. Interview. Ramallah. 22 June.

3

TANGLED WEBS OF COERCION

PARASTATAL PRODUCTION OF VIOLENCE IN ABU GHRAIB

Laleh Khalili

"It was all the contractors; the people who did terrible things to us, who told the soldiers to 'soften us up,' they were all contractors," says Haj Ali al-Qaisi, the founder of Association of The Former Iraqi Detainees of the United States, who was held in Abu Ghraib between October 2003 and March 2004.[1] Haj Ali's image, recognisable despite his hood because of the identifiable injuries to his left hand, appears in the vast cache of photographs taken by the US soldiers and leaked to the press. When I ask him how he knew they were employees of CACI or Titan, the private military contractors working in Abu Ghraib, he says that they wore civilian clothes and carried no guns.[2]

[1] Interview with Author, Amman, 6 November 2007.

[2] Although Qaisi is largely correct that the majority of the interrogators in Abu Ghraib were indeed contractors, his account excludes the military intelligence personnel involved in the interrogations, as well as the Central Intelligence Agency interrogators. We now know that CIA interrogators in civilian clothing were also involved in the Abu Ghraib interrogations of "high value detainees" and were responsible for at least the death of Manadel al-Jamadi. Furthermore, the ordinary military police wore civilian clothing during their

This chapter is about the complex apparatus of coercion at work in Abu Ghraib under the aegis of the United States' counterinsurgency campaigns in the "War on Terror." Based on interviews with former Abu Ghraib prisoners, contractors and military interrogators, and US military officers, as well as memoirs, news articles, and US government documents declassified under the Freedom of Information Act, this chapter argues that far from being an aberration, or being solely a pornography of violence, the operations at Abu Ghraib are instances of the mundane co-imbrication of what are too often dichotomised as the domains of the "state" and "the private sector." Indeed, the manner in which the administration, guard duty, and interrogations at Abu Ghraib are located in an interstitial no-man's-land of extraterritoriality, legal and procedural ambiguity, and a simultaneous visibility/invisibility (at once over-photographed for "inside" consumption and inaccessible to "outside" scrutiny) all speak to the kind of parastatal complexity reproduced by neoliberal forms of rule and coercion. In other words, contra the "return of the state" literature prevalent since 11 September 2001 (Hall 2002; Press-Barnathan 2004), I argue that the parastatal complex residing at the blurred boundaries between the state and the "private" sector has become more robust, further undermining a notion of a strong, unitary, coherent and bounded state (cf. Mitchell 1991).

What makes the case of Abu Ghraib particularly relevant in this regard is that it combines the two functions which are considered to be the conditions of "stateness" and the domains of the state's monopoly: control over modes of punishment and incarceration on the one hand, and military coercion on the other. The significance of parastatal coercion in Abu Ghraib is, of course, not only that the use of racialised violence is normalised and institutionalised beyond the bounds of the state, but also that the set of inextricable public/private institutions comprising the parastatal complex shore up the power of the United States in Iraq and are familiar modes of European colonial control. These complexes are particularly effective, because as they distribute the sites of exercise of power (while still allowing for central control of a dominant state), they implicitly and explicitly incorporate large constituencies in their tangled web of power, thus making for a far more

time off while still bearing arms. The latter is a violation of military regulations in a prisoner of war detention setting (Taguba 2004: 41).

institutionalised, powerful and enduring form of domination than tactical usage of short-term military power would indicate.

The simplest definition of the parastatal complex is of a series of interconnected institutions and organisations with political authority over a given constitutency, serving a given state.[3] In discussions of centrally planned economies, parastatal organisations are those in control of some economic function/institution *for* the state, and are often visually pictured as "surrounding the state." For my purposes, the parastate is not simply a set of semi–autonomous institutions demarcating the boundary of an extended state, but rather a socio-political space best illustrative of the inseparability of state and the social sphere, or as Mitchell describes it, "the porous edges where official practice mixes with the semi–official and the semi–official with unofficial to be turned into [fabricated] lines of separation" (Mitchell 1991: 82). Furthermore, the regulations, contracts, and shared understandings and practices which discipline the relations between different political actors within this parastatal complex are indicative extensions of broader regulations, contracts, and norms elsewhere, and they reproduce the same social relations in microcosm.

I do not intend the parastatal complex (or my insistence on the inextricability of state and the social) to obscure the incomparably large magnitude of the power that some states wield in the world, in this case the US. My visual metaphor for the power of the US working through the parastatal complex is not the same as Hardt and Negri's amorphous and decentralised "Empire" of network wars where equivalent nodes of power operate universally (cf. Duffield 2002). Rather, the parastatal complex is one space in and through which an imperial centre attempts to reproduce social hierarchies, political asymmetries, and relations of violence. Furthermore, the imperial centre's attempts at domination are all too often disrupted, distorted, and challenged, but the extent to which these disruptions and distortions transform its dominance depends on the specificities of context and the ongoing struggle therein.

[3] Here, I differ with standard description of parastatal organisations which point to self-contained corporations or businesses—such as the Saudi Aramco or utility firms—which are fully or partially state-owned. Rather, as the definition shall make clear, I am focusing on a series of corporations, all interwoven and all ostensibly independent, but very much tied in with the state. My use of the word "complex" is intended to invoke the "military-industrial" complex without necessarily being delimited by the definition of that term.

In this chapter, I will discuss the coercive parastatal complex that has emerged in the specific site of Abu Ghraib prison, because more than any other location in the cartography of the "War on Terror", Abu Ghraib acts as a fulcrum of the kinds of micropolitics that attempts to reproduce the world order that has the US at its economic, political and military apex. The specific areas in which the parastatal coercive complex does the work of reproduction are labour hierarchies, transnational disparities, zones of legal ambiguity, instantiation of imperial forms of authority, and carceral states in which carceral coercion is the normalised mode of domination.

We now know much about the ways in which a "permanent war economy" has shaped US policy (Melman 1984; 1997; Mills 1960). Jonathan Feldman (2007) writes eloquently about how war economies garner the loyalty of a US labour force who see in militarist production higher wages and the possibilities of economic advancement, while since the 1960s and the reign of Robert McNamara as Secretary of Defence, the US Department of Defense has increasingly consolidated its management and administration of "the military-industrial empire." Here, however, I am more interested in the coercive micropractices on the ground which instantiate the neoliberal order in the interaction between the US as an occupying power and the Iraqis as the occupied.

One of the most extraordinary features of the parastatal complex at Abu Ghraib has been the extent to which it penetrates every single aspect of the establishment and administration of the prison. Precisely because of this penetration, I argue that Abu Ghraib is *un*exceptional in any sense,[4] and that all activities therein, from the banal everyday functioning of the prison to the outrageous abuse and torture of the prisoners, reflect and reproduce global economic, political and military asymmetries and the intertwining of the ostensibly public and the allegedly private, even crossing national boundaries.

From its very inception, Abu Ghraib exemplifies these border-crossings. The radical coup that deposed a pro-British monarchy in Iraq in 1958 and ended the pro-US Baghdad Pact (to be superseded by other coups in the coming years) seems not to have been a barrier to trade in the technology of coercion between US firms and the Iraqi government. Begun at the behest of Abdul-Karim Qasim, and finally completed

[4] Like Puar 2004, I do not find Abu Ghraib exceptional; but my emphasis here is less on the torture or the sexualisation of the soldiers and the prisoners, and more on the running and management of a counterinsurgency prison.

under the rule of Ba'ath in March 1970, Abu Ghraib prison was constructed by an international consortium of architects, contractors, and civil engineers, coordinated centrally by the main contractor, a Long Island, New York civil engineering firm, Litchfield, Whiting, Browne, Panero and Severud.[5] The prison "met the international standards of the time" and included security features familiar from contemporaneous US prisons (Christianson 2004; McAllester 2004). The macabre history of the prison under the Ba'ath regime includes the execution of some four thousand political prisoners in 1984 and of a large number of Shi'a prisoners again in 1996.

Since 2003, the prison complex has acted as both a Forward Operating Base and as the main detention centre in Iraq. Until 2004/2005, it held a mixture of both criminal and security prisoners, but since then, it has become solely a security prison, to which detainees considered to have "useful intelligence" are sent from all over Iraq. The prison area is approximately one square kilometre, with four kilometres of security perimeter and twenty-four guard towers. To effectively police the planned population of some two thousand prisoners (though at points it has held five or six times as many, including in late 2003, when it held six to seven thousand prisoners), the vast prison complex was subdivided into five different compounds with varying degrees of security, and as a penal-military site allowing for the kind of carceral "management" practices familiar from a variety of different contexts (e.g. Long Kesh Prison in Northern Ireland is a particularly apt comparison; see Feldman 1991).

Because the US military and civilian administrators in Iraq had largely destroyed the country's coercive apparatus, disbanding the military and disarming the police, they required penal processing of the "common criminals" and, increasingly, counterinsurgency "detainees". From very early on, the occupation authorities brought in contractors, firstly to restore Saddam's prisons, damaged by war, bombing, and looting, and secondly to construct a series of "modern" prisons modelled after US carceral facilities and train the police in "democratic" methods of policing. This entailed the hiring by the US Department of Justice of "corrections consultants", to be paid under the provisions of the International Criminal Investigative Training Assistance Program (ICITAP).

[5] Before the construction of new prisons began in the 1950s, Iraqi prisons had been built by the British during their control of the country (McAllester 2004).

The program, established in 1986 and housed in the Criminal Division of Department of Justice, but providing services through the Department of State in post-intervention contexts (such as Haiti, Bosnia, and Kosovo), follows in the footsteps of the both historic and extant US programmes and organisations which export US methods of counter-insurgency incarceration and policing overseas (e.g. The School of Americas, now renamed the Western Hemisphere Institute for Security Cooperation, and the now defunct International Police Academy).

After the Abu Ghraib scandal, the ICITAP contractors—hired at the behest of the hastily established Office for Reconstruction and Humanitarian Assistance in Iraq (first convened in January 2003 and in turn replaced by the Coalition Provision Authority in April—came under some scrutiny both by congress and an anaemic Department of Justice internal investigation, which essentially cleared them of all charges. In my own interview with Janis Karpinski (Washington DC, 13 August 2007), the general who had initially been in charge of all the prisons in Iraq in 2003, she again and again emphasised the corruption of the private contractors. My intent, however, is not to focus on financial or administrative irregularities, but rather to interrogate the very basis of the contracts.

If the problems that arose around the prison construction and training programme were to be deconstructed layer by layer, we note ever more profound—though subtle—features of this parastatal coercive complex. The most observable problems (or the outer layers) are those of "corruption": the contractors would order $2000 replacement keys for prison locks from their friend and/or business partner in the US, where these probably could have been manufactured locally for a fraction of a dollar.[6] The occupation authorities would pay multiple times to perform simple tasks without keeping track of whether or not the task was completed. The contractors "had once taken photos of themselves holding fists full of US dollars, with more bills sticking out of their pockets. One time, they drew $3.1 million [in cash] to pay for prison contracts. They had photos taken of themselves sitting on the bricks of cash, which formed a pile about the height of a barbecue grill" (Karpinski 2005: 178). Setting aside the corruption, problems of incompetence were glaring: the occupation military and civilian administrators had no accounting system, no bank, and no capability to pay by checks or transfers. Bricks of cash were used to pay for services and

[6] Karpinsi, interview with author, Washington D.C., 13 August 2007.

products and the money was kept "in an unused bathroom in the prisons department". Karpinski (2005: 176) also recounts how in the accounting ledger, "one torn scrap of paper requested $25 for computer and printing support. Another entry ordered payment of $28,000 to an Iraqi prison contractor." When attempting to hire contactors, Karpinski notes the inter-agency rivalry between the Department of Defense and the Department of Justice who "was not going to let anybody tread on their turf" (Karpsinki 2005: 173).

Further, Karpinski recounts that despite the urgency of the need to restore the prisons to a functioning form (Abu Ghraib, for example, did not have running water until well into 2004), US occupation authorities only wanted to employ US, or Canadian, or British contractors, but certainly not Iraqis (Karpinski 2005: 172). The war had always been intended as an important strand of military Keynesianism, and handing of contracts to foreign firms have come under US congressional scrutiny because of the emphasis on the national security importance of military contracts "benefiting" US firms and employees.

Congressional oversight also found problems with the occupation authorities' inadequate vetting of the contractors hired to reconstruct Iraqi prisons (DoJ 2005). Terry Stewart, who during his brief tenure in Baghdad made openly racist comments about Iraqis, was the director of Arizona prison system (1995–2002) which, under his watch, the Department of Justice charged for the rape and sodomy of women prisoners by guards. After leaving Iraq, his company, Advanced Corrections Management, was put in charge of prisons in Haiti (Braziel 2006: 152 fn13). Lane McCotter, a former colonel in the US Army and Vietnam veteran, had been successively in charge of the Texas, New Mexico, and Utah state prisons. In Texas, the incidences of prisoner abuse skyrocketed under his watch, while he had to resign his post in Utah because during his tenure a mentally ill prisoner died from a coronary embolism after being strapped to a chair, naked, for sixteen hours. After leaving Utah, his management of a New Mexico jail as a private consultant for Management and Training Corporation, a private corrections consulting firm, was criticised by the same Department of Justice which employed him to "reform" Iraqi prisons (Forsch 2004; Simmons 2004; DoJ 2005). Several other private consultants were under investigations for a variety of mismanagement charges. In the wake of the Abu Ghraib scandal, and when the hiring of these prison officials came to light, a reporter for *The Nation* found that a former corrections officer who was "respected both by prison reformists and corrections administrators, turned down an offer to join the Justice Department's team." He told the reporter that "The philosophies of the individuals that were going did not match mine" (Forsch 2004).

But again, these are managerial and administrative deficiencies, which the Congressional oversight intends to monitor and repair. What is far more interesting and yet far less commented-upon is the carceral complex that is explicitly and aggressively exported through these contracts across international boundaries. In some senses, the ICITAP programme of the Department of Justice is an extension of the agenda of the School of Americas, or the International Police Academy, or the Public Safety Assistance programme of years gone by. These programmes trained state violence workers from Southern governments in the methods of policing necessary in Cold War (and subsequent) counterinsurgencies, had been implicated in training of death squads, teaching of torture (the film *Battle of Algiers* was a favourite teaching tool), and were only brought to task through the active and persistent mobilisation of US and Latin American activists both in direct action and through lobbying with less supine Congresses (Gill 2004). However, as the privatisation of state functions has proceeded apace, and as the coercive parastatal complex has thickened and deepened, these counterinsurgency functions have become far more diffuse, and correspondingly, Congressional debate about exporting such punitive practices has died down. Because of the multi–sitedness of these functions, many taken up by mega-corporations, but many more under the auspices of small and mid-sized innocuously named enterprises, popular mobilisation around them now requires the kind of research resources, geographic reach, and familiarity with transnational corporate structuring that is only slowly being acquired by activists. In the Congress, the difficulty of monitoring non-public entities on the one hand, and the ideological commitment to free market "entrepreneurship" on the other, have allowed for international corrections consulting to evade the kind of scrutiny that is often mobilised, for example, around the renewal of the mandate of the School of Americas.

The peculiarity of this transnational carceral network is that it is parastatal. The assimilation of counterinsurgency incarceration and policing into global trade in services distinguishes this coercive parastatal complex from its progenitors, the government-to-government military aid/training on the one hand, and the symbiotic relationship between the US government and defence technology firms, on the other.[7] The consequences are militarisation of police forces, creation of a web of personal and institutional contacts between violence workers of the police or military across borders, the creation of an interpenetrated network of public and private both vested in the export of violent methods from the US, and a penetration of US commercial/political/coercive interests into the sinews of state power overseas.

The coercive parastatal complex created through these export practices works in Abu Ghraib to reproduce labour hierarchies within the prison walls and far beyond it. Abu Ghraib cannot run without the labour of "expatriates, third party nationals, and local nationals." The International Peace Operations Association (IPOA), the US trade association representing primarily US and UK private security firms, describes these naturalised categories as follows:

> Expatriates tend to be from the same country as either the occupying military force or the companies that contract with that force. Therefore, expatriates are generally from countries such as Australia, Canada, the United Kingdom or the United States. Third country nationals are from countries that are essentially unconnected to the conflict, such as Bangladesh, Fiji, India, Nepal, Pakistan, the Philippines or Uruguay, among others. Finally, local nationals, as their description suggests, are drawn from the local population (Messner 2007: 32).

The description at first seems innocuous enough, but further reflection brings to the fore the unstated distinction made between the nationals of Britain and its former settler colonies on the one hand and the "other", southern, states on the other. The racialised difference is reflected not only in the kind of jobs these categories of contractors do, but also in their pay, their privileges and rights, and their treatment at Abu Ghraib and elsewhere in Iraq.

Tony Lagouranis, who was a military interrogator in Abu Ghraib in 2004, describes the "global" hierarchy of labour at the prison. At the bottom of the hierarchy are migrant workers from South Asia under contract to US corporations. They are often transported from Kuwait to Iraq without their consent (or sometimes even knowledge; they think

[7] The US and Boeing—for example—have long had an intimate relationship, in which the various administrative offices of the state (Department of Defense, the US Chamber of Commerce, the Department of the State, etc.) act to smooth the sales of Boeing products, while Boeing's sales of its products not only enriches US coffers, but also provides the state with a political lever it can use in projecting its international power.

they might be flying to Dubai, for example), sometimes forced to serve as indentured workers, and are all too often left without recourse to any diplomatic support since their passports have been confiscated by the contractors (PARC-Forces 2006; Phinney 2006). They serve the US military bases and prisons in the most menial positions. They are either hired by the large contractors that provide logistical support—such as KBR, Bechtel, or Halliburton—or by the local (Kuwait-, Qatar- or UAE-based) subcontractors these firms hired to do the recruitment. Watchdog groups in the US have pointed to the de facto indenture of these workers to their recruiters, and the extremely poor working and living conditions they have had to endure, notwithstanding the violence targeted at them specifically for being seen as foreign collaborators and enablers of the occupation. At Abu Ghraib, they cooked and cleaned for the soldiers and the prisoners. As Lagouranis (2007: 25) describes:

> They left their villages for a relatively safe enclave in the Persian Gulf for what seemed like great pay. Then, one day, their boss told them to pack up, and suddenly they were, without fully understanding what was happening in a place where insurgents were trying to kill them. They told me they had no choice in this terrible bait and switch. What could they do? Quit and catch a bus home?

In the hierarchy of labour, Iraqi labourers came above them. They often line up outside the gates of the prison (or elsewhere, where day labour is needed) and are often targeted by suicide bombers. Once inside the wire, "they deliver goods, clean toilets, rewire aid conditioners, and lay gravel. Some of them served as translators, but never in any interrogations or sensitive areas. Everyone suspected them of being spies" (Ibid.). Yet above them are the Iraqi police—guarding the "hard sites" in Abu Ghraib—"trusted even less than the Iraqi civilians" and distinguished from the ordinary labourers by their willingness to work as policemen, and by the network of political affiliations and familial connections that facilitate their joining.

The contract interpreters "who were provided to fill the gap between our immense need for Arabic speakers and our sparse actual numbers" were primarily native speakers with American citizenship and security clearances working with the Military Intelligence. While back in the US, these contractors had been "former construction workers, computer technicians, security guards, and assembly-line workers" (McKelvey 2007a: 49), their placement in a global hierarchy of labour had elevated their pay and prestige above people from other nations and from Iraq itself doing similar work.

Of course, in this global hierarchy of labour, the pay rates vary widely. A *Washington Post* reporter investigating a private security firm in Iraq found that it had a two-tier system: "Guards from the United States, Britain and other Western countries earned $7,000 a month or more. Iraqi guards earned $600—roughly $20 a day—but performed the most dangerous work" (Fainaru 2007). The managing partner of that contracting firm told the *Washington Post* reporter, that "the system was not ideal but was necessary to hold down costs. 'To put twelve white people on a team, it's not economically viable'" (Ibid.). This racialised gradation was not peculiar to this firm alone. In testimony to the US Congress about kidnapped Asian soldiers building the new US embassy in Iraq, a former foreman of the construction firm subcontracted to do the work stated that:

> The contract for these workers said they had to work twelve hours a day, seven days a week, with some time off on Friday for prayers. A few people from India told me they were making $240 a month. A guy from Sierra Leone got paid $300 a month. A Pakistani worker told me he got $900 a month, but that he had to pay additional costs for his work permit and visa, and that all told he was making about $300 a month after those costs (Oversight Committee 2007: 91).

Neither the racialisation of the pay-scale nor its astounding disparity is unusual in Iraq, or indeed in the coercive parastatal complex as a whole. The aforementioned editor-in-chief of the security contractors' trade associations justifies this pay differential by appealing to both familiar and new arguments. Firstly, the cost of living in the countries to which the contractors belong justifies the massive disparities, and in fact, Messner argues that in relative terms, a Fijian salary of $48,000 is far superior in its earning capacity at home than an American salary of $150,000. Secondly, "soldiers from western countries are some of the best trained in the world. So, based on experience, should someone who has worked twenty years for the US military be paid the same as someone who was part of an under-resourced developing country's military?" Finally, the pay disparity between expatriates and local nationals is justified, because "in an environment of reconstruction, it is critical that [local national] contractors do not earn too much" so that for example, teachers do not quit teaching to become security contractors (Messner 2007: 32).

A particular aspect of the coercive parastatal complex which brings together both the global labour hierarchy and the export of forms of policing is the manner in which low-level personnel involved in everyday forms of coercion in the Abu Ghraib prison circulated in the ambiguous space between public and private, policing and military, national and international. At Abu Ghraib, as elsewhere in Iraq, "the military personnel who are more likely to perform enemy prisoner of war and detention operations during war reside almost exclusively in the Army Reserve and Army National Guard" (Inch 2003: 79), while significant numbers of reservists are employed in law enforcement jobs. By April 2003, more than five thousand civilian correctional officers were on active duty (Inch 2003: 79), and many of them served in Abu Ghraib as military police. Indeed, two of the most notorious military policemen appearing in the Abu Ghraib torture photographs, Charles Graner and Ivan "Chip" Frederick, had both been prison wardens before active duty, with Graner having been investigated and sued for abusing prisoners, including hiding a razor in a prisoner's mashed potato (Davenport and Amon 2004).

The interconnection between civilian and military forms of policing and violence work was even more conspicuous among the private contractors employed by CACI and assigned to the 205th Military Intelligence Brigade, implicated at Abu Ghraib. While 65 per cent of the CACI contractors at Abu Ghraib had had prior training as military intelligence any time between one to twenty-five years before Abu Ghraib, 35 per cent had experience as civilian interrogators, policemen, or prison wardens (DAIG 2004: 87). In his assessment of the environment at Abu Ghraib, General Taguba wrote, "without adequate training for a civilian internee detention mission, Brigade personnel relied heavily on individuals within the Brigade who had civilian corrections experience, including many who worked as prison guards or corrections officials in their civilian jobs" (Taguba 2004: 37). These personnel, which included the contractors, also provided ad hoc training to others.[8]

In addition to their experience, as young soldiers testified to Army investigators, the CACI "contractors [were] typically more mature" than the young military interrogators who had had scant few weeks of training and no experience of war (DoD 2004: 018467; DoD 2004:

[8] This ad hoc training occurred before military intelligence personnel who had been in Afghanistan, or part of Guantanamo or Ft. Huachuca "Tiger Teams", arrived on the scene and brought with them the ingrained habits of torture learned in the prisons there (Jaffer and Singh 2007: xxxi; Fay/Jones 2004: 18; 29).

015942). As a former CACI interrogator, Eric Fair told me, his past experience (both as a military interrogator in the mid-1990s and as a former policeman) gave him a great deal of authority over and influence with the younger soldiers. He mentioned that the other interrogators "looked up" to him and, because of the blurry chain of command and the overlapping authorities of military commanders and contractor managers, they sought guidance from him.[9] As another soldier told the Army investigators, the CACI interrogators "seem[ed] to bring their police tactics to military interrogations" (DoD 2004: 018767).

This police/prison/military/private firm circuit became a conduit of bodily knowledge and corporeal practice structured around race, class, gender, and intimate and habitual brutality. Much has been written about the sexualised and pornographic forms of torture exercised in Abu Ghraib (McKelvey 2007a; 2007b; Puar 2004; Puar 2005), but the prison/military "synergy" (Inch 2003: 78) brought to Abu Ghraib the casual brutality of the super-max prisons, with their tacit condoning of rape (Mariner 2001), and their work in managing race in the US (Wacquant 2001).

While the coercive parastatal complex reproduces a global hierarchy of racialised labour, it also reinforces a transnational network of capital, where firms contract and subcontract to one another, and where managerial staff move comfortably between the various departments of the US government and the firms' high- and mid-level management, not to mention the firms' board of directors. A US government auditor's assessment of the manner in which CACI was hired in Iraq states that in drawing up the relevant contracts:

> the contractor effectively replaced government decision-makers in several aspects of the procurement process. For example, a contractor employee proposed the initial requirements package for human intelligence, which included interrogators, and provided information to the Army personnel regarding skill sets needed for positions. Contractor employees also identified the company's BPA [blanket purchase agreement] with Interior as the contract vehicle to provide the services. Contractor officials acknowledge they helped to draft statements of work, with contractor employees in Iraq sending the statements of work to company headquarters in the United States for suggestions. In fact, one of the statements of work we found in official contract files was on the contractor's letterhead. We also found that contractor employees wrote a draft justification and approval for Interior to award additional work noncompetitively to the company (GAO 2005: 14).

[9] Interview with author, Princeton, 31 July 2007.

The interchangeability of government functions resulted from the intimate knowledge of the CACI managers and the officers in the field. CACI managers "marketed their services directly to Army intelligence and logistics officials in Iraq because of relationships they had developed over time." In fact, the relationship between the managers and the officials was so intimate that the CACI personnel acted as mediators in the negotiations between the US Departments of Interior and Defence (Ibid.). Contractors also act as go-betweens with other firms, and sometimes beyond national borders, with other states and transnational corporations.

This "revolving door" has long been a feature of the military-industrial complex (Silverstein 2000). Former defence secretaries Dick Cheney and Frank Carlucci have moved from their government offices to Halliburton and the Carlyle group and back. The directorial boards of firms providing products and services to the US military are stacked with former military men and public servants with national security experience. But what is new is that while, until recently, private firms looked to the authority, connections, and influence of the military leaders they incorporated (Mills 1956), today, the infatuation is mutual, with the military looking to the managers and corporations to perform tasks and fill posts (Verkuil 2007). In this, the emergence of the coercive parastatal complex has followed the contours of the economic transformations in the US: the shift from a production-based economy to one primarily based on a trade in services is reflected in the political economy of the US military.

Much like the sluggishness of laws to catch up with this tidal shift in the economy, the laws dealing with military contracting of services have been slow to appear. Bodies of laws have always depended on the fabrication of boundaries around state institutions, such that the fiction of a fully autonomous state can be maintained. But as the coercive parastatal complex becomes increasingly institutionalised, or perhaps as it becomes more visible in the crimson glare emanating from the Iraqi killing fields, the law is left bereft. We already know about the sophistry of the US administration lawyers who tried to shroud their kidnapping and torture of combatants and non-combatants in Guantanamo, Afghanistan, rendition processes, and CIA "black sites" in the cloak of law (Cole 2005; Margulies 2006). Interestingly, the question of whether or not contractors are also legal or illegal combatants is a very urgent and pertinent one. Much uncertainty persists about whether and under which laws contractors can be prosecuted, perhaps because there is much ambiguity about which bodies of law they may have transgressed against.

Some of the complications emerge precisely because of the imbrication of the public and private in such a thorough manner. The contractors' extraterritoriality, the confusion over the contracting agency within the body of the state, the complications that come with subcontracting, and uncertainties about the applicability of military or civilian law all contribute to these difficulties. The Uniform Code of Military Justice does not apply to civilians, unless the Congress has declared war, which in the case of Iraq, it has not. If contractors are contracted to "inside" organisations (the Department of Interior, or the Department of Justice), but do their work and commit their crimes "outside", can they be prosecuted under the Alien Tort Claims Act? As regards US Federal Law, a Congressional researcher writes, "whether contract employees are subject to federal court jurisdiction for crimes depends on the crime alleged to have been committed, the place where it was committed, and the suspect's contractual relationship with DoD" (Elsea 2004: 15; Border 2007). Furthermore, precisely because of the private nature of the firms, any possibility of demand for transparency is heavily curtailed. The hard-won Freedom of Information Act does not apply to private firms, and given the shell games that can be played with fake subsidiary companies and forged regulatory statements, extraction of such material is nigh on impossible.

Indeed, it is perhaps the inability of the law to gain access to the affairs of the private firms that makes them attractive partners in the activities of government institutions that seek to evade scrutiny. In his rapturous paean to "imperial grunts," Robert Kaplan recounts an incident in the jungles of Colombia where a plane carrying American contractors had crashed in the jungle. Kaplan (2005: 72) writes:

> the civilians were grizzled old Special Forces veterans of Vietnam, now working for private contractors and government agencies at the rough edge of the counter-drug [and he might add, counterinsurgency] program…
>
> The Pentagon, the State Department, the CIA, and others had learned that there were many intelligence-related details more efficiently handled by private firms, which did not incur quite the degree of oversight by media and Congress. The Americans aboard the plane that had gone down were technically civilians doing contract work for the US government. But their work was classified, and in a slightly earlier era their job might well have been handled directly by the CIA. The men were examples of the privatization of war and clandestine operations.

But even if laws were made to monitor and regulate the coercive parastatal complex, how can one ignore the blanket immunity from any form of Iraqi prosecution that L. Paul Bremer granted the private military firms on the eve of his departure from Iraq (Cody 2004)? Even, or maybe especially, here, the hierarchies of power were reproduced through Bremer's viceregal edict. Citizenship was also what counted here, as the US citizens were the only ones granted immunity from prosecution while, after the departure of the CPA, "it would be up to the embassies of each country to work out arrangements for their own nationals;" as one "senior military official succinctly put it, "Every foreign citizen will have a certain status in Iraq" (Ibid.). A complicated—and codified or semi–codified—system of differences like the one created through fiat by Bremer has long been a characteristic of colonial rule.

The invocation of colonial pasts here is not gratuitous. The emergence of the coercive parastatal apparatus has a profoundly familiar historical precedent. The European private companies that colonised West and East Indies all served the sovereigns of their nations, while functioning in ways expected of the state in regards to taxation, military organisation, and bureaucratic administration (Boxer 1965: 5–28; Washbrook 1981; 2004; Bayly 1993; Thomson 1994). As forerunners of the modern parastate, these companies blurred the boundaries between public and private, and allowed for the imperial core to reach further shores. Like today's parastatal complex, they were not uncontroversial, and struggles over their control framed their history of expansion and profit-making.

Much more recently, the wars of decolonisation fought in the peripheries of the Cold War cannot be understood without some reference to mercenaries who served many sides, but especially that of the colonial powers, especially in Africa (Musah and Fayemi 2000).[10] In fact, among the major concerns of the United Nations General Assembly—which in the 1960s overwhelmingly reflected the anti–colonial mood in the Third World—was the rise of mercenaries, and the UNGA's resolution against their employment (1968) was later codified into the 1970 Declaration of Principles of International Law Concerning Friendly Rela-

[10] See McAleese, Marchant and Tomkins entries in the Imperial War Museum oral history archives for a narrative of the hiring of mercenaries by the CIA to exert influence in Angola.

tions and Cooperation Among States and in the 1977 Additional Protocols to the Geneva Conventions (Singer 2004: 527–8).

It is perhaps this colonial parallel that underlines the significance of the coercive parastatal complex coming onto the scene with such force today. In their practices of institutionalising globally racialised hierarchies of labour, exporting particular US military and carceral practices overseas, establishing tangled webs of cooperation between firms specialising in violence-work and the state(s), but always with the interests of the US protected at the centre (though not without challenges from within and without), these coercive parastatal complexes raise the spectre of another colonial moment.

Bibliography

Bayly, Christopher A. 1993. "The British Military Fiscal State and Indigenous Resistance" in Lawrence Stone (ed.) *Imperial State at War: Britain from 1869 to 1815*. London: Routledge; 322–354.

Border, John M. 2007. "Rice Says 'Hole' in U.S. Law Shields Contractors in Iraq" in the *New York Times* 26 October 2007.

Boxer, Charles R. 1965. *The Dutch Seaborne Empire 1600–1800*. London: Alfred A. Knopf.

Braziel, Jana Evans. 2006. "Haiti, Guantánamo, and the 'One Indispensable Nation': U.S. Imperialism, "Apparent States", and Postcolonial Problematics of Sovereignty" in *Cultural Critique* 64: 127–160.

Butterfield, Fox. 2004. "Mistreatment of Prisoners Is Called Routine in U.S." in *The New York Times* 8 May 2004.

Christianson, Scott. 2004. *Notorious Prisons: A Look at the World's Most Feared Institutions*. Guilford, CT: Lyons Press.

Cody, Edward. 2004. "Contractor Immunity a Divisive Issue" in *Washington Post* 16 June 2004.

Cole, David 2005. *Enemy Aliens: Double Standards and Constitutional Freedoms in the War on Terrorism*. New York: New Press.

Davenport, Christian and Michael Amon. 2004. "Three to Be Arraigned in Prison Abuse" in *The Washington Post* 19 May 2004.

Duffield, Mark. 2002. "War as a Network Enterprise: The New Security Terrain and its Implications" in *Cultural Values* 6(1&2): 153–165.

Elsea, Jennifer K. 2004. *U.S. Treatment of Prisoners in Iraq: Selected Legal Issues*. Washington D.C.: US Congress; Congressional Research Service.

Fainaru, Steve. 2007. "Cutting Costs, Bending Rules, and a Trail of Broken Lives" in *The Washington Post* (29 July 2007).

Feldman, Allen. 1991. *Formations of Violence: The Narrative of the Body and Political Terror in Northern Ireland*. Chicago: University of Chicago Press.

Feldman, Jonathan M. 2007. "From Warfare State to 'Shadow' State: Militarism, Economic Depletion and Reconstruction" in *Social Text* 25(2): 143–168.

Forsch, Dan. 2004. "Exporting America's Prison Problems" posted online on 12 May 2004 at http://www.thenation.com/doc/20040524/frosch; accessed on 1 November 2007.

Gill, Lesley. 2004. *The School of the Americas: Military Training and Political Violence in the Americas*. Durham: Duke University Press.

Hall, John A. 2002. "The Return of the State" in *After 9/11*. New York: Social Science Research Council.

Hersh, Seymour. 2007. "The General's Report: How Antonio Taguba, who investigated the Abu Ghraib scandal, became one of its casualties" in *The New Yorker* 25 June 2007.

Margulies, Joseph. 2006. *Guantanamo and the Abuse of Presidential Power*. New York: Simon & Schuster.

Mariner, Joanne. 2001. *No Escape: Male Rape in US Prisons*. New York: Human Rights Watch.

Inch, Mark S. 2003. "Twice the citizens" in *Corrections Today* 65(7): 78–80.

Kaplan, Robert D. 2005. *Imperial Grunts: On the Ground with the American Military, from Mongolia to the Philippines to Iraq and Beyond*. New York: Vintage.

Lagouranis, Tony and Allen Mikaelian. 2007. *Fear Up Harsh: An Army Interrogator's Dark Journey Through Iraq*. New York: NAL Caliber.

Liptak, Adam. 2004. "Who Would Try Civilians From U.S.? No One in Iraq" in *The New York Times* 26 May 2004.

Mathieu, Fabien and Nick Dearden. 2006. *Corporate Mercenaries: The Threat of Private Military and Security Companies*. London: War on Want.

McAllester, Matthew. 2004. "Prison with a Past: Abu Ghraib, now Focus of Scandal, Became a Symbol of Terror Under Saddam" in *Newsday* 6 May 2004.

McCarthy, Ellen. 2004. "CACI Contracts Blocked: Current Work in Iraq Can Continue" in *The Washington Post* 26 May 2004.

McKelvey, Tara. 2007a. *Monstering: Inside America's Policy of Secret Interrogations and Torture in the Terror War*. New York: Carroll and Graf.

McKelvey, Tara (ed.). 2007b. *One of the guys: women as aggressors and torturers*. Emeryville, CA: Seal Press.

Melman, Seymour. 1984. *The Permanent War Economy*. New York: Simon & Schuster.

Melman, Seymour. 1997. "From Private to State Capitalism: How the Permanent War Economy Transformed the Institutions of American Capitalism" in *Journal of Economic Issues* 31(2): 311–330.

Messner, J. J. 2007. "Expatriates, Third Country Nationals, Local Nationals and Pay Disparity" in *Journal of International Peace Operations* 3(2): 32.

Mills, C. Wright. 1956. *The Power Elite*. New York: Oxford University Press.

Mills, C. Wright. 1960. *The Causes of World War Three*. New York: Ballantine.

Mitchell, Timothy. 2001. "Limits of the State: Beyond Statist Approaches and Their Critics" in *Annual Review of Political Science* 85(1): 77–96.

Musah, Abdel-Fatau and Kayode Fayemi. 2000. *Mercenaries: An African Security Dilemma*. London: Pluto Press.

Phinney, David. 2006. "A U.S. Fortress Rises in Baghdad: Asian Workers Trafficked to Build World's Largest Embassy" in *CorpWatch* 17 October 2006. http://www.corpwatch.org/article.php?id=14173 accessed on 14 November 2007.

Press-Barnathan, Galia. 2004. "The War against Iraq and International Order: From Bull to Bush" in *International Studies Review* 6(2): 195–212.

Priest, Dana. 2004 "Violence, Turnover Blunt CIA Effort in Iraq" in *Washington Post*, (4 March 2004).

Puar, Jasbir. 2004. "Abu Ghraib: Arguing Against Exceptionalism" in *Feminist Studies* 30(2): 1–14.

Puar, Jasbir. 2005. "On Torture: Abu Ghraib" in *Radical History Review* 93(1): 13–38.

Silverstein, Ken. 2000. *Private Warriors*. New York: Verso.

Simmons, C. C. 2004. "Prisoner Abuse: From Texas to Baghdad: Former Texas Prison Chief Played Key Role at Abu Ghraib" *The Touchstone*, XIV(3).

Singer, Peter W. 2003. *Corporate Warriors: The Rise of the Privatized Military Industry*. Ithaca, NY: Cornell University Press.

Singer, Peter W. 2004. "War, Profits, and the Vacuum of Law: Privatized Military Firms and International Law" in *Columbia Journal of Transnational Law* 42(2): 521–549.

Singer, Peter W. 2007. "Can't Win with 'Em, Can't Go to War without 'Em: Private Military Contractors and Counterinsurgency," Brookings Policy Paper No. 4. Washington D.C.: Brookings Institute.

Thomson, Janice. 1994. *Mercenaries, Pirates and Sovereigns: State-Building and Extraterritoriality in Early Modern Europe*. Princeton: Princeton University Press.

Verkuil, Paul R. 2007. *Outsourcing Sovereignty: Why Privatization of Government Functions Threatens Democracy and What We Can Do About It.* Cambridge: Cambridge University Press.

Wacquant, Loic. 2001. "Deadly Symbiosis: When ghetto and Prison Meet and Mesh" in *Punishment and Society* 3(1): 95–134.

Washbrook, David A. 1981. "Law, State, and Agrarian Society in Modern India" in *Modern Asian Studies* 15(3): 649–721.

Washbrook, David A. 2004. "South India 1770–1840: The Colonial Transition" in *Modern Asian Studies* 38(3): 479–516.

Archival Documents

DAIG (Department of the Army's Inspector General) 2004. *Detainee Operations Inspection* (The "Mikolashek Report"). Washington D.C.: Department of the Army.

DoD (Department of Defense) 2004. Interviews conducted as part of the Department of the Army, The Inspector *General Detainee Operations Inspection* (The Mikolashek report). Documents released under ACLU FOIA. http://action.aclu.org/torturefoia/released/091505/ accessed on 1 November 2007.

DoJ (Department of Justice) 2005. *A Review of ICITAP's Screening Procedures for Contractors Sent to Iraq as Correctional Advisors*. Washington D.C.: DoJ Office of the Inspector General.

GAO (Government Accountability Office) 2005. *Interagency Contracting: Problems with DOD's and Interior's Orders to Support Military Operations* (Apr. 2005) (GAO-05–201). Washington D.C.: US Government Accountability Office.

Fay, Major General George R. and Lt. General Anthony R. Jones. 2004. *AR 15–6 Investigation of Abu Ghraib Detention Facility and 205th Military Intelligence Brigade*. Washington D.C.: Department of Defense. Officially released to the public.

Marchant, Kevin. Imperial War Museum Oral History Archives 13019/1. Description: British mercenary in Angola during 1970s and 1980s. Served prison sentence of eight years in Angola for atrocities against Angolan civilians.

McAleese, Peter. Imperial War Museum Oral History Archives 15433/20. Description: mercenary commander in Angola for FNLA 1976; mercenary for Rhodesian SAS and South African Police Security Branch in Southern Rhodesia, Mozambique and South Africa 1977–1980; mercenary for South African Defence Force 44 Parachute Bde Pathfinder Coy in search and destroy operations in Namibia and Angola 1980–1984; managed private security business in South Africa 1984–1986; mercenary commander on brief missions for drugs cartels in Colombia 1987–1990 during which he was rescued from plane crash.

Miller, Major General Geoffrey. 2003. *Assessment of DoD Counterterrorism Interrogation and Detention Operations in Iraq*. Washington D.C.: Department of Defense. Document leaked to the press.

Nelson, Colonel Henry. 2004. *AR 15–6 Investigation—Allegations of Detainee Abuse at Abu Ghraib: Psychological Assessment*. Washington D.C.: Department of Defense. Document leaked to the press.

Oversight Committee. 2007. "Allegations of Waste, Fraud, and Abuse at the New U.S. Embassy in Iraq—26 July 2007." Washington D.C.: US Congress, Committee on Oversight and Government Reform.

PARC-Forces (Principal Assistant Responsible for Contractors-Forces). 2006. *Memorandum for All Contractors; Subject: Withholding of Passports Trafficking in Persons*. (19 April). Baghdad: Joint Contracting Command Iraq/Afghanistan. Document released under FOIA.

Taguba, Major General Antonio M. 2004. *Article 15–6 Investigation of the 800th Military Police Brigade* (The "Taguba Report"). Washington D.C.: Department of Defense. Document leaked to the press.

Tomkins, Dave. Imperial War Museum Oral History Archives 19258/2. Description: British mercenary for FNLA in Angola, 1970s.

4

BARRING THE ALGERIAN SUBJECT

CARCERALITY AND RESISTANCE UNDER MARKET-STATISM

Sayres S. Rudy

The natives' challenge to the colonial world...is not a treatise on the universal, but the untidy affirmation of an original idea propounded as an absolute.

Frantz Fanon (1963: 41)

The camp is the sign of the system's inability to function without transforming itself into a lethal machine.

Giorgio Agamben (2000: 43)

This chapter explains the appearance of concentration camps in Algeria in the 1950s and 1990s as the pure-violence stage of the cyclical struggle between ruling elites and resistant activists over extremist market-statism.[1] State-citizen violence in Algeria was never a battle

[1] My thanks go to the members of the "Policing and Incarceration" workshop, Mediterranean Programme of the Robert Schuman Centre, European University Institute Conference (Florence, April 2007), especially Laleh Khalili, Jillian Schwedler, Ilana Feldman, Paul Amar, and Anthony Gorman; of the Middle East Seminar, Yale Law School (New Haven, Mar 2008), mostly Darryl

between modernity and identity, as the leading theories suggest. Rather, concentration camps and terrorism intensified conflict over a radically exploitative social regime. The contrapuntal killing machines of the citizenry and the state, or the terror-camp complex, emerged following the suppression of peaceful resistance. State coercion thus precipitated the carceral regime by defending market-statist absolutism from the realization, or even pursuit, or Algerians' social needs and rendering citizens material and political objects, a condition I call subjective compression. Between 1957 and 1992 Algerians rejected this suffocation, violently rebuffing extremist market-statism. The state then deployed mass internment, torture, extrajudicial executions, and disappearances: its immanent and ideal carceral form.

French and Algerian rulers built markets by disciplining labor, commodifying property, and centralizing political-legal authority. Military, entrepreneurial, and bureaucratic elites thus reconstituted communal Algerians as wage-workers and regulated citizens. Capitalists "freed" Algerian labor and land; the state then nationally collectivized them. Military-backed investors eroded Algeria's decentralized Muslim *zawaya* system of distinct ethical, regional, and moral-economic saintly lineages. Algerians uprooted by enclosure and parcellation of usufruct land worked in commercial agriculture, often as indebted laborers. The martial capitalization of value-added, export-oriented agriculture and later petroleum atomized Algerian life, replacing integrated productive and social life with centralized clientelism (Polanyi 1971). Urbanized and politicized Algerians confronted statist bureaucratic regimentation. They were officially standardized via legal regulations in a juridical order with secular citizenship criteria; absorbed into the political-economic hierarchy; or forced to comply. Maximizing market-statism turned Algerians into a subjectively compressed "'forced' object", fragmenting their local socioeconomic arrangements and reinscribing them as national political citizens (Balibar 1999: 164). This process combined "training…man-as-body" in the "disciplinary technology of labor" and "regulating…man-as-species" in the biopolitics of citizen-subjectivity (Foucault 2003: 242ff).

Algerians resisted this dual re-territorialization by dissimulating, mobilizing, or revolting (Appendix). Dissimulation refers to private

Li and Asli Bali; and Josh Barkan, Laura Hirschfield, Peter Sapira, and Anderson Mackenzie.

strategies in pursuit of particular interests, such as subterfuge or personal alliances. Mobilization implies public activism, such as founding parties, launching periodicals, or staging protests. Algerians prefered these peaceful modes against market-statist encroachment, but state exclusion forced them from reformism to violent uprising in defense of social autonomy (von Sivers 1988: 45; Roberts 2003: 53; Scheele 2007: 305). Betrayed hopes for equality triggered populist counter-aggression; unrewarded fealty to France in WWII and participation in Algerian elections 1990–1992 confirmed ruling class indifference to Algerian suffering, provoking social agitation. In a familiar intensification, state brutality evolved from exclusion to extermination (Razac 2000: 82). The camp's return has been a "negative *transmutation*" of one state-citizen struggle for the respatialized Algerian subject in several forms (Deleuze 2006: 191). The terror-camp complex fulfilled the logic of militant market-statism compressing a resistant people, not a dialectic of antinomian state and culture, much less reason and madness (Kalyvas 1999).

Yet the camp is often seen as the epitome of social rationality, terrorism the derivative of this rationality. The modern state is said to beget these evil twins by eradicating individual or collective social plurality. In one view the camp's purge of alterity evinces the "Enlightenment ... fully played out" (Gellner 1987: 77; Bauman 1989: 61ff.). Another abstraction detects in the coincidence of "new laws on citizenship" and mass internment "the new biopolitical *nomos* of the planet" (Agamben 2000: 43, 45). A more historical idea is that modernity makes the "camp the only 'country' [for] the stateless" when it "transform[s] the state from an instrument of law into [one] of the nation" (1979: 275, 284). The shared claim is that modern states replace ethical or deliberative communal life with political groups with isomorphic worker-citizens for efficient production and governance. But if the mechanics of modern state-building are conditions of possibility for concentration camps, state-citizen confrontations over the specific design of social regimes are their conditions of actuality. The camp enforces willful and aggressive social policies against their opponents; it does not enforce abstract social processes.

A related mystification links internment camps to imperial or authoritarian domination by forces "external" to society. By extension, incarceration under democracy is seen as upholding the rule of law against freely chosen criminality. Tying the camp to despotic political regimes is an ideological coding that exonerates the violence of the prison-industrial complex in radical liberal polities; mass prisons in the US are thus never seen as the camps of democratic capitalism. By fiat, the prisoner is guilty in liberal orders—in authoritarian orders, the prison is. The dichotomy fends off the anti–liberal criticism that democratic, moral, or biopolitical cohesion is totalizing, exclusionary, or genocidal (Mann 2005, Bull 2006, Foucault 2003). Unlike vague perceptions that camps enforce modern homogeneity, this critique emphasizes the standardizing violence at the inception of law, democracy, and state—the pre-existing coercion behind liberal regimes.[2]

That liberal democracy genetically conquers or silences value-conflict challenges common sense about Algerian violence. Analysts often blame the terror-camp complex on its immediate cause, the cancelation of elections in 1992, and infer that democratization would have avoided it. But political reforms were adopted to avoid the social and economic reforms activists demanded. Elections between 1990 and 1992 were meant to divide regime opponents and advance the crony capitalism, military-state sovereignty, and security apparatus that Algerians had furiously protested against in 1988. So it was deepened market-statism not abrogated electoralism that returned concentration camps and rampant terrorism to Algeria after forty years of independence. Previously autocratic rule, relaxing market-statist subjective compression (1962–1980s), avoided the terror-camp complex. This contrast in social and carceral regimes displaces authoritarianism and capitalism as merely alternative global causes of violence. Instead, the interaction of specific social deprivations and desires as they permit or hinder subjectivity explain terror and the camp (Rudy 2004).

French Rule

Imperial France met an "indigenous Algerian society" resistant to central rule and "ready for a dogged fight" (Abun-Nasr 1987: 158, Kiernan 1982: 73). French hopes to Christianize and capitalize Algeria through "agricultural colonization" led to "expulsion and extermination of the natives" (Buheiry 1989: 4, Khalidi 2005: 182–3). Algerians suffered France's "indiscriminate... tactics," such as the "burning of the crops of 'disloyal' tribes" and "incinerations of men, women, and children"

[2] Democratic harmonization is one "dogmatic basis of liberalism" (Merleau-Ponty 1969: 35).

(Moore 1970: 40ff.). Marshall Bugeaud called the live cremation of the Oulad Riah tribe (1845) the "salutary terror" of "total war," adding, "When the Arabs are subdued, I rule them with humanity" (Sullivan 1983: 105, 129). Alarmed by Islamist resistance, France was subject to a *fatwa* from rival *'ulema* letting "Muslim tribes...submit without becoming infidels so long as the French did not interfere with their practice of Islam" (Piscatori 1986: 79–80). All the while France cleared the land, destroyed small and communal farmers, and commodified agriculture (Owen 2005: 172ff.; Stora 2001: 6).

Market-statism began with ethnocidal militarism, cultural submission, and perilous dispossession. Commercial farming enclosed rural areas, ruining survival methods and yielding the 1867–8 famine-deaths of 300,000 (Ageron 1991: 44). Growing control allowed France to make politicized traders "choose...anticolonial resistance [or] assured food supplies" (Clancy-Smith 1994: 200). The secular naturalization decree (1870) "destroy[ed] the internal structures of Algerian society" (Sartre 2001: 132). Capturing Algerians' will-to-subjectivity 'Abd el-Qader implored, "Do you not understand [assimilation] would mean death for us?" (Clayton 1975: 242). The initial terror-camp carceral form deployed abusive relocation to island prisons and native penitentiaries where Algerians and French were configured by colonial status (Gorman 2007). The state provided free convict labor to capital, protected by the military, exemplifying the market-statist matrix of social forces (Prochaska 1990: 66ff.).

After the triumph of French settler-military capitalism, circa 1881, Algerians dissimulated. French "political authority over religious institutions [anointed] an official Muslim clergy" to subvert Muslim brotherhoods (Laremont 2000: 47). The latter, once centers of revolt, now housed Islamist quietists (Clancy-Smith 1993, Berque 1986: 42ff). Under shared jurisdictions *qadi* protection of dispersed communities caved under French plans for "a unified polity embracing different classes and interest groups" (Christelow 1992: 135). By 1890 *qadi–shuyukh* social intermediaries had become tax–farming French servants (Establet 1991). Worse still, the *code de l'indigénat* (1881) mandated the *corvée*, letting *colons* conscript native labor, often sharecroppers dispossessed by high taxation or subsidized manufacturing. French power over Algerian bodies presumed "whites 'had the authority to inflict punishment' on any native" (Mamdani 1996: 126, Harrison 1988: 180ff.). French carcerality thus moved from interning the resistant body to disciplining the dissimulating body (cf. Bâ 2007). Despite intensifying market-statism, the crushing war of 1830–1881 had commended strategic cooperation to Algerians.

The First World War led to Algerian mobilization. Conscription, migration, and work redeployments increased French reliance on indigenous mediation. France's temptation to naturalize Algerians with Muslim personal status signaled its flexibility. Algerians burst into public discourse and civic agitation. Ben Badis founded the reformist *Association des Ouléma d'Algérie* in 1931. Their main rivals were Ferhat Abbas's *Jeune Algérien* equal rights group and Messali Hadj's militant nationalist *Etoile Nord-Africaine*, ENA (McDougall 2002). By 1937 the ENA had five thousand militants and Hadj was arrested. The ENA reformed as the *Parti du Peuple Algérien*, PPA, with a manifesto "against repression, in service to the people, for union and emancipation." Algerian subjectivization had turned from dissimulation to mobilization of new ideologies, movements, and organizations—systemically peaceful, potentially violent.

Unrewarded for wartime loyalty, Algerians murdered *colons* in May 1945, prompting French reprisal massacres. The violence presaged the terror-camp complex in spirit and action. Sétif was excused, ironically while the Nuremberg trials were in session, as a slaughter of subhumans with risible demands (Sartre, Ali 2005: 195). France did grant Algerians citizenship but as a stratagem to deny them national autonomy. Political mobilization had exposed secular inclusion as another form of imperial *dirigisme*. In response, native subjectivization had changed its criteria from assimilationist survival and appeals to civic rights to militant anti–imperialism. Only autarky offered a solution to exploitation. By now *colons* were six times wealthier than Algerians, teeming in jobless cities or rural areas with 55 per cent of the population but 18 per cent of national income (Farsoun 1975: 3–4). The PPA founded a military wing "because…playing by the French rules, staying within the framework of French legality, French political norms, had got them nowhere" (Roberts 2002: 39–40). In August 1955 Algerian and French military and civilians killed 123 *colons* and 12,000 Muslims. The body politic was cannibalizing the political body.[3]

Algeria was at total war. French settlers, soldiers, counterinsurgents, and paramilitaries and Algerian revolutionaries and nationalists deci-

[3] The "somatic sovereignty" of French market-statism was, by then, shattered (Shapiro 2003).

mated one another. With an "icy feeling…of always knowing there is an enemy," Algerians fought with sacrificial abandon (Djebar 2005: 4). France adopted scorched-earth tactics. Mere "flight render[ed] one suspect: the authorization to shoot [any] 'runaways' constituted the legalization *a priori* of summary executions" (Branche 2004: 139). A March 1956 Special Powers Law encouraged officers to intern suspects, which "regularized arrests [with] no judicial authority" (Talbott 1980: 86). France executed prisoners in June and bombed the Casbah in August 1956, killing seventy-five. Algerians followed with café bombings but "counter-terrorism [had] preceded terrorism" (Stora, in Rotman 2002). It was, though, against the punishing Algerian general strike that France became "a police state" beyond morality, law, or legitimacy (Arendt 1979: 287–8; Maran 1989: 2, Robin 2005: 48).

France crushed the Algerian subject with internment, torture, massacres, executions, and disappearances. This objectification confined, damaged, or obliterated the body and tormented, broke, or silenced the mind. A place of total biopower, the camp reduced inmates to the death-in-life confinement over torture or erasure. It was a zone of neutralization between two sites of mutilation or death: the battlefield and the torture/execution chamber. The internment-torture-execution-disappearance series pacified by having prisoners choose their bounded fates. Obedience saved internees from torture, the tortured from execution, and the executed from posthumous mystification. Thus terror-camp territorialization intensified the mechanisms of market-state disciplinary sovereignty. Inmates were forced into hard labor and bureaucratic routinization. They were ideal workers (rightless, dependent, and propertyless) and citizens (isomorphic and subordinate)—disposable subject-objects of the regime's "prohibition and authorization" of torture (Branche 2004: 143). Capitalist citizenship is not incarceration, but the camp absolutized market-statist social control, producing *in extremis* the dynamics of wage-labor and national inscription. The panoptic serialization of internees, labor, and citizenry are cognate. Obedience saves worker/citizen from poverty/surveillance, shelter/arrest, starvation/denaturalization, and dismissal/expulsion. French sovereign, disciplinary, and biopolitical power cohered in the camp's purified market-statist social logic.

The horrific terror-camp carcerality of Algerian-French hostilities has been tied to the institutional contradictions of *l'Algérie française* or cultural contradictions of any "colonialist configuration" (Stora

2004; Fanon 1967: 64). The first posits a technical defect in political structure corrigible by uniform citizenship laws. The second fetishizes imperialist subjugation that uniquely creates a "unanimously revolutionary…wretched of the earth" (Shohat 2006: 235). Thus either local French error or global imperial necessity causes violence. Neither view grasps France's will to retain the market-statist social regime against its Algerian opponents. The camp did not betray but fulfilled French colonial practices. France's market-statist social regime made camp prisoners as its viticultural regime made wines. They enclosed, collected, and crushed the natives to avoid compromising their exploitation and domination of Algerian life.

Algerian Rule

The return of the terror-camp complex thirty years into independent modernization belies facile associations of imperial or authoritarian rule with political violence or pacific hegemony. Until the 1980s, Algerian military, party, and bureaucratic elites replaced market-statism with a social regime of multiple negotiated subjectivities and social decompression. The state relaxed national inscription, juridical centralization, and market domination to satisfy citizen demands. Algeria's *mukhabarat* state avoided the terror-camp complex by organizing and subjectivizing, rather than conquering and objectifying, its diverse constituencies. Algerians dissimulated at first, privately bargaining with authoritarian patrons. But resurgent market-statism from the late 1970s on prompted economic protests to challenge this new social regime, electoral reforms to stabilize it, and finally systemic political mobilization to remove it (1988–1992). When the state's scheme to trade democracy for militarized crony-capitalism brought an Islamist electoral triumph the generals abrogated democracy and interned opponents (1992–). Algerians, their desires denied and subjectivity compressed, turned to violence. I trace below the reciprocal revival of market-statism and camp carcerality in Algeria from private dissimulation and public mobilization to bloodcurdling terrorism and militarism.

From independence onward, Algerian rulers incorporated powerful civilians, notably Islamists, with concessions. The FLN repeatedly declared Algeria an Islamic state "against depersonalization" (UA 1976: 129). Land redistribution and agricultural *autogestion* yielded to Islamist landowner pressure (Bennoune 1988: 176ff.). To compensate popular classes the state decommodified and supported workers with coalition-building side payments (Waldner 1999). State rulers and social conservatives removed women deputies from government by 1982 and passed the patriarchal 1984 Family Code. Algeria's social regime comprised redistributive oil-rent patronage, and capital-intensive sectoral development, and satisfied regnant Islamist groups through its policies against linguistic, ethnic, or gender equality. Hostile to subalterns, the state cynically de-standardized national inscription, in the end coopting the agenda of the opposition forces. By the mid-1980s the economy, partially liberalized since 1982 and crippled by falling oil-prices, collapsed under fiscal crisis, inflation, currency overvaluation, high unemployment and urbanization rates, overcapacity and underproduction, decimated agriculture, foreign debt, and gaping income inequity. This intensified objectification led to the 1988 riots.

The year 1989 was a watershed for Algeria. The famous democratic experiment was, in fact, a delusional tactic to harmonize the radicalizing agendas of market-statists and Islamists. Moral anger swelled against the upper echelons of society, who flaunted "late-model cars, new villa construction and new businesses" (Layachi 1992: 3). Struggling Algerians wondered "why more than half of them are jobless 'while [Algeria earns] billions per year from natural gas'" (Vandewalle 1988: 2). Renowned for exposing the state's indifference by providing immediate relief after the 1989 Tipasa earthquake and by fighting the Soviets in Afghanistan, Islamists founded the *Front Islamique du Salut* (FIS) as the adversary of political, economic, and religious elites. Systemic opposition was manifest when "populist Islam" became "*the* counterhegemonic force [against] Islamic leaders and institutions... drafted into [the] hegemonic project" (Brumberg 2002: 57).

The crisis only energized Algerian market-statists—crony-capitalists seeking deregulated but uncompetitive environments for state-backed investment portfolios. Selective privatization had devasted most Algerians by reducing subsidies and employment, but also impeded ruling class interests with negative real interest rates, commercial debts to European financial houses, recession, and a burgeoning but uncontroled black market (Owen 1992: 144ff.; Frieden 1981: 408ff). Further liberalization permitted public and private sector "corruption and profiteering to distort the privatization process and prevent genuine competition" (UA 2001: 1, UA 2000: 4). The 1988 riots pushed "an abrupt transition to a free-market economy, with the liberalization of exchange rates, credit, customs, foreign trade and foreign investment, [and] establishment of [an independent] Central Bank" (Evans and Phillips 2007: 145). In effect, the mass uprising against encroaching corruption, inequality, and exclusion prompted market-statists to exacerbate those conditions for their own advancement.

To retain control, the state modified Algeria's security and political regimes. Ruling elites calculated that democratization, "tightly supervised [by] the *Sécurité Militaire*,...would enhance their illicit corruption networks" (Burgat and Gèze 2007: 15). Thus Algeria's political reforms presupposed improved state economic and security controls. Defense Minister Khaled Nezzar formed the *Département de Renseignement et de Sécurité* (DRS) under Mohamad Mediène to intimidate opponents and Prime Minister Mouloud Hamrouche against confronting ruling elites. More radically the generals withdrew from the FLN, so "they could no longer be held to account in any political institution...[T]hey forced President Chadli to surrender the defense portfolio; from [then] on, they were a law unto themselves to a degree...without precedent since 1965" (Roberts 2003: 253). By 1990 market-statists were readying the ground for martial law, should party politics prove more than a red-herring to facilitate their stranglehold on Algeria.

What matters most here is that Islamists mobilized peacefully—despite state coercion—as long as elections gave them systemic means to resist market-statism. Eventual cancelation of the election results thus provoked violent contention because it removed activists' only resource against political and economic corruption, not because it removed democracy *per se*. FIS leader Abbas Madani had threatened "to install Islamic rule and make the law conform to the...*Qur'an* and *sharia*" (Aziz 1990: 42). Moreover, after early victories FIS paraded its conservative intent including "gender apartheid," in local governance (UA 1999c: 16). FIS forged, then, a coalition not for democratic inclusion but against political-economic exclusion. One Algerian spoke for many on citizens' "four choices: you can remain unemployed and celibate because there are no jobs or apartments to live in; you can work in the black market and risk being arrested; you can try to emigrate to France to sweep the streets of Paris or Marseilles; or you can vote for FIS and vote for Islam" (Ibrahim 1990). FIS populists were furious over the Gulf crisis, state electoral machinations, new FLN concessions to the IMF, and Nezzar's state of emergency and the arrests of Madani and

Ali Benhadj, all in 1991 (Cf. Roberts 2003: 63ff.; Willis 1996: 162ff.; Stora 2001: 200ff.; Volpi 2003: 49; Frégosi 1994). Yet they eschewed violence as long as democratic participation might reform Algerian market-statism.

The generals annulled national elections in January 1992, banned FIS, and imposed martial law, completing systemic objectification and ensuring violence. Only then did FIS militarize, under the French, against "corruption [serving] narrow elites who control wealth or armed force" (Scott 1969: 1154; Ghannouchi 2000: 103, Sadiki 2004: 356). Democracy aside, violence was ensured since the military protected extreme market-statist corruption. In January 1992 a military presidency, the *Haut Comité d'État* (HCE), announced itself. Within a month:

> five detention centers opened in the Sahara to hold thousands of FIS activists, including five hundred mayors and councilors. Special courts,...banned under the 1989 constitution, were reestablished to prosecute 'terrorists'...[T]he state closed...cultural and charitable organizations of the FIS and ordered the destruction of all unofficial mosques, which were popular with Islamists (Hafez 2004: 46).

By March FIS was outlawed, 7,000 Algerians were interned in seven camps, and "new judicial councils created to expedite trials began handing down death sentences with chilling regularity" (Waltz 1995: 101).[4] By Autumn 1992, a military court had given FIS leaders Madani and Benhadj long prison terms; 400 officers, gendarmes, soldiers, and President Boudiaf had been murdered; and Algiers airport had become the first terrorist target since their independence. City-wide curfews were enforced, partly to protect the police from attacks. Whereas torture nearly "'disappeared between 1989 and 1991,' it was 'reported [now] regularly in twenty detention centers" (Stora 2001: 214, UA 2004). Algerians now suffered "torture, 'disappearances,' and...extra-judicial killing of suspected Islamists" (Hafez 2004: 46). Camp carcerality—lawless internment, torture, executions, and disappearances—was back, again to defend market-statism from challenge.

Salafis renounced reformism.[5] Deploring FIS's *hizbiyya*—corrupting participation in party competition—an Al-Qaeda emissary urged "total

[4] I am grateful to the Islamists and state officials I interviewed in Algiers and Paris at the time (Apr 1992).

[5] FIS's naïveté inspired Abdelkader Chebouti to revive Mustapha Bouyali's 1980 *Mouvement Islamique Armé*, and *Takfir wal-Hijra* (Evans and Phillips 2007: 128ff., 182ff.).

war" against the HCE and DRS. "This simple argument destroyed us," one reformist lamented (Wright 2006: 216). Returned Algerian "Afghan-Arabs" compared the USSR to the Algerian "state and its 'eradicationists,' who pass off their violence as the defense of modernity" (Ajami 1998: 201). But it was a homegrown, not imported, neo-Wahhabi drive "to plunge Algeria into a bloodbath" (Rashid 2000: 135–6). The protean *Groupe Islamique Armé* (GIA) adapted the state's exterminationist manicheanism: "There is no neutrality in the war we are waging. [Those not with us] are apostates and deserve to die" (quoted in Wright 2006: 216). The GIA slit women's and children's throats, burned babies alive, disemboweled pregnant women, and slew imams.

Soon market-statists and Islamists had again reterritorialized Algeria into a terror-camp complex, a social regime of extreme dehumanization. In prisons like Chateauneuf and Cavignac the state tortured suspects and bystanders with blowtorches, electric shocks and drills, and forks (in eyes); men and women were raped with cables, bottles, and brooms, often in front of loved ones. Mass arrests enabled perpetual torture of "terror" suspects. By 1995 116 prison-camps held 30,000 inmates. Torture-deaths and executions contributed to the 7,000 Algerians the state "disappeared" by 1997, the bodies dumped in hidden graves. The DRS and GIA infiltrated each other, purged traitors, and formed death squads (Samraoui 2003). Committing massacres to implicate Islamists, soldiers shot civilians at will. Official death tolls for 1992–1997 hit 70,000 but some estimates put the number at as high as 200,000.

Algeria's war had become pure violence: to live was to kill to be subject; not to kill was to be object, to die. Pacifism, flight, or neutrality became suspect under kleptocratic surveillance and the jurisprudence of forced confessions. Innocence signaled guilt. The reclaimed Algerian subject was a ghost, "only the victims [were] known, visible" (Charef 1998: 5). Shadow killers gauged and produced their freedom by civilian body-counts. Necropolitical Algeria modeled the "generalized instrumentalization of human existence and the material destruction of human bodies and populations" (Mbembe 2003: 14). In perverse strategic resubjectivizations secular and Islamist *éradicateurs* became indistinguishable to annihilate each other. They became each other not only in the mutual mimicry needed to penetrate enemy command structures, but also in joint actions. This dissolution of allies/enemies, means/ends, and complicity/innocence was absent from French camp carcerality because the French left. In this sense Algeria's self-immolation extended the anti–humanist logic of the war against France, where only extermination overcame resistance.[6] Algerians expelled France but cannibalized Algeria in their ongoing resistance to market-statism.[7] That basic continuity is again visible in the exhorbitant expression of social commodification and a disposable citizenry. Abducting, killing, and disappearing civilians, the state charged many Algerians for relatives' bodies or withheld their pensions and benefits for failing to confirm their deaths. Extrajudicial murders of "Islamist terrorists" were often pretexts for eliminating critics of corruption (Smith 2004: 2–3). Similarly, after the UK sent refugees back to Algeria to protect oil and arms investments, several disappeared (Sweeney 1997: 4).

President Bouteflika, peddling the DRS agenda, appeared to diminish this brutalization with the *concorde civile* of 1999, exchanging elite incumbency for a general amnesty. Market-statists who dominated import-export networks, the informal economy, and monocultural rent-distribution expected to secure uncompromised freedom without concessions. "Unconditional amnesty" freed ruling elites to reap "unofficial 'commissions'...on imports and exports" while promoting "Islamo-conservatives...to pacify social unrest and protect the economic interests of today's military decision-makers" (Burgat and Gèze 2007: 18). This strategy has chanelled war-weary Algerians back into strategic dissimulation under "multi–party authoritarianism" or "pluralism without enfranchisement" (McDougall 2007: 38; Roberts 2003: 263). Meanwhile, Algeria's integration into global capitalism has accelerated, with "regime insiders benefiting... from [bank] privatization, import-export[[8]] companies, and construction...Crony capitalism and corruption, fueled by oil rents, remain firmly entrenched" (Richards and Waterbury 2008: 256). As in previous eras, market-statism reduced welfare outlays despite rising unemployment and homelessness, now exacerbated by a million displaced persons subsisting in *bidonvilles*.

In this post-"civil war" period, Algerians' public activities, peaceful or violent, gave way to personal survival, sporadic fighting, and state

[6] This "becoming-(to kill)-enemy" inverts "killing-(to unbecome)-humanity," that is, killing to eradicate "the basic foldedness of human-being with the other" (Sanders 2002: 132).

[7] Thus both sides savagely targeted women in the 1990s, unlike in the 1950s (Turshen 2002).

[8] The Customs Police typify "mafia" networks tied to the 1990s war (UA 2006: 3, Martinez 1998).

dirigisme. Kabylie protests expressed broader hatred of "the brutal contempt with which the authorities [humiliate] ordinary people" (Roberts 2003: 293). In secret sites the DRS continued water-torturing, beating, electric-shocks, religiously insulting, raping, disappearing, collectively arresting, and forcing confessions from citizens with impunity. The state's juridical order used prolonged pre-trial detentions, secret trials, and denied access to prisons. Finally, harassment of journalists, protesters, NGOs, and mosques[9] completed Algeria's post-war camp carcerality. As usual, ruthless market-statism preceded and guaranteed a terrorist response, bolstered—as in the nineteenth century, the 1950s, and 1990s—by systemic compression, material objectification, and foreign-trained Islamists. But one discontinuity may present itself here. So far Algerians have divided into a dissimulated majority and a militant minority, without an interim public civil-societal mobilization.

When Benhadj, former *Armée Islamique du Salut* head Madani Mezrag, and GIA founder Abdelhaq Layada conciliated for amnesty, many Islamists saw them as collaborators in the wider global war of market-statism, known by its moralistic advocates as the "war on terror." After 11 September 2001, the US embraced Algerian statists' preemptive repression of Islamist activists, urged on by one-dimensional criticism that America was letting "the Algerians fight the Islamic-fascist wave without saying a word or lending a hand" (Hitchens 2004: 419). Dialectical extremism recurred—from state repression to Islamist militancy to cultural moralism. Having given no military aid to Algeria from 1995–2002, the US started giving it weapons and praise for its anti–terror campaign (Grimmett 2003: 59). The new US ally was the "army [that] 'kill[ed] indiscriminately' and 'exterminated' anyone who support[ed] the Islamists, not just terrorists" (Tremlett 2002). In consequence Al-Qaeda joined the *Groupe Salafiste pour la Prédication et le Combat* (GSPC), stating: "We strongly and fully support Usama bin Laden's *jihad* against the heretic America as we support our brothers in Afghanistan, the Philippines, and Chechnya" (UA 2003: 1).[10] As usual, Islamist resistance to occupation or tyranny would be attacked as nativist irrationalism rather than engaged as a lived rejection of Algeria's rapacious and vengeful social regime.

[9] The Penal Code forbids speech "contrary to the noble nature of the mosque or likely to offend the cohesion of society or serve as an apology for such actions" (UA 2006: 7).

[10] Algerians fighting the US in Iraq were training to bring that fight home (UA 2007a).

The escalation continued apace. US government militants advanced the Trans-Sahara Counter-Terrorism and AFRICOM initiatives to lead African armies in pacifying the continent, naming "especially Algeria" a key "lily pad" (Johnson 2006: 148). The *Organisation d'al-Qaida au Pays du Maghreb Islamique* (AQMI) then declared war, vowing in 2007, "We won't rest until every inch of Islamic land is liberated from foreign forces" (Gèze and Mellah 2007, UA 2007b: A10). AQMI has bombed the Algerian Prime Ministry, police convoys, security outposts, the site of a presidential visit, and UN offices. A horrific battle over a Kabylia AQMI training camp in April 2007 recalled the 1990s war. AQMI attacked the UN to repel "the Crusaders and their agents, the slaves of America and the sons of France" (Benhold and Smith 2007: A1). This convinced "counterterrorism officials...that Algeria was becoming a regional center for terrorist activity that could threaten Europe and even North America" (Smith 2007: A1). US President Bush echoed France in 1957 and the HCE in 1992: "The United States stands with the people of Algeria, as well as the United Nations, as they deal with this senseless violence."

Despite the episodic outbreaks of violence, an odd peace has settled over Algeria. In 2006 SIPRI lifted Algeria from its list of major armed conflict areas. But the state has perhaps institutionalized its camp carcerality. Market-statists may finally have reterritorialized Algeria. The state's "forcible depoliticization of the population" has silenced both civil society and voters (McDougall 2007: 41). Algeria's ruling classes may finally have their desired subjects: a population of docile bodies for market discipline and national biopower with enough volatile bodies to require statist sovereignty. The cycle may now be a pendulum swinging between militancy and dissimulation, murder and death.

Conclusion

Algerians have by turns dissimulated and mobilized against material and political deprivation and militated against subjective compression. These stages of resistance comprise a cyclical response to intensified market-statism in Algeria. The terror-camp complex reflects the immanent violence of incommensurable agendas that finally burst forth in extreme versions of state-capitalist power and cultural self-authentication. Such a brief case study can only qualify these causal trajectories and their normative, theoretical, and empirical inferences with the hope of provoking comparative research.

One normative extension is that incommensurable desires make aggression indeterminate. Value-pluralism threatens the very idea of a consensual scheme, but it is extremist differentiation and not mere difference that sparks political violence. Efforts to pacify by standardizing diverse identities are likely to militarize them instead. A related theoretical qualification is that Algeria's cyclical resistance to absolutizing market-statism is not a general theory of violence. Elsewhere, exploitation, exclusion, and compression have prompted non-violent rebellion or hegemonic acquiescence. This variation only apparently impeaches explanations of violence. Sustained collective violence expresses the perceived denial of systemic subjectivity rather than denied wants or needs; that systemic subjectivity can be portrayed reliably in a general causal account. Algeria's dialectic of peaceful to militant popular action is illustrative, if not dispositive, of this explanatory method. Empirically, Algeria—like Palestine, Colombia, Haiti, Somalia, Iraq, Afghanistan, Congo, and the "war on terror"—may exhibit the rise of lawless, improvisational, terroristic, and polycentric bourgeois-militant power over juridical sovereignty or moral authority. If this sanguinary *realpolitik* captures the cowering quietism and towering terrorism of Algerian politics, then it is not violence that needs to be explained, but violence that explains.

Appendix: Cycles of Algerian Resistance and Carcerality, 1830–present*

Dates	*Stage*	*Carceral complex*	*Social action*	*Subjectivity*
1830–1871	militancy	camp, exile	warfare, terrorism	compression
1871–1914	dissimulation	land appropriation	migration, mediation	private repression
1920–1945	mobilization	policing	campaigning	public expression
1945–1962	militancy	camp, torture, disappearance, execution	warfare, terrorism, statization	compression
1962–1988	assimilation	policing	bargaining	private expression
1989–1992	mobilization	military security	campaigning	public expression

1992–1999	militancy	camp, torture, disappearance, execution	warfare, terrorism, statization	compression
1999–2008	dissimulation	military policing	bargaining	private repression public repression
2002–2008	*militancy*	*camp, torture, regional war*	*terrorism*	*compression*

*Assimilation (1962–1988) reflects de-intensification of market-statism.

Bibliography

Abun-Nasr, Jamil. 1987. *A History of the Maghrib in the Islamic Period*. Cambridge: Cambridge University Press.

Agamben, Giorgio. 2000 [1994]. 'What is a Camp?' in *Means without End: Notes on Politics*. Trans. V. Binetti and C. Cesarino. Minneapolis: Minnesota University Press.

Ageron, Charles-Robert. 1991 [1964]. *Modern Algeria: A History from 1830 to the Present*. Trans. M. Brett. London: Hurst & Co.

Ajami, Fouad. 1998. *The Dream Palace of the Arabs: A Generation's Odyssey*. New York: Pantheon.

Ali, Tariq. 2005 [1987]. *Street Fighting Years: An Autobiography of the Sixties*. London: Verso.

Arendt, Hannah. 1979 [1951]. *The Origins of Totalitarianism*. New York: Harcourt Brace and Jovanovich.

Aziz, Philippe. 1990. 'Que nos frères de France reviennent au pays', *Le Point*, 919 (30 April 1990).

Bâ, Babacar. 2007. 'La prison coloniale au Sénégal, 1790–1960: Carcéral de conquête et défiances locales' in *French Colonial History* 8: 81–96.

Balibar, Etienne. 1999. 'Algeria, France: One Nation or Two?' in Joan Copjec and Michael Sorkin (eds.) *Giving Ground: The Politics of Propinquity*. London: Verso.

Bauman, Zygmunt. 1989. *Modernity and the Holocaust*. Ithaca: Cornell University Press.

Benhold, Katrin and Craig Smith. 2007. 'Twin Car Bombs Strike Algiers, Killing Dozens' in the *New York Times* (12 December 2007).

Bennoune, Mahfoud. 1988. *The making of contemporary Algeria, 1830–1987* Cambridge: Cambridge University Press.

Berque, Jacques. 1983. *Arab Rebirth: Pain & Ecstasy*. London: Al-Saqi.

Branche, Raphaëlle. 2004. 'Torture and Other Violations of the Law by the French Army during the Algerian War' in Adam Jones (ed.), *Genocide, War Crimes & the West*. London: Zed Books.

Brumberg, Daniel. 2002. 'The Trap of Liberalized Autocracy' in *Journal of Democracy* 13(4): 56–68.

Buheiry, Marwan. 1989. 'The Conquest of Algeria and the Apocalyptic Vision of La Gervaisai' in *The Formation and Perception of the Modern Arab World*. Princeton, NJ: Darwin Press.

Bull, Malcolm. 2006. 'Ultimate Choice', *London Review of Books*, 28(3).

Burgat, François and François Gèze. 2007. 'Algeria' in Toby Archer and Heidi Huuhtanen (eds.) *Islamist Opposition Parties and the Potential for EU Engagement*. Helsinki: Finnish Institute of International Affairs.

Charef, Abed. 1998. *Algérie: autopsie d'un massacre*. Paris: Éditions de l'Aube.

Christelow, Allan. 1992. 'The Muslim Judge and Municipal Politics in Colonial Algeria and Senegal' in Juan Cole, (ed.), *Comparing Muslim Societies: Knowledge and the State in a World Civilization*. Ann Arbor: Michigan University Press.

Clancy-Smith, Julia. 1993. 'The Shaykh and His Daughter: Coping in Colonial Algeria' in Edmund Burke III (ed.) *Struggle and Survival in the Middle East*. Berkeley: University of California Press.

Clancy-Smith, Julia. 1994. *Rebel and Saint: Muslim Notables, Populists Protest, Colonial Encounters, Algiers and Tunisia, 1800–1904*. Berkeley: University of California Press.

Clayton, Vista. 1975. *The Phantom Caravan of Abd El Kader, Emir of Algeria (1808–1883)*. Hicksville, NY: Exposition Press.

Deleuze, Gilles. 2006 [1962]. *Nietzsche and Philosophy*. Trans. Hugh Tomlinson. New York: Columbia University Press.

Djebar, Assia. 2005 [1962]. *Children of the New World*. Trans. Marjolijn de Jager. New York: CUNY Press.

Establet, Colette. 1991. *Être Caïd dans l'Algérie Coloniale*, Société Arabes et Musulmanes, no. 6. Paris: Editions du Centre National de la Researche Scientifique.

Evans, Martin and John Phillips. 2007. *Algeria: Anger of the Dispossessed*. New Haven: Yale University Press.

Fanon, Frantz. 1963. *The Wretched of the Earth*. Trans. Constance Farrington. Boston: Grove Press.

Fanon, Frantz. 1967 [1957]. 'Algeria Face to Face with the French Torturers' in *Toward the African Revolution*. Trans. Haakon Chevalier. Boston: Grove Press.

Farsoun, Karen. 1975. 'State Capitalism in Algeria', *MERIP Reports* 35.

Fisk, Robert. 1997. 'Lost Souls of the Algerian Night: Now Their Torturers Tell the Truth' in *The Independent* (30 October 1997), at http://www.algeria-watch.de/mrv/mrvtort/souls.htm.

Foucault, Michel. 2003 [1976]. 'Society Must Be Defended': *Lectures at the Collège de France, 1975–1976*. M. Bertani and A. Fontana (eds.). Trans. David Macey. London: Picador.

Frégosi, Franck. 1994. 'Fondamentalisme islamique et relations internationals: Le cas du FIS' in *Timestre du Monde*, #25 (Jan-Mar).

Frieden, Jeffry. 1981. 'Third World Indebted Industrialization: International Finance and State Capitalism in Mexico, Brazil, Algeria, and South Korea' in *International Organization* 35(3): 407–432.

Gellner, Ernest. 1987. 'From Königsberg to Manhattan (or Hannah, Rahel, Martin and Elfriede or Thy Neighbor's *Gemeinschaft*' in *Culture, Identity, and Politics*. Cambridge: Cambridge University Press.

Gèze, François and Salima Mellah. 2007. '"Al-Qaida au Maghreb", ou la très étrange histoire du GSPC Algérien' in *Algeria-Watch* (22 September 2007).

Ghannouchi, Rashid. 2000. 'Secularism in the Arab Maghreb' in John Esposito and Azzam Tamimi (eds.), *Islam and Secularism in the Middle East*. New York: NYU Press.

Gorman, Anthony. 2007a. 'Regulation, Reform and Resistance in the Middle Eastern Prison?' in Frank Dikötter and Ian Brown (eds.), *Cultures of Confinement: A History of the Prison in Asia, Africa and South America*. London: Hurst & Co.

Grimmett, Richard. 2003. *Conventional Arms Transfers to Developing Nations, 1995–2002*. Washington D.C.: Library of Congress, Congressional Research Service.

Hafez, Mohammed. 2004. 'From Marginalization to Massacres: A Political Process Explanation of GIA Violence in Algeria' in Quintan Wiktorowicz (ed.) *Islamic Activism*. Bloomington: Indiana University Press.

Harrison, Christopher. 1988. *France and Islam in West Africa, 1860–1960*. Cambridge: Cambridge University Press.

Hitchens, Christopher. 2004 [2001]. *Love, Poverty, and War*. New York: Nation Books.

Ibrahim, Youssef. 1990. 'Militant Muslims Grow Stronger as Algeria's Economy Grows Weaker' in the *New York Times* (25 June 1990).

Johnson, Chalmers. 2006. *Nemesis: The Last Days of the American Republic*. New York: Metropolitan Books.

Jones, Adam. 2004. 'Afghanistan and Beyond' in Adam Jones (ed.), *Genocide, War Crimes, and the West*. London: Zed Books.

Kalyvas, Stathis. 1999. 'Wanton and Senseless? The Logic of Massacres in Algeria' in *Rationality and Society*, 11(3): 243–85.

Khalidi, Rashid. 2005. *Resurrecting Empire: Western Footprints and America's Perilous Path in the Middle East*. Boston: Beacon Press.

Kiernan, V.G. 1982. *Colonial Empires and Armies 1815–1960*. London: Sutton.

Laremont, Ricardo. 2000. *Islam and the Politics of Resistance in Algeria, 1783–1992*. Lawrenceville NJ: Africa World.

Layachi, Azzedine. 1992. 'Government, Legitimacy and Democracy in Algeria' in *Maghreb Report* (Jan/Feb).

Mamdani, Mahmood. 1996. *Citizen and Subject: Contemporary Africa and the Legacy of Late Colonialism*. Princeton, NJ: Princeton University Press.

Mann, Michael. 2005. *The Dark Side of Democracy: Explaining Ethnic Cleansing*. Cambridge: Cambridge University Press.

Maran, Rita. 1989. *Torture: The Role of Ideology in the French-Algerian War*. New York: Praeger.

Martinez, Luis. 2000. *The Algerian Civil War 1990–1998*. Trans. Jonathan Derrick. New York: Columbia University Press.

Marx, Karl. 1978 [1843]. "On the Jewish Question" in Robert Tucker (ed.) *Marx–Engels Reader*. New York: W.W. Norton.

Mbembe, Achille. 2003. "Necropolitics". Trans. Libby Meintjes in *Public Culture*, 15(1): 11–40.

McDougall, James. 2002. "Colonial Words: Nationalism, Islam, and Languages of History in Algeria". Doctoral thesis, St. Anthony's College, Oxford University.

McDougall, James. 2006. *History and the Culture of Nationalism in Algeria*. Cambridge: Cambridge University Press.

McDougall, James. 2007. "After the War: Algeria's Transition to Uncertainty" in *Middle East Report* 245.

Merleau-Ponty. Maurice. 1969 [1947]. *Humanism and Terror*. Boston: Beacon Press.

Moore, Clement Henry. 1970. *Politics in North Africa*. Boston: Little, Brown & Co.

Owen, Roger. 1992. *State, power, and politics in the making of the modern Middle East*, New York: Routledge.

Owen, Roger. 2005. "Settler Colonialism in the Middle East and North Africa," Caroline Elkins and Susan Pedersen, eds., *Settler Colonialism in the Twentieth Century: Projects, Practices, Legacies* New York: Routledge.

Piscatori, James. 1986. *Islam in a World of Nation-States*. Cambridge: Cambridge University Press.

Polanyi, Karl. 1971 [1944]. *The Great Transformation: The Political and Economic Origins of Our Time*. Boston: Beacon Press.

Prochaska, David. 1990. *Making Algeria French: Colonialism in Bône, 1870–1920*. Cambridge: Cambridge University Press.

Rashid, Ahmed. 2000. *Taliban: The Story of the Afghan Warlords*. New Haven: Yale University Press.

Razac, Olivier. 2002. *Barbed Wire: A Political History*. Trans. Jonathan Kneight. New York: W.W. Norton and Co.

Richards, Alan and John Waterbury. 2008. *A Political Economy of the Middle East*, 2nd ed. Boulder, CO: Westview Press.

Roberts, Hugh. 2002. "Musical Chairs in Algeria" in *MERIP* Press Information Note 97 (June 4).

Roberts, Hugh. 2003. *The Battlefield Algeria 1988–2002: Studies in a Broken Polity*. London: Verso.

Robin, Marie-Monique. 2005. "Counterinsurgency and Torture: Exporting Torture Tactics from Indochina and Algeria to Latin America" in Kenneth Roth et al. (eds.). *Torture*. New York: New Press.

Rotman, Patrick. 2002. "États d'armes", *L'ennemi Intime* (Film), Part III.

Rudy, Sayres. 2004. "Subjectivity, Political Evaluation, and Islamist Trajectories" in Birgit Schaebler and Leif Stenberg (eds.), *Globalization and the Muslim World*. Syracuse: Syracuse University Press.

Sadiki, Larbi. 2004. *The Search for Arab Democracy: Discourses and Counter-discourses*. New York: Columbia University Press.

Samraoui, Mohammad. 2003. *Chronique des années de sang*. Paris: Denoël.

Sanders, Mark. 2002. *Complicities: The Intellectuals and Apartheid*. Durham: Duke University Press.

Sartre, Jean-Paul. 2001 [1956]. "Colonialism is a System" in *Interventions*, 3(1): 127–140.

Scheele, Judith. 2007. "Recycling *Baraka*: Knowledge, Politics, and Religion in Contemporary Algeria," *Comparative Studies in Society and History*, 49(2): 304–28.

Scott, James. 1969. "Corruption, Machine Politics, and Political Change," *APSR*, 63(4): 221–231.

Shapiro, Kam. 2003. *Sovereign Nations, Carnal States*. Ithaca: Cornell University Press.

Shohat, Ella. 2006. *Taboo Memories, Diasporic Voice*. Durham, NC: Duke University Press.

Smith, Craig. 2004. "Voices of the Dead Echo Across Algeria" in the *New York Times* (18 April 2004).

Smith, Craig. 2007. "Algerian Blasts by Qaeda Unit Kill at Least 23" in the *New York Times* (12 April 2007).

Stora, Benjamin. 2001. *Algeria 1830–2000, A Short History*. Ithaca: Cornell University Press.

Stora, Benjamin. 2004. Interview, "The Battle of Algiers: Remembering History" (Criterion Film).

Sullivan, Anthony. 1983. *Thomas-Robert Bugeaud, France and Algeria, 1784–1849: Politics, Power, and the Good Society*. New Haven, CT: Archon Press.

Sweeney, John. 1997. "Surviving Algeria," *Observer* (29 Jun), at http://www.algeria-watch.de/en/articles/1997_2000/surviving.htm.

Talbot, John. 1980. *The War without a Name: France in Algeria, 1954–1962*. New York: Alfred Knopf.

Tremlett, G. 2002. "US Arms Algeria for Fight against Islamic Terror," *Guardian* (10 Dec).

Turshen, Meredith. 2002. "Algerian Women in the Liberation Struggle and the Civil War: From Active Participants to Passive Victims?" *Social Research*, 69(3): 889–911.

Vandewalle, Dirk. 1988. *Autopsy of a Revolt: The October Riots in Algeria*. Washington D.C.: Institute of Current World Affairs.

Volpi, Frédéric. 2003. *Islam and Democracy: The Failure of Dialogue in Algeria*. London: Pluto Press.

von Sivers, Peter. 1988. "Rural Uprisings as Political Movements in Colonial Algeria, 1851–1914" in Edmund Burke III and Ira Lapidus (eds.), *Islam, Politics, and Social Movements*. Berkeley: University of California Press.

Waldner, David. 1999. *State Building and Late Development*. Ithaca: Cornell University Press.

Waltz, Susan. 1995. *Human Rights and Reform: Changing the Face of North African Politics*. Berkeley: University of California Press.

Willis, Michael. 1996. *The Islamist Challenge in Algeria*. New York: NYU Press.

Wright, Lawrence. 2006. *The Looming Tower: Al-Qaeda and the Road to 9/11*. New York: Vintage.

Unsigned Articles (UA)

1976. "National Charter of the Algerian Popular Democratic Republic", John Donohue and John Esposito (eds.), *Islam in Transition: Muslim Perspectives* (Oxford).

1999. "Shadow Report on Algeria", International Women's Human Rights Law Clinic and Women Living under Muslim Laws (Jan) at http://www.nodo50.org/mujeresred/argelia-shadowreport.html.

2000. "The Algerian Crisis: Not Over Yet", International Crisis Group Report 24 (20 October 2000), at http://www.crisisgroup.org/home/index.cfm?l=1&id=1414.

2001. "Algeria's Economy: The Vicious Circle of Oil and Violence", International Crisis Group Media Release, at http://www.algeria-watch.org/mrv.mrvrap/icg_eco.htm.

2003. "Algerian Group Backs al-Qaeda", *BBC News* (23 October 2003), at http://news.bbc.co.uk/go/pr/fr/-/2/hi/africa/3207363.stm.

2004. "Algeria Prison Conditions", *Library of Congress Country Studies and CIA World Factbook* (10 Nov), at http://www.photius.com/countries/algeria/national_security/algeria_national_security_prison_conditions.html.

2006. "US government report on Algeria's human rights", US Department of State (9 March 2006).

2007a. "January 1992–January 2007: 15 years of atrocities and impunity in Algeria", *Algeria-Watch* (11 January 2007), at http://www.algeria-watch.org/en/aw/15_years.htm.

2007b. "Suicide Bombing Outside Algiers Kills 10 Soldiers At Military Post", *The New York Times* (12 July 2007).

5

POST-COLONIAL POLICING AND THE "WOMAN" QUESTION

A HISTORY OF THE WOMEN'S POLICE DIRECTORATE IN BAHRAIN

Staci Strobl

Specialized female police units within national police forces exist in a majority of Arab, Muslim countries and many of them, including those in Bahrain, Lebanon, Oman and Tunisia, have existed since independence from colonial powers. However, Western academics in the fields of criminal justice and political science have failed to notice these policewomen, even as journalists occasionally reported their accomplishments. As such, Arab Muslim policewomen can be considered subaltern subjects relative to the international criminal justice and political science community by virtue of existing outside academic discourse during their nearly forty year history. The invisibility of Arab, Muslim policewomen reflects a larger selective viewing of the Middle East by Westerners with geopolitical agendas in the region, and a continuation of the colonial gaze which fails to "see" beyond stereotypical constructions of women in the region. As one United States embassy official in Bahrain, in charge of cooperating with local security forces as part of the Regional Security Office, stated to this police researcher in 2005: "Bahraini policewomen? They have those?"

Because no academic study of female police officers in an Arab, Muslim country has previously been undertaken, this research represents new academic territory. It lays the foundation for subsequent research by engaging in an archival exploration of the historical antecedents to the introduction of policewomen in Bahrain in 1970. As a historical case study of the implementation and development of one of the region's many female police units, it aims to answer the question of why, in a society with traditional notions of women as belonging in domestic roles as wives and mothers, they were invited into a male-dominated profession.

Using a post-colonial theoretical framework, the introduction of Bahraini policewomen is examined in relation to what is often termed the "woman question" by scholars—the way in which the colonial obsession with women's roles and status became one of the theatres of change in the transition to modernity (Abu-Lughod 1998; Kandiyoti 1998). This study contributes to an understanding of the larger historical narrative about the position of women within the post-colonial state. Similar micro-histories have served as powerful lenses for viewing the colonial and post-colonial narratives about women in India (Chatterjee 2003; Spivak 1999; Gupta 1998; Bhabha 1994; Chowdhry 1989) and Egypt (Fahmy 1998; Bier 2004). Similarly, Jafar (2005) uses modern Pakistani history to outline the role of women in state ideology and policy, arguing that women collectively served as a "boundary marker" between colonized Muslim societies and their imperial rulers (37). These works draw on Foucault's (1980) discussion of subjects made "other", according to which networks of power in society become starkly visible through a close viewing of marginalized and excluded subjects. This notion has been reworked to recognize that women do not necessarily constitute a monolithic, universal category, but rather their roles and positions are produced through social relations that have material and historical specificities (Mohanty 2003). Spivak (2005) has argued that such qualitative inquiries into the conditions of subalternity must consist of a series of "singular cases" from which larger theories can be formed—a learning "to learn from below" (482).

Gender-segregated Police Units

Contemporary Western examples of specialized policing range from anti–gang to special victims units. Specialization in policing has been heralded as having the advantage of delineating specific responsibilities to particular officers, developing expertise, promoting group cohesiveness and morale and increasing efficiency and effectiveness (Haberfeld 2002; Wilson & McLaren 1972). However, most Western countries no longer have specialized female police units. In non-Western societies, in which there may be a perceived inappropriateness of female or child victims describing their plights to male officers, a segregated unit may offer an alternative to a situation in which such problems are otherwise neglected by authorities. The policewomen themselves may also prefer to work in a parallel police environment out of respect for traditional notions of the female social role as belonging to the domestic sphere of women and children (Natarajan 2001). Contemporary gender-segregated units can be found in India and Brazil, as well as the Middle East.

As this historical exploration shows, it is precisely because the social and cultural contexts in Middle Eastern nations are often gender-segregated that opportunities for women to enter policing have arisen. Policewomen in these countries solve a historical and culturally-specific social problem—how to provide government services to women and children despite cultural codes around gender segregation in public settings.

At the same time, these segregated units may themselves also reflect the gender inequality that remains characteristic of many Arab nations, despite overtures to constitutional and legal equality (Ammar 2004; AbuKhalil 1993). Feminist theorists who emphasize the social construction of gender (Martin and Jurik 1996) may view segregated units as yet another manifestation of gender-based social control, particularly because women are largely relegated to tasks involving women and children, a reification of the more traditional notions of women as nurturers and protectors of the family.

Contemporary Policewomen in Bahrain

Bahrain's female participation in policing is similar in scope to neighboring Qatar, the United Arab Emirates and Oman. Bahraini policewomen work in the Women's Police Directorate (WPD) within the Ministry of the Interior in Bahrain, headquartered in Isa Town (*Madinat Isa*). The directorate was composed of 447 policewomen at the end of 2006 (Brigadier Awatif Hasan Al-Jishi, Director of the Women's

Police Directorate, personal communication, 3 April 2007). Policewomen are estimated to compose approximately 10 per cent of the Bahraini police force (Strobl 2008). The WPD is headed by the highest ranking female officer in the history of Bahraini policing, Brigadier Awatif Hasan Al-Jishi, who achieved this rank in May of 2006 after thirty-six years of service. She is one of five police officers who currently hold this rank within the Ministry of the Interior. Her earlier promotion to colonel preceded women achieving the same rank within the military.

Within every police station in Bahrain, there is a female police unit to handle cases involving women or child victims and offenders. They address domestic violence by helping victims with medical and psychiatric treatment as well as confronting the abusers in a process akin to victim-offender mediation (Al-Jishi 2003). However, studies have shown that in "serious" cases of domestic abuse, such as those involving serious physical injuries, prosecution is sought rather than mediation (Al-Jishi 2003). Additionally, female police and police station workers accompany women during any legal medical examination occurring as part of an investigation, court case or prison intake procedure. They can also be found working in the country's traffic directorate, immigration section, the Criminal Investigation Division (CID), social care (juvenile probation) unit and a child protection unit. Finally, policewomen develop and present educational awareness programs for children in schools, and for adults and families in the community, on topics like family violence and drug abuse (UNESCO 1998).

Policing as a Colonial Legacy

In the Arabian Peninsula, social responses to violence and other transgressions were originally the domain of tribal or *qāđi* justice. In traditional forms of dispute resolution, conflicts around deviant behavior were managed within tribes, villages and families, as related men and women gave evidence in each other's presence before the *qāđi*, indigenous tribal judges learned in Muslim law. Pre-colonial law in the region can be considered a fusion of both customary and Islamic typologies. Bracey (2006) defines customary law as kinship- or tribal-based systems which place the rights of the group ahead of the rights of the individual. Third parties are often involved as arbiters, drawn from people who have kinship ties to the disputed parties and have social status as elders or, in this case, religious authorities. In the event of inter-family and inter-tribal disputes, male members of the clan handled the negotiations—and sometimes embarked on violent confrontations in the case of blood feuds (Lienhardt 2001). As modern policing was established in the region, the centrality of traditional *qāđi* justice waned, representing the larger shift of power from the family or tribe to the colonial state.

Modern policing in the Middle East originates in the colonial experience and, therefore, the cultural hegemony of the West cannot be overlooked as a factor in shaping gender and policing in the Middle East, even post-colonially. The first modern police force in Bahrain was established in 1920 in the capital city of Manama. Its ranks were largely drawn from non-Bahraini British colonial subjects, particularly Baluchis and Punjabis. According to colonial reports, the first modern court, the Bahrain Court, opened in 1926 in central Manama by the decree of the Emir, Shaikh Hamid bin Isa bin Ali Al-Khalifa, and was intended to replace previous local courts run by *qāđis*. The Bahrain Court's first judges were Charles Belgrave, British advisor to the Emir, and Sheikh Mohammed bin Abdul Rahman. The court followed the *Indian Code of Criminal Procedure* which the British established in India. Another "small court" was opened the following year in order to take less serious cases and relieve the Bahrain Court of some of its caseload. In addition, two *shari'ah* courts opened in the 1920s, one for the Sunni and the other for the Shi'a, as well as a *majlis tijāra* which heard commercial disputes (Annual reports, Volume II 1987).

The heavy hand of British influence on the system of justice in Bahrain is clear; the newly-arrived political advisor (*mustashār*) in the 1920s put himself on the bench despite not having ever been legally trained in Britain and not having any experience in Bahraini dispute resolution. Interestingly, local sensibilities regarding justice attempted to penetrate the colonial court. Reports indicate that the court had difficulty obtaining "impartiality" because "... people who are not really affected by a case frequently involve themselves in it with a laudable desire to make a compromise"; such people were labeled "interceders" (Annual reports, Volume II 1987: 18) and were perhaps indicative of the inherent conflict between the narrow delineation of parties in British-style legal cases and the community context in which dispute resolution traditionally occurred in Bahrain. In 1936, another court opened which specialized in cases related to commercial disputes within the fishing and pearl diving industries, the most important industries before the development of oil extraction and refining.

As a result of discriminatory hiring, indigenous Bahrainis avoided seeking employment in policing. Only about 20 per cent of the thousand-strong force were Bahraini in the early 1930s (Khuri 1980). Popular demonstrations for reform began as early as 1938. Concurrently, the government clamped down on the printing of the first local newspaper, *Al-Bahrain*, in 1944, when publisher Abdullah al-Zayed called for uniting Bahrain into one Gulf Arab principality with other emirates (Hanna 1991), a Pan-Arabic call to usurp the control of the British political advisors and the Bahraini royal family.

In the 1950s, the police were headquartered at Riffa' Fort, southwest of Manama. At that time, additional Iraqi troops were required to shore up the ruling family against Shi'a demonstrations and popular violence. In 1953 a state of emergency was declared (Fakhro 1997) and a special branch of the police was established to handle political affairs and internal unrest. Second-in-charge of the political unit was a British officer. Additionally, tribal militias, primarily from the village of al-Hasa (Saudi Arabia) who were loyal to the Bahraini Emir, suppressed local disorder. These two hundred volunteers were later recruited into an anti–riot team (Lawson 1989).

In 1965 a strike at Bahrain Petroleum Company (BAPCO) involved demonstrators calling for the right to organize labor unions, a lifting of the state of emergency, and freedom of the press (Fakhro 1997). By the 1960s, given the sectarian unrest and growing opposition to the ruling family, the Emir preferred to have British officers in "positions of trust" in policing rather than Bahrainis or other foreigners (Joyce 2003). British officers remained in high-level positions in Bahrain's national police force after independence and well into the 1990s (Strobl 2007), reflective of a larger, regional trend in which the same officials are present post-independence as before independence (Crystal 2001).

Post-colonial Historiography

As Spivak (1999) writes in her exploration of widow suicides (*sati/suttee*) in India during the colonial period, studies of women in the post-colonial context often involve "...groping in the margins of official Western history" (239) and reflect "the neglected details of the everyday" (238). The official history primarily involves colonial annual reports reflecting what Said (1993) refers to as the era of "high imperialism" (204). Said argues that the business of administrative surveillance of colonial possessions had become a well-oiled machine and was not merely sustained by heavy-handed military control, but rather the more subtle control of report-writing, a narrative "...positing a world universally available to trans-national impersonal scrutiny" (204).

Colonists categorized and ordered the colony through textual representation of its people, places and practices, and the penetration of scientific, aggregate information was utilized to manage both space and bodies (Mitchell 1988; Foucault 1975). The colonial period was a historical disruption that could not easily be overcome, for the imperial episteme involved colonialists cloaking their discussions of locals as disinterested social science, when in fact, they adhered to a narrative which understands everything in relation to European social, economic and political formations (Said 1993; Spivak 1999). Because of this, it becomes difficult to study women and other subaltern groups in post-colonial societies:

> ...the mode of production narrative is the final reference, these women are insufficiently represented or representable in that narration. We can docket them, but we cannot grasp them at all. The possibility of possession, of being haunted, is cut by the imposition of the tough reasonableness of capital's mode of exploitation (Spivak 1999: 244).

Any reading of colonial documents for information about under-represented people becomes a deconstructionist enterprise by default, cutting through the narrative for underlying, latent content which may or may not elucidate historical dimensions explicitly intended by the writer (Quayson 2000). This reading "up the ladder of privilege" (Mohanty 2003: 231) or "against the grain" (46) involves challenging the assumptions and meanings in official, dominant discourse through a historical materialist lens, interpreting the texts in relation to marginalized people such as women. Yet, the texts often barely see, or fail to see, women as active agents, but rather construct them as symbolic markers and passive recipients of the specifications of both the old traditions and the new modernity, appearing in the narrative only when required to fit imperialistic constructions. In this way, the limits of historiography are two-fold, concerning both what is written and what is excluded. This leads to the question of whether a text written from the vantage point of one social actor can be said to speak for those documented as subjects, occupyinig a distinctly different social location (Birla 2002).

Archival Documents Referencing Bahraini Women and Justice

Originally, this researcher hoped to obtain historical documents about the creation of the policewomen's unit directly from the Ministry of the Interior. The Ministry claimed to have no such documents. However, colonial records viewed at the government's Historical Documents Center in Riffa', as well as other historical materials found there, proved helpful. This research primarily drew upon *The Bahrain Government Annual Reports, 1924–1970*, a collection of reports that the British Political Advisor to the Emir of Bahrain presented to London as accounts relating to the use of imperial funds to develop and control the country. These sources were consulted as to any mention of women working in the burgeoning criminal justice system.

The number of colonial and postcolonial sources that describe Bahraini policewomen is relatively low considering their near forty year history in policing. Only a handful of articles could be found in the local press regarding the moment of their inception and early years of their deployment. The country's main newspapers at the time were published by the Bahraini Petroleum Company (BAPCO) and included *The Islander* (1956 to 1969), the English language paper, and *al-Najmah al-Usbū'iya* (*The Weekly Star*; 1956 to 1978), the Arabic language paper. In addition, the Ministry of Information's *Hunā al-Bahrain* magazine was also examined. Contemporary newspaper coverage was also monitored for articles related to women in policing. Newspapers formed a major part of this research as one of the primary sources of ideological discourse in modern society.

Archival Research Findings

The archives and newspaper articles document changes in the pursuit of justice in Bahraini society during the transition from the colonial to post-colonial period and bring to the fore important questions about the interplay of customary, Islamic and colonial (Western) law and law enforcement. Despite colonial imposition of Western justice systems, there remained the customary segregation of women from public life, including police stations and courtrooms, where they were sometimes required to appear in connection with criminal cases.

Bahraini women as crime victims

The British encouraged the criminalization of behavior that victimized women—behavior that in some communities was not customarily considered deviant. Charles Belgrave, the Political Advisor to the Emir from 1926 to 1957 (Belgrave, 1993), often wrote in his annual reports to London about honor killings, in which women who were discovered to have had sexual relationships outside of wedlock were killed by their male relatives. He explained in 1937:

> Although in recent years Bahrain has progressed in many ways, there are still a number of Arabs living in [Hidd] and Muharraq who consider they are justified in murdering their female relations if the woman brings shame on the family. A few of the very old-fashioned Arabs even consider that because the Government does not ignore such murders it is encouraging immorality. The [*qadi*s] though ultra conservative in their outlook, disapprove of men taking the law into their own hands and murdering women who misbehave (Annual reports, Volume II 1987: 10).

And in 1938:

> A murder took place in [Hidd], a girl drowned by her father for the usual reasons, but the father escaped arrest and took refuge in [Qatar]. The reputation of [Hidd], as being a place where women are frequently murdered, is notorious (Annual reports, Volume II, 1987, p. 17).

Belgrave lamented in a 1947 report the problem of detecting such crimes when many communities kept such incidents hidden from public view:

> It is possible that during the first decade of the last twenty years murders occasionally took place that were not discovered by the police but these crimes were mostly defined to the destruction of newly born unwanted children or women who went wrong. Such cases, taking place inside the harems of Arabs' homes, were difficult to detect (Annual reports, Volume III, 1987).

The Emir and the leading *qāđi* supported the criminalization of honor killings showing that internal, local opposition to honor killings was present; the difference was that the colonial court, rather than customary dispute resolution, was the new response to such incidents. By the 1930s, the court was routinely hearing cases involving women as victims who were required to appear in court as part of the official proceedings.

Wakīl *justice*

The phenomenon of women appearing in public courts was a contested occurrence and served as the subject of a petition to the Emir, Shaikh Hamad bin Isa bin Ali Al-Khalifa, dated Muslim year 1354 (1935 in the Gregorian calendar). Approximately 115 male representatives of Bahraini families called for a solution to the perceived problem of women having to appear and testify in the Bahrain Court. According to those who signed the petition, based on Muslim tradition and the requirements of *shari'ah*, it was inappropriate for women to testify in public and to be interrogated by policemen. As such, they demanded that a male representative (*tawkīl/ wakīl*) of a summoned women's family be permitted to testify on her behalf (original document on display at the Historical Documents Center in Riffa', Bahrain). A *wakīl* is distinct from someone acting as a legal representative of a party, such as a lawyer (*muḥām*). Instead, the *wakīl* is the legal proxy of the female victim or witness.

Wakīl justice was debated by British advisors and Bahraini sheikhs as early as 1933 when, according to the government reports, it was permitted. A system of professional *wakīls* had developed in which women paid males unrelated to them to act as their proxies in court. The system, however, was suffering from corruption as several *wakīls* "...had misappropriated funds which had been paid to them on behalf of their principals by the court"; two of them were convicted of the offense and sentenced to hard labor (Annual reports, Volume I 1987: 366). Belgrave proposed to the Emir that professional *wakīls* be subjected to a cash deposit, retained by the court, in order to be permitted to practice their trade. This would serve to secure women in the event their *wakīls* stole their court-awarded funds. *Wakīls* who were related to the woman represented would not be subjected to this regulatory measure (Annual reports, Volume I 1987). Complete information about *wakīls* could not be obtained from available historical records; however, based on the aforementioned petition it can be surmised that the Emir may have attempted to abolish *wakīls* altogether, a move unpopular with many men in the community. *Wakīl* justice, however, lived on. According to a subsequent report in 1937, the Emir adopted the following regulatory measure:

> A proclamation was issued laying down the conditions under which *wakils* should be permitted to appear in court and specifying their rates of fees. This

became necessary after criminal charges had been proved against certain *wakils* who had cheated their clients. (Annual reports, Volume II 1987: 22).

And in 1947 regulation continues to be defined by the Emir and the *mustashār*:

No persons who are not Bahraini subjects are allowed to appear in Bahraini courts as *wakils* and only those *wakils* who are granted licences by the courts are permitted to practice (Annual reports, Volume III 1987: 66).

The colonial record is relatively silent about *wakīls* after 1947, and never mentions how women related to the criminal justice system in general until 1965. It is here that Spivak's (1999: 239) "groping in the margins" seems particularly relevant. The links between *wakīls* and policewomen are implied by the return of narration about women in public courts and police stations in the late colonial period. Bahraini policewomen become those granted the authority to shuttle between customary practices of gender segregation and the modern courts and police stations. Press reports discussed below, though few in number, appear to fill in the margins of the colonial reports.

The arrival of policewomen in the late colonial period

Prior to 1970 and the country's transition to independence from Britain, there is no record of indigenous Bahraini women serving in the police force. However, Brigadier Awatif Hasan Al-Jishi recalled that several British women worked for the police in the intelligence sector prior to independence (personal communication, 8 April 2006). Searches through the English and Arabic language newspapers published during the colonial era revealed no mention of British policewomen in Bahrain. However, the *Bahrain Government Annual Reports, 1924–1970*, documents the advent of sworn-in female personnel in 1965. At this time six women sub-inspectors from Britain arrived to perform primarily administrative support to police officers in the Criminal Investigation Department (CID). British policewomen working in the empire's colonial possessions and protectorates was a common occurrence throughout the imperial period. For example, Egypt's first two female police officers were British and introduced to the Alexandria police force in 1923; six more arrived in 1930 (Rizk 2002). Regarding the policewomen dispatched to Bahrain, the 1965 annual report states:

[CID] is functioning more satisfactorily than in previous years mainly owing to an increase in suitable clerical staff, and particularly 6 policewomen recruited from U.K. (Annual report, Volume VIII 1987: 70).

Notably, similar to trends in policing in Britain at the time, British policewomen in Bahrain were also being utilized as clerical adjuncts to male officers. The above quotation might imply that women were perceived to be superior workers in these types of assignments, a common theme in the development of policewomen around the world (Brown and Heidensohn 2000).

A snapshot of the Bahraini force at the time British policewomen became part of the force, in 1965, reveals that there were a total of 1,021 sworn-in police personnel serving a population of approximately 150,000. Of the forty-two commissioned officers, 45 per cent were British and the remaining officers were Arab, not of Bahraini origin. As sub-inspectors, the policewomen enjoyed a position below that of the forty-two officers, but above Deputy Sub-Inspectors, Assistant Sub-Inspectors, and non-commissioned officers. However, their clerical duties suggest that their formal rank may not reflect the nature of their actual duties. In 1965, there were five cases of murder investigated, with only two leading to prosecution and conviction. There were 2,967 complaints investigated by police, of which 45 per cent pertained to alleged violent crimes.

By 1968, one British woman, I.M. Darragh, had been promoted to the rank of Inspector and became the highest-ranking policewoman in the history of the colonial forces. However, at this time only one additional woman in the force worked as a sub-inspector and performed administrative duties.

Indigenous policewomen first entered Bahraini policing in 1970. Awatif Hasan al-Jishi and Aisha Isa Thawadi, graduates of Cairo University's sociology program, enlisted as policewoman cadets and trained under I.M. Darragh. The two cadets were selected from among forty candidates who applied (*al-Bahrain thānī dūlah* 1971). They were the first female policewomen in the Arabian Gulf (*Aūla fitātayn* 1971) and considered the second in the Arab world; Tunisia had women in police support positions at an earlier date (*al*-Bahrain *thānī dūlah* 1971). According to al-Jishi:

When I went to work with [Bahrain's] social affairs department, they told me [the police] were thinking of establishing women police for women's cases and juveniles. They said you can try to do this and if you don't like it, you can just leave it... (personal communication, 11 January 2005).

The following statement from the 1970 annual report to London reflects the perceived mission of the indigenous women police at their inception:

> The Women Police Division is required for the investigation of cases, especially sexual cases involving women and children. During the year there were twenty-seven criminal cases and thirty-four miscellaneous involving women and children (Annual report, Volume VIII 1987: 93).

This mission of reaching out to women and children victims of abuse has remained one of the stated reasons for the current Women's Police Directorate. Yet, several other aims have since been added to the perceived mission of policewomen—for example, the ability of policewomen to get more and better information from those women in the community who are only comfortable talking candidly with other women (Strobl 2007).

The introduction of indigenous policewomen can be considered a deliberate move by the British and their Bahraini subjects to set up a lasting legacy of policewomen in Bahrain after independence. The British signed an agreement with the Emir of Bahrain in January 1968 to withdraw their control of the Gulf region by the end of 1971 (Albaharana 1975). The training of policewomen by the British was part of the transitional program implemented by the British government in which teams would be put into place in the Gulf Trucial states in order to develop their security forces prior to independence (Albaharna 1975).

However, the British and Bahraini perspectives differed in the cultural and social meaning they attached to the introduction of policewomen. The British saw policewomen as part of their modernizing mission, the liberation of women from the shackles of tradition, and a legacy of their imprint on the region. The Bahrainis, also committed to modernization of Bahrain's government and infrastructure, nonetheless emphasized the preservation of women's honor in the customary sense and the role of policewomen as restricted to supporting and helping policemen. In a 1971 article describing the new female policing unit in *Hūna al-Bahrain* (published by the Ministry of Information), the unit was characterized as part of an overall plan to develop the country and to have men and women share the responsibility of serving the newly independent nation. The article particularly emphasizes that policewomen are in a supportive position, required for handling women and children as victims of physical and sexual abuse. The article states that women are better at nurturing and caring for women and children and that among women, their problems can be handled with dignity and respect in the context of local cultural sensibilities (*al-Bahrain thānī dūlah* 1971; Brigadier Awatif al-Jishi, personal communication, 11 January 2005). As such, the introduction of police women represents ironically, an area of cross-cultural common ground in the final hour of the colonial experience.

Conclusion

It would be incorrect to argue that Bahraini policewomen directly replaced the *wakils* in the historical development of the Bahraini criminal justice system. Instead, they solve the same problem as the *wakīl* system, and their presence signals the *wakīl* system's demise. By bringing policewomen into the criminal justice system to process female victims, witnesses and offenders, and to accompany them into male-dominated public spaces, they effectively addressed the problem of offending the sensibilities of local families in summoning women to the police stations and court. As such, the entry of women into the police in Bahrain was socially and politically possible precisely because of the customary gender segregation—the same customs which ultimately may limit their full deployment in a male-dominated profession today.

The continued presence of Bahraini policewomen in segregated units may serve as a symbolic or cultural marker of a slowly disappearing custom given increased urbanization and the casual meeting of men and women in public spaces throughout Bahrain. It is possible that the solution has outlived the problem and policewomen in gender-segregated units today are more nostalgic relics than socially necessary. At the same time, recent Islamisation trends have selectively reinforced traditional gender roles; therefore, policewomen in segregated units can also be considered an important compromise for conflicting social forces that provide occupational opportunities for women, but also restrict them to tasks which reify their traditional roles as nurturers.

Policewomen are liminal actors in the post-colonial context, exhibiting the "hybrid sensibility" of both the colonizers and the colonized (Quayson 2000: 78). At the moment of their inception, they were not constructed by colonial or press reports as fully representing the dominant status of male, authoritarian police officers as the indigenous extension of the former colonizers. Nor did their public role as female authority figures make them ideal carriers of tradition; they were framed as necessary tools in preserving tradition for other women. Therefore, they exhibit aspects of tradition and the potential weakening of tradition at the same time, in a poignant example of the "unhoused, decentered, and exilic energies" of the postcolonial milieu (Said 1993: 403). Their identities can be considered to be mediated through the colonial and post-colonial hegemonic social and political forces, in which space is carved out for the negotiative possibilities of their roles among state actors (Kapoor 2003; Bhabha 1994) in a socially interpellated performance of gender and culture (Butler 1990). As such, this account of policewomen in Bahrain falls into what Cooke (2000: 169) has called a "counter-memory", where a gendered formation of official governmental and historical epistemology is confronted.

Further research should pay close attention to the public discourse about police in Muslim, Arab societies as an evolving and contested site at which gender constructions are produced and maintained. These constructions poignantly illuminate the larger discourse about the position of women within post-colonial Arab, Muslim states. Such research should aim to deconstruct and discern the social, cultural and political ingredients which make women in policing possible in most Muslim, Arab countries, as well as account for their notable absence in a minority of countries such as Saudi Arabia.

Bibliography

AbuKhalil, As'ad. 1993. "Toward the study of women and politics in the Arab world: The debate and the reality" in *Feminist Issues* 13: 3–22.

Abu-Lughod, Lila. 1998. "Feminist longings and post-colonial conditions" in Abu Lughod (ed.). *Remaking women: Feminism and modernity in the Middle East* Princeton, NJ: Princeton University Press; 3–31.

Albaharna, Husain M. 1975. *The Arabian Gulf states: Their legal and political status and their international problems* (2nd ed.). Beirut: Librarie Du Liban.

Ammar, Nawal H. 2004. "Arab women in their constitutions." Paper presented at the forty-first Annual Meeting of the Academy of Criminal Justice Sciences, 12 March in Las Vegas, NV.

Aūla fitātayn baĥraynitayn fi al-būlis al-nisā'ī tazūran al-sharkah. 1971. *Al-Najmah Usbū'iyah*, 2 February.

Bahrain Government Annual Reports, 1924–1970 (Annual Reports) (1987). Bahrain: Oriental Press.

Al-Bahrain thānī dūlah 'arabiya tash'al shurtah nisā'iyah. 1971. *Hunā al-Bahrain*, February 1971. Bahrain: Ministry of Information.

Belgrave, Robert. 1993. "C. Dalrymple Belgrave: The early years as Adviser in Bahrain" in Abdullah bin Khalid Al-Khalifa and Michael Rice (eds.). *Bahrain through the ages: The History*. London: Kegan Paul International; 104–122.

Bhabha, Homi K. 1994. *The location of culture*. London: Routledge Press.

Bier, Laura. 2004. "Modernity and the other woman: Gender and national identity in the Egyptian Women's Press" in *Gender & History* 16: 99–112.

Birla, Ritu. 2002. "History and the critique of postcolonial reason: Limits, secret, value" in *Interventions* 4: 175–185.

Bracey, Dorothy. 2006. *Exploring law and culture*. Long Grove, IL: Waveland Press.

Brown, Jennifer & Frances Heidensohn. 2000. *Gender and policing: Comparative perspectives*. New York: St. Martin's Press.

Butler, Judith. 1990. *Gender trouble: Feminism and the subversion of identity*. New York: Routledge.

Chatterjee, Partha. 2003. "An empire of drink: Gender, labor and the historical economies of alcohol" in *Journal of Historical Sociology* 16: 183–208.

Chowdhry, Prem 1989. "Customs in a peasant economy: Women in colonial Haryana" in J. Sangari and S. Vaid (eds.) *Recasting women: Essays in colonial history* New Delhi: Kali Press.

Cooke, Miriam. (2000). "Women, religion and the postcolonial Arab world" in *Cultural Critique* 45: 150–184.

Crystal, Jill. 2001. "Criminal justice in the Middle East" in *Journal of Criminal Justice* 29: 469–483.

Fahmy, Khaled. 1998. "Women, medicine and power in Egypt" in Lila Abu-Lughod (ed.) *Remaking women: Feminism and modernity in the Middle East*. Princeton, NJ: Princeton University Press; 35–72.

Fakhro, Munira. 1997. "The uprising in Bahrain: An assessment" in Gary Sick and Larry G. Potter (eds.). *Gulf at the millennium: Essay in politics, economy, security and religion*. New York: St. Martin's Press; 167–188.

Foucault, Michel. 1975. *Discipline and punish*. New York: Vintage.

Foucault, Michel. 1980. *Power/Knowledge: Selected Interviews and Other Writings 1972–1977*, edited by Colin Gordon. London: Harvester.

Gupta, Akhil. 1998. *Postcolonial developments*. Durham: Duke University Press.

Haberfeld, Maria. 2002. *Critical issues in police training*. Upper Saddle River, NJ: Prentice Hall.

Hanna, Sami. 1991. *A modern cultural history of Bahrain*. Bahrain: The National Council for Culture, Arts and Literature, Ministry of Information.

Jafar, Afshan. 2005. "Women, Islam and State in Pakistan" in *Gender Issues* 22: 35–55.

Al-Jishi, Awatif. 2003. "Women police and the community: Kingdom of Bahrain, Ministry of the Interior." Paper presented at the 10th International Police Executive Symposium, 12–15 October, Manama, Bahrain.

Joyce, Miriam. 2003. *Ruling sheikhs and Her Majesty's government: 1960–1969*. Abingdon, United Kingdom: Taylor & Francis Group.

Kandiyoti, Deniz. 1998. "Some awkward questions on women and modernity in Turkey" in Lila Abu-Lughod (ed.) *Remaking women: Feminism and modernity in the Middle East*. Princeton, NJ: Princeton University Press; 270–287.

Kapoor, Ilan. 2003. "Acting in a tight spot: Homi Bhabha's postcolonial politics" in *New Political Science* 25: 561–577.

Khuri, Fuad. 1980. *Tribe and state in Bahrain*. Chicago, IL: University of Chicago.

Lawson, Fred. 1989. *Bahrain: The modernization of autocracy*. Boulder, CO: Westview Press.

Lienhardt, Peter. 2001. *Shaikhdoms of Eastern Arabia*. New York: Palgrave.

Martin, Susan E. & Nancy C. Jurik. 1996. *Doing justice, doing gender*. Thousand Oaks, CA: Sage Publications.

Mitchell, Timothy. 1988. *Colonising Egypt*. Cambridge: Cambridge University Press.

Mohanty, Chandra Talpade. 2003. *Feminism without borders: Decolonizing theory, practicing solidarity*. Durham, NC: Duke University Press.

Natarajan, Mangai. 2001. "Women police in a traditional society: Test of a Western model of integration" in *International Journal of Comparative Sociology* 42: 211–233.

Quayson, Ato. 2000. *Postcolonialism: Theory practice or process?* Malden, MA: Polity Press.

Rizk, Yunan L. 2002. "A *diwan* of contemporary life: Women police" in *al-Ahrām* (5–11 September). Retrieved from http://weekly.ahram.org/2002/602/chrncls.htm.

Said, Edward W. 1993. *Culture and imperialism*. London: Vintage.

Spivak, Gayatri C. 1999. *A critique of postcolonial reason: Toward a history of the vanishing present*. Cambridge, Massachusetts: Harvard University Press.

Spivak, Gayatri C. 2005. "Scattered speculations on the subaltern and the popular" in *Postcolonial Studies* 8: 475–486.

Strobl, Staci. 2007. *Women and policing in Bahrain*. New York: City University of New York Graduate Center Doctoral Dissertation.

Strobl, Staci. 2008. "The Women's Police Directorate in Bahrain: An ethnographic observation of a gender segregated unit and the likelihood of integration" in *International Criminal Justice Review* 18: 39–58.

Sulaibekh, Khalifa. 2004. *Tales from al-Hoora* (2nd ed.). Bahrain: Al Sayah Public Relations.

United Nations Educational, Social and Cultural Organization (UNESCO). 1998. *Manthūmāt al-'afwa al-dūliyah*. Document number: 4/30/98 POL. Received from Chief Public Prosecutor Ali bin Fadhl Ghanim Al-Bouainain, Bahrain Ministry of Justice, on 18 January 2005.

Wilson, Orlando Winfield and Roy C. McLaren. 1972. *Police administration*. New York: McGraw-Hill.

6

THE POLICE ORGANIZATION IN TURKEY IN THE POST-1980 PERIOD AND THE RE-CONSTRUCTION OF THE SOCIAL FORMATION

Biriz Berksoy

Introduction

This chapter aims to examine the re-structuring of the police organization in Turkey, in the post-1980 period, during the neo-liberalization process. Throughout the period, the police occupied a more extensive and serious part in everyday life. After the military coup of 1980, the organization initially entered a phase of expansion and militarization, during which it was structurally and legally strengthened with the help of the military, and it began to apply violence more frequently and intensively via the newly established paramilitary units. While this trend has not yet ceased, from the mid-1990s onwards it internalized the market-oriented rationality, engaged in "proactive policing" and increased its surveillance capacity by the installation of electronic cameras on the streets to minimize risk.

It is argued here that during this period in Turkey, the police organization acquired an increasing significance as a gateway of the state to reconstruct the social formation on a neo-liberal trajectory. The police augmented its capabilities to regulate, incapacitate and repress the "internal enemies", which expanded to include the resistant labor unions, leftist groups, ethnic/religious groups posing a challenge to political power and the "under-class" of the big cities, whose ranks swelled due to the new accumulation regime and forced internal migration waves caused by the war waged in Southeastern Turkey against the Kurdish guerillas of PKK (*Partiya Karkerên Kürdistan*, Kurdistan Workers' Party). Moreover, by using these "enemies", it also set out to construct a model of "citizens" as prudent subjects who conduct their own "risk assessments" and cooperate with the police as "informants".

This re-structuring of the police organization in Turkey is examined here by theorizing the capitalist state as a "social relation" (Poulantzas 2000) and by taking into account changes in social relations, which acted on the state, which is a "strategically selective terrain" (Jessop 1990: 342) to produce these new power strategies. Additionally, emphasis is put upon the concept of "internal enemy", for it occupies an important place within Turkey's hegemonic discursive formations and thereby the sub-culture of the police. To present its place within these discursive formations will be illuminating for conceiving the police's everyday practices.

This chapter is composed of two parts. In the first part, the reasons for the re-structuring process are analyzed by focusing on the reconfiguration of social relations. In the second part, the police's subculture is depicted in order to investigate the motivations behind their practices. For this purpose, primary resources published by the police, like the journals *Polis* (Police) and *Polis Dergisi* (Police Journal), as well as the in-depth interviews conducted with police officers,[1] are utilized.

The Police Organization and its Restructuring in Turkey in the post-1980 Period

As Bittner asserts "no human problem exists, or is imaginable about which it would be said with finality that this certainly could not become the proper business of police" (Bittner 1980; cited in Neocleous 2000: 93). The conventional image of the police as "enforcers of the law" or "fighters against crime" does not enclose the rationality behind the

[1] The author conducted twenty-seven interviews throughout April-June 2005 with police officers working in a police station in Ankara, the Directorates of Security of five districts (Bağcılar, Sultanbeyli, Gaziosmanpaşa, Beyoğlu, Kadıköy), the Rapid Action Units and Motorcycled Police Teams in Istanbul as well as with the instructors of the Police Academy in Ankara.

overwhelming interventions of the police in everyday life (Neocleous 2000: 92). While the state, through law, constructs injunctions, points to an object of violence and provides the terrain of its execution (Poulantzas 2000: 77), the police, symbolizing "the capacity of the state to intervene and the concern of the state for the affairs of its citizenry" (Manning 1997: 20), constitute the gateway of the state to penetrate every corner of social life. The discretionary powers held by the police mean that they are able to draw a line which, when crossed, will invoke "intervention" and "correction". With their incessant and omnipresent interventions, they create subject positions and conduct attitudes, and "interpellate" (Althusser 1994: 131) each and every person on behalf of the state. They have the role in society of acting upon the possible consequences of other people's actions (see Foucault 2000). This role does not amount solely to the reproduction of order but, as Neocleous asserts, to its fabrication (Neocleous 2000: 5).

What differentiates the police organization (and gendarmerie in some countries) from other institutions infiltrating everyday life is that at the core of the police's actions there lies the possibility that violence may be used (Bittner 1974: 35): it may surface or remain as a possibility, solely depending upon the decision of the officer. Enjoying discretionary powers and a substantial opacity, the police, therefore, have a similar position to that of a sovereign. They have the power to make a decision in the moment about whether to dispense violence or any other form of coercive action (Agamben 2000: 103).

The police occupy a crucial position in the ordering of social relations, but they acquire further importance at times when a comprehensive re-construction of the web of social relations, especially if it is on an exclusionary basis, is being attempted.[2] The post-1980 era was such a period for Turkey. Hence, although the police organization[3] had had a modest place among the state institutions until the 1980s, the only significant addition to the organization being the Society Police (*Toplum Polisi*, the first professional public order squads), from 1980 onwards it entered a far-reaching re-structuring process that has not halted yet.

[2] See Wacquant (1999; 2001), Brewer et al. (1996) for analyses of similar processes experienced in the USA, Britain and Continental Europe in the post-1980 period.

[3] The police organization in Turkey, whose origin goes back to the Ottoman era, is part of the civil administration system and organized within a centralized and hierarchical scheme under the Ministry of Internal Affairs.

The process started immediately after the 1980 military coup with extensive evaluations made to specify the organization's needs regarding its structure, cadre and equipments. Consequently, its budget was increased; new police schools were opened, and the number of personnel was increased at a faster pace (EGM 1983: 42–53). Two paramilitary units were established in the first three years with the initiative of the military. One of them incorporated the militarized public order squads formed out of the Society Police and re-named Rapid Action Units (*Çevik Kuvvet*, 1982); the other comprised the Special Operation Teams (*Özel Harekat Timleri*) established in 1983. In the following years, high-tech weapons and armored vehicles were supplied and several new departments, such as the Anti–Terrorism and Operation Department (1986), were established. A draconian Anti–Terrorism Act was ratified in 1991. While community policing strategies were utilized from the mid-1990s onwards, the Motorcycle Police Teams were organized in 1993 and an electronic surveillance system was launched in 2005. The police authorities were substantially increased in 1985, 2002, 2005 and 2007.

The diverse and intermingling reasons behind this process are located within the changing web of social relations, which were given a new shape by the re-structuring state in the 1980s and have to be related to the expanding category of "internal enemies".

The post-1980 period started in Turkey with a violent military coup, which terminated the organic crisis of the late 1970s caused by the deadlock within the developmentalist accumulation regime and the running social struggles between labor unions/leftist students/politicized shantytowns and the power block incorporating the industrial capital, military and the nationalist-conservative governments (Savran 2002; Yalman 2002). The coup helped the state to restore its power, to eliminate the anarchists/communists, included by state terminology in the category of "internal enemies", and to reconfigure social relations on a neo-liberal trajectory, while the state itself went through a re-structuring process. The 1982 Constitution was re-organized in such a way that the executive (the military[4] and civil bureaucracy as well as the President of the Republic), with the exception of the cabinet, acquired substantial new authority. The terms of their accountability became

[4] Through the newly established National Security Council, the military bureaucracy attained the prerogative to take binding decisions concerning "national security" (Bayramoğlu 2002: 87–91).

vague enough to give them a considerably free-hand. The basic rights and freedoms were so restricted that even the "right to live" ceased to be absolute (Parla 2002: 45–54, 87–99).

After the coup, the militarized state quickly set out to re-structure the accumulation regime in accordance with the "structural adjustment program" of the IMF and the desires of local industrial capital (Ercan 2002: 25). The import substitution industrialization scheme was replaced with an exclusionary neo-liberal one. Accordingly, the state supported industrial capital with credits and tax exemptions to increase its exports; while the production costs, especially the wages, were decreased to the lowest possible rates (Ercan 2002: 26, 27). The laws concerning the rights of labor and conditions of social opposition were re-formulated so as to prevent any resistance to these policies (Akkaya 2000: 212), which soon led to high public debts and inflation rates, the shrinking of the industrial sector and the swelling of unemployment rates. The financial liberalization of the late 1980s contributed to the financial crises of 1994, 2000 and 2001. Consequently, a big army of cheap, unorganized and marginalized labor emerged to be increasingly employed within the informal sector, which substantially expanded. Poverty became severe and widespread (Yeldan 2002: 27–63).

The military junta of the first three years and the succeeding civilian governments tried to achieve pacification and mobilization around these policies by criminalizing all political opponents who were allegedly endangering the needed "order and stability" (Mert 2002: 65; Yalman 2002: 41). The state utilized the doctrine of "Turkish-Islamic Synthesis" to construct hegemony. The doctrine, built upon the anti–communist legacy of the previous period, incorporated the authoritarian-fascist interpretation of Kemalism, Islamic elements endorsing the Sunni sect and an emphasis put upon the ever-present themes of the "perpetuity and sacredness of the state" and its "indivisibility with its nation and territory" (Bora and Can 1990: 24). From the mid-1980s onwards, the promotion of "market society" and "entrepreneurial individual" were adjoined to this discursive formation. One of the most emphasized discursive constructs of the 1980s became the concept of "middle-pillar" (*orta direk*), signifying the social group to whom upward mobilization was promised. The concept did not denote a particular class and, as a vague concept, raised expectations among many sections of society; it also implied that there existed a limit to these upwardly-mobilized groups and, thereby, indicated the existence of class preferences (Taşkın 2004: 112, 113). Therefore, unlike the pre-1980 period, it became explicit that there were the "preferred ones" and "the others". The latter, whose "content was rendered vague by the political power to make maneuvers" (Taşkın 2004: 113, 114), would be composed of those who, somehow, did not get integrated to the system and, thereby, endangered the "tranquility" provided by the coup.

Throughout the 1980s, "the others" came to be composed of the resistant labor unions, leftist groups, the poverty-stricken population who agreed to be represented by them and, as ethnic/cultural differences became visible due to claims of rights over identities, the politically active Kurdish[5] and Alevi people[6] (ibid.). The coup was a blow to the dissidents of the pre-1980 period, mostly gathered around a leftist paradigm. Hence, each social group was scattered around and, especially with the end of the Cold War, turned into a "threat" on its own, joining the ranks of the marginalized non-Muslim minorities. These groups fell outside the social order, within which unquestioned obedience was rendered as an integral part of the fragile neo-liberal balance, and no ethnic identity/religious sect other than the Turkish identity/ Sunni Islam (except for the non-Muslim minorities) was officially recognized. As the Kurdish movement incorporating the armed struggle of the PKK starting in 1984 was accompanied by extreme violence in Southeastern Turkey, particularly in the 1990s, the potential of the state to treat the "others" as "internal enemies" crystallized once more, some of whom were accused of connections with "foreign sources" (Taşkın 2004). Human rights associations, political parties, and those criticizing the state's repressive policies were adjoined to this category.

[5] Until very recently, the state did not recognize the existence of Kurds as an ethnic group. When it could no longer deny their reality, it insisted on defining them as a "kinfolk" of Turks, who forgot their Turkishness. Nevertheless, this approach also entailed the possibility of "estranging" the Kurds from the "cluster of citizens" if they failed to appreciate this offer of assimilation (see Yeğen 2006).

[6] Three factors account for the marginalization of the Alevi community: firstly, as the state endorsed the Sunni sect and promoted it more aggressively since the 1980s, the Alevi people constituted a factor of disharmony for the state's vision of a homogeneous national identity. Secondly, leftist orientation has always been widespread among the Alevi community. This was also a source of "threat" for the state. Thirdly, in several places, the Alevi identity coincided with Kurdishness. Thus, towards the late 1980s as the political claims over identities were expressed more explicitly, they consolidated their place among the "internal threats" (see Küçük 2003).

In the 1990s, while the state's strategies implemented in Southeastern Turkey became increasingly repressive, the police organization acquired dominance along with the military and contributed to the formation of a "national-security state". As the military gained further prerogatives[7] and engaged in daily policy-making processes (Öngen 2003: 181; Bayramoğlu 2002: 45, 46), the "national-security/terror" discourse became predominant (Öngen 2003: 181, 182). Within this context, a substantial part of the Kurdish population living in Southeastern Turkey was forced by the state to migrate because of the war against the PKK. They mostly ended up in big cities to constitute a large part of the marginalized labor and unemployed "under-class" (Öngen 2003: 178). Most of them amassed in poverty-ridden shantytowns. As crimes against property increased and became visible in the 1990s, they became targets of the "enemization" mechanism. While a security obsession was constructed, they were usually blamed for the increasing mugging incidents.

From the late 1990s onwards, although democratization policies were adopted, under pressure from the European Union, they did not result in any substantial changes in basic rights and freedoms, or the powers of the police and the military.

Thus, as the social relations were reconfigured in an exclusionary and un-egalitarian manner, it became strategically preferable for the state to strengthen the police to interfere in every social incident before it threatened the new social order. One member of the military junta evaluated this process in the following way:

> The Police Organization which attained huge success with the multi–dimensional support of the Turkish Armed Forces has launched a re-organization project to effectually carry out its duties *that will become heavier after the termination of martial law* (*Danışma Meclisi Tutanak Dergisi* [The Journal of the Consultative Assembly Minutes] 21.1.1982 [40/1]: 409; italics added).

It will be appropriate now to take a look at some major steps in this re-structuring process and how they served the state in establishing a permanent "state of exception" (see Agamben 2005).

[7] For example, in 1997 a new regulation concerning the Prime Ministry Crisis Management Center was promulgated, according to which some social movements could also be categorized as crises. During crises, the military bureaucracy would be able to take control of the administration (Bayramoğlu 2002: 46, 47).

The replacement of the Society Police with Rapid Action Units (RAU) constituted an important step in this process. These new units were given substantial legal powers.[8] They would take reactive and proactive measures about legal and illegal demonstrations/strikes/lock-outs, prevent illegal acts in public places, and patrol the streets where social movements undermining public order might break out. In contrast to the Society Police, the RAU made use of advanced weapons like electrified truncheons, fog/gas bombs, machine guns and gas/water-spurting armored vehicles. Concerning illegal gatherings, the police chiefs were given the prerogative to decide on the degree of the threat that the crowd posed and the degree of force to be applied (EGM 2001: 111). In this way, the police's discretionary powers to decide on which groups to subject to violence were officially amplified, and unlike the former public order squads, they were encouraged in every way to intervene in all social incidents.

Throughout the period, the units staged forceful interventions in workers' and public employees' collective actions, sometimes leading to fatalities, as in the 1 May celebrations of 1989 and 1996, and to detention of numerous protesters (*Milliyet*, 2 May 1989; *Milliyet* 2 May 1996). They exerted systematic violence at the demonstrations of leftist students, especially at those held every year on 4 November to protest the Higher Education Council. They also used extreme coercion against ethnic and religious groups. For example, in nearly every year, they intervened in the Kurdish groups celebrating Newroz on 21 March, declared by the PKK as a Kurdish national holiday. Another paradigmatic example in this respect was the intervention of these units in an Alevi neighborhood named Gazi Mahallesi in March 1995, after the shooting death of an Alevi elder led to clashes between residents and the police. As a result, more than twenty people died (Dural 1995). Throughout the 2000s, RAU also participated in home raids in certain Kurdish- and gypsy-inhabited shanty-towns (i.e. Karabayır, Sarıgöl, Gaziosmanpaşa), which were blamed for the increasing crime rates (i.e. *Radikal*, 24 February 2006). They took part in the destruction of these shanty-towns too. The demolitions were implemented as part of "urban transformation projects" which entailed the provision

[8] They were legally strengthened by the amendment of laws such as the "Law on Strikes, Lockouts and Collective Bargainings" and the "Law on Meetings and Demonstrations", which contained heavier punishments and increased the discretionary powers of the police and civil administrators.

of large city spaces to construction firms, leading to brutal clashes between the inhabitants and the police. Thus, these units were mobilized to repress and deter any politically opponent group that could endanger the new order and regulate/incapacitate the expanding "underclass" of this new period.

The second unit to be mentioned is the Special Operation Teams (SOTs), which were initially trained by the former vice-commander of the army's Special War Department according to guerilla warfare techniques as part of broader state strategies in the Kurdish issue, which was considered a "public security problem". Accordingly, they were supplied with high-tech heavy arms and mobilized in Southeastern provinces and countryside against the PKK in collaboration with the army (Bora 1997: 119). Especially during the 1990s, they were composed of the ultra nationalist youth (Bora and Can 2000: 70). The Director-General of Security in 1987 illuminated how these teams were utilized:

> It must be known that these *inhumane* people [the rebelling Kurds] are pursued closely by the Provincial Directorates of Security and their specialized personnel throughout Turkey...To be able to annihilate these divisive bandits, our police cooperate with our military troops (*Polis* 1987 [419]: 38, 39, italics added).

Thus, the aim was to get rid of people who were excluded not only from the category of "citizenship" but even the category of "humanity". From the mid-1990s onwards, after the teams engaged in demonstrations against government and their ill-treatment of the local people became highly visible, some were moved to Western cities (*Milliyet* 2 August, 1995) where they were used in "no-knock entries"[9] together with the RAU. Thus they initially helped the state to deal with "terrorists", degraded to the level of "bare-lives" (Agamben 1998) and later to regulate and repress the marginalized groups that amassed in certain neighborhoods. Thereby, they further militarized police practices in the cities.

The Anti–Terrorism and Operation Department (ATOD) was another department set up in the 1980s to intervene in the "destructive, leftist and right-wing terror" (EGM 2000: 131). However, it was

[9] They started to function just like the SWATs in the USA, which were mobilized for "no-knock entries" in criminal cases in most police units from the 1980s onwards, (see Kraska and Kappeler 1999: 466–471).

used primarily in relation to the Kurdish question and secondarily against leftist organizations. Towards the mid-1990s, while claims of extra-judicial killings and torture substantially increased, especially in Southeastern Turkey, a new unit, the Psychological Operation Branch Directorate, was set up within the department in 1994 to:

> support the struggle against terrorist organizations by taking into account its psychological dimension via preparing written, visual or audio propaganda materials and engaging in propaganda activities...(EGM 2000: 132).

This was a crucial development. This directorate arguably buttressed the police's ability to shape the highly nationalist political climate of the 1990s and to legitimize police practices.

The proceedings of ATOD were backed by a draconic Anti–Terrorism Act (no: 3713, 1991). With this Act, "terror" was so defined that even the "crimes" like "counterfeiting of official documents" or "estranging people from military service" fell within its scope, together with "engaging in armed activities of a terrorist organization", if "intent" to perpetrate terrorism was identified in these criminal acts.[10] Hence, the Act covered not only "acts" but "intent" and thereby enabled the monitoring of a large portion of the population. It contributed to the formation of a "national-security state" in these years. It also provided the police with the authority "to use fire arms, directly and without hesitation...to render the perpetrators ineffectual in case of their noncompliance with the call for surrender or intention to use arms". The provision, having been annulled in 1999 by the Constitutional Court for violating the "right to live", was reinstated in 2006.

In the mid-1990s, as poverty deepened and crimes against property became more visible, leading to a media panic, the police organization started to utilize a new strategy named "community policing". It began to place emphasis on public relations and attempted to initiate a restructuring process for achieving productivity and effectiveness, the two important principles of market-oriented rationality.[11] As part of

[10] For an evalution of the Act see the website of the Association of Jurists (*Hukukçular Derneği*): http://www.hukukcular.org.tr/haber_detay.php?haber_id=165&Grup=NORMAL

[11] The police drew on the policing strategies implemented in the USA and Britain in these years. In fact, the close contact with the police of these countries had existed since the Second World War. Aspects of policing such as the anti–communist mobilization in the US, the riot police (i.e. Police Support Units) of Britain, SWAT teams, and community policing strategies and the

the "total quality management" program, the police aimed to establish close relations with people and turn them into informers, to collect data for taking proactive measures, especially regarding certain neighborhoods,[12] and to create a central computer data bank.[13] In this context, the Motorcycle Police Teams, whose members were selected according to physical appearance and ability to interact with people, were established in 1993 to improve relations with the public, to deal with mugging incidents and to take proactive measures for public security. Billboards announcing that the police were there "to help" proliferated; brochures and CDs containing recommendations for reducing risks were distributed. Electronic cameras were installed on streets in Istanbul in 2005 to achieve permanent surveillance and gather as much data as possible.

These measures were devised to construct the "citizens" as much as they sought to target the increasing number of people who transgressed this new order. The citizens, defined in the journal *Polis Dergisi* as "external customers" (*Polis Dergisi* 2004 [41]: 295), were to be molded, through improved public relations, into "suspicious" subjects responsible for their own "risk assessments". Thus, while the police aimed to reduce crime, achieve quick results, and control, regulate and incapacitate the "under-class", they also attempted to mold the attitudes of "citizens", turn each one into a police and create a sense of security at a time of insecurity.

Throughout the post-1980 period, therefore, the police acquired the capacity to penetrate every corner of the social formation with maximum impact. They frequently applied intense coercive force to eliminate those who resisted this exclusionary social order. Thereby, it enabled the state to extensively re-configure the social relations and create "prudent", "obedient" and "informant-like" subjects sustaining it.

---

installation of surveillance cameras on public streets, all constituted models for Turkey, whose police frequently visited these countries to participate in in-service training courses. Collaboration with the US police reached its peak in 1999 when an institute named the "Turkish Institute for Police Studies" was established at the University of North Texas.

[12] The General Directorate of Security declared that there were ten criminogenic neighborhoods which were "swamps that had to be dried out" (*Radikal*, 24 February 2006).

[13] See *Polis Dergisi* 2004 [41]: 202–209, *Polis Dergisi* 2004 [39]: 245–251.

The Sub-Culture of the Police and "Internal Enemies"

In addition to structural transformations, it is also important to consider the police's sub-culture to grasp the motivations behind their everyday practices. Examination of several volumes of the journals *Polis* published between the years 1963 and 1989 by the Social Support Association for Turkey's Retired and Serving Police Officers (*Türkiye Polis Emeklileri ve Mensupları Sosyal Yardım Derneği*), and *Polis Dergisi* published from 1995 onwards by the General Directorate of Security, reveals that the dominant political orientation among the police is persistently and manifestly "nationalist-conservatism". Interviews conducted by the author confirm this conclusion. This "nationalist-conservative" orientation incorporates the fervent endorsement of Turkishness and Sunni Islam, construction of a division between "citizens" and those so-called "terrorists/criminals", self-representation of the police as an altruistic "public order army", "enemization" of ethnic and religious groups which could not be assimilated, emphasis placed on the "perpetuity of the state" and the "wholeness and homogeneity of the social body", stigmatization of certain neighborhoods as hotbeds of crime and criminalization of those who engage in social opposition, criticize police practices or defend human rights.

This depiction can be elucidated by scrutinizing expressions from the interviews and journals. Starting with the nationalist-Islamic tendencies of the police organization, the description made by an instructor of the Police Academy, during an interview, is illuminating. He underlined that, among the police "chauvinism and intolerance are dominant. They are nationalist and statist; Turkish and Muslim... [There is] the 'otherization' of non-Muslim and ethnic groups, like considering Kurdish and Alevi groups as 'divisive' groups". Another police officer from the RAU depicted police personnel as the children of tradesmen and petty public employees living in small towns of Anatolia and as having loyalties to the motherland, national flag and religion as well as customs, traditions and honor. Accordingly, a police officer from the Motorcycle Police Teams declared that there were no varied political orientations in the organization: "we are all nationalists, there is no deviation"[14]. These show that the police's nationalist-

[14] Moreover, a police chief working in a police station in Ankara admitted that, there was a "patriarchal culture" within the organization "based on violence and bullying".

conservative orientation is highly in line with the state's desire to construct a homogeneous national identity. Substantiating this quality are the words of a police chief uttered to students at a conference in Varto, a district mostly populated by Kurdish people: "...[Y]ou, as the Turkish youth, carry a noble blood...Our ancestors, race and religion are more certain than those of anybody else. All of us are Turkish, Muslim... Kurdish people are Turks living in mountains" (*Polis Dergisi* 1995 [3]: 41–43). This homogenizing perspective bears the potential for "enemization" of those who oppose this vision of national identity.

In fact, the potential for "enemization" frequently solidifies in everyday practices of the police. A police officer from the RAU candidly stated in an interview that: "[a] person cannot be a police officer if s/he cannot distinguish citizens from terrorists". This paradigmatic example shows that the police consider certain people as falling out of the scope of the "cluster of citizens" and thereby, as a "bare-life" or enemy with no rights (Agamben 1998). They deem themselves to be the agency which decides on this division[15]. This tendency to "enemize" materializes both in the journal articles and interviews. In an article from *Polis Dergisi* (1996 [7]: 67, 68) it is reported that, during a visit to the RAU in Istanbul, the General-Director of Security pointed at: "...the existence of people who aim to divide the country and make people stand against each other via fabricated distinctions like Turks-Kurds, Alevi–Sunni". According to the news, he emphasized that the RAU had the mission to establish tranquility. Hence, the head of the police organization implied that the people demanding recognition for their identities were "working against Turkey" and mobilized the RAU against them. There are other exemplary articles in *Polis Dergisi*. In a seminar given at the Police Academy, the instructor claims that Kurds are a "kinfolk" of Turks and the activities trying to establish a separate Kurdish identity are non-scientific and "rely on the PKK terror" (*Polis Dergisi* 1995 [4]: 3–8). In an article written by a head official of a dis-

[15] Similarly, a police officer working in Motorcycle Police Teams declared that: "there are people who do not deserve our laws". This tendency to "enemize" must be borne in mind when considering the use of violence against suspects during police interrogations. During an interview, an instructor of the Police Academy stated that the police had, until recently, relied on confessions for collecting evidence and admitted that this had led to torture incidents. The use of torture (TİHV 1996) can also be evaluated as a way of punishing the "enemy" first-hand by the police.

trict and titled "Armenian Terror from the Past to This Day" it is asserted that there are internal and external threats and that "the Armenian terror", whose extension is the "PKK terror", is supported by the Russians (*Polis Dergisi* 1998 [15]: 53–69). Hence, while the struggle for the recognition of identities and cultural rights is represented as "treason", symbolic relations are constructed between the Alevis and Kurdish people, PKK, the Armenians and Russia, all of whom are represented as engaging in plots against Turkey.

This discursive orientation within police circles has also led to the stigmatization of certain neighborhoods inhabited by these perceived enemies. In an interview, a police officer from the RAU claimed that various shanty-towns constituted breeding grounds for terrorism. According to him, terrorist groups gave support to these people in order to resist the destruction of their towns, and encouraged them to take action against the state in 1 May demonstrations. In a similar manner, a police officer working in Bağcılar claimed that:

> There are certain neighborhoods whose residents are sympathizers of terrorist organizations like the PKK, DHKP-C or TIKKO. They are known people. On special days, for example Nevruz, which is, by the way, a Turkish celebration[16], we clash with these people... We gather intelligence and then a collective force is deployed to these places.

In other interviews, particular districts such as Taksim, Armutlu, and Gazi, inhabited by ethnic/religious/politically active groups, were mentioned several times as creating problems for the police. A police officer from a Motorcycle Police Team named other districts such as:

> Zeytinburnu, Kazım Karabekir, Mustafa Kemal, Örnek, Gazi, Karabayır districts. The dwellers are from East, from Kars, Van, Ağrı, Diyarbakır...a population, which we can call "Kurds". The special units of the police such as Anti–Terrorism, National Intelligence Organization and Anti–Organized Crimes Department are monitoring these districts... There are, for example, one hundred people [living in the district], eighty of them are bad and the remaining twenty are good. These twenty people are also ruined because they have no choice but to support the majority in the district.

It is not only the residents of these certain districts that are marginalized. A police officer from the RAU claimed that the members of the

[16] After unsuccessful attempts to repress these celebrations, the state eventually endorsed "Nevruz" in 1995 as a Turkish celebration. Nevertheless, it continued to surveil and repress them, especially in Southeastern Turkey.

Confederation of Revolutionary Labor Unions (*Devrimci İşçi Sendikaları Konfederasyonu*)—which is a legal organization)—always supported the "divisive organization" (the PKK) with their slogans and, thereby, criminalized the organization; another one claimed the same thing for another active labor union, *Eğitim-Sen*. According to a third one, those who do not heed the call of the police to disperse during demonstrations are "terrorists": "Before intervening, first a call is made to disperse. If there are any terrorists it becomes clear at this point". With this threshold for labeling people as "terrorists", every person insisting on his/her rights can easily fall into the "terrorist" category, and thus can be subjected to violence by the police.

Besides these groups, which are stigmatized for "being engaged in terrorism", there are also those who are turned into "the usual suspects" of crimes against property. In several interviews, the police officers stated that they knew who the burglars, thieves, and pickpockets were in their area and that when a robbery occurred, they knew where to look. Certain people have thus become "police property" (Reiner 1992: 137). This conclusion is in line with the results of the reports prepared by the Turkish Grand National Assembly Human Rights Observation Commission in 1998 and 2000. They show that "the usual suspects" are detained often and tortured into confessing crimes they did not commit (Pişkinsüt 2001). During the interviews, several police officers depicted the uneducated and unemployed people as "potential criminals" and pointed to the neighborhoods (like Sarıgöl, Çukurmahalle, Küçükbakkalköy) inhabited by immigrants from Southeastern Turkey and gypsies as the source of crime. One paradigmatic example is a police officer (working in Kadıköy) depicting "dark-skinned people" (a euphemism for gypsies) as "suspects". That same police officer, during a car ride to a gypsy neighborhood in Küçükbakkalköy, expressed his perception of these people while pointing to the children: "children with no identification...They are not citizens; they are animals. If their huts are pulled down, they cut themselves. Let them cut themselves, in this way it will be possible to get rid of the dirt".

This tendency to "enemization" is also fed by the self-representation of the police as the altruistic "public order army". The Director-General of Security stated in 1995 that their main task was the protection of the regime and the unity of the country (*Polis Dergisi* 1995 [2]: 10) and mentioned that the police also produced martyrs and veterans (*Polis Dergisi* 1995 [1]: 2). Throughout the police journal issues, symbolic elisions are made between the army and the police as the "protectors of the motherland". Furthermore, the police also acknowledge themselves as "the visualization of the state". A police chief in Sultanbeyli evaluated the "patrolling of streets" as a necessary task "for making people see the state". As indicated above, this position of being the "embodiment of the sovereign" puts the police officer at a decision point in each case. Many police officers hint at how these decisions were made. For instance, a police officer, working in Sultanbeyli, revealed their method in this way: "we have understood the psychology of the people, we are keeping their pulse". Another one working in Kadıköy stated that the police acted with greater sensitivity in certain districts of Kadıköy because they were home to elites with connections to influential people. Several police officers mentioned the flexible nature of the laws. According to a motorcycle police officer: "expressions in laws are vague, like 'reasonable doubt'... 'Reasonable doubt' is a very broad concept. Both the defendant and the police can use it for their benefit." When asked about the disciplinary mechanism, another motorcycle police officer explained it in this way: "the disciplinary mechanism works according to the case at hand. For example, if marijuana or cocaine is found in the vehicle, even if it was against the procedures for me to stop and search the car, the case is in favor of the police. It cannot be reversed." Thus, discretionary powers and the loose disciplinary mechanism provide a free hand for the police to implement adjusted strategies.

Hence, Turkish nationalism, conservatism with an Islamic predisposition, militarism and the substantial place of the "internal enemies" are discernible within the meaning maps of the police personnel. This orientation contributes to the shaping of strategies implemented by the police for different people, the motivations behind their practices and the goals they aim to achieve.

Conclusion

The period following the 1980 coup was marked in Turkey by its unegalitarian and exploitative qualities. In this period, the militarized state violently repressed the "communists/anarchists", put the accumulation regime on a neo-liberal track, readjusted the class balances in favor of industrial capital and boosted nationalist and Islamic tendencies to establish hegemony. It constructed poverty and unemployment as acceptable phenomena and rendered individuals responsible for their own well-being. It re-formulated the laws to criminalize oppositional groups. The "others" of the period became those who were perceived as challenging notions of stability and order and the imposition of a homogeneous national identity. The poverty-ridden and expanding "under-class", which intimidated the upwardly mobilized middle-classes, joined these groups in the mid-1990s.

Within this context, the police acquired further importance as a tool used by the state to implement its strategies for the reconstruction of the social structure. Via its new paramilitary units, increased authority and various strategies within which violence started to play a more important role, the police acquired the capacity to penetrate and control every corner of society. Embedded within the hegemonic discursive formations of the period, based mainly on nationalist-conservatism and militarism, the police controlled/regulated/repressed groups criminalized by the state as "enemies" inimical to the social order's perpetuity, applied adjusted strategies in accordance with the identity of the interlocutor and tried to mold the "citizens" into "responsible" subjects who would collaborate with the police. In this way, the state tried to construct the dissidents into obedient subjects, discard those who resisted, fashion a new mode of subjectivity and alleviate anxieties around "social insecurity". The police constituted an important mediation point for the state in fabricating this new social order.

Bibliography

Agamben, Giorgio. 1998. *Homo sacer: Sovereign power and bare life*. Stanford: Stanford University Press.

Agamben, Giorgio. 2000. *Means without end: Notes on politics*. Minneapolis: University of Minnesota Press.

Agamben, Giorgio. 2005. *State of exception*. Chicago: The University of Chicago Press.

Akkaya, Yüksel. 2000. "Türkiye'de 1980 sonrası emek-sermaye arasındaki bölüşüm mücadelesinde grevlerin yeri" in *Toplum ve Bilim* 86: 211–40.

Althusser, Luis. 1994. "Ideology and ideological state apparatuses" in Slavoj Zizek (ed.) *Mapping Ideology*. London: Verso; 100–140.

Bayramoğlu, Ali. 2002. "Asker ve siyaset" in *Birikim* 160–161: 28–48.

Bittner, Egon. 1974. "Florence nightingale in pursuit of Willie Sutton: A theory of the Police" in Herbert Jacob (ed.) *The potential for reform of criminal justice*. Beverly Hills: Sage; 17–44.

Bittner, Egon. 1980. *The functions of the police in modern society*. Cambridge: Oelgeschlager, Gunn & Hain Publishers.

Bora, Tanıl. 1997. "Devletin polisi, polisin devleti" in *Birikim* 93–94: 116–21.

Bora, Tanıl, and Kemal Can. 1990. "12 Eylül'ün resmi ideolojisi, faşist entelejensiya ve 'Türk-İslam sentezi'" in *Birikim* 18: 24–39.

Bora, Tanıl, and Kemal Can. 2000. "MHP'nin güç kaynağı olarak Kürt meselesi" in *Birikim* 134–135: 56–77.

Brewer, John, Adrian Guelke, Ian Hume, Edward Moxon-Browne, and Rick Wilford. 1996. *The police, public order and the state*. London: Macmillan Press Ltd.

Dural, Tamaşa. 1995. *Aleviler ve Gazi olayları*. İstanbul: Ant Yayınları.

Emniyet Genel Müdürlüğü (EGM).1983. *Cumhuriyet'in 60. yılında Türk polisi*. Ankara: Türk Polis TeşkilatınıGüçlendirme Vakfı.

Emniyet Genel Müdürlüğü. 2000. *2000 yılında Türk polisi*. Ankara: Emniyet Genel Müdürlüğü.

Emniyet Genel Müdürlüğü. 2001. *Çevik kuvvet polisinin toplumsal olaylardaki çalışmasına tesir eden faktörler*. Ankara: Emniyet Genel Müdürlüğü.

Ercan, Fuat. 2002. "The contradictory continuity of the Turkish capital accumulation process: Critical perspective on the internationalization of the Turkish economy" in Neşecan Balkan and Sungur Savran (eds.) *The ravages of neo-liberalism: Economy, society and gender in Turkey*. New York: Nova Science Publishers; 21–37.

Foucault, Michel. 2000. "The subject and power" in James Faubion (ed.) *Power: Essential works of Foucault 1954–1984 Volume 3*. New York: The New Press; 326–48.

Jessop, Bob. 1990. *State theory: Putting the capitalist state in its place*. Cambridge: Polity Press.

Kraska, Peter, and Victor Kappeler. 1999. "Militarizing American police: The rise and normalization of paramilitary units" in Victor Kappeler (ed.) *The police and society*. Illinois: Waveland Press, Inc; 463–79.

Küçük, Murat. 2003. "Mezhepten millete: Aleviler ve Türk milliyetçiliği" in Tanıl Bora (ed.) *Modern Türkiye'de siyasi düşünce: Milliyeçilik*. İstanbul: İletişim Yayınları; 901–10.

Manning, Peter. 1997. *Police work: The social organization of policing*. Illinois: Waveland Press, Inc.

Mert, Nuray. 2002. "Türkiye'de merkez sağ siyaset: Merkez sağ politikaların oluşumu" in Stefanos Yerasimos et. al. (eds.) *Türkiye'de sivil toplum ve milliyetçilik*. İstanbul: İletişim Yayınları; 45–83.

Neocleous, Mark. 2000. *Fabrication of social order: A critical theory of police power*. London: Pluto Press.

Öngen, Tülin. 2003. "'Yeni liberal': dönüşüm projesi ve Türkiye deneyimi" in Ahmet Köse, Fikret Şenses and Erinç Yeldan (eds.) *Küresel Düzen: Birikim, Devlet ve ınıflar*. İstanbul: İletişim Yayınları; 161–89.

Parla, Taha. 2002. *Türkiye'de anayasalar*. İstanbul: İletişim Yayınları.

Pişkinsüt, Sema. 2001. *Filistin askısından fezlekeye: İşkencenin kitabı*. Ankara: Bilgi Yayınevi.

Poulantzas, Nicos. 2000. *State, power, socialism*. London: Verso.

Reiner, Robert. 1992. *The politics of the police*. Toronto: University of Toronto Press.

Savran, Sungur. 2002. "The legacy of the twentieth century" in Neşecan Balkan and Sungur Savran (eds.) *The politics of permanent crisis: Class, ideology and state in Turkey*. New York: Nova Science Publishers; 1–20.

Taşkın, Yüksel. 2004. "Milliyetçi muhafazakarlık çözülürken merkez sağda miras kavgası ve AKP'nin imkanları" in *Birikim* 186: 108–19.

Türkiye İnsan Hakları Vakfı (TİHV). 1996. *İşkence Dosyası: Gözaltında ya da cezaevinde ölenler 12 Eylül 1980–12 Eylül 1995*. Ankara: TİHV Yayınları.

Wacquant, Loic. 2001. "The penalisation of poverty and the rise of neo-liberalism" in *European Journal on Criminal Policy and Research* 9: 401–412.

Yalman, Galip. 2002. "The Turkish state and bourgeoisie in historical perspective" in Neşecan Balkan and Sungur Savran (eds.) *The politics of permanent crisis: Class, ideology and state in Turkey*. New York: Nova Science Publishers; 21–53.

Yeğen, Mesut. 2006. *Müstakbel Türk'ten sözde vatandaşa: Cumhuriyet ve Kürtler*. İstanbul: İletişim Yayınları.

Yeldan, Erinç. 2002. *Küreselleşme sürecinde Türkiye ekonomisi–bölüşüm birikim ve büyüme*. İstanbul: İletişim Yayınları.

Journals

Danışma Meclisi Tutanak Dergisi 21.1.1982 [40/1].

Polis 1987 [419].

Polis Dergisi 1995 [1], 1995 [2], 1995 [3], 1995 [4], 1996 [7], 1998 [15], 2004 [39], 2004 [41].

Websites

Website of the Association of Jurists concerning the Anti–Terrorism Act: http://www.hukukcular.org.tr/haber_detay.php?haber_id=165&Grup=NORMAL.

Newspapers

Milliyet, 2 May 1989.

Milliyet, 2 August 1995.

Milliyet, 2 May 1996.

Radikal, 24 February 2006.

Reiner, Robert. 1992. *The politics of the police*. Toronto: University of Toronto Press.
Savran, Sungur. 2002. "The legacy of the twentieth century," in Nesecan Balkan and Sungur Savran (eds.) *The politics of permanent crisis: Class, ideology and state in Turkey*. New York: Nova Science Publishers: 1–20.
Tuckun, Yüksel. 2004. "Milliyetçi muhafazakarlık cozumlenen merkez sagda miras kavgası ve AKP'nin mekanları" in *Birikim* 186: 103–19.
Türkiye İnsan Hakları Vakfı (TİHV). 1996. *İşkence Dosyası Gözaltında ya da cezaevinde ölenler 12 Eylül 1980–12 Eylül 1995*. Ankara: TİHV Yayınları.
Wacquant, Loïc. 2001. "The penalisation of poverty and the rise of neo-liberalism," in *European Journal on Criminal Policy and Research* 9: 401–412.
Yalman, Galip. 2002. "The Turkish state and bourgeoisie in historical perspective," in Nesecan Balkan and Sungur Savran (eds.) *The politics of permanent crisis: Class, ideology and state in Turkey*. New York: Nova Science Publishers: 21–53.
Yeğen, Mesut. 2006. *Müstakbel Türk'ten sözde vatandaşa: Cumhuriyet ve Kürtler*. İstanbul: İletişim Yayınları.
Yeldan, Erinç. 2002. *Küreselleşme sürecinde Türkiye ekonomisi: bölüşüm, birikim ve büyüme*. İstanbul: İletişim Yayınları.

Journals

Dünya'nın Mesleki Teknik Dergisi 2:1 1992 [4671].
Polis 1987 [49].
Polis Dergisi: 1995 [1], 1995 [2], 1995 [3], 1995 [4], 1996 [7], 1998 [15], 2004 [39], 2004 [41].

Websites

Website of the Association of Jurists concerning the Anti-Terrorism Act: http://www.hukukcular.org.tr/haber_detay.php?haber_id=1657&Grup=NORMAL

Newspapers

Milliyet, 2 May 1989.
Milliyet, 2 August 1995.
Milliyet, 2 May 1996.
Radikal, 24 February 2006.

PART II

CONSTITUTING STATES AND CITIZENS

7

CONFINING POLITICAL DISSENT IN EGYPT BEFORE 1952

Anthony Gorman

The policing of political activity is a basic technique of the modern state. Governments set boundaries around what is legally acceptable in political word and deed not simply to protect themselves from criticism and attack but also, purportedly at least, to counter the threat that hostile political activism might pose to society at large. In Egypt this conception of political dissidence developed over time. Before 1882, political offenders were most often defined in terms of personal hostility towards the ruler. Thereafter the term "political prisoner" came to be applied to those regarded as antagonistic to the state itself, whether the British-backed administration (1882 to 1919), or, after 1923, the Egyptian state whose law spoke in terms of defending the constitution against the enemies of the social order.

The way in which the penal system addressed these perceived political threats also changed over time. At the beginning of the nineteenth century, exile, capital and corporal punishment were most often employed to punish political dissent. However, during the second half of the century a prison system, developed primarily with ordinary crime in mind, provided obvious potential for dealing with political dissidents, especially with the rise of mass political participation at the beginning of the twentieth century. Though not the only penalty employed, imprisonment came to be applied systematically as an instrument for deterring and confining political criticism and activism. By the middle of the twentieth century, political detention had become part of the standard armoury the regime used to defend its position.

The term political prisoner requires some brief discussion. Defined by one scholar as "someone who is incarcerated for his or her beliefs or for peaceful expression or association" (Neier 1995: 352), a political prisoner is necessarily determined by the ideological character and interests of the hegemonic political order. For these reasons, the definition of what constitutes "political" is susceptible to manipulation, misrepresentation and distortion. Governments have long sought to criminalise political acts to avoid giving standing to a particular cause or serving as a basis for criticism of its repressive character. In 1952, for example, after coming to power, the Free Officers announced that all political prisoners would be amnestied except for communists, who had been guilty of a "social crime", not a political one (Ismael and El-Sa'id 1990: 73). Conversely, some activists (and scholars) have, with considerable justification, claimed that economic or social protests, such as tax revolts, riots and evasion of military service, are also political in the sense that they express dissent with the system (Brown 1990). Political convictions might also mask personal conflicts or quarrels. Despite these important qualifications, the practice of incarceration has clearly been employed to restrict political debate and promote the state's conception of loyal citizens.

Despite its significance to Egyptian public life, political imprisonment has received surprisingly little attention in the scholarly literature.[1] This chapter focuses on two groups and examines the way the Egyptian state framed the definition of political offences and applied imprisonment to repress political opposition in the period before 1952. The first are political activists, principally nationalists, communists and Muslim Brothers, who bore the brunt of state repression due to their ideological positions towards the state; the second are journalists and other practitioners of free speech who were targets of government censure because of their criticism and sometimes condemnation of government policies and practices. These two groups are neither mutually exclusive in terms of personnel nor distinct in terms of government sensitivities. Quite the contrary, periods of political

[1] However, for two recent contributions see Bakr 2005, Gorman 2007.

repression in Egypt have invariably been accompanied by a government campaign against critical voices in the press. As a clear embodiment of the coercive power of the emerging modern state, political imprisonment would not just mould public attitudes towards the state but would, ironically, come to nurture the prison as a site of political resistance.

An Expanding Prison System

Our knowledge of political imprisonment in Egypt before 1882 remains sketchy. During the Mamluk period rulers had incarcerated personal enemies at their own pleasure, while preventative detention, such as the taking of hostages to guarantee the behaviour of a Bedouin tribe, is attested in the 1850s but probably was practiced much earlier (Peters 2002: 40). Even during the nineteenth century, rulers may more often have sent political opponents into exile. Sudan served as a place of internal exile (Hill 1959: 87) but certain individuals, such as Ya'qub Sannu' in 1878, were banished from the country entirely.

Although a more definitive assessment of political imprisonment before the British occupation awaits further research, it is clear that the political prisoner was already an established category of inmate in the Egyptian penal system by 1882. The series of prison inspections carried out by the British at the end of that year, listed up to a thousand political prisoners held throughout the country, even if there was some scepticism about the genuine basis of their offence.[2] During this period of political turbulence, both those accused of "assisting the rebels" and "stirring up public feeling against the Khedive" and the partisans of 'Urabi were imprisoned as the political fortunes of each group ebbed and flowed.[3] The subsequent release of the pro-Khedive elements and the prosecution of the 'Urabists highlighted the important symbolic role that prisoners could play in legitimating the new political order.

[2] Further Correspondence respecting the Affairs of Egypt [henceforth FCAE] no. 5, *Parliamentary Papers* [henceforth *PP*] LXXXIII no. 5 (1883) 5–31 (General Report by Major Chermside on the Prisons of Lower Egypt, 5 Dec 1882); *PP* LXXXIII no. 1 (1883) 65 (Dufferin to Granville, 18 Nov 1882).

[3] FCAE no. 1, *PP* LXXXIII (1883) 77–78, Memo, C.W. Wilson, 12 Nov 1882.

In the period before the First World War, the British authorities reorganised the Egyptian prison system, setting up a Prisons Department within the Ministry of the Interior in 1884 that administered a system of local, central and hard labour prisons with capacity expanded three-fold. Specialised institutions of confinement for youth, women, the insane and habitual offenders, were also established. Although these changes drew significant inspiration from British metropolitan and imperial practice, they accelerated a local process ongoing since the 1820s of moving away from corporal and capital punishment towards incarceration as the chief penalty (Gorman 2007: 103). Increasingly, imprisonment became the primary instrument for dealing with a broad range of social, and in time, political dissension.

Ordinary criminals were the primary clientele of the expanding prison system but in time it offered obvious potential for dealing with political dissent. At the very beginning of the twentieth century only a small number of offences in the penal code might be regarded as political in nature with no more than a handful of inmates serving prison sentences for such crimes in 1904.[4] However, as the decade progressed the state developed its capability and capacity for dealing with perceived threats to public security. While not specifically targeting political offenders, the Law of Police Supervision passed in 1909 that allowed for the indefinite internment of "notoriously dangerous persons" at the Kharga Oasis was a worrying development.[5] Against those regarded as politically suspect, and particularly the revitalised Egyptian nationalist movement, the state employed a range of measures including close surveillance, infiltration, censorship and imprisonment.

The clampdown on political action was accompanied by a move against freedom of political expression. Regulation of the press in Egypt was far from new, with licensing procedures, censorship, and the occasional closing down of newspaper titles punctuating relations between the Egyptian government and the fourth estate since at least 1879. In that year Bishara Taqla, co-owner of *al-Ahram*, was briefly detained by order of Khedive Isma'il for publishing an article critical of the authorities (Rizq 1999c). The Publications Law of 1881, Egypt's first such law, provided for imprisonment as a possible punishment.

[4] Prisons Department, *Report for the year 1904*, Table VI (articles 150–158, and 169).

[5] Reports by His Majesty's Agent and Consul-General on the Finances, Administration and Condition of Egypt and the Soudan, *PP* CIII (1911) 34–36.

Although shelved for a time after 1894 (with occasional exceptions), the legislation was reinstated and amended as the Press and Publications Law in early 1909 amid growing fears of nationalist agitation (Rizq 2003a; Ayalon 1995: 116). Ominously, the new law reassigned the authority to deal with offences committed by journalists from the court of misdemeanours to the criminal court.

These legal changes signalled the beginning of a campaign against the nationalist press that saw newspapers closed and journalists imprisoned. Ahmad Hilmi was convicted of libelling the Khedive, the first journalist to be imprisoned for such an offence (Rizq 1999a). He was followed by a number of distinguished nationalists given prison sentences for political and press offences: Muhammad Farid, 'Abd al-'Aziz Jawish (on two occasions), and 'Ali Fahmi Kamil (brother of Mustafa Kamil) (Tollefson 1999: 144). The campaign intensified following the outbreak of the First World War and for the next four years a general clampdown on all nationalist activities through detention, surveillance, and banning of newspapers remained in force (Rizq 2002).

Domestic imprisonment was not the only means to remove agitators from the political scene. Resident foreign activists, such as anarchists, were routinely deported, and the far-flung nature of the British Empire meant that imprisonment or exile abroad could also be imposed on Egyptian nationals. Ahmad 'Urabi was exiled to Ceylon and some of his supporters banished to the Sudan after the suppression of the revolt in 1882 (Hill 1959: 163). Later in 1919, British authorities sought to diffuse the clamour for independence by removing Egyptian nationalist leaders, Sa'd Zaghlul, Isma'il Sidqi and others to internment in Malta and again two years later Zaghlul, with another group of comrades, to the Seychelles and Gibraltar (Rizq 1999b). These measures had mixed results. 'Urabi and Muhammad Farid lost political influence in exile while for Sa'd Zaghlul and the Wafd, exile arguably enhanced the popularity of the nationalist cause.

The New National Order

The stalemate between nationwide opposition to continued British rule in Egypt and the British determination to maintain its position was broken, at least for a time, when Britain granted Egypt self-government in 1922. Formalised in the constitution of 1923, the new arrangements reconfigured a domestic political landscape that now became a field of contestation between moderate nationalists and the will of the palace, while Britain continued to play a critical and often decisive role in the background.

Now in control of the coercive organs of state, the Egyptian political elite set about the task of upholding the new constitution as it constructed and enforced its own vision of those deserving of its protection and those hostile to the new national order. The first Wafdist government elected in January 1924 was quick to put this conception into action. One of its earliest acts was to secure the release of Egyptians who, in the course of furthering the nationalist cause during the unrest of 1919–1921, had been imprisoned by order of the military courts. The mass release of nationalists provoked enthusiastic public demonstrations in Cairo and Alexandria and once again demonstrated the important legitimising role that prisoners played in a period of political transition.[6]

Yet, just at the time that the government was making political capital out of the liberation of Egyptian nationals, it was readying itself to strike against domestic opposition deemed hostile to the new national order. Communism had already been perceived as a danger by the authorities, fuelled by a press that reported the activities of Bolshevik agents, the circulation of subversive political material and the discovery of bombs.[7] Following the establishment of the Egyptian Communist Party (ECP) at the end of 1922, the government launched a prosecution against the party leadership in the summer of 1923 before the otherwise detested military courts, since the civil code had no relevant provision for dealing with their alleged offences.[8] The failure to secure a conviction prompted a change in the law to plug the loophole. Prison terms were now prescribed for those who "excited hatred and contempt for the established order and the government in Egypt", and who spread "subversive ideas contrary to the fundamental principles of the constitution and advocated the use of violence and intimidation in pursuing these aims."[9] Political offences which until recently had been applied to the nationalist opposition to the British occupation, were now cast as inimical to the Egyptian state and social order.

[6] *Egyptian Gazette* 8–15 February 1924.
[7] *The Times* 4, 6 July 1921.
[8] *The Times* 10 June 1924
[9] *L'Egypte Nouvelle* 12 April 1924, 227.

In February 1924 the Wafd government resumed the anti–communist campaign following a wave of strikes in Alexandria in which it accused the communists of a central (probably exaggerated) role (Beinin and Lockman 1998: 149). Party leaders including Husni al-'Urabi and Anton Marun were arrested and communist cadres around the country rounded up the following month. Found guilty of inciting workers to commit criminal acts against employers and of spreading "revolutionary ideas contradicting the principles of the constitution", a number of the leaders were sentenced to imprisonment for terms ranging from six months to three years (quoted Ismael and El-Sa'id 1990: 28). Even with the Wafd out of power, the government campaign, described by the international communist press as "white terrorism", was kept up into the next decade (Kokkinos 1927; Ahmed 1925: 44). Communist suspects were routinely arrested, tried and either imprisoned (if Egyptian nationals) or expelled (if foreigners).[10] Charges consistently cited revolutionary literature, subversive ideas, intimidation and violence, and the threat to the constitution. Concerned that the publication of the speeches of defendants might serve as communist propaganda, the court ordered that a trial in January 1926 be heard in camera, a practice continued in later years.[11] By the end of the twenties, the ECP had ceased to function as an effective organisation, closed down by a combined strategy of close surveillance and infiltration of communist groups followed by prison sentences and deportation.

Repressing Dissent

The arrest and gaoling of the editor and staff of *al-Hisab*, the communist party newspaper, in 1925 (Ismael and El-Sa'id 1990: 30) made clear how important the government held the connection between political activism and the press to be. Indeed, at the same time as the government was pressing its campaign against the communists it was seeking to tighten the freedom of the press. The press law of 1925 was amended to increase prison sentences, principally for the publishing of false or inaccurate information that could endanger public order, and quickly employed to prosecute a series of opposition newspapers and politicians (Rizq 2000).

[10] "Communists sentenced in Egypt",*The Times* 20 Jan 1926, *Egyptian Gazette* 14 Dec 1931; *Egyptian Gazette* 29 Dec 1932.

[11] *Egyptian Gazette* 23 Nov 1932.

This increasing use of prison sentences as well as financial penalties and closure to muzzle the press and punish criticism of the government picked up momentum over the next decade with the selective application of press laws closely reflecting the interests of those in power (Ayalon 1995: 119–120). Legislation passed under the Sidqi government in the early thirties was used to convict offenders for the use of "expressions that could incite hatred or contempt for the established system of government in Egypt or cast aspersions on its legitimacy or authority" (Rizq 2004b quoting Tawfiq Diab). Among those journalists imprisoned were Salama Musa, and Tawfiq Diab, owner of *al-Jihad*, who was found guilty of defaming parliament in February 1933, the first case of a "freedom of opinion" offence involving a sentence of hard labour. With the Wafd back in government in mid-1936, prison sentences for slandering public officials and for publishing false or fabricated documents with malicious intent were increased. Opponents of the Wafd soon found themselves targeted: Ahmad Husayn, leader of *Misr al-Fatat* (*Young Egypt*) and editor-in-chief of its newspaper, was sentenced to three months' prison for defaming a judge in June 1937; Fatima al-Yusuf, owner of *Ruz al-Yusuf* and a former Wafdist, was imprisoned for criticising the government; writer Mahmud 'Abbas al-'Aqqad served time on two occasions in 1937 for lambasting the Wafd for its attitude towards big business and the constitution. When the Wafd fell from power at the end of the year the tables were turned. The new government of Muhammad Mahmud issued an amnesty to those convicted under the press law and now began to target Wafdist journalists. In the pages of the Wafdist *al-Misri*, one writer asked in protest, "...[W]ould the government please explain to us how it is that while hundreds of Wafdist journalists are being dragged before the prosecution, shoved into prison and put on trial, not a single government journalist has been so much as brought in for simple questioning" (Rizq 2005).

By restricting what was permitted in the press, governments sought to manufacture political advantage and curb criticism. Even *suspension* of the press law could be used to advance a political agenda. When the British Foreign Secretary, Sir Samuel Hoare, stated that Egypt should not have its constitution restored in 1935—a view opposed by all Egyptian political parties—the Egyptian Prime Minister Tawfiq Nasim Pasha announced that the press would be given a free hand to respond to the Hoare's statement without any repercussions under the press law (Rizq 2004c). This exemption aside, the imprisonment of journalists and those guilty of "crimes of opinion" had become such a regular feature of Egyptian political life that in 1936 the prison regulations were amended to cater for this particular category of inmate.

Pre-Revolutionary Dissent

While Egyptian governments continued to use imprisonment against political activists during the Second World War, the practice took a backseat to the prosecution of the war effort (with the exception of the wartime policy of mass internment of enemy aliens). However, between 1945 and 1952 the conflict between an increasingly impatient nationalist movement and a series of unimaginative governments saw the political fabric in Egypt increasingly fray amidst an atmosphere of political violence and volatility. The massive demonstrations in Cairo in February 1946 signalled the looming confrontation between a government and a political opposition that began to agitate not only for political independence but also for a program of social and economic reform that the traditional political class had failed to deliver.

In July, the Sidqi government took on the left in a more systematic fashion, again targeting activists and the press. Progressive associations and communist fronts were banned, and opposition newspapers and publishing houses closed down (Botman 1988: 64–65). Large numbers of "young revolutionaries" were arrested and detained, many at al-Tur camp in the Sinai (Abdel-Malek 2006). Over the next two years, the government pursued this campaign against its political opponents with vigour. The penal code, again amended to deal with a changing political environment, now singled out "the promoters of revolutionary societies whose aims included the subordination of one social class to another, the overthrow of a social class, or the destruction of the fundamental social or economic principles of the state". Organisations of "an international character" were singled out for particular attention (Botman 1988: 66). The new law again stressed that these measures were necessary to protect the integrity of the constitution. This was ironic not only because Sidqi himself had presided over the abrogation of the constitution in 1930, but also because, following a practice established by the British practice between 1914 and 1923, Egyptian governments declared martial law on a number of occasions in 1947, in May 1948, and again in January 1952, to facilitate state repression without constitutional constraints.[12]

Yet the left was not the only group that sought to challenge the government. The Society of the Muslim Brotherhood had already clashed with authorities in October 1941 when its founder Hasan al-Banna and others were imprisoned after an anti–British demonstration. Although released soon after, the incident marked the beginning of an increasingly fractious relationship between the government and the Society. In the years after 1945, the Muslim Brothers suffered what they regarded as the "great *mihna*" (persecution) at the hands of the state (Mitchell 1993: 34). Events in Palestine in 1948 ramped up political tensions and reached a climax when, after banning the Society, Prime Minister al-Nuqrashi was assassinated at the end of 1948. Al-Banna himself was gunned down two months later. The government response was uncompromising. Thousands of Brothers were detained in camps at al-Tur, Huckstepp and 'Uyun Musa by the middle of the year and Brotherhood publications were effectively banned (Mitchell 1993: 72, 186). The state repression against those groups regarded as serious challenges to the political and social order—communists, Zionists, Muslim Brothers, and labour activists—would continue into the fifties and serve as one of the reasons for the popular reception of the Free Officers' coup and the fall of the *Ancien Regime* in July 1952 (Botman 1988: 15; Ismael and el-Sa'id 1990: 52; Beinin and Lockman 1998: 368).

The Practice of State Coercion

The increasing use of political imprisonment in Egypt was not simply the result of political conflict between opposition and the government but a product of the increasing coercive capability of the state. The police force, specialised security services, and a sophisticated surveillance system supported a justice system empowered to prescribe a range of penalties for political crimes. The prison system played a central role in the application of this regime of force.

Although Egyptian prison regulations in the nineteenth century do not seem to have made any formal distinction between the treatment of ordinary inmates and political prisoners, a convention, not always

[12] This practice of overriding the civil code continues in the present day guise of the Law of the State of Emergency (Kassem 2004: 37).

observed, held that the latter, as most often men of means and social status, should be given preferential treatment.[13] The practice was given a certain standing in the prison legislation of 1901 which stipulated that prisoners be treated according to "their accustomed lifestyle", in effect allowing for preferential treatment of those political prisoners (and others) drawn from middle class backgrounds.

Despite this oblique concession, the proper conditions in which those convicted of political crimes should be held remained an unresolved issue and a regular subject of public dispute. In 1924 the matter came before the public eye during the trials of communist activists. In the Egyptian Chamber of Deputies a debate, dubbed by one journal as "Le Scandale des Prisons", raged at the manner in which political offenders were being treated as ordinary criminals.[14] Given the public clamour surrounding the release of nationalists detained by the military courts two months earlier, the issue had more than academic interest. The government, for its part, insisted that there was no legal basis for the preferential treatment of political prisoners. Nevertheless, it granted, at least for a time, an improvement in conditions, partly as a result of direct action by the prisoners themselves. Similar public concerns were voiced regarding the treatment of imprisoned journalists. During the 1920s the journalists' syndicate successfully appealed to the Minister of Interior to treat imprisoned journalists "with compassion" and "as their counterparts were treated in civilised countries". Journalists were granted privileges such as separate rooms, the right to bring their own bed and have food brought to them by their families, greater visiting rights and exercise privileges, and the right to read the daily press (Rizq 2003b).

This victory did not last. When Tawfiq Diab was imprisoned in 1933, an outcry in the press erupted about the conditions of his confinement. On an issue where altruism met self-interest, *al-Ahram* expressed its profound concerns that:

> a journalist and master of the pen, a man of ideas and a leader of public opinion, and a person of refinement and erudition could be treated as an inveterate thief, a bloodthirsty killer or a hardened criminal who cannot be deterred from perpetrating crime and evil (quoted Rizq 2003b).

The government responded by insisting that since Diab had been sentenced to hard labour there could be given no special considera-

[13] FCAE no. 5, *PP* LXXXIII (1883), 5–31.
[14] *L'Egypte Nouvelle* 12 April 1924

tion, but conceded after a time and allowed him the use of a lamp and extra blankets.

Formal recognition of the special status of journalists in prison came in the Press law of 1936, which provided for those convicted of press offences to be held in special prisons. In practice, they were more likely held in designated cells. This provision was subsequently incorporated into the 1949 prison law along with a clearer expression that prisoners should be treated according to their "customary way of life, the nature and circumstances of the crime committed, or because of their social situation" (art. 9). Generally speaking, political prisoners enjoyed better conditions than ordinary prisoners, being held in a separate section of the prison and allowed better quality clothes, medical care, and reading materials. This practice had the benefit of avoiding any potential proselytising between ordinary and political prisoners but it stemmed from social attitudes that held a different view of middle class inmates convicted of crimes of opinion. Yet, if social considerations favoured preferential treatment for politicals, changes in the political climate outside could adversely impact on their conditions inside, as happened often during the 1950s (Darwish 2003, Gazis 2003).

The Camps (mu'taqalat)

Prisons were not the only place of confinement for political inmates. From the late 1930s internment or concentration camps (*mu'taqalat*) were established far from urban centres to contain a burgeoning detainee population. In the years during and after the Second World War these camps came to be employed with greater regularity. One reason for this development was the sheer weight of numbers. Always overcrowded, the prison system was simply unable to cope with the great influx of detainees. Muslim Brother inmates alone were estimated to number 4,000 in 1949 (Mitchell 1993: 72). After 1952, the number of prisoners dramatically increased to at least 25,000, accompanied by a significant expansion in the camp system (Domenach 1957).

Internment camps had the advantage not only of greater capacity but of relative invisibility. Prisons for the most part were located in and around population centres. The Central Prison in Cairo, Hadra Prison in Alexandria and provincial prisons were familiar parts of the urban landscape. Even the hard labour prisons of Tura, Abu Za'bal and al-Qanatir (the Barrage) on the outskirts of Cairo were well-known locations. Proximity to urban centers facilitated visits by the families of detainees but also increased the danger, as far as the government was concerned, that the plight of inmates would be more apparent and thus more likely to engender popular sympathy. The camps, by contrast, were usually set up in more isolated locations. While Huckstepp was only just outside Heliopolis, al-Tur (a former pilgrimage quarantine station on the Red Sea), 'Uyun Musa (in the Sinai), and later Wahat (in the Western Desert) were all remote. More inaccessible to visitors, they were less subject to the public gaze.

Prison Resistance and Negotiation

A clear expression of the coercive power of the state, political imprisonment nevertheless also served as a site of resistance and negotiation. Sustained by a set of practices that ranged from passive compliance with prison rules to direct protest and defiance of the authorities, prisoners sought both to ameliorate the conditions of prison life and to nurture a sense of group identity and purpose. Amongst political prisoners the phenomenon and development of prison subculture could take on a more ideological and politically focused sense grounded in an ethic of struggle.

The hunger strike was a favoured protest. Refusal of food only became feasible in Egypt after the state undertook the responsibility to feed inmates at the end of the nineteenth century. In the years before the First World War, ordinary prisoners at Tura and the Barrage regularly employed the tactic to protest against the poor quality of food and their conditions of confinement. Perhaps one of the first hunger strikes of a political character occurred when Muhammad Kamil Husayn, a trade unionist, reportedly refused food in early 1922.[15] The practice was soon taken up by communist inmates who successfully won the right to wear their own clothes, read books and see relatives once a fortnight in 1924 (Ahmed 1925: 44–45). The death of Anton Marun during another hunger strike the next year demonstrated the hazards of such a tactic (A.S. 1926). Nevertheless, the hunger strike remained an effective way of protesting prison conditions particularly when publicised. Journalist Tawfiq Diab (May 1933) and union leader Prince 'Abbas Halim (July 1934) refused food, although the latter for

[15] *The Times* 26 Jan 1922.

only three days and from the relative comfort of the foreigners' prison. Nevertheless the tactic, assisted by his high profile, proved successful. By the late 1940s the collective hunger strike had become a well-established part of the political prisoners' stock in trade. In 1949 political detainees at Huckstepp went on hunger strike for better conditions and later a similar action by communists in Cairo Prison won an improvement in their status (Darwish 2003).

Inmates pursued a less dramatic but arguably more effective means of resisting the psychological pressure of imprisonment through collective organization, that is, by taking control of the management of their daily prison routines themselves. Although a regular feature of prison life, the practice was probably strongest among political prisoners whose solidarity provided a solid basis for common agreement and disciplined practice. In Cairo Prison in 1950, for example, communist and other political inmates formed a "General Assembly of Life", which represented members in negotiations with prison authorities and was subsequently adopted by Marxist groups throughout the Egyptian prison system (Darwish 2003). Muslim Brotherhood detainees also organized themselves, if on different, more hierarchical lines.

Internment camps offered greater opportunity for detainees to determine the order of prison life. Camp authorities were often content to maintain external security while inmates, less physically constrained in large sheds or tents (rather than in cells), managed their daily routines. The practice of separating political cadres from ordinary criminals and of segregating different political tendencies reinforced feelings of solidarity. Under these conditions the prison experience could radicalise inmates, as happened to labour activist Mahmud al-'Askari (Beinin and Lockman 1998: 320). Indeed it is ironic that the communist movement in Egypt, forced underground and chronically fragmented during the 1940s and 1950s, was arguably at its most united in prison. On occasion, camp life even allowed for political discussions between communists and Muslim Brothers in the same camp (Botman 1988: 92).[16] As well as reinforcing political identity, prison life could also foster personal development through collective cultural and educational activities, such as providing the opportunity of performing theatre and studying languages and literature.

[16] Yusuf Darwish, a communist inmate, reported discussing socialism with 'Umar Tilmisani, later head of the Muslim Brotherhood, while detained (Personal Interview).

Despite these positive manifestations of prison subculture, the prison camp as a site of constructive resistance should not be exaggerated. Ideological divisions and personal disagreements within political movements were not expunged by the shared experience of prison (Ismael and el-Sa'id 1990: 66). Moreover, as Voglis (2002) has pointed out, the so-called solidarity of prison life has its own coercive dimension. On a practical level, there is little doubt that for many individuals imprisonment and torture was often a brutal experience that convinced them that political activism was not worth the personal price (Mitchell 1993: 69–70). After 1952, the evidence suggests that prison conditions got significantly worse. Indeed, the decision of the Communist Party to dissolve itself in 1965 was in part due to the toll that years of imprisonment and harsh treatment had taken on the membership (Darwish 2003).

Conclusion

In the century before 1952, political imprisonment closely mirrored the changing conceptions of political dissidence in Egypt and served as a barometer of contemporary sensibilities. As the field of politics expanded, the early nineteenth century notion of the political prisoner as a personal enemy of the ruler gave way to that of the the enemy of the state, applied to those accused of subverting the constitution and the social order in the 1920s. Techniques of coercion that had been developed though not necessarily created by the colonial regime were, with Egyptian self-government, embraced by the indigenous elites to deal with those whose actions and expression were deemed to have exceeded acceptable limits. The political prison was central to this strategy as it sought to contain, constrain and confine those who threatened hegemonic social values. When this opposition developed on a mass scale, internment camps were established as part of the carceral regime on an industrial scale.

Despite its increasing use as an instrument of state repression, preventative and punitive political imprisonment had only limited success in the period before 1952. Egyptian nationalists before the First World War were neutralised for a time but would capture the state in the 1920s. The communist movement, ruthlessly suppressed in the 1920s, would again rise as an important oppositional force in the 1940s and influence the trajectory of the 1950s. The banning of the Muslim

Brotherhood in the late 1940s and imprisonment of thousands of its members would be only one setback in a much longer record of Islamic militancy. Indeed, it might be argued that the government record against the non-parliamentary opposition after 1945 was symptomatic of the decline and ultimate overthrow of the old order. Employed en masse, political imprisonment became counter-productive for a regime already leaking legitimacy and increasingly characterised as repressive in nature. Yet just as political imprisonment became a central instrument for the defence of the regime, so it contributed to the construction of an ethic of political opposition and resistance. With the coup of July 1952, the by now well-established ritual was observed: political prisoners were released, a new campaign of political repression instigated, this time with a greater ferocity, and political imprisonment became more deeply inscribed in Egyptian political practice.

Author's Note: A longer version of this chapter was originally published in *Interventions: International Journal of Postcolonial Studies* in 2007 (http://www.informaworld.com/smpp/title~content=t713702083) and is reprinted here with permission.

Bibliography

Ahmed, Nefnil. 1925. "Communists' Hunger Strike in Egypt" in *Communist International* 9: 44–45.

A.S. 1926. "Dans les prisons anglo-égyptiennes" in *La Correspondance Internationale* 94 (21 Aug): 1048.

Ayalon, Ami. 1995. *The Press in the Arab Middle East, A History*. New York & Oxford: Oxford University Press.

Bakr, "Abd al-Wahab. 2005. 'al-Jarima wa falsafa al-'aqab fi al-sujun al-misriyya fi al-qarnayn al-tisa' 'ashar wa al-'ishrin" in *Misr al-haditha* 4: 357–382.

Beinin, Joel and Zachary Lockman. 1998. *Workers on the Nile*. Cairo: AUC Press.

Botman, Selma. 1988. *The Rise of Egyptian Communism, 1939–70*. Syracuse: Syracuse University Press.

Brown, Nathan. 1990. *Peasant Politics in Modern Egypt: The Struggle against the State*. New Haven & London: Yale University Press.

Darwish, Yusuf. 2003. "Communist", interview with the author, Cairo.

Domenach, J.M. 1957. "Tribunaux et bagnes d'Egypte", unpublished.

Gazis, Nikolas. 2003. Communist, interview with the author, Athens.

Gorman, Anthony. 2006. "Regulation, Reform and Resistance in the Middle East Prison" in Frank Dikötter and Ian Brown (eds). *Cultures of Confinement*. London: Hurst & Co; 95–146.

Hill, Richard. 1959. *Egypt in the Sudan, 1820–1881*. Oxford: Oxford University Press.

Ismael, Tareq Y. and Rifa'at El-Sa'id. 1990. *The Communist Movement in Egypt, 1920–1988*. Syracuse: Syracuse University Press.

Kassem, Maye. 2004. *Egyptian Politics, The Dynamics of Authoritarian Rule*. Boulder & London: Lynne Rienner.

Kokkinos, Apostolos. 1927. "White Terrorism in Egypt" (in Greek), *Rizospastis* 28 Jan.

Abdel-Malek, Anouar. 2006. "Three Scenes from a Genuine Life" in *al-Ahram Weekly* 23 Feb-1 March.

Mitchell, Richard P. 1993. *The Society of the Muslim Brothers*. Oxford: Oxford University Press.

Neier, Aryeh. 1995. "Confining Dissent" in Norval Morris and David J. Rothman (eds). *The Oxford History of the Prison. The Practice of Punishment in Western Society*. New York & Oxford: Oxford University Press.

Peters, Rudolph. 2002. "Prisons and marginalisation in nineteenth-century Egypt" in Eugene Rogan (ed.) *Outside In*. London & New York: IB Tauris.

Rizq, Yunan Labib. 1999a. "Al-Ahram: A Diwan of contemporary life" in *al-Ahram Weekly* 10–16 June.

Rizq, Yunan Labib. 1999b. "The Cataclysm" in *al-Ahram Weekly* 4–10 Nov.

Rizq, Yunan Labib. 1999c. "On the Censor's Block" in *al-Ahram Weekly* 9–15 Dec.

Rizq, Yunan Labib. 2000. "Muzzling the Press" in *al-Ahram Weekly* 14–20 Dec.

Rizq, Yunan Labib. 2002. "Men of Calibre" in *al-Ahram Weekly* 10–16 Jan.

Rizq, Yunan Labib. 2003a. "Laws in Print" in *al-Ahram Weekly* 13–19 Feb

Rizq, Yunan Labib. 2003b. "Stop Press" in *al-Ahram Weekly* 13–19 Nov.

Rizq, Yunan Labib. 2004a. "Noble Rebel" in *al-Ahram Weekly* 19–24 Feb.

Rizq, Yunan Labib. 2004b. "When They Gathered" in *al-Ahram Weekly* 26 Aug-1 Sept.

Rizq, Yunan Labib. 2004c. "Because of the British" in *al-Ahram Weekly* 30 Sept-6 Oct.

Rizq, Yunan Labib. 2005. "When Papers Shift" in *al-Ahram Weekly* 17–23 Nov.

Tollefson, Harold. 1999. *Policing Islam: the British occupation of Egypt and the Anglo-Egyptian struggle over control of the police, 1882–1914*. Westport CT & London: Greenwood.

Voglis, Polymeris. 2002. "Political Prisoners in the Greek Civil War, 1945–50: Greece in Comparative Perspective" in *Journal of Contemporary History* 37(4): 523–540.

8

OBSERVING THE EVERYDAY

POLICING AND THE CONDITIONS OF POSSIBILITY IN GAZA (1948–1967)

Ilana Feldman

In January 1967 a police officer in the Criminal Investigation Department [*mabahith al-'amma*] in Gaza filed his daily activity report. According to this report, he had observed nothing unusual during his tour:

> On the 25th, at exactly 11am, I passed by the Household Cooperative Society, the Center for Youth Protection, and the Price Control Council, and everything is calm there. At exactly 1:00 I passed by the UNRWA [United Nations Relief and Works Agency] clinic, where they are giving injections and medicine in an orderly fashion, and things are calm. I passed by the provisioning storehouse and they were distributing rations with considerable order. At exactly 2:00 I went to the Bir Saba secondary school and asked one of the students about whether there was any lack of teachers or teaching materials, and he told me that there was nothing negative and education is well ordered. There is nothing happening that is contradictory to public order.[1]

The policing files of the Egyptian Administration of the Gaza Strip (1948–1967) are filled with reports such as this—policemen reporting

[1] Israel State Archives [ISA], RG 2024, File 4, Report from *shurti*, 26 January 1967. All translations from Arabic are my own.

back on their hours spent in surveillance where nothing happened, of the completion of their rounds where no troubling activity occurred. These reports were products of a condition of expansive policing, where the police were occupied with the business of surveilling (and perhaps curtailing) political activity, as well as the work of investigating crimes and catching criminals. No space or moment was deemed beyond the interest of the police and surveillance was trained on all aspects of people's activities, speech, and opinions. Given this expansiveness, it was inevitable that often as not surveillance provided little or no information about either criminal or political activity—that it produced, that is, reports of nothing.

In this article, I consider what light police records, and particularly these seemingly useless reports of nothing, shed on conditions in Gaza. These reports are both sources, albeit particularly located ones, about aspects of life in Gaza and artifacts and instruments of the security regime in place there. They were not, I argue, simply the detritus of a broader policing regime that was uncovering criminal and political activity, but were effective in their own right. Even as reports of non-activity were of limited immediate use for police investigation, they participated in describing and shaping the contours of public life. Both people's awareness of the persistence of surveillance and the collection and circulation of the reports from this activity helped shape life in Gaza. Understanding the place of policing in Gaza requires an exploration of this feature of police work—the surveillance of regular activity, the observation of the everyday.

This kind of policing is certainly not unique to Gaza, or to the Middle East. Across the Arab world, post-colonial states have frequently become security states—often referred to as *mukhabarat* [intelligence] states—where security services "have virtually unchecked powers and a long record of encroachments on the freedom and property of citizens" (Perthes 2000:154; see also Korany, Noble, and Brynen 1993). The conflict with Israel—long a condition of an ongoing, suspended war—as well as persistent internal threats to regime stability, encouraged the development of highly elaborate security apparatuses. These were not created entirely afresh in the post-independence period, but were often developments of policing mechanisms established under colonial rule (Rathmell 1996; Eickelman and Dennison 1994). Security states have flourished in many locales, with many different histories and concerns, suggesting that an understanding of the effects of policing has broad significance.[2] In this chapter I explore a particular instance of this security condition, not in order to define the character of the state, but to understand its implications for civic life under these conditions.

When, in the course of research in Gaza in 1998 and 1999, I spoke with people about life under the Egyptian Administration, policing was one of its frequently mentioned features—and not always in negative terms. People sometimes expressed an almost nostalgic recollection of these practices—a recollection that has to be understood as refracted through the experience of forty years of Israeli occupation after 1967. As one woman told me in a fairly typical comment: "The Egyptians had a great role in security, people used to sleep with their doors open."[3] Equally typically, however, other people described the restrictions this policing imposed on their lives: "[The Egyptians] were afraid of anyone who expressed his opinion.... So they said let's get rid of him and put him in jail."[4] These two sorts of recollections are each products of the policing of everything that characterized this time, a practice that created a public space that was relatively free of crime and where politics was severely constrained.

Gaza is a somewhat anomalous place, with a history that does not fit in a colonial to post-colonial trajectory. The Egyptian Administration followed the end of the colonialism of the British Mandate. For the most part, Palestinians do not describe Egyptian rule in Gaza as colonial; this period is thus not easily categorized.[5] The Egyptian Administration began and ended in war. When active fighting ceased after the 1948 war, and armistice negotiations began, Egyptian forces were recognized as the administrators of Gaza by the armistice agreement. With the exception of a four-month occupation by Israel in the context of the 1956 Suez Crisis, Egypt governed Gaza until its defeat in the 1967 War, which began the Israeli occupation of the West Bank and Gaza.

In 1948, not only was the economy of the area almost entirely destroyed by the loss of land and markets and the dramatic overcrowd-

[2] For explorations of policing in other places see, for example, Piccato 2001; Salvatore, Aguirre, and Joseph, eds. 2001; Garland 2001 and 1990; Caldeira 2000.

[3] Interview, Gaza City, 11 April 1999.

[4] Interview, Gaza City, 20 March 1999.

[5] See Feldman 2008 and 2005b.

ing of the territory, its political future was tremendously uncertain. A large majority of the population survived on rations provided by the United Nations Relief and Works Agency (UNRWA). While conditions improved in the later years of the Administration—in part due to Egyptian policies that made Gaza a free-trade zone, created a tourism industry, dramatically expanded civil service employment, and made state land available at low cost to many Gazans—Palestinian demands for independent political action only increased over this period. Security, therefore, remained a concern throughout.

Just as significantly, the concomitant elaboration of expansive policing within Egypt under Gamal Abdul Nasser's rule provided models and mechanisms that were deployed in Gaza. In the spectrum of *mukhabarat* states, Egypt was not the most repressive, but it certainly exercised broad control. In Gaza the most popular parties were the Muslim Brotherhood and the Communist Party.[6] Political events beyond Gaza led to the repression of each of these parties at different moments. For the Muslim Brotherhood the turning point was the 1954 assassination attempt on Nasser by a member of the group. For the Communist Party it was the Iraqi Revolution of 14 July, 1958, and the increasing rivalry which developed between Nasser's Egypt and the Communist supported regime of 'Abd al-Karim Qasim.[7] In these moments of heightened concern about party activity, people who were known as "activists" were especially susceptible to arrest and detention.

Considerable attention has been paid to the relation between police practices and citizenship possibilities, much of it concerned with the ways in which aggressive policing inhibits democracy and civic action (Caldeira 2002 & 2000; Milton-Edwards 1998). In this essay I utilize archival records of police work in Gaza to examine a similar terrain, but from a somewhat different perspective.[8] Rather than measuring the

[6] For more on the history of political parties in Gaza during this period see Abu 'Amr (1987).

[7] On the control of politics in Egypt under Nasser see Jankowski (2002); Beattie (1994); and Waterbury (1983).

[8] These records were taken by Israeli forces when they occupied Gaza in 1967 and are housed in the Israel State Archives. They have never been catalogued, or fully de-classified. Everything appears to have been kept—evidenced by, among other things, the existence of files that appear to be quite literally trash—ripped up papers, random documents. Because these records were taken "mid-life"—that is before they were archived—documents that might

possibilities for political freedom in "better", less oppressive, police practices, I trace ways that the surveillance of everything worked to "foreclose political action and depoliticize citizens" (Wedeen 1999: 45) as well as the sometimes surprising opportunities for civic effect that arose under these conditions.

Policing and Possibility

Conditions in Gaza very acutely raise the question of what preconditions enable people to make claims of government, to act civically or even politically. Addressing exactly this problem, Hannah Arendt identified statelessness as one status that marked a boundary of such possibility. In her view, what people were most deprived of in the loss of a polity were not the specific rights of citizens, but their ability to be human. She described the capacity to make "opinions significant and actions effective" (1968: 296) as the essential requirement of the "human condition" (1958). According to Arendt, relations of policing were central in this process. Those expelled from humanity, and from politics, were outside the domain of law and were left at the mercy of the police. It was, in fact, only by committing a crime and violating the law that stateless persons could acquire legal protection, hence crossing into the space generally reserved for citizens.[9]

While Arendt describes a European landscape ever more starkly divided between privileged citizens and utterly disenfranchised stateless people—people treated as "the scum of the earth" (1968: 269)—the case of Gaza after 1948 illuminates a somewhat different condition, and hence sheds a different light on the question of political possibility. Unlike the West Bank under Jordanian rule, Egypt administered Gaza, but did not claim sovereignty over it. Rather than being distinguished from a group of privileged citizens by their statelessness, however, Gazans (whether refugees or native inhabitants) were all to some degree both citizens and stateless. Furthermore, there was not a group

---

normally have been discarded in the normal course of police work have been preserved. These records are thus an exceptionally rich archive for capturing details of police work in action. For further discussion of the circuitous life of archival materials about Gaza, see Feldman (2008).

[9] As Arendt says of the stateless, "only as an offender against the law can he gain protection from it" (1969: 286).

of people in the realm of law and another at the mercy of the police. Nor was there a spatial delineation of a "territory of exception within the juridical space" (Ticktin 2005: 258; see also Fassin 2005; Agamben 1998). Rather, police and law were expansively indistinct, and everyone, everywhere, was subject to both. In fact, policing was one of a relatively few areas of government service that was administered by the same agency to the entire population. Education, healthcare, rations, even public utilities were provided to people by different bodies depending on refugee status—refugees being serviced by UNRWA and natives by the Administration. In contrast, whether living in refugee camps or in towns, everyone was policed by the same force. Policing and surveillance were important for the elaboration of civic space and political possibility in part by constituting a domain—a "zone of indistinction" in Agamben's terms (1998: 90)—that was both criminal and lawful, subversive and obedient, orderly and disorderly. In this case, the police did not only represent the limits of opportunity for action, but its condition of possibility as well.

The exploration of policing in Gaza, then, demands a somewhat distinctive approach. Building on Michel Foucault's (1979) work, a great deal of the literature on policing explores the ways that it works as a form of disciplining, as a means through which people are evermore precisely defined and categorized. Advances in policing technologies allow for increasing specificity of the observed subject, and thereby permit a population to be searched for its "criminal elements". Very often this disciplining works in the service of particular political projects of social control—as studies of the centrality of policing to colonial projects make clear (Anderson 1994; Anderson and Killingray 1991; Arnold 1977). The dynamics of policing in Gaza during the Egyptian Administration certainly support the general diagnosis of its disciplinary operations, but also highlight a practice that frequently relied more on indistinction than on precision.

How did indistinction operate in this context? Policing in Gaza operated with a principle of vagueness, according to which not only did it not always matter whether people and practices were precisely categorized, but sometimes it was "better" if they were not. Here I use vagueness in the particular way that C.S. Peirce defined it, as a condition where "the principle of contradiction does not apply," where multiple meanings may all be true. For Peirce, vagueness was a significant condition of being that made action possible. As we will see, the instrumental value of vagueness for policing in Gaza intersected in perhaps surprising ways with the ontological value accorded it by Peirce.

Just as vagueness can be important in enabling human action, it has considerable significance in governing dynamics. In a circumstance like that of the Egyptian Administration in Gaza—where the status of territory and of the governing relation was so uncertain—vagueness as a policing technique worked to shore up, rather than undermine, governmental power. As an instrument of indistinction, vagueness helped to deflect potential crises and challenges to government control. The practices of observing and recording everyday activity were of particular importance here; by making of any possible action a "case" and by turning each event into a "report," surveillance helped produce an indeterminacy even between the everyday and the extraordinary. If any word, any deed, could signal subversion or crime, then no word or deed could be entirely perceived as ordinary. The citizen could easily become the criminal, perhaps even without awareness or intent. This vagueness injected uncertainty—and sometimes fear—into the most mundane of activities, as one could never be sure what they might turn out to mean. At the same time, this zone of indistinction sometimes created opportunities for independent action, even within a space that was heavily patrolled. It provided, without any intention toward this end, a limited opportunity for Gazans to influence government, through making their "opinions significant and actions effective."

Surveillance of Political Life

As in any security state, Gazans were aware that any of their activity might be observed by police, and they knew with certainty that political organizing would be surveilled. People were questioned by the police about things as diverse as the mail they received, the books they read, the people they knew, and sometimes people they may have simply seen in the streets. While Gazans frequently protested that there was nothing untoward in any of their actions, they rarely seemed surprised by the interrogation itself. While to a certain degree one can ascribe people's compliance to their fear of punishment, this does not seem to have been the only factor. Elsewhere I have argued that bureaucratic authority is in significant part engendered by its expansiveness and its repetitions (Feldman 2005b, 2008). Something similar seems to be at work in policing. This familiarity with police surveillance bred a certain kind of acceptance in the breadth of the police domain—not necessarily an acceptance that it was right, but rather a recognition that it was actual. This normalization was crucially important for the effectiveness of the police, and further underscores the imprecision of the boundary between legal and illegal, between upstanding citizen and criminal threat.

While the condition of surveillance is in many ways an isolating experience, injecting distrust and insecurity into relations between people, it was at the same time an experience that was certainly shared by all, and it shaped everyone's experience of community and place, albeit in different ways. The isolation effect of security states has received a great deal of attention. Lisa Wedeen argues that in Syria under Assad (a much more heavily controlled space than Gaza) state practices "operate to kill politics prophylactically before it emerges, to depoliticize people by orchestrating public performances in which people's compliance ensures their safety but, more importantly, forecloses the individual and group engagement associated with ideas of political fulfillment" (1999:147–8). In both Syria and Gaza, the experience of public space was shaped by these isolating effects of perpetual surveillance. At the same time, while surveillance constrained public life and relationships in some ways, people were clearly also engaged in a variety of networks of relation, some more explicitly political than others—many apparently not political at all—but each potentially able to have an effect on government policy.

As noted above, much of the impetus behind the broad surveillance practice was concern about possible political activity among the population. Not surprisingly, then, police files indicate a clear interest in determining who might engage in political organizing. Lists of supporters of various political parties were regularly compiled; in addition to Communists and Muslim Brothers, Ba'ath Party affiliates were tracked. Even in these efforts to differentiate among the population, however, the recording of everything meant that indistinction remained a crucial mechanism. The files include many reports of police officers following people to meetings, noting who was there, how long they talked, but often saying nothing about the content of their conversation.[10] In this

[10] For examples of this sort of mundane police report, see ISA, RG 115, Box, 2005, File 3, Report from *shurti* to *mabahith* director, 12 December, 1960 and Box 2096, File 21. Reports from police officers, n.d. 1967.

context, the fact that there was nothing to report was an indication of some success of the policy of repression, though the fact that people could still be identified as in some way "members" of these outlawed organizations also indicates the limits of that success.

In a typical series of reports on the Nuseirat camp (one of a group of refugee camps in the middle of the Strip), police described their surveillance of known Communist sympathizers. On 4 January 1960: "The persons I was asked to watch did not have any meeting yesterday. They did not meet at the barber's place as usual. I have seen some of them walking alone, or talking to others not from the same group."[11] The next day's report indicated that: "This is to inform you that after watching the barber's shop, we observed that some people from the Communist Party visited him but did not stay for long. The party does not yet have obvious activities."[12] Another police officer reported: "This is to inform you that the supporters of the Communist Party met at the school, and then everyone returned home. Two of them walked back and forth in the street, then went to [so-and-so's] house where they stayed for half an hour, and then each went home." The file continues in this vein.

The possible effect of this extensive surveillance is that everybody knows that it is happening, but they can't always pinpoint exactly when or by whom. That people knew these files existed, but could never see them, could never know for sure which of their activities or words were recorded, without doubt contributed both to their vagueness and to their power. That people were afraid of the police seems clear, but it is equally clear that this fear did not eliminate political activity and indeed may have engendered activism on some people's part.

Mu'in Basisu's (poet, teacher, and Communist activist) account of his prison experiences during the Administration—the beatings and torture during interrogations—makes clear that fear was appropriate (Basisu 1980: 68). While Basisu's four years in prison did not dissuade him from activism, people in Gaza indicated to me that much of the population was hesitant to engage in organized political activity. As one person told me, describing conditions among government

[11] ISA, RG 115, Box 2096, File 22, from police officer to Deir Belah *Mabahith* inspector, 4 January 1960.

[12] ISA, RG 115, Box 2024 file 10, Policeman's report to police inspector, 25 January 1966.

employees, "The civil servant was afraid.... Other than teachers, most civil servants did not participate in political activities, but teachers did. They were active with either the Communist Party or Muslim Brotherhood." Even widespread reticence to engage in formal politics should not be taken to mean that Gazans were wholly apolitical in public. Police reports indicate, in fact, that among ordinary folk there was considerable political conversation on the street and in other public spaces.

Police were aware of this conversation in part because the imperative to observe political activity required that surveillance extend beyond those actually active. While the reports from Nuseirat describe known "suspects" doing very little that was suspicious, other reports describe a similar lack of activity among people who had no known political ties. A case in point is a report on a Palestinian woman, who had moved to Gaza from Baghdad when she married a Gaza resident. While it was no doubt her residence in Iraq that provoked this interest, she was not otherwise a suspicious person. Not surprisingly, according to the report: "No harmful activity has been observed since she arrived until this date." The demand for such breadth of surveillance in the service of control meant that its targets, and its effects, regularly exceeded the instrumental.

Surveillance as Social Control

Before discussing the surveillance of political conversation, I want to turn to another important feature of policing in Gaza, one which further highlights the effects of policing on public behavior. While political activity was an obvious issue of concern for the police, it was only one of many objects of surveillance. Considerable police attention was also directed towards behavior that fell within the domain of society. The surveillance of the social illuminates the indistinction both between issues of "public concern" and the arena of "private behavior" and between the social management of such behavior and the state's efforts to shape this domain.

In some ways, society itself operated as a form of policing, but it never did so independently. As Arendt argues, "society expects from each of its members a certain kind of behavior, imposing innumerable and various rules, all of which tend to "normalize" its members, to make them behave, to exclude spontaneous action or outstanding achievement" (1998 [1958]: 40). Here Arendt identifies a particular form of human organization as constraining action. Pierre Mayol describes the constraints of "propriety" in similar terms: "it represses what is 'not proper', 'what one does not do'.... it takes care of decreeing the 'rules' of social custom, inasmuch as the social is the space of the other, and the medium for the position of self as a public being" (1998: 17). This interest in normalizing behavior is clear in the policing of society in Gaza, as society is not an autonomous domain.

The different techniques police deployed in surveilling the social indicate how society could appear more or less autonomous depending on the style of policing. In one mode, the police occupy the role of mere observers of independent "social processes", suggesting that where society was functioning well active intervention was not required. In other instances, however, surveillance led to intervention, with police working directly to manage the behavior of individual members of society.

A typical sort of report on social misbehavior described the police questioning of a photographer, Hussein Sharif, who had been observed photographing women. Police frequently relied on rumor, gossip, reputation, and other "vague" sources to guide their investigations, and this instance was no different. Hussein was reported to be known for flirting with women and to have a bad reputation. The particular incident which provoked his questioning was a report that he had taken a picture of two teenage girls with a boy. In Hussein's statement he insisted that while he did photograph women he only did so "within the general morals." He denied this particular accusation, saying that when it became clear that the boy wanted to be in the picture he had refused to take it. Despite Hussein's insistence that he had done nothing wrong, being brought in for questioning was enough to enable the police to extract from him the declaration that: "I the undersigned, Photographer Hussein Sharif, hereby undertake not to take any photograph that does not go with our morals, customs and traditions or can affect the reputation of the Gaza Strip." Hussein was willing to promise not to do anything wrong, even as he denied having done so. The questioning itself was an effective means of control, and did not require any formal adjudication. It was in part the very condition of expansive policing—and the vagueness that was part of this practice—that lent it this power.

In the domain of social "crimes" there was a further indistinction between the police and the public as agents of surveillance and interdiction. A case in point is described in police reports about the behavior of *shabab* [young men] in Shati camp, next to Gaza City. A police officer reported in January 1967 that he had seen a group of young men harassing girls on the street. In this instance, the police did not intervene to stop this behavior, though the report described the efforts of other people to do so. At least one observer chastized them, saying: "shame on you, *shabab*, each of you has a sister or a mother. Protect the honor of people, as it will reflect on your own honor." The report concluded with a list of the young men's names, each also identified by their town of origin. This attention to detail underscores that it was neither lack of interest nor absence of concern about stopping this behavior that led the police officer to take an observer position in this case. While there might have been some vagueness here about where surveillance intersected with interdiction, there was precision about the violators. A follow-up report from a month later indicated that there had been further intervention from the public. People had spoken with the young men's families, who exercised their influence, and the harassment had ceased. Clearly surveillance did not only come from the police.

One cannot say with certainty why the first incident demanded an active response, and the second simply reporting. Perhaps it is because the first seemed a more serious violation of proper norms, while harassment, even while clearly frowned upon, was a common feature of social life. Or, perhaps it was the readiness of members of the public to take on this policing task with the young men that rendered it unnecessary for the police to get involved. These possibilities remain speculative, however. What is significant for my purposes here is the availability to the police of different means of surveilling social life. That people might not know what sort of police response a particular behavior might generate was another source of vagueness in police power. That people could count on someone paying attention to their actions (or behavior) certainly helped shape public space. Both instances underscore the indistinction between threats to social order and threats to security. Administration officials recognized that the one could easily lead to the other and responded to this danger both by providing social services that could improve social life (Feldman 2005a) and by the policing we have encountered here.

'On People's Tongues': Surveillance, Circulation, and Possibilities for Civic Effect

While the policing of the social illuminates a public space where everyone seemed to be watching everyone else, other aspects of policing produced a much more opaque public space. In fact, one effect of surveillance was to constitute a "public sphere" to which the public did not have unfettered access. Reports produced by the police about public opinion, about meetings, about gossip and rumors, circulated this talk far beyond its immediate domain, giving it life and significance that it might not have otherwise acquired. To be sure, most members of the Gazan public did not have access to these reports, and could not even know for sure that they existed. They were nonetheless significant in shaping the contours of public life—in part by shaping government policies, in part by functioning as a spectral presence around this life.

In addition to organized expression in public meetings, police investigators searched for public opinion in everyday talk—"on people's tongues [*ala lisanat al-nass*]." The police tracked discussions about politics and government policy, about civil service salaries and UNRWA ration distributions. They also recorded the mundane frustrations of everyday life. Talk could be both banal and important, and it was not always easy to determine what it might be at any given moment. Indistinction did not only operate as an instrument of social control, but provided opportunities for political challenge.

In 1965 and 1966, for instance, there was a crisis surrounding the dearth of *fakka* [small change] in circulation. A police report from January 1966 noted that "there is a lot of complaining about *fakka*. This is especially a problem in relation to taxis. It is said that the money does exist to solve the problem." Another report from later the same month elaborated on the problem, and the talk: "Everyone is wondering why there is this shortage, what has created it and what the role of the government is in this problem which is harmful to social and economic life in the Strip." There is no suggestion in the reports that anyone was organizing around this issue yet—and there was no direct petition to government to solve the problem—but the possibility of talk leading to political action was clearly concerning. In the case of the absent *fakka*, even as public frustration was being recorded, government efforts—even if inefficient–were under way to address the problem.

In October 1965 the Director of Finance and Economic Affairs wrote to the Director of Internal Affairs and Public Security asking him to intervene in this matter. A few days later, the Governor General wrote to the Director of Internal Affairs and Public Security telling him to ask the Director of Finance and Economic Affairs to talk to the banks about the problem. In November the *Mabahith* Director also wrote to the Director of Internal Affairs and Public Security asking him to "be in touch with all the banks and ask them to put a lot of small change—5, 10, and 50 mils—into circulation." The circularity of these requests for action may explain why, in January of the following year, there was still "a lot of wondering among the people who are waiting for the government to take an active role." What is significant here is not the efficiency of government response, but the fact of it. Not only did surveillance operate as a vector for circulation of talk, it lent this aggregated talk a weight that its repeated individual articulations did not have. Even without a clearly petitioned demand, this talk came to be a means of having an effect on government. The fact that people would not necessarily have been aware of the effects of their talk renders this an admittedly strange version of participation. Vagueness did not only produce fear, but sometimes possibility.

Conclusion

In this investigation of policing and possibility in Gaza I have highlighted the variety of ways that indistinction and vagueness shaped these domains, and the relation among them. While it is clear that indistinction could be a potent instrument of social control, injecting fear, destabilizing people, it also could work to provide some space of civic action. Vagueness, that is, could be a two-way instrument. The indistinction that characterized police practice in Gaza did not only restrict possibility, though it surely did this, but also on occasion created an opening for influence and effect. This insight into the conditions of possibility in Gaza has, I think, a broader import as well. Not only does Gaza shed light on conditions widespread in the post-colonial Middle East, it also opens up new ways of thinking about the effects of living in security states more generally.

As we think about what conditions are necessary for civic and political action now—a question that has tremendous importance—it is worth remembering that the possibility of such action can exist even in highly policed and constrained circumstances. I do not mean to inject an overly optimistic note into what looks like a fairly bleak picture of contemporary political control, but simply to suggest that such control is never total and that, furthermore, even the mechanisms designed to ensure such control sometimes also work to create possibilities for people to have an effect on government. Whether these "vague" opportunities can be harnessed for the purpose of making a broader transformation in the conditions of our existence remains an open question.

Bibliography

Abu 'Amr, Ziyad. 1987. *Usul al-Harakat al-Siyasiyyah fi Qita' Ghazzah, 1948–1967*. Acre: Dar al-Aswar.

Agamben, Giorgio. 1998. *Homo Sacer: Sovereign Power and Bare Life*. Stanford: Stanford University Press.

Anderson, David. 1994. "Policing the Settler State: Colonial Hegemony in Kenya, 1900–1952", in Dagmar and Shula Marks Engels (eds.) *Contesting Colonial Hegemony: State and Society in Africa and India*. London: British Academic Press; 248–64.

Anderson, David and Killingray, David (eds.). 1991. *Policing the Empire: Government, Authority, and Control, 1830–1940*. Manchester: Manchester University Press.

Arendt, Hannah. 1968. *The Origins of Totalitarianism*. San Diego: Harcourt Brace Jovanovich.

Arendt, Hannah. 1998 (1958). *The Human Condition*. Chicago: University of Chicago Press.

Arnold, David. 1977. "The armed police and colonial rule in South India, 1914–1947" in *Modern Asian Studies* 11(1): 101–25.

Basisu, Mu'in. 1980. *Descent into the Water: Palestinian Notes from Arab Exile*. Wilmette, Illinois: Medina Press.

Beattie, Kirk J. 1994. *Egypt during the Nasser years: ideology, politics, and civil society*. Boulder: Westview Press.

Caldeira, Teresa. 2000. *City of Walls: Crime, Segregation, and Citizenship in Sao Paulo*. Berkeley: University of California Press.

Caldeira, Teresa. 2002. "The Paradox of Police Violence in Democratic Brazil" in *Ethnography* 3(3): 235–63.

Eickelman, Dale and Dennison, M.G. 1994. "Arabizing the Omani Intelligence Services: Clash of Cultures?" in *International Journal of Intelligence and Counterintelligence* 7: 1–28.

Feldman, Ilana. 2005a. "Government Without Expertise? Competence, Capacity, and Civil Service Practice in Gaza (1917–1967)" in *International Journal of Middle East Studies* 37(4): 485–507.

Feldman, Ilana. 2005b. "Everyday Government in Extraordinary Times: Persistence and Authority in Gaza's Civil Service (1917–1967)" in *Comparative Studies in Society and History* 47(4): 863–91.

Feldman, Ilana. 2008. *Governing Gaza: Bureaucracy, Authority, and the Work of Rule (1917–1967)*. Durham, NC: Duke University Press.

Fassin, Didier. 2005. "Compassion and Repression: The Moral Economy of Immigration Policies in France" in *Cultural Anthropology* 20(3): 362–387.

Foucault, Michel. 1979. *Discipline and Punish: The Birth of the Prison*. Trans. A. Sheridan. New York: Vintage Books.

Garland, David. 2001. *The Culture of Control: Crime and Social Order in Contemporary Society*. Chicago: University of Chicago Press.

Garland, David. 1990. *Punishment and Modern society: a Study in Social Theory*. Chicago: University of Chicago Press.

Jankowski, James. 2002. *Nasser's Egypt, Arab Nationalism, and the United Arab Republic*. Boulder: Lynne Rienner Publishers.

Korany, Bahgat, Paul Noble and Rex Brynen (eds.). 1993. *The Many Faces of National Security in the Arab World*. New York: St. Martin's Press.

Mayol, Pierre. 1998. "Propriety" in Luce Giard (ed.) *The Practice of Everyday Life, Volume 2: Living and Cooking*. Minneapolis: University of Minnesota Press; 15–34.

Milton-Edwards, Beverley. 1998. "Palestinian State-building: Police and Citizens As Test of Democracy" in *British Journal of Middle Eastern Studies* 25(1): 95–119.

Peirce, Charles Sanders. 1955. *Philosophical Writings of Peirce*. New York: Dover Publications.

Perthes, Volker. 2000. "Si Vis Stabilitatem, Para Bellum: State Building, National Security, and War Preparation in Syria" in Steven Heydemann (ed.) *War, Institutions, and Social Change in the Middle East*. Berkeley: University of California Press. 149–173.

Piccato, Pablo. 2001. *City of Suspects: Crime in Mexico City, 1900–1931*. Durham: Duke University Press.

Rathmell, Andrew. 1996. "Syria's Intelligence Services: Origins and Development" in *Journal of Conflict Studies* 16(2).

Salvatore, Ricardo, Carlos Aguirre and Gilbert Joseph (eds.). 2001. *Crime and Punishment in Latin America*. Durham: Duke University Press.

Ticktin, Miriam. 2005. "Policing and Humanitarianism in France: Immigration and the Turn to Law as State of Exception" in *Interventions: International Journal of Postcolonial Studies* 7(3): 346–68.

United Nations Relief and Works Agency for Palestinian Refugees in the Near East. 1982. *UNRWA: A Brief History, 1950–1982*. Vienna: UNRWA.

Waterbury, John. 1983. *The Egypt of Nasser and Sadat: the Political Economy of Two Regimes*. Princeton: Princeton University Press.

Wedeen, Lisa. 1999. *Ambiguities of Domination: Politics, Rhetoric, and Symbols in Contemporary Syria*. Chicago: University of Chicago Press.

9

RIOT POLICE AND POLICING PROTEST IN TURKEY[1]

Ayşen Uysal

On 1 May 2007 Istanbul witnessed exceptional measures and police violence. The unions had wanted to organize a meeting to commemorate the thirty-year anniversary of the 1 May demonstrations in Taksim, which had ended in bloodshed; the resulting clash with the Governor of Istanbul and the Chief of Police saw the *Çevik Kuvvet* police's measures turn various districts of Istanbul into battlefields. Participants coming from outside Istanbul were not allowed to enter the city. Buses coming from İzmir to the west were made to wait near Gebze in ferry boats. In Taksim Square, police forces used tear gas; one person who suffered its effects subsequently died. In order not to allow demonstrators to enter Taksim Square and to force them to disperse, teams of riot police wielded their batons with indiscriminate violence. Approximately a thousand people were taken into custody. People eating at nearby restaurants were also affected by the gas. When one of these people, Masis Kürkçügil, a well known left wing activitst and founder of the Liberty and Solidarity Party (ODP), protested to the police, he was slapped by a riot officer. The governor of Istanbul, Muammer Güler, explained these public order measures by emphasising

[1] I would like to thank Daniel Neep and Demet Lüküslü for their contribution.

that: "provocative actions will be realized" and "Taksim square is forbidden to mass demonstrations."

How can this police violence be explained? What was it about the demonstration which led to violence? What were the police's perceptions of the demonstrators and what factors shaped their perceptions? These are some of the questions that this study seeks to answer through an investigation of a specialized police force that concentrates on the control of demonstrations and protests in Turkey.

But what do we mean when we talk about a specialized force for demonstrations? Even though the modern police apparatus in Turkey was founded in 1845, the specialization of police in order to deal with collective action only happened on 14 July 1965 with the formation of *Toplum Polisi* (Community Police). In 1982, *Toplum Polisi* ceded its place to *Çevik Kuvvet* (Rapid Intervention Forces). The foundation of *Çevik Kuvvet* took place after the military coup of 12 September 1980, and its conception of the state and of civil rights is particularly influenced by the political specificities of that period.

Four departments collaborate in order to control the demonstrations. The first three are the Security Department (*Güvenlik Dairesi*, and particularly its sub-section *Çevik Kuvvet*), the Intelligence Department (*Istihbarat Dairesi*), and the Photography and Film Department. In certain cases, the Anti–terrorism Department (*Terörle Mücadele Dairesi*)[2] can also intervene. The Security Department takes primary responsibility in maintaining order during demonstrations. As part of the institutional reforms of the police, on 11 August 2003, *Çevik Kuvvet*, which was linked to the Public Order Direction (*Asayiş Şube Müdürlüğü*) in the 1990s, was attached to the Security Section. Not every city has a Special Forces branch: in those that don't collective action is supervised by urban police.[3] Nevertheless, the governor and the assistant governor have the power to call the nearest *Çevik Kuvvet* forces if "serious" developments occur, giving the force a mobile character.

[2] This police section was attached to the Security Section until 1986 and was organized in an autonomous way after the emergence of Kurdish guerilla movement in 1984.

[3] Here we should note that, as is the case with the French model, gendarmerie forces maintain order in the rural areas where the police is not charged by security. In the city centers, they accompany the police forces when the latter are not sufficient in number for managing the crowd.

Police officers see *Çevik Kuvvet* as a compulsory stage of their career in which working conditions are intense (*Polis Dergisi* 1998). A period of up to three years in the Rapid Forces Section forms the first part of an officer's career but can be extended at the request of the officer. However, the poor reputation this section suffers among the police makes such a request unlikely.

Here I focus on state perceptions and strategies, especially those of the police. My evidence is drawn from the archives of the General Directorate of Police in Ankara (*Emniyet Genel Müdürlüğü*, EGM), which have not yet been opened to researchers. My study of social movements and police practice based on police archives was the first in its field. These archives are now accessible, after a long process. The General Directorate of Police's archives are based on the fax messages that were sent to the Directorate in real time or just after the event. These messages are recorded in Access format. This type of archiving has existed since 1994. I collected the protests from all over Turkey during a period of seven years (1994–2000). This data provides the date, the time, the place (region and city/district), the name of the organizer, the aim, the demands, type of action, number of participants, police arrests, and number of injuries and deaths among civil people or police forces. They also include an account of the events. The data obtained include 12,853 records of open air demonstrations, 6,249 records of meetings closed to the public and 1,639 records which are undetermined (not qualified as "closed" or "open air") over a period of seven years. After excluding the closed demonstrations, I was left with a corpus of 11,909 events.

Apart from police archives, I also consulted police training materials. Interviews with police officers and leaders and members of organizations responsible for or participating in demonstrations were also conducted.

Through a study of these sources, I first demonstrate that governing with a focus on security is not simply a police strategy, but a more general government approach of the state in Turkey. Following this, I examine the police perceptions of security and the factors which contribute to the formation of these perceptions. Finally, I discuss the relationship between police's definition and categorization of the "internal enemy," and its regulation of, and participant deterrence strategies against, the collective movements.

Governing focused on Security Perception

In Turkey there exists an overemphasis of security issues in the country's administration, which has had an immediate impact on the right to engage in political activity, as well as the right of assembly and demonstration. The emphasis on security issues provides an important reference point for the concept of the "internal enemy."

Perceptions of the terms "internal security" and "state security" are historically contingent. State officials and their security forces redefine the "internal enemy" according to the specificities of a particular period—they react not only against insecurity and "the enemy", but determine the identity of that enemy and define the meaning of internal and external security (Bigo 1996: 54). Designating the enemy allows the executive authorities "to reaffirm their own engagements and to mobilize allies" (Edelman 1991: 129). In this way, the discursive construction of the enemy helps to legitimize the policies adopted and the relationships put in place. The interior enemy "is both an indeterminate figure with shadowy outlines and a figure capable of being defined as a result of the metaphorical construction of the 'interior' in which its putative action unfolds" (Ceyhan & Peries 2001: 5). The enemy is a "discursive production of one or more interlocutors who express themselves through various social and institutional spaces" (Ibid.: 6). Even if the concept of the interior enemy exists through different periods, it has a different—often multiple—face in each new context. Security agents are assigned the role of identifying internal enemies.

This conception of the "internal enemy", whether associated with an "external enemy" or not, has given the authorities a quite specific perception of the history of collective action and social protest. In a broader historical perspective, they might see political opponents (*siyasi muhalifler*) as "internal enemies." In this mental universe, mobilization can only be the work of "hidden powers" (internal or external, but more often external) that want to destroy the country (Tilly 1978). In fact, mobilization is not perceived as an ordinary mode of political participation. Instead, it is seen as a threat to state security. From this perspective, the assembly of groups and populations for a cause considered illegitimate and "subversive" offers to those who construct the figure of the internal enemy the very "reasons for perpetuating and exaggerating the danger" (Edelman 1991: 130). This way of perceiving demonstrations has coined a phrase unique to Turkish political life:

"someone has pushed the button" (Sav 1996: 19) (*birileri düğmeye bastı*[4]). When violence emerges again on the streets, this expression is used by agents of the state. Such a perception of security increases the risks faced by protestors.

This security perception means that the Turkish political system is characterized by disconnections between the entrepreneurs of collective action and the authorities, as well as the ordinary citizens. While connections between citizens and collective organizations are severed by legal restrictions and repressive practices, connections with the authorities are destroyed by the refusal of the authorities to recognize these organizations as potential interlocutors. Disconnections are also generated by the delegitimization of social movements, often achieved by the construction of their supposed links with illegal organizations designated as "terrorist."

The security perception of the Turkish state is also embodied in police *savoir-faire*. How is the police's perception nourished by the "security regime" (Dorronsoro 2005)? How do the police officers of *Çevik Kuvvet* perceive their role and the outside reality?

Effects of professional perception

"Police *savoir-faire*" refers to police officer's perception of their own role (professional culture) and to their vision of the external world (environmental culture) (Della Porta 1998: 229). The social profile of police officers constitutes an important factor that has an impact on professional and environmental cultures. Who becomes a police officer in Turkey? Police officers are recruited from specific social and political categories. The Security Section is mostly composed of police officers with a certain cultural capital, most of them having a PhD in the social sciences, often from the United States. On the other hand, the Section's visible appearance on the street—the Rapid Intervention Forces—also attracts young, inexperienced, and less able or recently graduated police officers of Anatolian origins (Cerrah 1997: 136). According to

[4] This expression was introduced into the Turkish political language to designate the automatic arrival of a danger exterior to the system. More precisely, this expression implies that administration is not in the hands of the government and that the exterior powers had launched a process not controllable by the authorities. According to that perspective, this process aims at establishing chaos in the country.

an internal police survey, 80 per cent of police candidates are the children of workers, small tradesmen, merchants and farmers. They belong to provincial families (82 per cent from villages and small towns) with numerous children and with low incomes. 69 per cent of the candidates had experienced unemployment for at least one year after their high school education (*Zaman*, 5 October 2000; Kul and Demir 2001).

Apart from these particular socio-demographic characteristics, *Çevik Kuvvet* police officers are recruited among people with right-wing tendencies—especially the radical right following the military coup of 12 September 1980—though membership of a political party prohibits entry into the police force, a demand which is seen as a way of ensuring that officers do not become political tools. The political sympathies of the police forces that handle demonstrations tend to lead them to perceive demonstrators as "internal enemies" who can, on occasion, collaborate with the external enemy. This perception was particularly strong in the 1980s and 1990s (Uysal 2006b: 265–66).

The police officers see the police force as the guarantor of the security of the state. The perception of the state as "The Sacred State," and the importance subsequently given to *raison d'Etat* (*devletin bekaası*) and the designation of the internal enemy that threatens the state's security, generates a professional culture which regards the existence of the police officers as a *sine qua non* of the "healthy continuity" of the state.[5] This official perception of "chronic insecurity" (Bora 1996: 1071) has two important consequences in practice: arbitrary behavior (derived from a relatively autonomous structure of the police) and *de facto* sanctions (such as extrajudicial killings). The harsh repression of demonstrations, the harassment of demonstrators who have already been cautioned, insults and even practices of torture all seem to follow from this perception. As the words of a *Çevik Kuvvet* police officer indicate, harassment is seen as an ordinary means of sanctioning dem-

[5] In certain cases, police officers question their relationship with the state. After the assassination of their colleagues in December 2000, riot police officers who went out onto the streets had chanted the following slogan: "Today police officers do not believe any more in the sacredness of the state and the state playing the role of a father. Can a father 'sell' his son?" (*Polis artık devletin kutsallığına, babalığına inanan eski polis değil. Baba evladını satar mı?*) Once again, we see an intimate and hierarchical relationship established by the police officers between the state and the police officers.

onstrators: "If I am given a gun, I use it. If they demonstrate on the street, I beat them. I did not become a police officer to let them swear at my mother". (*Elime silah veriyorlarsa kullanırım. Gösteri yapılıyorsa döverim. Anama küfrettirmek için polis olmadım*).

Since police officers identify themselves with the state, government legislation that provides rights to the demonstrators can become the target of protests by the Rapid Forces. For example, police forces carried out a number of demonstrations as a reaction to amendments in the Penal Code accepted by the Turkish Parliament on 18 November 1992, which were intended to prevent torture and poor treatment in police custody. At the 17 November funeral of four police officers who were murdered by DHKP-C[6] during a shoot out, the police officers chanted "human rights are the enemy of the police force!" (*Milliyet*, 20 November 1992), which aptly captures their image of the outside world.

Despite the designation of demonstrators as the internal enemy, the practices of left-wing demonstrators have influenced Turkish police officers. In fact, the repertoire of action and the slogans used by the police evokes the protests of the militant left. The slogan "Ankara, Ankara hear our voice, this is the voice of the rapid forces" is adapted from the workers unions slogan "Ankara, Ankara hear our voice, this is the voice of the steps of workers." Similarly, the slogan "this homeland will be a tomb for Apo"[7] recalls the slogan of radical leftist students, "this homeland will be a tomb for fascism." It is interesting that police officers adopted the kinds of slogan that they had been used to hearing throughout their whole professional life. There is an accumulation and transmission of protestors' knowledge, not only between protestors, but also from leftist protest groups to the police forces.

How are these police perceptions formed? How are they generalized to the police members in the organization? In order to answer these questions, it is necessary to explore the training of police officers.

Effects of Training

In addition to their identification with the state, the training given in Police Academies and Colleges has also contributed to the perception

[6] Revolutionary Party/Front of the People's liberation, one of the armed and illegal radical leftist organizations.

[7] Apo is the nickname of Abdullah Őcalan, the leader of the PKK (Party pro-kurde).

of protests and to police practices. For example, in the Police Academy, the demonstrations are analyzed in Social Psychology courses which follow the theories of Gustave Le Bon (see Büyükdöğerli 1992; Göksu 2000). More recently, the "theory of the crowd" was abandoned with the introduction of a new handbook (Cerrah & Sevindik & Kavruk 2002; Kartal & Kızılırmak 2006), which also contained Ted Gurr's "theory of frustration."[8] This contribution to police officer training made their perception of demonstrations even more complex. For example, a document I obtained from the Security Section of the General Directorate of Police on the policy of intervening in public events demonstrates the extent to which these two theories are utilized to inform the police perceptions of protests, albeit without forming a coherent doctrine. The introduction to this file sees protests as a way in which opposition is expressed in democratic states. In democracies, demonstrations do not constitute a danger to the regime because they are carried out by people who seek to resolve their complaints within the legal framework. However, the same file maintains that in repressive and authoritarian regimes, where fewer disputes take place, it is much more likely that any challenge will assume an explosive form (*sosyal patlama*). In spite of this, collective action is seen as both "clandestine activity based on specific strategy and programme" (Emniyet Genel Müdürlüğü, no date: 381) and "an irrational and emotional gathering" (Ibid.: 382). Moreover, the bibliographies of books and articles written by police officers contain many references to social psychology, which inevitably has important practical consequences. First of all, "rational" individuals making choices are totally absent in these texts (Korkusuz 1999; Türkmen 2001); demonstrators are thus portrayed as irrational, emotional people, a tactic which serves to delegitimize them (Contamin 2003: 399). From such a perspective, dem-

[8] Explaining violent demonstrations by the concept of frustration appears also in the discourses of some ministers of internal affairs. The Minister of Internal Affairs of the ANAP government, Ülkü Güney explains the violent demonstrations of 1 May, 1996 as follows: "Can we imagine that each year around 300–400 thousand people come to Istanbul and the shanty towns of Istanbul, particularly from Southeast of Turkey? And these people cannot be placed well; they try to stay in Istanbul living at overpopulated houses [that is to say several families in the same house]. The illegal construction and unemployment generates their feelings of hostility and vengeance" (*TBMM Tutanak Dergisi*, 1996).

onstrators are constituted as mere "puppets" of illegal organizations, stripped of any cognitive capacity:

> People lose most of their ability to criticize in a crowd situation. They cannot develop personal ideas and make personal decisions... In collective action it is emotions which dominate, not rationality...
>
> ...
>
> The notions of copycat behavior and the crowd mentality are found at the heart of all social protests... (Göksu 2000: 173–75).

In addition, the leaders—who are the (active, masculine) guides of the crowd (feminine and passive)—occupy an important place in the work of Le Bon and in social psychology in general (Thiec 1981: 409–28). Leaders act as catalysts (Mariot 2001: 715) for the development of events, and they easily influence young and naive people (Emniyet Genel Müdürlüğü, no date: 381). In this worldview, the surveillance and arrest of leaders (before, during, or after the demonstration), attempts to discredit them, and sentencing them with severe prison terms all appear as means to control the crowd (Uysal 2001: 64–84):

> Leaders are the brain of the crowd. Separating the leaders from the crowd is an effective measure since the crowd finds itself in a state where it does not know what to do (Göksu 2000: 190).

Distinctions made between the various categories of participant in the same demonstration also reveal the specific perceptions of the police.[9] The police place demonstrators in six categories: professional agitators (*profesyonel kışkırtıcılar*), risk-takers (*atılganlar*), the easily influenced (*tesir altında kalanlar*), the cautious (*ihtiyatlılar*), supporters (*destekleyiciler*) and spectators (*seyirciler*) (Kartal & Kızılırmak 2006: 24). Professional agitators, according to the police, have been trained to start the action and to keep it going. Risk-takers are considered to be irrational as they make decisions without thinking about the consequences; this category of demonstrators has no other aim than to ascend the ranks of the movement's hierarchy. The police perceive the easily-influenced to be people who are insufficiently courageous to begin protests, but who are led on by the risk-takers. Cautious participants are individuals ready to participate in a protest begun by agita-

[9] These distinctions are, however, inscribed into written texts rather than translated into practice.

tors but who do not take the initiative, unlike the risk takers. As for supporters, they are sympathizers who do not directly participate in the protest but who try to persuade others to take part. Last but not least, spectators deliver moral support since they follow the protest with interest (Kartal & Kızılırmak 2006: 24).

Crowd policing envisages a specific management strategy particularly for those agitators who are active. This strategy requires a particular surveillance process, notably by cameras. It is considered essential to prevent these people from infiltrating through to the protest march. According to the Turkish police, these most active participants in the gatherings need to be kept away from the rest of the participants and sympathizers. Therefore, they are kept under close watch during the demonstration (Emniyet Genel Müdürlüğü: 5). In other words, according to police logic, the "brain" of the protest has to be separated from its "body" to render its movements ineffectual.

In fact, protests are considered by police officers in the field (and until recently by police commanders as well) as events which should be prevented, not as an accepted mode of political participation. This perception of the police demonstrates that on the streets in Turkey, a protest constitutes a means of engaging in politics without it being considered an ordinary means of political participation. However, in most democracies, demonstration has become a normal mode of political participation (Barnes & Kaase 1979: 523 and sq.).

The perception of collective action as a deviant means of political participation brings with it the attempt by state forces to dissuade participants from protest.

Dissuasive strategy for maintenance of order and categorization of internal enemy

We can use pressurized, colored water to identify protestors easily for questioning. Using this liquid might have a dissuasive effect on those who intend to join meetings. To put it simply, no one wants to get their clothes stained (Göksu 2000: 193).

The Turkish model of policing demonstrations is characterized by arbitrariness and the use of dissuasive strategies to maintain order. In "a zero sum game," its arbitrary character "prevents any of the players from gathering any information about the adversary's intended strategy." In contrast, in "a non-zero sum game," the partner is brought around to recognizing the layout of the game by instrumentalizing the game plan as a threat (Schelling 1986: 215). In the Turkish model of maintaining order, the arbitrary element incorporates both of these meanings, which leads to police intervention that can be unpredictable in spite of an explicit threat. Before the start of events that are publicly announced but not formally declared to the authorities, the directors of the police and the chief administrator threaten the organizers and potential participants by police repression via the media. This also applies to declared meetings that seek to be held in prohibited places. Regardless of the threats made by the public authorities, police actions towards the gathering may be repressive or tolerant. However, the increased risk appears to constitute by itself "a veritable dissuasive threat" (Schelling 1986: 232) for potential participants.

In Turkey, the criterion of legality does not constitute a way to predict whether or not protests will be suppressed: some illegal demonstrations are tolerated whereas others are heavily clamped down upon. This can be explained by the distinction made between "good" and "bad" demonstrators:

> The most important criteria vis-à-vis the legality of a street parade is the purpose of the demonstration [....]. The distinction between illegal and legitimate demonstrations should be remembered. Even though certain protests are illegal because they are organized without authorization,[10] they can be legitimate because they are supported by public opinion and because they do not constitute a danger to the morals, health or security of society (Kartal & Kızılırmak 2006: 25).

My analysis of the police database of protests, in particular "incidents" that give rise to arrests or prosecutions, suggests that the Turkish police makes a certain distinction between "good" and "bad" protestors.[11] The five groups that the police considers to be the most dangerous are also the groups most affected by police violence.

Some 69 per cent of protests organized by armed revolutionary organizations result in legal sanctions. This highlights the importance given to the purpose of the protest in making decisions about how best to maintain order. Similarly, the police suppress more harshly organi-

[10] According to Turkish legislation, a declaration (not an authorization) is required 48 hours prior to the beginning of the demonstration. It is curious to note the use of the word "authorization" in official police discourse.

[11] In the French case, for example, "bad demonstrators" are considered to be "autonomous/leftist" groups, "hooligans" and "non-citizens" as Olivier Fillieule (1997) has demonstrated.

zations that question the state's monopoly of legitimate violence. Events with "unknown author" or events initiated by "a group" are the second most frequently persecuted group, with 48 per cent of their protests giving rise to prosecution. Handbooks demonstrate the skeptical attitude of the police towards unidentified initiators (Kartal & Kızılırmak 2006: 17–18). Islamist organizations also score highly (with 41 per cent of their protests resulting in arrests or prosecutions), disproving the widely-held perception that the police is more tolerant of religious groups. Students constitute one of the "privileged" targets for police repression (20 per cent of their actions).[12] Finally, the police intervened in fifty-three protests by *HADEP*,[13] even though forty-nine of these actions were peaceful (in other words 14 per cent of all their actions). Moreover, the police refuse to negotiate with illegal organizations and with groups considered to act as wings of illegal organizations. This explains its intolerance towards the Association of Prisoners' Families, which is an organization both linked to DHKP-C (Revolutionary Party/Front for Popular Liberation) and benefiting from legal status. The demonstrations organized by the families of prisoners and missing persons, and human rights organizations, especially the Human Rights Association (*Insan Hakları Derneği*, founded in 1986) included 118 events "with incidents" (11 per cent of all their demonstrations). These incidents led to arrests and judicial prosecutions, even though the meetings were all non-violent.

On the other hand, traditional and legal collective action organizations such as unions (4 per cent of their actions) and political parties (7 per cent of the total of their actions) experience proportionally less police repression if we consider that they are the groups most represented on the street. We can conclude that the more the street is used as a site of protest, the fewer chances there are for violence, even though the number of "incidents" remains high. Does the example of 1 May 2007 constitute an exception to this finding? The police make distinctions between different unions. On the very same day, while police

[12] Students have neither the right to form a union nor the right to join one. Only a certain number of students' associations were authorized after the military coup of 12 September 1980. Until the constitutional amendment in 1995, students' membership of political parties was explicitly banned.

[13] A pro-Kurdish party banned by the Constitutional Court in March 2003. It preceded the current DTP (*Demokratik Toplum Partisi*, Party of Democratic Society).

officers were intervening in demonstrations organized by DISK (Revolutionary Confederation of Workers' Unions), they tolerated the march of TURK-IS (Turkey's Confederation of Workers' Unions). The participation of other leftist groups, and especially of small revolutionary leftist groups, in the DISK demonstrations facilitates their designation as "bad" demonstrators by the police.

Table: Demonstrations leading to "incidents" by group (1994–2000)

Organizations	*Total number of occurrences*	*Occurrences with incidents*	*Violence/Total of actions (%)*
Unions	5962	220	4
Political Parties	2205	160	7
IHD, TAYAD, Disappeared People's Families	1046	118	11
Students	1029	208	20
Unknown Author	684	331	48
HADEP	383	53	14
Islamist Groups	181	75	41
Armed Organizations	137	95	69

Source: Based on data from the General Directorate of Police.

Dispersing protestors through police intervention is one way of suppressing collective action. There are, however, many other forms of repression employed during protests by Turkish police. The massive armed presence of police forces with the aim of dissuading participation in street protests is just one of these. Nevertheless, this repression excludes neither negotiation and compromise nor the preventative management of collective action. Several management strategies operate simultaneously (Goldstone & Tilly 2001: 180). These may be, for instance, the massive armed presence of police, the encircling of demonstrators, negotiations with protest leaders, and the detention of the "instigators" while the remainder of the protesters are left alone.

Conclusion

The belief of state security agents that collective action is a security threat and that it should be actively discouraged characterizes the maintenance of order in Turkey. This notion is not unique to the police, but is widespread across different state institutions. The self-identification of police officers with a state considered sacred, and the professional education they receive, reinforce their negative perception of demonstrations as an extraordinary means of political participation. The strategies and forms of dissuasive control demonstrate the point to which protests are not seen as a normal means of political activism by the security forces.

This conception of protest among police officers does not totally prevent the streets being used for political purposes. Protestors and protest entrepreneurs develop their own strategies for survival. Thus, the streets become a space of intersection between the different strategies of the state and the protestors.

Bibliography

Aminzade, Ronald & Doug McAdam. 2001. "Emotions and Contentious Politics" in Ronald Aminzade, Jack A. Goldstone, Doug McAdam et al. (eds.). *Silence and Voice in the Study of Contentious Politics*. Cambridge: Cambridge University Press; 14–50.

Aminzade, Ronald, Jack A. Goldstone and Doug McAdam et al. 2001. *Silence and Voice in the Study of Contentious Politics*. Cambridge: Cambridge University Press.

Barnes, Samuel Henry & Max Kaase. 1979. *Political Action. Mass Participation in Five Western Democracies*. London: Sage Publications.

Bigo, Didier, 1996. *Police en réseaux. L'expérience européenne*. Paris: Presses de la FNSP.

Bora, Tanıl. 1996. "Polis devleti" in *Cumhuriyet Dönemi Türkiye Ansiklopedisi*. Istanbul, Iletişim Yayınları.

Büyükdöğerli, Ethem. 1992. *Toplumsal Olaylar ve Müdahale Esasları*. Ankara: Polis Okulları Ders Kitabı.

Cerrah, Ibrahim, M. Sevindik & M. Kavruk. 2002. *Güvenlik Güçleri için Yakın Savunma Teknikleri. Teori ve Pratik*. Emniyet Genel Müdürlüğü Polis Akademisi Başkanlığı.

Cerrah, Ibrahim. 1997. "Toplumsal Olaylar ve Çevik Kuvvet Eğitimi" in *Amme Idaresi Dergisi* 30(3): 135–49.

Ceyhan Ayşe & Gabriel Peries, 2001. "L'ennemi intérieur : une construction discursive et Politique," in *Cultures et Conflits* 43: 5–11.

Contamin, Jean-Gabriel. 2003. "De la fécondité épistémologique d'un rapprochement historique incongru: La pétition guillotine et ce qu'elle enseigne sur une forme d'action publique citoyenne" in *Historicité de l'action publique*. Paris: Presses Universitaire de France.

Della Porta, Donatella. 1998. "Police Knowledge and Protest Policing: Some Reflections on the Italian Case" in Della Porta, & Reiter (eds.). *Policing*

Protest. The Control of Mass Demonstrations in Western Democracies. Minneapolis: University of Minnesota Press; 228–252.

Della Porta, Donatella & Olivier Fillieule. 2006. *Police et Manifestants. Maintien de l'ordre et gestion des conflits.* Paris: Presses de Sciences Po.

Della Porta, Donatella & Herbert Reiter (eds.). 1998. *Policing Protest. The Control of Mass Demonstrations in Western Democracies.* Minneapolis: University of Minnesota Press.

Dorronsoro, Gilles (eds.). 2005. *La Turquie conteste. Mobilisations sociales et régime sécuritaire.* Paris : CNRS éditions.

Edelman, Murray. 1991. *Pièces et règles du jeu politique.* Paris: Editions du Seuil.

Emniyet Genel Müdürlüğü. *Toplumsal Olaylar ve Müdahale Esasları.* Unpublished notes.

Favre, Pierre. 1990. *La Manifestation.* Paris: Presses de Science Po.

Goldstone, Jack A. & Charles Tilly. 2001. "Threat (and Opportunity): Popular Action and State Response in the Dynamics of Contentious Action" in Aminzade et al. (eds.) *Silence and Voice in the Study of Contentious Politics.* Cambridge: Cambridge University Press; 179–194.

Göksu, Turkut. 2000. *Toplumsal Psikoloji: Toplumsal Olaylar ve Müdahale Esasları.* Ankara: Özen Yayımcılık.

Kartal, Nusret & Kızılırmak, Öner. 2006. *Kalabalık Yönetimi Ders Notu.* Ankara: Çubuk Ofset Matbaacılık.

Korkusuz, Hakan. 1999. "Öğrenci Olaylarının Perde Arkası" in *Polis Dergisi* 18: 123–137.

Mariot, Nicolas. 2001. "Les formes élémentaires de l'effervescence collective ou l'état d'esprit prêté aux foules" in *RFSP* 51(5): 707–738.

Offerlé, Michel. 1990. "Descendre dans la rue : de la 'journée' à la 'manif'", in Pierre Favre, *La Manifestation.* Paris: Presses de Science Po.; 90–122.

Sav, Önder. 1996. *TBMM Tutanak Dergisi*, cilt 5, 48. Oturum, 7 Mayıs.

Schelling, Thomas. 1986. *Stratégie du conflit.* Trans. Raymond Manicacci. Paris: PUF.

T.C. Içişleri Bakanlığı. 2005. Emniyet Genel Müdürlüğü Araştırma Planlama ve Koordinasyon. Dairesi Başkanlığı. 1998. "Çevik Kuvvet Polisinin Toplumsal Olaylardaki Çalışmasına Tesir Eden Faktörler" in *Polis Dergisi* (supplement) 21.

Thiec, Yvon. J. 1981. "Gustave Le Bon, prophète de l'irrationalisme de masse" in *Revue Française de Sociologie* XXII (3): 409–428.

Tilly, Charles. 1978. *From Mobilization to Revolution.* Reading, Mass.: Addison-Wesley Publishing Company.

Türkmen, Mustafa. 2001. "Toplumsal Olay Psikolojisi ve Polisin Rolü" in *Polis Dergisi* 26: 617–618.

Uysal, Ayşen. 2001. "Devletin güvenliği ve toplumsal muhalefet eylemleri : Kalemli Çete örneği" in *Birikim* 146: 64–84.

Uysal, Ayşen. 2005. "Maintien de l'ordre et risques liés aux manifestations de rue" in Dorronsoro (eds). *La Turquie conteste. Mobilisations sociales et régime sécuritaire*, Paris: CNRS editions: 31–49.

Uysal, Ayşen. 2006a. "Cop Gölgesinde politika : Türkiye'de Toplumsal Olay Polisliği ve Sokak Eylemleri" in *Mülkiye Dergisi* 253: 79–94.
Uysal, Ayşen. 2006b. "Maintien de l'ordre et répression policière en Turquie" in Della Porta & Fillieule (eds.). *Police et Manifestants. Maintien de l'ordre et gestion des conflits*. Paris: Presses de Sciences Po: 257–78.

10

INCARCERATED WOMEN, HONORABLE WOMEN

Roberta Micallef

As a means of controlling the deviant and disobedient, corporal and capital punishment, as well as financial penalties and incarceration, have a long history in the Middle East. However, the emergence of women's prisons in the late eighteenth century (Gorman 2005) marks a change in the state's assumptions about who had the obligation and the authority to punish disobedient women. Women have remained part of the penal system in the Middle East since then, but they represent a small segment of the prison population in Turkey as throughout the Middle East. The International Centre for Prison Studies reported on 8 January 2007 that women constituted 3.7 per cent of the Turkish prison population (International Centre for Prison Studies 2007). While many of these women are in prison for crimes ranging from prostitution to murder, a significant number are incarcerated for their political views.

This chapter examines two multi–layered texts by Turkish female political prisoners in order to gain a better understanding of the culture of women's prisons and the gender-specific aspects of being a female political prisoner. Asiye Güzel and Leyla Zana's texts offer us a glimpse of a new society created outside the bounds of the community in the exilic realm of the prison. An examination of their narratives reveals the prisoners' survival strategies, the encounters among prisoners incarcerated for non-political crimes and those incarcerated for acts of political defiance, as well as the interactions between the prisoners and the representatives of the state. Furthermore, these narratives illuminate the dynamics between the prisoners and those on the outside and expose the conjunctions or ruptures in contemporary intellectual currents relating to prisons, incarceration and women in Turkey.

In much of the literature on Mediterranean and Middle Eastern societies men have been portrayed as obsessed with maintaining honor and upholding the family name at all costs, and women have been stereotyped as silent, passive, and marginal figures who were secluded in their houses, modestly covered from head to toe (Weidman 2003: 520). Both these texts dispute the traditional understanding of honor. Both Güzel and Zana challenge patriarchal norms and this stereotype, first by claiming a public voice and second by their defiant actions.

Asiye's Story narrates the torture and gang rape to which Güzel was subjected, allowing for an in-depth examination of the use of sexual violence against women prisoners. Torture, and in particular sexual violence against women, she argues, is part of daily life in Turkey, and the state is not dealing adequately with these problems (Güzel 2003: 9–10). The text underscores that rape is a unique torture tool used against women, a punishment that is effective because of prevalent patriarchal norms and practices. She describes rape as a crime against humanity, a crime that is committed in the homes, the street and at the hands of the agents of the state to punish women who do not know their place and the men who cannot control them. But by writing about her ordeal, Güzel manages to transform rape from a silencing mechanism, a gendered punishment, into a topic of discussion and a re-evaluation of the concept of honor.

Leyla Zana raises issues regarding women's duties and obligations to their children and families vs. their political activism that could benefit their community. Women are challenged not only by the opposition but also often by their own group because of their gender. Zana's text reveals her struggles in maintaining her role as a "good" mother while in prison. She refuses to leave prison for medical reasons when given a choice: she wants the state to acknowledge that it was wrong to imprison her. Both these texts also reveal that the assumptions of the state and its agents may have been out of touch with social transformations taking place within the society. Studies on early incarcerations of women in the Middle East reveal that women suffered a greater social stigma from being viewed as criminal deviants (Güzel 2003: 6; Gorman 2007: 5). These narratives suggest that this may no longer be the case, especially when it comes to political prisoners.

Rape as a Gendered Torture Tool: Asiye's Story

Asiye's Story is a well-written, autobiographical prison memoir that chronicles a transformation in the face of horrific atrocities. Her story does not begin with a birth or a marriage but with a terrifying scene. On 22 February 1997, Güzel comes home to find a group of police officers searching the apartment where she has been living in hiding with her husband, who is also a political activist. The editor of a socialist Turkish newspaper, she is then taken into custody and accused of involvement in an "illegal" organization. She is interrogated and tortured and gang raped during the following thirteen days at the security headquarters. After signing a forced confession, she spends five and a half years in untried detention. While in custody she commits evidence of rape and torture to paper, and the resulting diaries are smuggled out and made into a book—published in 1999 while she is still in prison.[1] In June 2002, Güzel has a court appearance during which she is charged with being a member of an illegal Marxist-Leninist organization. She is released pending the final decision of the Supreme Court. In October 2002, she travels to Sweden to receive the prestigious Tucholsky Prize, awarded to writers who show courage when their freedom of expression is in danger. Two days after the ceremony, the court sentences her in absentia to twelve-and-a-half years imprisonment. Güzel is granted political asylum in Sweden, where she continues to reside.

Her book, like her story, is fragmented. Time flows backwards as the narrative unfolds. First, we read the foreword written in February 2003 and then the preface to the English edition written in January 2003. This is followed by the translated preface to the Turkish edition originally written in October 2000. After this preface we reach the introduction and then finally the story itself. Each layer we uncover presents a different frame through which this book can be read and understood. These frames, while not competing, reveal what each actor

[1] The diaries were published by the English Centre of International PEN, translated by Richard McKane, then Deputy Chair of English PEN's Writers in Prison Committee.

involved in the English production of the book considers most important and where the local discourse intersects and diverges with the global discourse. Each frame also adds a layer of current events, which demonstrates that torture in Turkey is not on the wane.

The English translation of *Asiye's Story* is presented in a "human-rights" frame. In the pursuit of justice, rights campaigns depend upon victim stories to gain support for rights activism. The personal story makes the atrocity concrete for the reader (Schaffer and Smith 2004: 15–17). The very cover of *Asiye's Story* reveals that it won the 2002 Tucholsky Prize for Human Rights Writing, awarded by the Swedish Pen Club. The PEN club's charter tells us that they are the oldest organization to fight for human rights and in particular for the freedom of expression (International Pen 1948). The foreword to the English edition published in 2003 confirms that this is a "human rights" narrative. The forward was penned by Helen Bamber, a leading campaigner against torture and the founder of the Medical Foundation for the Care of Victims of Torture. Here Bamber declares that Güzel is a brave woman for having spoken out against "torture, rape and judicial manipulation" (Güzel 2003: 5). Her foreword accomplishes three objectives: it tells us how brave Güzel is as an individual; it links her story to similar ones and it calls attention to the fact that human rights abuses are everyone's concern. Human rights are a transnational issue. Bamber poses a question for the reader to consider: "What is my society prepared to do about such a stain on the conscience of the world?"

The preface to the English edition (January 2003) is marked by important dates that witness the fragmentation of Güzel's life, the narrative and her geographic dislocation. The author tells us that this preface was written "three years since my book came out, seven months since I have put distance between myself and the thick walls of prison" (Güzel 1999: 7). She writes that this marks the beginning of a new period in her life, "away from the country and people that I love" (Ibid.). She has also put some distance between her and her experiences in the security headquarters and calmly looks back on the period of her life covered in this book. She tells us that she learned that human beings could overcome anything. In addition to seeing the lowest form of humanity, she also experienced the highest form. The prison school was tough but it made her stronger.

Whereas the foreword ties Güzel's highly personal story into a global discussion of human rights, the preface to the English edition presents her story in two local frames. Here the author contextualizes her story first in the frame of the Turkish prison systems. She tells us about large-scale abuses that took place in the prison systems when the operation to implement F Type prisons, along with the policy of isolation called 'Return to Life', was launched.[2] She narrates the stories of prisoners who committed suicide by starvation or self-immolation to protest the State's policies (Güzel 2003: 7–8). Torture and resistance in Turkish prisons are commonplace.

The preface to the Turkish edition of her book—written three years earlier than the English one while Güzel was still incarcerated but after the book came out—is roughly twice as long and serves to clarify why she wrote this book. She describes her emotional and psychological state in detail. Whereas in the preface to the English edition she writes about the "fascist revenge" and "capitalist-imperialist" invasions (Güzel 2003: 9), here her language is poetic and more emotional. She quotes revolutionary poetry: "The friends gave the signal/ it's time/in the shouts of the people/ a revolution will blossom like flags." Güzel describes how the book became part of her healing process. She also discusses her fear of reactions to her book and is most concerned with her family's and comrades' reactions to her having been raped. She takes great pains to express that she is not only a socialist but also a woman and that therefore she is doubly punished in patriarchal Turkey. She is certain that her book will open up a much needed discussion about sexual violence, for even among "revolutionaries" rape remained a taboo topic (Güzel 2003: 13). The author describes a dull ache that she wakes up with occasionally. This ache is telling her she should have resisted more. Although she was blindfolded, naked, tied up and assaulted by five armed men, she is haunted by the idea that she should not have allowed herself to be sexually abused. She attributes this to her having internalized patriarchal, "false values" that put her "identity as a socialist and a human being under siege" (Güzel 2003: 15).

The book describes what happened to her but also focuses on her healing process. When she is being tortured by the suspension method, her tormentors strip her upper body, tie her hands behind her and suspend her from a wooden beam. At first, she does not feel anything but

[2] See Bargu, "Spectacles of Death: Dignity, Dissent, and Sacrifice in Turkey's Prisons" in this volume.

then they bring her down, rub her arms to get the circulation going again, remove the rest of her clothes and then re-suspend her. This time she is in agony and cannot breathe, but she finds that she can think only about her nudity in front of the male gaze. She is tortured by thoughts of her husband: "if they touch you what will you say to your husband?" (Güzel 2003: 32–33). Although rationally she knows that as socialists they both acknowledged that their political activism might lead to this, she has internalized societal norms: "If you don't ask for your clothes, he will hate you" (Ibid.) The next time they bring her down, she cannot feel her body; she is thrown on an icy concrete floor, held down and raped by her torturers. The only thought going through her head is, "No you can't do that—murder me, tear me apart but don't touch me. Don't dirty me, don't stain me!" (Güzel 2003: 34).

Even in times of peace, rape is widespread but under conditions of political chaos and war, violence against women including sexual violence increases exponentially within society as a whole. Güzel's case is neither the first documented case of torture in custody, nor the first case of the rape of a political prisoner, male or female. In her article narrating the rapes of women who have been either vocal in their opposition to political parties or are related to men supporting the opposition parties in Pakistan, Shahla Haeri writes that "political rape" is a modern improvisation on the theme of "feudal honor rape." The target of humiliation and shame is not necessarily a specific woman; it is a political rival. In its modern context, political rape has the tacit and at times explicit legitimation of the state, just as honor rape has continued to have cultural support and collective sanctions (Haeri 1999: 56).

According to an Amnesty International report (26 February 2003), every day many women across Turkey experience sexual and other physical violence. Women from all social and cultural backgrounds have been abused, assaulted and raped by state security forces, acquaintances, complete strangers, and even by family members. In addition to the physical and psychological effects of the rape, women who have been sexually assaulted risk death, further violence, forced marriage or ostracism by their families or communities as a result of their experiences. The concept of "honor" is used as an excuse for inaction and as a means of silencing survivors of sexual violence (Amnesty International 2003: 1/5). The vast majority of assaults in custody go unreported due to psychological distress and shame experienced by the survivor, fear of retribution at the hands of the state, fear of shame in the woman's family or her community. Some women do not disclose sexual assaults because they believe it will not bring about any justice. Women who organized and spoke at a conference on "Sexual Violence in Custody" in Istanbul in June 2000, were charged with having insulted the security forces by denouncing rape in custody (Amnesty International 2003: 3/5). As a consequence of their speaking openly against rape, they themselves faced prison sentences. Güzel's concerns are founded on solid reasons.

But a battle between ideologies and changing perspectives of individualism and gender roles is taking place in Turkish society. The first time Güzel tells a male activist that she was raped his response shocks her: "'Look at my face, look into my eyes,' Arif said. 'All our hatred is against those who did this. Why are you ashamed? It's those bastards who should be ashamed. Hold your head up high'" (Güzel 2003: 82). Furthermore, Güzel was not ostracized by her family or loved ones. The first time she revealed that she was raped publicly was at her trial in front of her family, her husband's family and her friends. On her way to the court where she was planning to reveal what had been done to her, she was so nervous that she was sweating profusely and felt as if she would die any second. As she read her prepared statement in public, with every word she uttered she believed she would die. When she looked over at her father, her heart was broken: he was crying. She discovered, however, that he was not crying because she had brought dishonor on the family but because his daughter had been hurt. He cried because she could not bring herself to tell him earlier. He cried because he could not protect his little girl. After her admission in court, her family and her husband's family continued to visit her in prison and to tell her that rape was just another form of torture. She received many letters and cards repeating this message: "You gave us courage too. It is not you who should be ashamed, but the perpetrators. You have taken an honorable step. You are our honor" (Güzel 2003: 92–93). She decided finally that she is the one who should have simply treated rape as she did suspension torture or beatings (Güzel 2003: 91–92). Yet she remained at war with herself: she is still ashamed of what happened to her, even though no one else in her family treated her as "sullied."

Gender roles are constructed at particular historical moments in complex relations with colonialism, nationalism and capitalism (Weidman

2003: 525). Rape at the hands of agents of the state that are charged with protecting its citizens has allowed for a culturally constituted and sanctioned discourse for expressing interpersonal experiences, in which citizens are able to express sentiments that would otherwise violate the codes of honor and modesty. Changing notions of femininity and female respectability are challenging the honor/shame model. Women and men in Turkey are redefining masculinity, femininity, and the traditional view of honor. Güzel's book brings forth the conflict in perceptions of honor, shame, responsibility, individual rights and ownership of the female body in contemporary Turkey. Until 2005, rape was classified as a crime against societal order and the family: a woman's body belonged to her natal family first and then to her husband. As Canan Arin states, this meant that the woman's body was property that needed to be protected. Under the new law, rape or a crime against a woman's body is simply violence against an individual.[3]

Finally, Güzel pays special homage to the women of the Female Workers' Union who in 2000 organized a campaign against rape and sexual assault in Istanbul titled The Congress against Rape and Sexual Assault in Custody. *Asiye's Story* was a powerful catalyst that contributed to a discussion in Turkey about the concept of honor. The story came out at a time when a global dialogue on human rights intersected with the local dialogue on the position of women in society. Because the book was first written while she was in prison with parts added for the English edition, Güzel has been able to include information about its reception. She writes that men and women from all segments of society wrote to her. She accuses the state and its protectors, both internal and external, of allowing and perpetrating such crimes. The acts of violence and specifically the rape that she had to endure, along with the time she spent in prison sorting out what had happened to her, transformed this socialist activist into a feminist and forced her to discover her adult, female voice.

Leyla Zana: Political Prisoner/Nurturing Mother

In 1991, Leyla Zana became the first Kurdish woman elected to the Turkish parliament. At her inauguration after reciting the required loyalty oath, she added in Kurdish, "I take this oath for the brotherhood between the Turkish people and the Kurdish people" (Kürkçü 2003).

[3] Interview with Canan Arin, "Kadının birey olma hakkı" 8 March 2005.

The last sentence uttered in Kurdish—in combination with her headband in the Kurdish tri–color of red, yellow and green—created turmoil in the Parliament and the country. In March 1994, she was stripped of her parliamentary immunity and arrested on charges of separatism and engaging in illegal activities. She was given a fifteen-year prison sentence that was increased by two years while she was in prison because of an article she wrote in 1998. During her incarceration, she was awarded many prizes by international organizations in recognition of her "uncompromising stand for human rights" (Bonner in Zana 1999: viii). She received the Sakharov Prize for Freedom of Thought in 1996 from the European Parliament, an award she collected in 2004 upon her release from prison.

Zana and Güzel are considerably different, but their stories are presented in a remarkably similar manner and intersect at many points. In both works, the reader is exposed to several layers of commentary before reaching the words these women wrote while in prison. The cover of Zana's *Writings From Prison*, a collection of her personal letters and articles written from Ankara prison during her incarceration from 1994–2004, makes it clear that the book falls within the category of "human rights," literally spelling out the words "HUMAN RIGHTS AND DEMOCRACY" in capital letters. There are two forewords, written by Elena Bonner and Betty Williams respectively, and, like Güzel's book, Zana's story unfolds backwards in time. Elena Bonner, Andre Sakharov's widow and founder of Andre Sakharov Institute for Peace, is the author of the first preface (Zana 1999). Bonner pays homage to Zana as a political activist and a woman. Zana, she writes, was born in 1961 in a small village and is married to Mehdi Zana, a much older man and former mayor of Diyarbakir, who introduced her to political activism. At fifteen, she gave birth to her first child. When she was twenty and pregnant with her second child, her husband was arrested (Bonner in Zana 1999: vii). Bonner's foreword emphasizes Zana's role as a mother and a wife and the plight of her children and family due to her imprisonment (Ibid.: viii–ix). In March 2003, Zana herself told a Turkish court that she was a woman first, then a mother and then a politician; she did not mention the word wife (Kürkçü 2003). Bonner also includes a letter she wrote to Hillary Clinton regarding Zana and the hunger strike supporting her. However, Bonner ends her foreword with a plea much like Helena Bamber did in the foreword for Güzel. She asks the reader to think about what he or she can do to hasten the day that the entire Zana family can celebrate a birthday together. Both texts emphasize that these women were in prison for their beliefs. While Bamber connects Güzel to other tortured political prisoners across the world, Bonner links Zana to other families separated by oppressive regimes.

In her 1999 foreword to Zana's book, Betty Williams, a Nobel Peace Laureate and the Founder and President of World Center of Compassion for Children, emphasizes the role of women in bringing peace to their communities. She calls the readers, men and women alike, to listen when women raise their voices in courage and determination to announce a gentle but firm commitment to change, to doing things differently, to exposing the insanity of war and all forms of violence (Williams in Zana 1999: xi). Both forewords emphasize the fact that Zana is a woman, a wife and a mother.

Then the reader encounters two letters written by prominent men in the international political arena. The first letter by John Edward Porter, a member of the US Congress, nominates Leyla Zana for the Nobel Peace Prize. This section includes a list of other prominent international politicians who supported Leyla Zana's nominations for the Nobel Peace Prize in 1998. The second letter, by François Mitterrand, is a reply to Zana in which he tells her that the European Union is aware of her situation and will do what it can to help her. These letters are followed by the preface to the French edition by Claudia Roth, President of the European Parliament Greens Group, also written in 1995. Roth emphasizes Zana's role as an activist and the price she has paid for her political stance. She writes about the first time she met Zana, in 1988, who was at work despite the fact that she had been bruised and beaten by the police for participating in a protest. She talks about Zana's courage in the face of adversity but also her separation from her children (Roth in Zana 1999: xvii–xxi).

Finally, a biographical piece about Zana frames her political activism in terms of her origins. This piece does not have a date or an author. Here we find out that at fifteen and with very little formal schooling she was married against her will to her father's cousin, a man twenty years her senior. Her son Rona was born in 1976, within a year of her marriage. That year her husband was elected the mayor of Diyarbakir, the largest city in Southeastern Anatolia with a large Kurdish population. The 1980 military coup brought about many changes. Political and individual freedoms were limited due to national security concerns. Her husband was arrested and sentenced to thirty years in prison. While traveling from prison to prison she learned Turkish and managed to take her high-school equivalency test. Her first political concerns were related to women. She founded and chaired a women's group and she worked for the Diyarbakir branch of the Human Rights Association. In 1988, she was held, beaten and tortured by security forces. The narrative takes us from her arrest to her many awards and the prolongation of her sentence in 1998 for her contribution to an article published in the HADEP[4] bulletin. At the time her book was published, like Güzel, Zana was still in prison.

The readers cannot but ask why they must go through twenty-seven pages authored by six different contributors before they get to Zana's words. Apart from the fact that each text is authored by a well-known figure demonstrating Zana's importance—especially for the reader who may not know anything about Zana or the Kurds—each text also links her to a wider network of women's organizations, human rights organizations and international politics. The biographical piece is also necessary because Zana's is not a traditional autobiography: it begins with an act of verbal violence perpetrated by the very people who are supposed to be her colleagues. Zana had worked with women's organizations before she was elected to Parliament. She was shocked at the level of sexism among the men of her own progressive political party. When she tried to speak, she was told to "Shut up!" She had to point out that she had been elected by twice as many votes as her male counterparts and that she had just as much a right to speak as they did, before she could proceed.

Güzel and Zana discovered that they were at a disadvantage not just in society at large because of their political beliefs, but even among their own communities because of their gender. In Zana's first page we feel her frustration at first being told to "shut up and let the men speak" by a man known as a progressive and a democrat in her own political party. She simply wants to be treated as an equal by her own party members and even this requires much effort and struggle. The biographical piece allows the reader to contextualize this interaction in a regional framework and elucidates Zana's emphasis on gender and on being a woman first.

[4] HADEP is the Turkish acronym for the People's Democracy Party founded in 1994. HADEP made The Kurdish Question a debate issue as its first political act.

The section of the text written by Zana herself is a collection of articles on diverse topics and various letters. In her articles, we read her political rhetoric. We see clearly where she stands on the situation of the Kurds in Turkey, as well as her hopes for the future of Kurds and Turks. There is very little of the personal or private in these works. In her first article, "Speaking Out", she describes her inauguration moment in the parliament as a little Kurdish peasant girl encountering an imposing group of decorated generals. Then she tells us in her own words about the path leading to her international contacts, the attempts on her life and finally her imprisonment. She tells us that her fragmented book is a modest contribution to the cause of women. She calls on Kurdish women to "Speak out!", to speak freely, to take a decisive step forward on the road to freedom (Zana 1999: 7). In her article on diversity, she vehemently argues for the individual and the preservation of language, culture and identity. She argues that without the individual there cannot be a universal. In the article entitled "Taslima Nasrin"[5] Zana argues for a sisterhood of women oppressed by interpretations of monotheistic religious texts by men. She suggests that all women suffer the consequences of patriarchy and that a few token women cannot change the established order. "Facing the Death Penalty" is her challenge to the world to take action against oppression and injustice. Here Zana points out the contradiction in being condemned as a separatist for talking about the Kurds even though two prior Turkish presidents had acknowledged the Kurds' existence. "On Trial for Being a Kurd" allows the author to emphasize the need for a resolution to Turkish-Kurdish relations. She calls on the world to look beyond Turkey's important geographic location and challenges the world to encourage Turkey to become more democratic. Her final article, "Before the Turkish Inquisition", articulates her refusal to defend herself to a court set up by a military government when neither her voters nor "institutions that symbolize the public, democratic conscience of the civilized world find the court incompatible with the principles of the rule of law and of democratic life" (Zana 1999: 24–25). In all of these

[5] Taslima Nasrin was born in 1962 in what is now Bangladesh. She received a medical degree in 1984 and began to practice as a gynaecologist. She gained worldwide fame and prominence as an author. Her works were highly critical of fundamentalism and traditional societies. Her criticism of Islam and its treatment of women led to her receiving many death threats and a life in exile.

articles, her concern is the situation of Kurds, the sorry state of democracy in Turkey and the situation of women. Even in the final article, written at a time when she may have been facing death, she is hopeful that there will come a day when Kurds and Turks will be able to live together with mutual respect.

The first three letters are written to prominent French women. The first two are written to Danielle Mitterrand, whom she calls "mother," thus revealing their close relationship, and the third letter is written to Ségolène Royal, a prominent French politician. In all three letters she maintains pressure on France when it comes to the Kurdish issue, and she is grateful to France for seeing to it that she is not tortured in prison. After a night in dungeon-like conditions, Zana is brought to a crowded ward for common criminals. She demands to be taken out of that ward and ends up in a solitary cell where she can read and write. She credits the pressure brought upon Turkey by France and the European Union for her move to a solitary cell. In describing the prison conditions, she cannot help but reveal the sympathy she feels for the guards: these women cannot make ends meet, and Zana shares her dinner with them. In fact, she spends most of her time with these two women.

In two letters, we find the mother who misses her children and yearns for more information about their daily lives. These touching letters were written in response to letters her children had sent her and warned them not to follow the same path as her. Although Zana is a woman who has not hesitated to cause trouble for the men in her community or the Turkish government, she advises her daughter not to do the same. Zana, who has put her political goals above all else, including a peaceful life, good health, and physical comfort, advises her son to enjoy his life. "You live only once", she writes (Zana 1999: 48). In her letter to her close friend and exiled Kurdish intellectual Kendal Nezan, she reiterates how much she misses her children. She asks him to send her news of them because she is not able to get any herself. In this letter, we are even permitted to see her genuine affection for her husband, whose visits lift her spirits. In prison, she survives because of her dreams and her visitors.

While her letters to heads of state and important organizations reveal her public persona, her dedication to the Kurdish cause and her fight for women who have been doubly punished for being Kurdish and female, it is in her letters to her friends and family that we understand the depth of her suffering for being separated from her family and especially her children. The question of why she is not with her children, especially when the Turkish government offers to release her from prison early for medical reasons, haunts her. This question faces all parents who choose a life of political activism. What is honorable: being a nurturing, caring parent or a political activist? Zana's stand is that being a political activist is a good role model for her children. In trying to improve the world for all children, she is being a nurturing mother for them all.

Conclusion

Asiye Güzel and Leyla Zana paid a heavy price for voicing their political opinions. They both suffered torture, spent years in Turkish prisons, and became poster women for humanitarian organizations. Yet their books are as much about patriarchy and sexism as they are about the right to some basic freedoms such as thought and speech. *Asiye's Story* and *Writings from Prison* are also very specifically about gender-based oppression, which the authors face at the hands of both those who oppose and those who share their political convictions.

The battle against this particular brand of patriarchy is not one that will be won any time soon. In June 2007, the Turkish prime Minister, Recep Tayyip Erdoğan asked a highly esteemed constitutional lawyer to form a commission to draft a new constitution. The new constitution, which would replace the 1982 constitution drawn up by the military, is to be "civilian" and "democratic" (White 2007: 430). A draft that was leaked to the media revealed that a clause that ensures the equality for women is to be eliminated and replaced with a description of women, children, the elderly and infirm as a vulnerable group in need of special protection (Ibid.). Thus it is not surprising that both books suggest emphatically that what is needed in Turkey is for each individual regardless of gender, ethnicity or political conviction to be treated with respect and dignity as equally worthy citizens whether in the house or in the public space.

Bibliography

Amnesty International. 2003. "Media Briefing: Turkey: End Sexual Violence against Women in Custody".

Gorman, Anthony. 2005. "In Her Aunt's House: Women in Prison in the Middle East", *International Institute for Asian Studies Newsletter* 39, December 7.

Güzel, Asiye. 2003. *Asiye's Story*. Trans. Richard McKane. London: Saqi Books.

Haeri, Shahla. 1999. "Women's Body, Nation's Honor: Rape in Pakistan" in Asma Afsaruddin (ed.) *Hermeneutics and Honor: Negotiating Female "Public Space" in Islamicate Societies*. Cambridge: Harvard University Press, 55–69.

International Centre for Prison Studies. 2007. "Prison Brief for Turkey". http://www.kcl.ac.uk/depsta/law/research/icps/worldbrief/wpb_country.php?country=119 accessed on 30 October 2008.

International PEN. 1948. *Charter*. http://www.internationalpen.org.uk/internationalpen/index.cfm?objectid=E9B6DCB1–E0C4–ED84–0D36261F33550103 accessed on 30 October 2008.

Kürkçü, Ertuğrul. 2003. "Defiance Under Fire: Leyla Zana: Prisoner of Conscience" *Amnesty International Magazine* (Fall).

Schaffer, Kay and Sidonie Smith. 2004. "Conjunctions: Life Narratives in the Field of Human Rights Biography" in *Biography* 27(1):15–17.

Weidman, Amy. 2003. "Beyond Honor and Shame: Performing Gender in the Mediterranean" in *Anthropological Quarterly* 76(3): 519–530.

White, Jenny. 2007. "The Ebbing Power of Turkey's Secularist Elite" in *Current History* (December).

Zana, Leyla. 1999. *Writings from Prison*. Cambridge, MA: Blue Crane Books.

PART III

REFUSALS, RESISTANCES AND PROTESTS

11

THE VICTIM'S TALE IN SYRIA

IMPRISONMENT, INDIVIDUALISM, AND LIBERALISM

Sune Haugbolle

Political prisoners and prison narratives have, since the period of intense political and social debate of 2000–2001 known as the Damascus Spring, become a *cause célèbre* for Syrian intellectuals, and a central issue for the civil society movement (*harakat al-mujtama' al-madani*) for political liberalisation in one of the Middle East's most authoritarian regimes. Through autobiographical writings, films, websites, reports and social work, intellectuals and activists aim to break the silence over the Syrian state's often abhorrent treatment of its own citizens, and of its political opposition in particular.[1] This chapter examines the political and cultural field of imprisonment in Syria. I argue that prison stories exemplify a correlation between the politics of memory, human rights and democracy that is changing the meaning of individualism and liberalism in contemporary Arab politics. Ex–prisoners use the realm of memory as a form of cultural resistance, a Prometheus-like metaphor for the assertion of self in the face of external constraints, and in so doing produce a focus on the body and individual suffering (Carnochan 1995) that seeks to separate the individual life story from

[1] The interviews were conducted in Damascus in May and June 2007, with the generous support of the Council for British Research in the Levant.

the collectivistic tropes that dominate traditional narratives of Syrian and other Arab forms of nationalism. Their stories and activism can therefore be read as a renegotiation of individual and collective suffering, heroism and victimisation that has implications in politics across the Middle East, but also as an indicator of the troubled interplay between international human rights discourse and the complexities of activism on the ground in Arab countries.

Politics of the Abstract Spectacle

Bashar al-Asad has been a disappointment to those who initially touted him as a reformist president. The Damascus Spring has been followed by several crackdowns on freedom of speech and association, and civil society today is squeezed to breaking point. Despite radical changes in media and technology, the conditions for public discourse in Syria continue to be structured by tacit fear of incarceration and torture. State violence in Syria is, as Frank Graziano has written about Junta violence in Argentina, "ever present in its absence, vague but insistent, never completed nor resolved, an endless, ephemeral, indefinable, uncertain torture" (Graziano 1992: 73). When reduced to rumours and whispers, the stories of victims actually function as parts of the punitive system by ensuring that an abstract sense of fear hangs over the heads of citizens like the Sword of Damocles. Rumours of violence render the public both 'audience,' "because it 'witnesses' the abstract spectacle of the detention centers, [and] 'actor' because its status as audience—however passive it may appear—is a function integral to the efficacy of the spectacle by which power is being generated" (Graziano 1992: 76). In this way, the knowledge that not just punishment, but cruelty is taking place establishes the power relationship meant to be produced by subjugation of subjects (Humphrey 2002: 91). The uncertainty at the same time terrorises the population and involves it as "silent witnesses," complicit in the perpetuation of violence and repression. As Lisa Wedeen has pointed out in her well-known study of spectacle and domination, the Syrian regime is powerful not because it controls and censors the public realm but because it has disciplined its people to act as if they believed and supported every word that is said. This politics of "as if" has created a public sphere full of ambiguity, where the truth that is trumpeted cannot be publicly questioned but only mimicked or tolerated, and the truth that is obvious to most cannot find public expression (Wedeen 1999: 1–31). The resulting pollution of language, aesthetics and common sense was very pronounced during the rule of Hafiz al-Asad but has become less overtly ridiculous and propagandistic under Bashar. However, even if dialogue and occasional critique have been allowed, the regime's grip on power cannot be challenged, and those who try still risk intimidation or arrest (Becker 2006).[2]

Since the 1970s, Syrian artists and intellectuals have sought to subvert this reality of unspoken fear, violence and self-policing in books, plays and films.[3] Their cultural production is full of frustrated, self-censoring individuals (Cooke 2007). It reflects a system of obedience, deterrence and discipline which ultimately depends on raw monopoly of violence and the extra-judicial exercise of institutions of incarceration. This system is dehumanising because it produces participation. Whereas cultural resistance traditionally approaches imprisonment in allegorical form, the new genre of prison memoirs seeks to redress the regime's monopoly over the interpretation of national history by turning illicit speech into public expression and openly acknowledging the crimes committed by the Syrian regime, both in the present and in the past. In particular, they aim to break longstanding taboos surrounding the Islamist and leftist rebellion between 1976 and 1982 that left thousands dead and imprisoned.[4] In the wake of the conflict, at the height of political oppression in the 1980s, Syria held as many as ten thousand political prisoners. Most were released during the 1990s as the regime sought to rely on less overtly discriminating means of domination. This opening concurred with an international trend in the early 1990s, when imprisonment gradually came to be seen as a politically expensive means of repression. In an era dominated by human rights

[2] For the most up-to-date assessment of the human rights situation in Syria and particularly political imprisonment, see http://www.shrc.org.

[3] Syrian writers whose work tackles imprisonment include Faraj Bayqadar, May al-Hafiz, Haditha Murad and Hasiba 'Abd al-Rahman. In theatre, the plays of Walid Ikhlassi, Sa'adallah Wannus, Muhammad al-Maghut and Mamduh 'Adwan all deal with trials and freedom of speech, just as the films of Nabil al-Malih, 'Umar Amiralay, Ussama Muhammad and Muhammad Malas. Most of these artists operate within Syria, which has fostered an often symbolist artistic language designed to circumvent state censors (Cooke 2007; Salti 2006).

[4] For an explicit discussion of collective memories of 1976–82, see Haugbolle 2008.

discourse, it became hard to imprison individuals, particularly famous intellectuals, without being labelled a pariah state. Instead, many repressive regimes through the 1990s replaced political imprisonment with other, less visible forms of punishment and repression (Neier 1995: 379). Since 2001, Iraq, Guantanamo, and anti–terror legislation have undermined the alleged Western moral high ground and universal standard for human rights by putting national security before basic human rights. Several Arab states have observed this normative turn, some undoubtedly with a certain glee. Hence the days are practically gone when singular cases of imprisonment would urge international action. Western political and economic interests in the Middle East have become too intricate to allow a foreign policy based on ethical or moral concerns. This was perhaps always true but became evident after 2001. Today it is only too easy for Syria to continue incarcerating prisoners of conscience.

Despite the general feeling of *plus ça change* in Bashar al-Asad's Syria, some things have indeed changed. Human rights organisations inside and outside Syria now monitor and document violations.[5] Testimonies by ex–prisoners have also been published in Jordan and Lebanon. The Beirut Press in particular has become a refuge for Syrian writers and several testimonies have appeared in an-Nahar and other Lebanese newspapers. Furthermore, Lebanon has, since the end of Syrian control over Lebanon in 2005 seen an increased focus on the plight of Lebanese prisoners in Syrian prisons. As a whole, these narratives form a political field and a multi–vocal counter-discourse of memory that allows us to gauge what used to remain shrouded in fear and rumours: the Syrian prison experience.

Imprisonment

A Syrian who enters the prison gates will already have an idea of what awaits him. Details of the brutal conduct of prison guards and police circulate in Syria and are the subject of stories and even jokes (Wedeen 1999: 120–129). He or she will know that some political prisoners share overcrowded, smelly cells with regular criminals, while others are kept in confinement and rarely allowed the sight of day. Many are

[5] See http://hrw.org/english/docs/2006/01/18/syria12231.htm, http://web.amnesty.org/library/eng-syr/index, http://www.hrassy.org/english/reports.htm, http://www.shrc.org.uk/default.aspx.

beaten, burned, whipped, given electric shocks or sexually assaulted during interrogation, and he will have heard of some of the methods with evocative nicknames like "the German Chair," "the Chicken" and "the Tyre". Even outside the torture chambers, prison life is hard. He or she may have heard that conditions in some prisons, like the Saydnaya Prison close to Damascus, have improved in the last couple of years.[6] But even in "modernised" prisons food rations are still sparse, and there is little heating in cells. At least he or she will take heart from the fact that prisoners often form bonds of friendships to help and support each other and keep up their spirits in the face of uncertainty. Those who succumb to depression quickly wither in the gruelling circumstances.[7]

Reports by Syrian and international human rights organisations confirm that confinement, torture, disillusion, humiliation and, conversely, moments of solidarity and hope, are all typical ingredients in a prisoner's ordeal.[8] However, the image of the confined prisoner closed upon himself and his entrapment fails to capture the collective consequences of individual suffering. There is another prison, the prison of fear, that permeates daily life and touches family and friends of the imprisoned. More generally, there is the prison of living in a restrictive society. Four people, the leader of the Communist Party-Political Bureau[9] Riyadh al-Turk, journalist Yassin al-Haj Salih, writer Faraj Bayrqadar and Beirut-based journalist Muhammad Ali al-Atassi, have made particular efforts to lift the veil from the Syrian prison. Al-Atassi's text *The Other Prison*, which appeared in an-Nahar in July 2004, is an attempt to come to terms with the existential and social effects of imprisonment (al-Atassi 2004c). For that, he chooses a collective narrative form. The writer is at once a "we" of all Syrian prisoners of conscience and their families—many of whom he has met or whose narratives he has read—and, more subdued, an "I" whose personal experience of growing up with a father in prison shines through the text. By focussing on the combined effect of physical and psychological torture, he achieves a synthesis of the torturous effects of imprisonment in a repressive political system. To begin with, al-Atassi

[6] See http://www.hrassy.org/english/english/sednayaprisonreport.doc.

[7] For prison conditions before 1991, see (Human Rights Watch 1991). For conditions today, see the webpages listed at the end of this article.

[8] See in particular www.dchrs.com.

[9] Splinter group of the Syrian Communist Party founded in 1974.

asks a very difficult question: "Can we understand the experience of being a prisoner without ever being in a prison cell?" Probably not, but we can approach the effects of extensive unlawful imprisonment by relating the details of those who have survived it and, like al-Atassi, have the courage to talk about it. Through his texts and other narratives of imprisonment we can construct a typology of the prison experience in Syria.

How does an imprisonment begin? Usually with threats, fear, hiding, and sometimes schemes to avoid the attention of the omnipresent *mukhabarat*. Being a member of the wrong political organisation is often enough. The moment that seals one's fate, the point of no return when the prisoner is captured, is a recurrent scene in prison narratives. One account published in 1998 by Hiba Dabbagh, a woman from Hama who was imprisoned as a young student in 1980, is simply titled *Khamsa Daqiqa wa Hasab* (Just Five Minutes), with reference to the five minutes that her interrogation was meant to take.[10] She ended up spending nine years in prison. Another example is the poet and member of the League of Communist Action[11] Faraj Bayrqadar, whose short essay about his imprisonment *A Father To the Point of Tears* was published in the journal *al-Jadid* in 2006 (Bayrqadar 2006). Bayrqadar knew that he was under suspicion. In order not to arouse attention, he taught his four-year old daughter only to call him Baba, but he let her keep a note with his real name hidden in her little suitcase, fearing that she might otherwise never know who he was in case he was to be arrested. One day in 1987 the suitcase was stolen, the name found inside, and Bayrqadar apprehended. His essay relates how he struggles to keep in touch with his daughter through his imprisonment. During the first five years he is denied access to visitors. Later he meets with her and discovers that she remembers him and adores him. His daughter is his consolation. At the same time, he feels:

> as if there is nothing left but absence, and I, like any prisoner, am unable to accept comfort.
>
> It seems to me that language is emptiness [...]
>
> My daughter is now eleven years old, and I have yet to experience the full extent of fatherhood (Bayrqadar 2006).

[10] The book can be read in full on http://www.shrc.org.uk/data/aspx/010BOOKS.aspx.

[11] Small Communist splinter group formed in 1980.

Imprisonment disfigures individuals through extended absence from the ones they love and leaves them with a sense of broken personal history, wasted time and emptiness. To wait is an active verb, as they quickly discover. Uncertainty forms part of the psychological torture designed to break political prisoners. It can kill an individual not to know where he is going. In equal measures, it affects the happiness, dignity and cohesion of their families. Al-Atassi describes how the absence of the beloved seeps into daily routines and poisons the joy of life; how contact with the imprisoned is sometimes made impossible and the link therefore severed; how photos of family members become sorry replacements for daily contact and create illusions that sometimes clash with reality when the prisoner is finally released; and how eagerly awaited visits are supervised and recorded by prison guards and therefore bereft of intimacy. Political prisoners feel robbed of their very humanity, to the point that it becomes difficult for them to believe that they are being held by fellow humans. One woman in al-Atassi's text relates how her punisher receives a phone call in the midst of torturing her:

> The master punisher takes the handset and his voice transforms into one of loving whispers: 'How are you my son? I won't be late. What do you want me to bring home, my darling son?'
>
> The bloodied woman on the floor wakes up to the gentle whisper of the master punisher, and she thinks to herself, "Oh my God, he is human like us!" (al-Atassi 2004c).

The theme of humanity and inhumanity of prisoners and guards alike recurs in many narratives. Some, like the Jordanian Muhammad Hammad who was imprisoned in Tadmur Prison[12] and wrote about it in his book *Tadmur shahid wa mashhud* (Palmyra A Witness and Witnessed), see their masters as "devils" or at least representatives of an inhumane system.[13] Others, like Bayrqadar, pity their torturers. Even when they tortured him, he knew that they were forced by circumstances and he often felt that they lessened his suffering if they were left unsupervised. In approaching an explanation for their behaviour, Bayrqadar, interviewed by al-Atassi, relates:

[12] The most feared prison in Syria described by one ex–prisoner as "Syria's Guantanamo." Conversation in Damascus, 22 May, 2007.

[13] The book has been published in whole on the Syrian Human Rights Committee's webpage, http://www.shrc.org.uk/data/aspx/005BOOKS.aspx.

When I returned to my solitude and had the chance to reflect and contemplate, I felt sorry for them because they [the torturers] had become sick; their humanity had been destroyed. When it comes down to it, they are part of my people and they are destroying my people. They destroy the prisoner, they destroy the executioner, and even the citizen outside the prison is destroyed, too. Today after my release, I do not hate any torturers who were simple soldiers. But I despise some of the officers, and I'm not willing to even deal with them (al-Atassi 2004b).

The goal of al-Turk as a politician, Bayrqadar as a writer, and al-Atassi as a journalist is to restore humanity, not just to the victims, but to the whole of the society which has produced, lives with and in some sense tolerates, the regime. These men represent the liberal, secular Left and are all affiliated to some degree with the Civil Society Movement that emerged in the late 1990s. Their memories are inscribed in that political project and are not merely memories for the sake of personal redemption. They are also the thoughts of intellectuals, who are able to step back from their experience and analyse it in structural terms. In fact, Riyadh al-Turk believes that it was this ability to see his own suffering in a larger perspective and force himself not to think that got him through fourteen years of detention. He even claims to have minimised visits from his family in order to avoid facing the painful reality of being restricted from the outside world. Instead he devoted himself to Zen-like routines such as painting prayer beads made of dried peas. Another former prisoner related to me how he and others, forced by necessity, began to talk and think about prison life as a "natural" part of their struggle. They even invented a word for living in prison, *yustahbis*, which can be translated as "doing prison" or "prisoning."[14] For al-Turk, this steely determination and austerity became not just a tactic to get himself through imprisonment or a defence of his political cause, but a fight for humanity as such:

During my first imprisonment, I was consciously strong. I faced barbaric conditions ready to die as though I were in a battle. Why is a person strong if not to defend his humanity? No one in history has stayed strong in conditions like that for the sake of something inhuman. I didn't see myself as a victim [sic] and I didn't look for anyone's sympathy. In prison, I paid the price of sticking to my positions, even if that price was harsh and unjust (al-Atassi 2004b).

Bayrqadar, very much the poet, adopted the opposite tactic. To him it was the ability to remain sensitive and emotionally alert that pre-

[14] Interview in Damascus 22 May, 2007.

served his humanity. Getting his hands on scraps of paper to write down poetry, memorising it and passing it on to fellow prisoners, not collaborating or disclosing information about his party: these things gave him strength. He allowed himself to cry, but only in solidarity with the suffering of other inmates. In front of his torturers, he remained calm and collected, apart from during sessions of electrical torture when he would howl like an animal (al-Atassi 2004a).

Individualism

The imputed heroism comes out clearly in the essays and poetry of Faraj Bayrqadar, but can be found to a lesser extent in most accounts.[15] These are survivors' narratives, the stories of men who endured imprisonment, resisted collaboration, and even escaped the fear of the abstract spectacle that forces many other ex-prisoners to silence their memories. They are victims, but victims who write back. The question remains: what about the rest, the countless "subalterns" who have less strength to resist with, and whose voices only resound anonymously in the reports of human right groups? Their fate is the norm around which these heroic narratives are written. Bayrqadar relates how many of his fellow inmates collaborated in order to escape torture. Others broke down or perished altogether (al-Atassi 2004a). But even their stories are constructed in a heroic language of victimisation and the promise of freedom. The belief in changing politics and healing society by resisting the pollution of language is profound. As the prominent writer and ex-prisoner Yassin al-Haj Salih has put it, all the different aspects of the prison experience should be brought into light, "until nothing remains unknown or overburdened with suppressed memory."[16]

The wish to tell the whole story of crimes in the past is a powerful motivation for retribution and remembering, but also a rather unrealistic notion. The fact remains that the memories we, as outside observers, receive, are intellectual representations of a much larger predicament. State repression has created an inside-outside dialectic, which means that intellectual discourse, powerful and representative as it may be, is

[15] Bayrqadar's poetry has received some attention in the West and is currently being translated into English. For a collection of poetry that deals explicitly with imprisonment, see (Bayrqadar 2006b).

[16] al-Haj Salih, Yassin, in *Mulhaq an-Nahar* 27 July, 2004.

relegated to a transnational counter-public that only overlaps with a small and rather elitist Syrian public. Mass mediation in Syria continues to be dominated by regime representations of national identity and history. A significant part of Ba'thist nationalist propaganda revolves around depictions of Syria's modern history that highlight the qualities of Hafiz al-Asad who drove the country forward, and of his son who is continuing his line. While official rhetoric generally celebrates Asad and his sons Basil and Bashar as individuals, the Syrian people mostly appear as an amorphous entity or as stereotypical Stalinist-inspired peasant folklore and other imaginaries of "the people." An idea of "the Syrian collective family" is established through endlessly repeated narratives of sacrifice and familial loyalty to Asad. Significantly, these narratives rarely stray from abstractions. In the fifty or sixty key sentences[17] that have been repeated endlessly since the 1970s, individual suffering is by definition heroic and heroically offered in sacrifice for the greater good of the nation—resisting Zionism and imperialism, regaining the Golan Heights and uniting the Syrian people and the Arab nation—while obedience and compliance are construed as natural givens for Syrians as acts that confer their membership of the national family (Wedeen 1999: 32–66). This lofty idealism in fact means little to anyone anymore, in an era when socialist, pan-Arabist ideology formulated in the 1950s and 60s has been all but emptied of meaning and replaced by sheer power politics, in Syria and in the region as a whole. Still, the collective illusion—the politics of "as if"—remains intact for now.

Individualism is a common response to failed collectivism, as developments in post-Communist societies have shown. In Syria, individualism from the late 1990s onwards found expression in a liberal secularism that was pursued politically during the Damascus Spring. As I will discuss later, this political project was killed in its infancy. Instead resistance has been relegated to bits of disjointed action and discourse. It is not wholly impossible to resist the Ba'thist fabrication of history and the present with action and words, but stoic heroism undeniably has a different face in Damascus than in a Stockholm parlour, as one Damascus-based dissident told me. This, he stressed, was not said to belittle those who leave, but to point out the different social

[17] According to a former Syrian official interviewed by Lisa Wedeen (Wedeen 1999: 46).

contexts of internally and externally produced resistance.[18] Instead of fleeing the country, this veteran writer had chosen to stay and continue his work despite the inevitable and recurrent confrontations with the *mukhabarat*. Having spent most of his youth behind bars, he, along with many other activists from his generation, feels he has nothing to lose, and continues to defy the regime by publishing critical articles in Lebanese and Arab newspapers. On one occasion an article he wrote in al-Hayat really incensed the leadership. "One more like that, and you're back in jail," an apparatchik told him to his face. Instead of shutting up, he described the incident in his next column in a slapstick fashion that made the officer look like the semi–literate goon he was. To the writer's surprise, the *mukhabarat* actually left him alone after that.

If dissidents want to make space for themselves they can either create public awareness of their presence and hope that it suffices to protect them, or they can observe the rules of the regime. In order to work with human rights in Syria it is acutely important to know the red lines of acceptable behaviour. As one young female activist put it, those red lines are essentially drawn between politics and civil society.[19] Any activity that tends towards political organisation—especially if it has an Islamist character—will be curbed, while activism as "chatter" in limited milieus can be monitored, co-opted and therefore tolerated. NGOs under Bashar have been allowed to publish reports on human rights issues, including the plight of former prisoners, simply because they are not deemed politically dangerous.[20] Similarly, the regime has adopted a tactic of allowing "commissioned criticism" by what Miriam Cooke calls "court jesters," particularly manageable artists and intellectuals who unwittingly become showcases for the regime's ostensible tolerance towards its critics (Cooke 2007: 72, 92). For said young activist, the task was to circumvent this de-politicisation of dissent by being "more than just discourse" to current and former prisoners living with the predicament of their experience. In her work helping the families of prisoners, she made informal contacts with the affected, "by building trust, like an anthropologist," and then used these networks to facilitate financial help and legal advice. She would go to the

[18] Interview with Syrian human rights activists in Damascus 22 May, 2007.
[19] Interview with former prisoner in Damascus 20 May, 2007.
[20] See http://www.dchrs.com/english/show.php?cat=article&id=2.

State Security Court in Damascus and mingle with people waiting outside the trial. Their first reaction would often be sceptical, but later they welcomed her help.

> They really need it! But they have no idea. People come from the countryside, especially the Islamists, and they don't know that there are any organisations, they haven't even heard about human rights! They don't know why they are in prison, and they don't know how to deal with the trial. They don't know their rights. And they need the support (...) The most important thing is relations with people, with victims here. But to deal with people who don't even know what human rights are, who don't know their rights, don't know who you are, what you do... They know that something unfair happened to them, but they don't know why, they don't know why it's against the law, and that there are human rights organisations that can help them. They think it will harm them, because security tells them so. By dealing with them you can open windows in their minds, by dealing with them you educate them.

This quote clearly demonstrates the limited impact of human rights and civil society. Without a social base, intellectual interlocutors are indeed in danger of being "nothing more than just discourse" to the vast majority, and hence easy to ignore for the regime. This is neither their fault nor their responsibility. Rather, individualism, victimisation and heroism have become the dominant tropes of resistance as a result of the Ba'ath party's systematic destruction of political life in Syria. In the 1960s and 70s, members of the intellectual Left organised in unions and leftist parties sought to check the state's treatment of its citizens (Dam 1979; Lobmeyer 1995). After the opposition, many of whom later formed the backbone of the civil rights movement, were forced into prisons or subservience during the 1970s and 1980s, they gradually replaced their original political programme for civil rights with one for international human rights. Indeed, their experience of imprisonment was formative in helping them formulate a human rights agenda.[21]

This move from civil rights to human rights has wide-ranging implications for activism and for oppositional politics in general. In the international system established after World War II, civil rights are supposed to embody and spell out in the forms of laws the eternal Rights of Man (Arendt 1966: 293). When they fail to do so, the international community still lacks coherent mechanisms to protect individuals and groups. Since the end of the Cold War, international powers have legitimised diverse forms of intervention in national

[21] Interview with former prisoner in Damascus 23 May, 2007.

affairs with reference to universal human rights. Such instrumentalisation is problematic because human rights, as Talal Asad points out, are not universal, timeless, or otherwise "natural," but a secular system of thought which today has become entwined with the global ruling ideology of liberal democracy and capitalism (Asad 2003: 127–158). The conflation between liberalism, human rights and Western hegemony exposes human rights advocates in anti–hegemonic states like Syria to accusations of treason and makes it even harder for them to operate. Furthermore, as Laleh Khalili argues, human rights discourse can de-politicise and internationalise by putting the onus for action on outside forces (Khalili 2007: 36–37). When political groups are enticed or forced to give up petitioning the state that denies them their rights as individuals, civil rights become replaced by a discourse of human rights that envisage individuals as enfeebled victims and society as a public in need of assistance, but stripped of agency. In Syria, the symptom of this dynamic is a de-nationalised memory discourse crafted for most parts outside Syria and with little impact on the majority of the Syrian population.

Liberalism

Perhaps civil society could have grown into a mass movement. In 2000, when an atmosphere of new possibilities still reigned, Riyadh al-Turk met with Muhammad Ali al-Atassi in a filmed interview titled *Ibn al-'Am* (Cousin) that achieved wide circulation in Syria and Lebanon (al-Atassi 2001). In this short film, al-Turk elaborates on his prison experience. The film is crudely shot but very effectively conveys the ordeal of the man, his worn-out features and yet determined spirit. Sitting in his simple Damascus office, he slowly and often humorously recounts and reflects on the meaning of suffering and the hopes for change in Syria. This filmic image of the old veteran coming out and speaking out seemed to symbolise a time of openness and promise. After his release from prison, al-Turk had become a central figure in the increasingly vocal attempts to revitalise Syrian civil society in 1998 and 1999. These years saw a number of initiatives for the advancement of civil society and political freedoms, such as a declaration signed by Syrian filmmakers in 1999 which stressed that creativity is intrinsically linked to freedom. This was the beginning of the revitalisation of collective actions by intellectuals, which had been limited since the late

1970s.[22] Along with this collective movement also came a new sensibility to individual rights. The new activism gave rise to a whole new terminology: "citizen," "freedoms" and "participation," words imported from Western liberal lingo and now transplanted to the context of a long struggle for political freedom in Syria (Majid, 2005 #278: 121). Through truth telling of the individual ordeal, the political philosophy of the regime based on national unity and "popular" committees would be exposed as a failure that had undermined individual freedom. The goal was to radically change the political realm.

The Damascus Spring came to an abrupt end when its proponents crossed the red line between civil society and politics by calling on the Syrian leadership to withdraw from Lebanon and end the Ba'th Party's monopoly of power. After the publication of their second manifesto, the so-called "Declaration of the 1000" on 9 January, 2001, which included a sweeping critique of the regime, the newly opened salons and committees were gradually shut down and many of their members imprisoned (George 2003: chapter 3). The text called for sweeping changes in Syria designed to create "a society based on individual freedom, human rights and citizenship." At the same time, the Statement urged a national exercise of *travail de mémoire*. It stated that Syria needs to draw lessons from its past in order to move forward. In the same manner that the postcolonial state sought to distance itself from colonialism and its related values in the 1950s, the Syrian civil society movement in 2000–2001 created itself in opposition to the Ba'thist state and its values. By re-evaluating the state's practices of punishment, its negative influence on inter-sectarian relations and national security and economy, the signatories hoped that human rights and individual freedoms would emerge as common values which, all Syrians would agree, must never be superseded by "revolutionary legitimacy" or "national interests" (George 2003: 184).

The strategy of linking individual suffering to political reforms was not restricted to the secular civil society movement. During the same period, members of Syria's forbidden Islamist organisations have engaged in re-appropriation of the past. For the Muslim Brotherhood and other Islamist groups, the massacre in Hama in 1982, in which anywhere between ten and twenty thousand people were killed, has become a symbol of their subjugation under the Ba'th Party. At the

[22] Al-Atassi, Muhammad Ali, in *Mulhaq an-Nahar* 7 October, 2000.

same time, some secular human rights organisations have converged with Islamist sympathisers in efforts to shed light on Hama and on the mass arrests that followed it through the 1980s.[23] Their prison stories are strikingly similar to the secular ex-prisoners mostly discussed in this chapter. All focus on the individual body tortured by the state, and on the individual mind exiled, censured or otherwise restricted from expressing itself. They frame their victimisation in heroic tropes of survival, resistance and hope for a more humane political system in Syria that protects human rights and the rule of law.[24]

By killing off the civil society movement, the regime not only strangled a budding movement of liberal activism, it also stopped dead a possible collusion between Islamist and secular opposition groups. Ostensibly, it was the Jamal al-Atassi Forum's decision to read a statement by leader of the outlawed Muslim Brotherhood, Sadr al-Din al-Bayanuni that provoked its closure in May 2005, as the last such salon (Gambil 2006). Without the ability to organise, interaction between the two currents is today limited to personal contact, and such contacts are rare. Most prisons separate Islamist convicts from their secular inmates.[25] Once released, former prisoners replicate those patterns of socialisation. Islamists move in particular circles, while former prisoners of secular persuasion have their forums and informal support groups (Saleh 2006). Islamist and leftist ex-prisoners also have different historical experiences and collective memories. Many more Islamists have been killed and imprisoned, and their ideology is more fundamentally at odds with Ba'thist secularism. Whereas the Left is struggling to re-inscribe their suffering and struggle for democratic reform in the 1976–82 rebellion into national collective memory, the Muslim Brotherhood is attempting to come to terms with its own violence and the widely held notion, successfully promulgated by the regime, that the group attempted to create an Islamic state (Zisser 2005). The combined effect of these factors complicates a truly national alliance over a liberal project of truth telling and reform.

[23] In particular the Syrian Human Rights Committee and Damascus Centre for Human Rights Studies.

[24] For a closer analysis of Islamist memories, see Haugbolle 2008.

[25] Interview in Damascus, 23 May, 2007.

Conclusion

Telling the truth promises to revert the negative energy of victimisation and to create a language of hope and freedom that allows subjects to overcome their role as acted-upon victims. By undoing the state's appropriation of language, truth-telling cleanses the polluted language and imbues it with meaning that corresponds to lived experience. As Godwin Phelps has written in her study of storytelling, truth and reconciliation:

> In multiple ways, an oppressive regime appropriates and manipulates language to shatter the voices of victims and any unified voices of opposition. It uses the appropriated language to create itself as a state, to deny the worth of any who dares to oppose it, and to silence the populace. The misuse of language pollutes the land. Thus, for a "polluted" nation to give justice to its citizens, to cleanse itself, and to move forward without repression, it must take back for itself and its citizens the ability to use language. It must allow the victims, even empower them, to tell their own stories, to re-member by remembering (Phelps 2004: 50–51).

Such empowerment necessitates a civil society of interlocutors who represent and channel the experience of subaltern victims. However, truth-telling and civil society can become surrogates for democratisation if they allow people to formulate liberal agendas but not influence policy making. A polluted nation cannot be empowered to engage in critical memory work without first re-membering the broken body politic. Without a state that supports political pluralism and memory work, such an effort is forced to remain on the fringes of the public sphere, in civil society, or in a de-nationalised public of foreign books, newspapers, journals, reports and web pages. In 2000–2001, counter-hegemonic remembrance inspired a liberal political project aimed against the regime and its practices, a project which may have had the potential to unite Islamist and secular opposition groups. Today, that project has been reduced to individual efforts; brave people left with the Sisyphean task of piercing the silence in the hope that truth-telling may eventually contribute to the demise of authoritarianism in Syria.

Bibliography

al-Atassi, Muhammad Ali. 2001. *Ibn al-'Am* (Cousin). Syria. CD-Rom.

al-Atassi, Muhammad Ali. 2004a. "An Interview with the Syrian Poet Faraj Bayrqadar, Released after 14 Years of Detention" in *Al-Jadid* 10 (49).

al-Atassi, Muhammad Ali. 2004b. "Noted Former Syrian Prisoner Riyadh al-Turk Speaks Out of Life Inside Prison" in *Al-Jadid* 10 (49).

al-Atassi, Muhammad Ali. 2004c. "The Other Prison" in *Al-Jadid* 10 (49).

Asad, Talal. 2003. *Formations of the Secular*. Stanford: Stanford University Press.

Arendt, Hannah. 1966. *The Origins of Totalitarianism*. New York: Harcourt Brace Jovanovich.

Bayrqadar, F. 2006. "A Father to the Point of Tears" in *al-Jadid* 12 (54/55).

Bayrqadar, F. 2006b. *Khiyanat al-lugha wa al-samt*. Beirut: Dar al-Jadid.

Becker, Carmen. 2006. "Strategies of Power Consolidation in Syria under Bashar al-Asad: Modernising Control over Resources" in *Arab Studies Journal* XIII/XIV (1–2):65–91.

Carnochan, W. B. 1995. "The Literature of Confinement" in N. Morris and J. D. Rothman (eds.) *The Oxford History of the Prison*. Oxford: Oxford University Press; 381–406.

Cooke, Miriam. 2007. *Dissident Syria: Making official Arts Official*. Durham, NC: Duke University Press.

Dam, Nikolas van. 1979. *The Struggle for Power in Syria: Sectarianism, Regionalism and Tribalism in Politics*. London: Croom Held.

Gambil, Gary C. 2006. "Dossier: The Syrian Muslim Brotherhood" in *Mideast Monitor* April/May 2006, http://www.mideastmonitor.org/issues/0604/0604_2.htm.

George, Alan. 2003. *Syria: Neither Bread nor Freedom*. London: Zed.

Graziano, Frank. 1992. *Divine Violence: Spectacle, Psyhosexuality, and Radical Christianity in the Argentine "Dirty War"*. Oxford: Westview.

Haugbolle, Sune. 2008. "Imprisonment, Truth Telling and Historical Memory in Syria" in *Mediterranean Politics* 13(2).

Human Rights Watch. 1991. *Syria Unmasked: The Repression of Human Rights by the Asad Regime*. New Haven: Yale University Press.

Humphrey, Michael. 2002. *The Politics of Atrocity and Reconciliation: From Terror to Trauma*. London: Routledge.

Khalili, Laleh. 2007. *Heroes and Martyrs of Palestine: the Politics of National Commemoration*. Cambridge: Cambridge University Press.

Lobmeyer, Hans Günther. 1995. *Opposition und Widerstand in Syrien*. Hamburg: Deutches Orient-Institut.

Majid, Z. 2005. "Des Espoir à Damas" in *L'Orient-Express* Hors-Série, Hommage à Samir Kassir: 120–124.

Neier, Arieh. 1995. "Confining Dissent: The Political Prison" in Norval Morris and David J. Rothman, (eds.) *The Oxford History of the Prison*. Oxford: Oxford University Press; 350–380.

Phelps, Teresa Godwin. 2004. *Shattered Voices: Language, Violence, and the Work of Truth Commissions*. Philadelphia: University of Pennsylvania Press.

Saleh, Yassin al-Haj. 2006. "L'Univers des anciens prisonniers politiques en Syrie" in *La Revue des mondes musulmans et de la Méditerranée* 115–116: 249–265.

Salti, Rasha, ed. 2006. *Insights into Syrian Cinema: Essays and Conversations with Contemporary Filmmakers*. New York: Arte East.
Wedeen, Lisa. 1999. *Ambiguities of Domination—Politics, Rhetoric, and Symbols in Contemporary Syria*. Chicago: The University of Chicago Press.
Zisser, Eyal. 2005. "Syria, the Ba'ath Regime and the Islamic Movement: Stepping on a New Path?" in *The Muslim World* 95 (1): 43–65.

Web pages

Damascus Centre for Human Rights Studies: www.dchrs.com.
The Syrian Human Rights Committee: http://www.shrc.org.
The Human Rights Association in Syria: http://www.hrassy.org.
Human Rights Watch: http://hrw.org.
Amnesty International: http://web.amnesty.org.

12

SPECTACLES OF DEATH

DIGNITY, DISSENT, AND SACRIFICE IN TURKEY'S PRISONS

Banu Bargu

"I would rather live a day with dignity than a dishonorable life that lasts hundreds of years."[1]

"They will not be able to put even our corpses into the cells."[2]

"We have come to the point where death will speak, where our dead will speak."[3]

Turkey's Death Fast Struggle (2000–2007) began as a protest against the introduction of high security prisons, known as F Types. These

[1] Interview, 1 July 2005. Unless otherwise indicated, interviews involve participants of the Death Fast. Interviews were conducted in full confidentiality during June 2004–August 2005 in Turkey. No interview was carried out while an interviewee was imprisoned or on hunger strike. I am deeply indebted to Richard Bensel, Susan Buck-Morss, Michael Gasper, Merveh Mısırlı, Anna Terwiel, and the editors of this volume.

[2] Veysel Eroğlu, "Letter to Oral Çalışlar from Special Type Prison," 8 August 2000, private collection.

[3] Ali Nazik, "Letter to Oral Çalışlar from Sincan F Type Prison," 15 February 2001, private collection.

prisons were part of a disciplinary penal regime in which isolated confinement in cells would replace collective confinement in wards. The primary target of this regime was Turkey's large constituency of political prisoners.[4] Since the 1970s, political prisoners had transformed prison wards into self-governing communes through struggles that came to spearhead opposition to military rule after the 1980 coup d'état. In their large and crowded wards, political prisoners were segregated from those imprisoned for "common" crimes and voluntarily separated according to distinct political causes (such as Kurdish nationalism, Islamism, and socialism). Against the imminent threat of transition to the F Types, leftist prisoners prepared to defend their wards, where they lived a communism-in-practice, by forging their lives into weapons.

The central component of the movement was a hunger strike, launched on 20 October 2000. Over eight hundred militants, affiliated with three outlawed leftist parties, embarked on a path of self-starvation, destroying the precarious peace in the country's prisons not by a clamorous mutiny but by the silent refusal to eat (HRW 2001; TIHV 2001; TAYAD 2002).[5] On 19 November 2000, the hunger strike was converted into a "fast until death" and prisoners restricted their intake to sugary water and salt.[6] Initially, there was some dialogue between the government and prisoner representatives. Under pressure of public criticism and popular mobilizations outside prisons, the Minister of Justice announced a reprieve soliciting a wider consensus around the new prisons. Soon after this declaration, however, negotiations fell apart. On 19 December 2000, the state launched a coordinated security operation called "Return to Life" upon the prisons in resistance,

[4] At the time, Turkey had 9,642 political prisoners, corresponding to 13 per cent of the total prison population of 73,748 (Adalet Bakanlığı [hereafter AB] 2007a).

[5] The prisoners who initiated the hunger strike were parties to lawsuits connected to DHKP-C [Revolutionary People's Liberation Party-Front], TKP(ML)/TIKKO [Communist Party of Turkey (Marxist-Leninist)/Workers' and Peasants' Liberation Army of Turkey], and TKIP [Communist Workers' Party of Turkey].

[6] Prisoners also used Vitamin B1 (thiamin) to lessen the aftereffects of starvation in case the hunger strike was called off, but not to prolong the process of dying in case it was not called off. However, the first death occurred on 21 March, 2001—152 days into the strike (Interviews with physicians, 20 and 25 June; 1, 5, and 13 July 2005).

claiming thirty-two lives and forcibly relocating 942 prisoners to F Type prisons (HRW 2001; IHD 2001, 2002; TIHV 2001; Le Pennec and Eberhardt 2001; TAYAD 2002).[7]

In response to the state's televised display of power, the movement spread more widely. At its peak, around 1,500 militants with a dozen different leftist affiliations participated in the struggle. Beginning in May 2001, hunger strikers were discharged from prison *en masse*, either through the provisional suspension of their sentences or by presidential pardon, on grounds of their deteriorating health. While some ex–prisoners continued to fast in "resistance houses" located in urban shantytowns—the constituent spaces of the radical left—participation soon began to wane.[8] Meanwhile, instances of self-immolation and suicide attacks complemented the hunger strike. On 22 January 2007, the strike was finally called off after 2,286 consecutive days as a result of a rather minimal concession by the state that allowed a maximum of ten prisoners at a time to come together for social activities for up to ten hours per week in the new prisons (AB 2007b). While the spectacular performances of violence resulted in 122 casualties, hundreds of veterans impaired for life, and countless personal tragedies, high security prisons had become entrenched in Turkey's penal landscape.[9]

How may we understand these spectacles of sacrificial death instigated by F Type prisons? Why did prisoners resort to this radical strategy of protest, to making life itself a weapon? How did they interpret their own goals and actions? To pursue these questions, I rely upon oral narrations, prison letters, and written propaganda, collected as part of a political ethnography of the Death Fast Struggle (Bargu 2008). My argument is that the Death Fast had multiple significations, revealed by the diverse and, at times, contradictory interpretations held by its participants. The Death Fast's polyvalence stemmed from the central, yet equivocal status of the weaponization of life as its main strategy of political action. Although this movement ostensibly emerged as a circumscribed struggle against prison conditions, neither its demands, nor its aspirations were limited to prisons. On the contrary:

[7] At the time of the operation, 277 prisoners were on a "fast until death" while 802 prisoners were on hunger strike, totaling 1,079. After the operation, participation increased to 396 death fasters and 1,039 hunger strikers, totaling 1,435 (AB 2003).

[8] Interviews with relatives of death fasters, May 2005.

[9] Today, 60 per cent of Turkey's prison population is kept in security prisons.

as an act of resistance, the movement sought both to defend human dignity against cellular confinement, which it saw as a form of torture, and to articulate itself with the broader struggle for the deepening of democracy. As an act of war, the movement viewed itself as advancing the anti–capitalist struggle, demonizing the state as the representative of the class enemy. As an act of insurgent sacrifice, the movement launched an ideological offensive upon state sovereignty, puncturing its hegemony based on the sanctity of human life by the prisoners' fatal exodus from the existing order.

Demands of the Death Fast Struggle

The formal self-portrait of the movement helps illuminate its aspirations. According to the public declaration issued at the launch of the hunger strike, the central demand was the closing down of F Type prisons, which, political prisoners argued, were aimed at "breaking [them] body and soul."[10] The Turkish state sought to import the disciplinary penal regime practiced in Europe and the United States.[11] This project was modeled on controversial institutions such as Stammheim (Germany), H-Blocks (Northern Ireland), Marion (Illinois), Pelican Bay (California), Red Onion (Virginia), and Florence ADX (Colorado)—prisons subject to ongoing criticism (HRW 1997, 1999, 2000; Kurki and Morris 2001; Lutsky 2001; Mears and Watson 2006; Parenti 1999; Perkinson 1994).

The high security prison project involved building new prisons based on single or three-prisoner cells and converting wards in existing pris-

[10] Interviews, February 2005. For this declaration, see *Bağımsız Vatan* 2000: 13. A different declaration was signed by nine organizations (TIKB, MLKP, MLSPB, TDP, TKEP/L, TKP/ML, TKP/Kıvılcım, Devrimci Yol, and Direniş Hareketi), arguing that the hunger strike was prematurely launched without sufficient publicity (*Atılım* 2000). Despite initial disagreements, these organizations joined in the Death Fast after the state's security operation on 19 December 2000. Other disagreements, regarding the use of self-immolation and suicide bombing, the handling of negotiations, the decision to fast outside prisons, and, finally, the apposite timing to end the strike, tore the coalition apart. After May 2002, only two parties (DHKP-C and TKIP) continued the strike.

[11] For analyses of the disciplinary penal regime in these contexts, see Churchill and Vander Wall 1992; Immarigeon 1992; King 1999; Mears and Reisig 2006; Pizarro and Stenius 2004; Sparks, Bottoms, and Hay 1996; Ward and Werlich 2003.

ons into similar units for two to ten prisoners by architectural adjustments.[12] The new units (called "rooms" by state authorities, as opposed to "cells" to avoid the latter's pejorative connotations in the public imagination) would replace the dormitory wards that had hitherto characterized penal space, making not only collective living arrangements but also social relations in prisons extremely difficult, if not impossible. The Ministry of Justice praised these prisons as venues for establishing order and discipline, ensuring prisoner participation in modern rehabilitation programs, and solving the problems caused by overcrowding (such as lack of privacy, hygiene, and individual freedom). State authorities repeatedly denied that F Type prisons would entail abusive and inhumane practices of confinement and claimed that these institutions were in complete conformity with prison standards recommended by the United Nations and the European Council, as well as international human rights (TBMM 2000). Even though these prisons did include common social spaces for education, sports, and occupational training, access to these spaces was conditional on the prisoners' "successful" participation in rehabilitation programs and a "clean" file, free of infractions. Given political prisoners' behavioral patterns, these spaces were bound to remain more for display than for actual use, confirming prisoners' suspicions that F Type prisons were in fact intended for solitary confinement.

High security prisons were legislated through the 1991 Law for the Struggle against Terror. The Anti–Terror Law defined terrorism in broad and vague terms, considering membership of terrorist organizations the equivalent of committing terrorist offenses. It prohibited written or oral propaganda against the constitutional order and the unity and security of the state, along with demonstrations and marches (TMK 1991).[13] While restricting the freedom of expression, the law created a two-tier criminal justice system with different standards for "common" and "terrorist" offenses. It stipulated that those detained as

[12] Previously, Eskişehir Special Type Prison had been the symbolic space of contestation between the state and political prisoners. The prison was closed down after mass hunger strikes; first by 206 prisoners in November 1991, and then by over 1500 prisoners in July 1996 (IHD 2001; TIHV 1992).

[13] Several legal amendments were later made that relaxed some of these stipulations. For example, the state was obliged to prove criminal intent and reduce sentences for "thought crimes," and detainees were granted the right to remain silent, to inform family members, and to meet with legal counsel.

terrorist suspects would not be subject to the Criminal Procedural Code, but rather could be held in *incommunicado* detention for up to four days for certain crimes, without being reminded of their rights or given access to legal counsel. State Security Courts, endowed with discretionary powers, were assigned the responsibility of conducting the trials of terrorist suspects and given the authority to increase prisoners' sentences. Most importantly, the law stipulated that suspects and offenders alike should be confined in "special institutions" without open visitation and communication, erasing the distinction between those arrested and those convicted while legalizing solitary and small-group isolation.[14]

Hence, the prisoners' call for the abolition of F Types actually involved the holistic transformation of the state's penal apparatus, including the abrogation of the Anti–Terror Law and State Security Courts. Prisoners also demanded the cancellation of the "Tripartite Protocol" between the Ministries of Justice, Internal Affairs, and Health, which restricted prisoners' access to confidential legal counsel and medical care, limited family visitations, and sanctioned artificial feeding upon hunger strikers (AB 2000; IHD 2001). Furthermore, prisoners wanted the periodic inspection of prisons by non-official public committees, consisting of lawyers, doctors, prisoner families, and representatives of human rights organizations. Prisoners sought reparations for previous abuses and injustices, particularly the prosecution of those responsible for conducting torture in custody and inflicting violence in previous security operations in the Buca, Ümraniye, Diyarbakır, Ulucanlar, and Burdur Prisons in which twenty-seven prisoners had died and many were seriously wounded. Another demand was the discharge of prisoners who had been denied medical treatment. Finally, prisoners called for the abolition of all anti–democratic laws and, specifically, the end to oppression of ethnic minorities—a demand which, seeking to obtain the support of the Kurdish movement, could not be met without constitutional reform.[15]

[14] The 1999 Law for the Struggle against Organized Crime stipulated that those imprisoned for crimes related to the "Mafia" and "gangs" were also to be kept in F Types. Furthermore, prisoners of "common" crimes who created unrest and were not responsive to rehabilitation were to be transferred to these institutions due to the By-Law for the Execution of Sentences (Article 78/B).

[15] However, except for individual acts of solidarity, the Kurdish move-

Tripartite Character of the Death Fast Struggle

While prisoner grievances were articulated around the problem of F Type prisons, more was at stake than the conditions of confinement. We can identify three different interpretations of the Death Fast through the window provided by the multiplicity of meanings that rank-and-file militants imputed to their actions in general and the weaponization of life in particular.[16] These interpretations enable us to situate the struggle in relation to broader political concerns: democracy and human rights, neoliberalism, and state sovereignty.

Human Dignity against the Cell

For political prisoners, the cell represented a "prison inside the prison" and a modality of torture (Kamel and Kerness 2003). This "double confinement" involved the deepening of their punishment, no longer limited to the suspension of their liberty but violating their basic human right to bodily and mental integrity.[17] Isolation in cellular prisons implied the exercise of state power to break their will and secure their submission through torture. Accepting to be put in the cells therefore meant "surrender": an exchange of human dignity for physical survival.

In Turkey, the association of cellular confinement with torture emanated from several sources. First, it was a remnant of the unbridled violence of the "state of exception" created by the military's 1980 coup

ment neither participated in nor gave organized support to the 2000 Death Fast.

16 These interpretations do not neatly correspond to views held by the various groups participating in the movement, nor do they constitute a diachronic representation of the different stages of the struggle. Rather, they are composites that are derived from the accounts of individual participants and that bracket the contradictions, overlaps, and inconsistencies in a single narrative or among narratives belonging to the members of the same political organization.

17 Solitary confinement is considered a human rights violation, "inhuman treatment" (HRW 1997, 2000, Evans and Morgan 1998), and a form of torture, even "psycho-terror" (IHD 2001). Its deleterious impact on mental integrity has been an area of substantial research (see, among others, Andersen et al. 2000; Glancy and Murray 2006; Haney 2003; Hrassian 1983; Miller 1994; Miller and Young 1997; Rhodes 2005; Way et al. 2007).

d'état (Schmitt 2005, Agamben 2005). The suspension of the constitutional order was experienced at its most intense in the cell, a space that concretized the fierce confrontation between the individual, who strove to keep his integrity and identity as a dissident intact, and the state, which resorted to naked and arbitrary violence in order to compel obedience and compound punishment (Çelik 2005; Kukul 1984; Yetkin and Tanboğa 1990). The cell served as an instrument of violent de-politicization that induced prisoners to renounce political affiliations (Mavioğlu 2004). The way out of the cell could be bought by accepting the administration's terms, spying, or joining the "independents' ward," thereby leaving the "political" wards in which prisoners lived communally and resisted the state collectively.

Secondly, the cell was associated with torture because its solitary individualism stood in stark contrast with the prisoners' conception of individuality defined in and through the revolutionary collective. Prisoners condemned isolation as a method of de-individualization, strongly opposing the state's claim that the new prison "rooms" would induce freedom by liberating individuals from communal pressures. The individuality promoted by cellular prisons was predicated on having privacy, but prisoners interpreted privacy as deprivation, both sensory and human (TTB 2000). They worried about being compelled to make concessions to guarantee their basic human need of sociability which, as a basic human need, should be beyond contestation. Conceding to the administration's doctrinal "treatment" programs in order to access common spaces would imply showing remorse—the sign of being "broken," fatally injuring their "nature" as human beings.

Thirdly, cellular confinement stood for torture because prisoners expected that the solitude of cells would place them at the mercy of the administration, rendering them individually vulnerable and collectively weaker. In ward-based prisons, prisoners weathered the intrusions of authorities much more effectively not only because they could act as human shields for one another, but also because they could rely on each other as witnesses. Cellular isolation in the prisons was compounded by their geographical isolation. Constructed in remote rural locales, F Type prisons were shielded from public view (Istanbul Barosu 2000; Ankara Barosu 2000). Their administrative practices were protected from outside observers by the absence of non-official public channels to inspect prisoner grievances. Prisoners believed that their isolation would expose them to arbitrary rights infringements, whimsical waves of violence, and only too familiar forms of intimidation (such as random searches, confiscation of personal belongings, limitations on visits, legal counsel, and health care), leaving them without anyone to bear witness to the actions of the authorities and thus granting the authorities illegitimate impunity.

For these reasons, prisoners envisioned their struggle against the cell as part of a democratic resistance movement seeking to stop rights violations in the name of a universal humanity that transcended prison walls. Theirs was a struggle for the deepening of civic liberties, both inside and outside prisons, motivated by global norms of human rights. From this perspective, the reliance on the body amounted to the exercise of the "right of resistance" against torture and oppression that targeted the same bodies as their objects. Prisoners argued that the means of collective action were severely limited in prison, rendering the use of the body unavoidable. The state had victimized these bodies by subjecting them to violence, pain, and deprivation, making them into spaces of a struggle for power (Scarry 1985). The Death Fast merely exploited these contested corporeal spaces, by transforming the objects of violence into the subjects of resistance.

While this transformation was paradoxical because it relied on voluntary starvation, which appeared to be a form of internalized and self-inflicted torture, participants saw the Death Fast as a redeeming reversal of torture. While the scars of torture were not thereby erased, they were reclaimed as a source of empowerment. The Death Fast mimicked the "slow and torturous death" in the cells, but it restored prisoners' agency over their own lives. By taking death into their own hands, prisoners made their bodies into bargaining chips against state authorities.[18] According to a participant, "We did not have any other means of resistance than our bodies at hand. Either our bodies would be transformed into weapons against us, through torture, or we would use those bodies as means of resistance against the state."[19]

Skeptical about any affinity of their action with self-sacrifice, these prisoners argued that they participated in the struggle in order to resist and not, as they were often criticized, in order to die. In fact, they tried to prolong the hunger strike as much as possible because it

[18] Interviews with human rights defenders, 2 and 11 August 2004; 18 January 2005; and 6 July 2005.

[19] Interview, 17 June 2005.

was important to live longer, if only one more day, "in spite of the enemy."[20] Death was not a certain or even intended outcome of the struggle, only a risk to bear: "You can die while you are hanging placards, you can be shot, you can die while you are beaten up. But the Death Fast is on the agenda when there is no other means left to use, when all other means are exhausted and in the last stage. Otherwise, it would not mean anything other than squandering oneself."[21] Instead of a willingness to die, these prisoners argued, the Death Fast expressed a willingness to live, an extremely passionate desire for life. In fact, self-starvation could only be sustained by a strong "life drive" whereas acts of suicide bombing and self-immolation were oriented toward death with a blind, emotive, almost religious devotion. Refusing these forms of protest, a participant explained: "A person who wants to die cannot do what it takes to sustain a hunger strike: drinking water, eating salt, eating sugar, maintaining oneself on these through the day, being face to face with wardens all the time, dealing with those who come to intervene [medically]. A person not tied to life, not wanting to live cannot do these. [...] It is very difficult to fight with one's own body."[22] Starving oneself without letting go of life took great effort, persistence, and self-discipline; a "war of the will" was fought daily in order to defend the democratic right to a dignified life in prison.

Class War against Neoliberalism

Other prisoners saw in the cell more than torture—it was the embodiment of the interests of the ruling class. The project of "cellularization" was not limited to prisons but sought to make the cell the basic unit of society by dissolving ties of community, collective action, and solidarity. Each citizen would eventually be transformed into a vulnerable, docile, obedient, and contained subject (Foucault 1977). Prisoners cautioned that "cellularization" would soon turn the entire country into an unbounded prison, a prison without walls and yet a prison from which there was no escape: "They are trying to make everywhere into an F Type. This is what they are doing to perpetuate the

[20] Interviews, 17 January and 1 July 2005.
[21] Interviews, 26 January 2005.
[22] Interview, 24 January 2005.

system."[23] If "the inside is a cell *with* walls," a death faster sharply argued, "the outside is a cell *without* walls."[24]

Prisoners viewed "cellularization" as a necessary corollary of neoliberal policies whose implementation required the state to "confine dissent" (Neier 1995). They saw an intimate connection between the F Type Prison Project and the International Monetary Fund that prescribed and supported the dismantling of the welfare state and the curbing of rights to social security, collective bargaining, and political expression. Prisoners maintained that opposition to neoliberalism would be eliminated through a selective revamping of the state's penal apparatus, by increasing the punitive might of the state while decreasing its welfare functions. Characterizing the F Type Prison Project as "IM(F)," they argued that the security interests of the state and the class interests of capital formed a unified, historic bloc (Gramsci 1971).

Viewing themselves as the vanguards of the people and the negation of the existing order, political prisoners waged war against this bloc by confronting the state, which they perceived to be the institutional agent of the global bourgeoisie. The Death Fast became the most recent act in the theater of permanent class war against the people's "enemy," staged now in the cells, then on the streets, at the factories, and in the universities. Even though the prison was only one trench in the ever-expanding war zone, it came to be at the forefront of the struggle against neoliberalism. A team of death fasters wrote from prison: "A war has been going on in prisons for many years. And this war does not consist of a war between us revolutionaries and the state. It is a class war between the oppressors and the oppressed, between political government and the people."[25]

In this protracted war, the prisoner's body was a weapon of strategic resort more than a tactic of last resort. Its deployment was not a necessity but an option, not dictated by circumstances in which other means were not available but, rather, suggested by calculations in which other means were not preferable. The uneasy coalition of outlawed parties, representing the prisoners participating in the Death Fast, was the real agent of this strategic political calculation (cf. Anderson 2004) while individuals participated in the construction of a revolutionary collec-

[23] Interview, 22 May, 2005.

[24] Interview, 17 January, 2005.

[25] Ilhan Demirel, Barış Kaya, Murat Çoban, "Letter to the Press and to the Public from Aydın Prison," 29 November 2000.

tive by fatally committing their own bodies. Prisoners were militants, no different to the revolutionary collective than other fighters whose very expendability made them pawns on a chessboard upon which two much greater powers clashed—the bourgeoisie and the proletariat: "Let's imagine we are playing chess. There, in order to win, you would give away the pawn if need be. Because you don't value each piece individually, you value winning. [...] What is important is the continuation of the political warfare. If my death is necessary for that, I will die."[26]

These prisoners' relation to death was predicated on responsibility. Their accountability and reputation depended on whether they were able to fulfill the duty that their party assigned them. The goal was less to win immediate concessions that ameliorated prison conditions than to advance the anti–capitalist struggle. In evaluating the impact of the Death Fast, these prisoners contended, we must think in terms of the abysmal counterfactual in which the class war has been completely suppressed: What might have happened if there had been no Death Fast? "In [its] absence, not a single voice would be heard."[27]

In the political calculus of leftist parties, each prisoner became the embodiment of the class war. The emaciation of each body was a proof that death was the basic denominator of struggle. Constituting silent indictments of the moral legitimacy of the neoliberal state, these bodies served as a metaphor outlining the relationship between political prisoners and the people: prisoners as the vanguards whose starvation in the face of "IM(F)" dictated prisons figuratively pre-empted and enacted the starvation of the people in the face of IMF dictated capitalism. The images of their deformed bodies were expected to prompt the public into action while also symbolizing their role as human barricades that would stand in the way of the state's direct attack on the people. The calculated and coordinated emergence of prisoners' corpses into the world out of prison walls (Feldman 1991) would demonstrate the state's failure in fulfilling its most basic responsibility toward its own citizens: the protection of their lives. The images of prisoners' famished bodies carried in funeral processions were envisaged to shame the state into giving up on the project of cellular confinement.

These prisoners insisted that their relation to death should not be overemphasized, but rather viewed as something ordinary. Just as they

[26] Interview, 15 July 2005.

[27] Ibid.

live for the communist cause, dedicated militants must be able to die for the communist cause. As a participant put it, "One must know how to die for what one lives for."[28] They perceived self-starvation as a modest rendition of what was routinely expected of militants of a lofty political cause. This view erased unbridgeable differences between being a guerrilla fighter, death faster, and suicide bomber: "[The suicide bomber] has a weapon around his waist, whereas our bodies are weapons."[29] Not sacrifice but the ideology of sacrifice was dangerous: it set those who performed sacrificial acts apart from the rest, attributing to them a heroism and exceptionality that singled them out from the masses. Communist sacrifice must be de-sacralized. Rejecting its heroic implications, a participant of the Death Fast argued: "[T]here is no difference between our actions today and those of the workers who have died fighting at the barricades of the Paris Commune. [...] These types of action are the same in essence: a guerrilla, a militant who distributes flyers on the street, a death faster...these are all the same. *It is necessary to routinize death*."[30]

Armored with such militancy and communist consciousness, however, these prisoners were also aware that their extensive, repeated reliance on life as their primary weapon complicated the war they were fighting. While they wanted to distance themselves from a "politics conducted over corpses," they also admitted that this was the path to victory: "We don't conduct politics over the death of people. But we also know that after a point, class struggle can only secure its achievements with the death of people."[31] Their struggle diverged from its textbook formulations because of its self-sacrificial quality, blurring the distinction between the war against the neoliberal state and the counter-hegemonic insurrection against a more spectral, more elusive power: sovereignty.

Insurgent Sacrifice and the Politics of Exodus

The state's sovereignty, defined as the political community's power of self-determination, based on its right over the life and death of its individual members, requires legitimacy. The legitimation of the sovereign

[28] Interview, 17 June 2005.

[29] Interview, 17 January 2005.

[30] Interviews, 7 April 2005, my emphasis.

[31] Ibid.

order depends primarily on the state's commitment to the preservation of its citizens and the sanctity of human life. From this perspective, disciplinary confinement was not an emblematic shift in the workings of power, displacing or replacing sovereign power (Foucault 1977), but it was intimately connected to the ideological reproduction of the instrumental rationality of modern state sovereignty, particularly in its liberal-democratic version, whose legitimacy is built on the idea of individual preservation. Despite this legitimation, not only does the modern state privilege the preservation of the collective, it also institutionally and ideologically facilitates the sacrifice of individuals for that collective. It monopolizes the right over physical existence as well as the right to sacrifice that physical existence. When individuals fights to create a new object of sacrifice—the revolutionary collective—and attempt to fight by self-sacrifice, they have to be "tamed" ideologically.

With cellular isolation, the Turkish state threatened prisoners not only with violent force, but as a more insidious power compelling them to consent to the discourses of its legitimation by which its ideological hegemony was reproduced. For these prisoners, the challenge was to create a new order while staying *in* the order, without becoming *of* the order. They experienced the sovereign order as pervasive, colonizing, and intolerant of its alternatives, striving to contain and eliminate its enemies. Such an existential threat could not be overcome by conventional means. It had to be countered by the public demonstration that the state could neither prevail over individuals in life, nor prevent their sacrificial death for a dissident cause. By (re)appropriating the right over life, these prisoners chose to subtract themselves from the order—an exodus not only defying the state's sovereign power, but also its hegemonic allure based on "mak[ing] live" (Foucault 2003: 241). Their action was an "engaged withdrawal" (Virno 1996: 196), calling forth an alternative order that would thrive on the destruction and the very absence of its agents.

To these prisoners, death was the only medium through which they could claim political voice. If nothing short of death seemed to make an impact in the public sphere, prisoners sought to make their deaths say what their lives could not: "What is forced upon us is this: 'to die as we live.' Our alternative is this: 'To become immortal as we die.'"[32] By weaponizing their lives, they became "revolutionary martyrs," not

[32] Interview, 8 April 2005.

only to reject the state's sovereign power but also to continue the fight toward the creation of a future order as martyrs. Informed by a theological conception of militancy and a collective understanding of individuality, the ideology of self-sacrifice provided prisoners with an alternative matrix that would nourish their actions and puncture the ideological hegemony of the existing order (Gramsci 1971: 57, 129, 161).

Sacrificial ideology constituted the new source of legitimation for an alternative, non-political sovereignty, based on the ideological survival of the counter-collective. The counter-collective's communal power would not be political in the old sense because it would eliminate both the antagonism between social classes and the opposition between the individual and the collective. At the same time, it would collapse the tension between self-preservation and collective preservation, a tension that underlies liberal democracy. It would thus relegate the sacrifice of prisoners' physical existence to a secondary status before the more dangerous possibility of the sacrifice of their ideological existence. "Our bodies are not unsacrificeable," a death faster argued. "When our thoughts and our bodies contend with one another, we relinquish our bodies, not our thoughts."[33] As another death faster put it, "To give up on one's thoughts is real sacrifice. [...] *We understand that death is not connected to self-preservation.*"[34]

Sacrificial ideology implied a latent but prevalent logic based on exchange between death and existence: "They are trying to annihilate us," a participant asserted. "'Revolutionism will come to an end on the soil of this country'—this is the calculation of the sovereign. We are *dying to exist* as revolutionaries."[35] Prisoners' relation to death was established through the mediation of a new category: price or toll [*bedel*]. The quid pro quo between different forms of existence operated in an economy of recompense. The worth of securing a political existence was, at the same time, its toll: the forgoing of physical existence. Similarly, the toll paid for physical self-preservation was the loss of political identity and the potential of a new sovereignty. Each sacrificial death called for due measure: "We have paid our price," the common slogan of the Death Fast went, "and we will make them pay!"

[33] Interview, 17 January 2005.

[34] Interview, 24 January 2005, my emphasis.

[35] Interview, 30 May 2005, my emphasis.

However, this exchange transformed self-inflicted violence upon the body into an abstract value, a "price to pay", functioning to neutralize it. The "price" of death mediated the exchange between different forms of existence, thereby abstracting violence from the real suffering of the concrete body. The neutralization of corporeal violence through the intermediary category of "price" in this exchange constituted the performance of sacrificial death as the equivalent of political voice, at the cost of human voice. A participant of the movement wryly summarized this substitution: "A death faster is *not* harming himself. This is an illusion. He is shouting with his body. Day by day, hour by hour, minute by minute, he is *shouting*."[36]

According to these prisoners, spectacles of death could be performed because a sacrificial consciousness already existed in nascent form in popular morality, indigenous culture, and a predominantly Alevi interpretation of Islam.[37] However, this subterranean tradition had to be reworked with the values of communism to be converted into a revolutionary morality that channeled ordinary acts of self-sacrifice into political insurgency. "One who does not have the consciousness to sacrifice has no chance of victory," a death faster explained.[38] Ironically, revolutionary consciousness depended on a legacy of heroic martyrdom that became constitutive of militancy. Just as equivalent exchange in the "free" market did not prevent the creation of surplus value (Marx 1976), equivalent exchange in the political market did not prevent the creation of a surplus spectrality—martyrdom.

Erasing the differences between various forms of the weaponization of life, sacrificial ideology sanctified martyrdom as the agent of irreversible damage, but damage of a different, counter-hegemonic caliber. Suicide bombing and self-immolation differed from the death fast only with respect to form, not content: they are "all the highest forms of [political] action."[39] While the prisoners' sacrificial exodus was expected to awaken the oppressed, defying the state's sovereignty while ruptur-

[36] Interview, 17 January 2005, my emphasis.

[37] The participants of the Death Fast Struggle did not act out of religious motivation, nor did they hold explicit religious beliefs. However, a significant portion of them were of Alevi origin (the local interpretation of Shi'i Islam, historically subjugated and oppressed by the Sunni majority). Being Alevi was an important part of one's dissident political identity and chimed with the notion of sacrifice derived from the Shi'i narrative of Hüseyin's death.

[38] Interview, 17 June, 2005.

[39] Interview, 30 May, 2005.

ing its hegemony (much in the spirit of the "propaganda of the deed"), it was the grandeur of sacrificial death which would earn militants recognition, create the unity of the revolutionary collective, and become the harbinger of a new order. The growing centrality of the "falling martyr" in the struggle attested to the glorification of death and its celebration as the vehicle for the calling forth of an alternative sovereignty—a sovereignty based on the haunting presence of militant-martyrs asserted through their physical absence.

As an insurrection against sovereignty, the Death Fast Struggle was a rejection of the order through fatal and non-compromising withdrawal—an act of insurgent sacrifice. This was an ideological war-without-end whose victory was paradoxically already won: "[The state] wants to annihilate you; you claim that you will exist *with* deaths. We are now carrying out a war upon deaths—upon deaths, disabilities, veterans. To take the decision to fast *is* our victory."[40] Victory was won and yet always deferred, in waiting for the people to claim their own sovereignty through death.

Conclusion

As resistance, class war, and insurgent sacrifice, the Death Fast was the unstable amalgam of different conceptions of struggle. In its advocacy of prisoner rights, it sought to resist arbitrary intrusions upon the exercise of those rights in an ostensibly liberal-democratic regime. As part of the anti–capitalist struggle, it acted as the vanguard of the oppressed in fighting neoliberal "cellularization." Finally, it launched an offensive against the state's ideological hegemony through an insurrection that usurped the right over life and death and adopted sacrifice as its ideological matrix. The struggle's divergent significations enveloped the weaponization of life and characterized the movement's oscillation, working within, through, and against sovereignty.

Bibliography

AB. 2003. "Cezaevi Reformu Çalışmaları ve Insan Hakları." [Progress on Prison Reform and Human Rights.] Press Release. http://www.cte.adalet.gov.tr/inshak/insan_hak.htm accessed on 15 March 2007.

AB. 2000. *Protokol.* [Working Agreement.] No: KS: 4V. R 1–E-2 3/18 Ankara (14 January).

[40] Ibid., my emphases.

AB. (Adalet Bakanlığı Ceza ve Tevkifevleri Genel Müdürlüğü.) [Ministry of Justice General Directorate of Prisons and Detention Houses.] 2007a. "Istatistikler." [Statistics.] http://www.cte.adalet.gov.tr/ist/c_ist/cezaevleri.htm accessed on 15 March 2007.

AB. 2007b. *Genelge 45/1*. [Decree 45/1.] No: B:03.0.CTE.0.00.00.04 / Ankara (22 January).

Agamben, Giorgio. 2005. *State of Exception*. Trans. Kevin Attell. Chicago and London: University of Chicago Press.

Andersen, H. S., D. Sestoft, T. Lillebæk, G. Gabrielsen, R. Hemmingsen, and P. Kramp. 2000. "A longitudinal Study of Prisoners on Remand: Psychiatric Prevalence, Incidence and Psychopathology in Solitary vs. Non-Solitary Confinement" in *Acta Psychiatrica Scandinavica* 102 (1): 19–25.

Anderson, Patrick. 2004. "'To Lie Down to Death for Days': The Turkish Hunger Strike, 2000–2003'" in *Cultural Studies* 18 (6): 816–46.

Ankara Barosu. [Ankara Bar Organization.] 2000. *Sincan F Tipi Cezaevi Gözlem Raporu ve 'Cezaevleri Sorunu' üzerine Görüşler*. [Sincan F Type Prison Observation Report and Views on the "Prisons Problem"]. Special Report.

Atılım. 2000. 28 October.

Bağımsız Vatan. 2000. 23 October.

Bargu, Ayse Banu. 2008. *Martyrs of Hunger: Sovereignty in the Age of Sacrifice*. PhD Diss., Cornell University.

Çelik, Mukaddes Erdoğdu. 2005. *Demir Parmaklıklar Ortak Düşler: Üç Dönem Üç Kuşak Kadınlar*. [Iron Bars Common Dreams: Three Eras Three Generations of Women.] Istanbul: Ceylan Yayınları.

Churcill, Ward and J. J. Vander Wall, eds. 1992. *Cages of Steel: The Politics of Imprisonment in the United States*. Washington, D.C.: Maisonneuve Press.

Evans, Malcolm D. and Rod Morgan. 1998. *Preventing Torture: A Study of the European Convention for the Prevention of Torture and Inhuman or Degrading Treatment or Punishment*. Oxford: Clarendon.

Feldman, Allen. 1991. *Formations of Violence: The Narrative of the Body and Political Terror in Northern Ireland*. Chicago and London: University of Chicago Press.

Foucault, Michel. 1977. *Discipline & Punish: The Birth of the Prison*. Trans. Alan Sheridan. New York: Vintage.

Foucault, Michel. 2003. "Society Must Be Defended": *Lectures at the Collège de France, 1975–76*. Ed. Arnold I. Davidson. Trans. David Macey. New York: Picador.

Glancy, Graham D. and Erin L. Murray. 2006. "Psychiatric Aspects of Solitary Confinement" in *Victims & Offenders* 1 (4): 361–68.

Gramsci, Antonio. 1971. *Selections from the Prison Notebooks*. Eds. and trans. Quintin Hoare and Geoffrey Nowell Smith. New York: International Publishers.

Haney, Craig. 2003. "Mental Health Issues in Long-Term Solitary and 'Supermax' Confinement SW6 4QP" in *Crime and Delinquency* 49 (1): 124–56.

Hrassian, Stuart. 1983. "Psychopathological Effects of Solitary Confinement" in *American Journal of Psychiatry* 140 (11): 1450–54.

HRW. (Human Rights Watch.) 1997. *Cold Storage: Super-Maximum Security Confinement in Indiana*. New York: Human Rights Watch. http://www.hrw.org/en/reports/1997/10/01/cold-storage accessed on 22 March 2010.

HRW. 1999. *Red Onion State Prison: Super-maximum Security Confinement in Virginia*. New York: Human Rights Watch. http://www.hrw.org/legacy/reports/1999/redonion/ accessed on 22 March 2010.

HRW. 2000. *Out of Sight: Super-Maximum Security Confinement in the United States*. Special Report 12, no. 1 (G). http://www.hrw.org/legacy/reports/1997/usind/ accessed on 22 March 2010.

HRW. 2001. *Turkey: Small Group Isolation in F-type Prisons and the Violent Transfers of Prisoners to Sincan, Kandira, and Edirne Prisons on December 19, 2000*. Report 13, no. 2 (D). http://www.hrw.org/legacy/reports/2001/turkey/index.htm

IHD. (Insan Hakları Derneği Istanbul Şubesi). [Human Rights Association Istanbul Branch.] 2001. *Sessiz Çığlık: Hücreler*. [Silent Scream: The Cells.] Special Report.

IHD. 2002. *F Tipi Cezaevleri Raporu 2*. [F Type Prisons Report 2.] Special Report.

Immarigeon, Russ. 1992. "The Marionization of American Prisons" in *The National Prison Project Journal* 7 (4): 1–5.

Istanbul Barosu Insan Hakları Merkezi Cezaevi Çalışma Grubu. [Istanbul Bar Organization Human Rights Center Prisons Working Group.] 2000. *"Kocaeli F Tipi Cezaevi" Gözlem Raporu*. ["Kocaeli F Type Prison" Observation Report.] Special Report.

Kamel, Rachael and Bonnie Kerness. 2003. "The Prison Inside the Prison: Control Units, Supermax Prisons, and Devices of Torture". *Justice Visions Briefing Paper*. Philadelphia: Community Relations Unit, American Friends Service Committee. http://www.afsc.org/stopmax/ht/d/ContentDetails/i/35525 accessed on 22 March 2010.

King, Roy D. 1999. "The Rise and Rise of Supermax: An American Solution in Search of a Problem?" in *Punishment and Society* 1 (2): 163–86.

Kukul, Sinan. 1984. *Bir Direniş Odağı Metris: Metris Tarihi*. [Metris, A Focus of Resistance: History of Metris.] Istanbul: Haziran Yayınevi.

Kurki, Leena and Norval Morris. 2001. "The Purposes, Practices, and Problems of Supermax Prisons" in *Crime and Justice* 28: 385–424.

Le Pennec, Elsa and Sally Eberhardt. 2001. *The F-Type Prison Crisis and the Repression of Human Rights Defenders in Turkey: Report from the Fact-Finding Mission to Istanbul and Ankara on 5, 11 May 2001 with Updates*. Copenhagen, Denmark: Euro-Mediterranean Human Rights Network, Kurdish Human Rights Project and the World Organization against Torture.

Lutsky, Julia, ed. 2001. *Torture in U.S. Prisons: Evidence of U.S. Human Rights Violations*. Newark: American Friends Service Committee Criminal Justice Program. http://afsc.org/stopmax/ht/d/ContentDetails/i/3987 accessed on 22 March 2010.

Marx, Karl. 1976. *Capital*. Vol. 1. Intro. Ernest Mandel. Trans. Ben Fowkes. London: Penguin.

Mavioğlu, Ertuğrul. 2004. *Asılmayıp da Beslenenler: Bir 12 Eylül Hesaplaşması*. [Those Who Were Not Hanged But Fed: Settling Accounts with September 12.] Istanbul: Babil Yayınları.

Mears, Daniel P. and Jamie Watson. 2006. "Towards a Fair and Balanced Assessment of Supermax Prisons" in *Justice Quarterly* 23 (2): 232–70.

Mears, Daniel P. and Michael D. Reisig. 2006. "The Theory and Practice of Supermax Prisons" in *Punishment & Society* 8 (1): 33–57.

Miller, Holly A. 1994. "Reexamining Psychological Distress in the Current Conditions of Segregation" in *Journal of Correctional Health Care* 1 (1): 39–53.

Miller, Holly A. and Glenn R. Young. 1997. "Prison Segregations: Administrative Detention Remedy or Mental Health Problem?" in *Criminal Behavior and Mental Health* 7 (1): 85–94.

Neier, Aryeh. 1995. "Confining Dissent: The Political Prison" in Norval Morris and David J. Rothman (eds.) *The Oxford History of the Prison: The Practice of Punishment in Western Society*. New York and Oxford: Oxford University Press. 350–80.

Parenti, Christian. 1999. *Lockdown America: Police and Prisons in the Age of Crisis*. London and New York: Verso.

Perkinson, Robert. 1994. "Shackled Justice: Florence Federal Penitentiary and the New Politics of Punishment" in *Social Justice* 21 (3): 117–132.

Pizarro, Jesenia and Vanja M. K. Stenius. 2004. "Supermax Prisons: Their Rise, Current Practices, and Effect on Inmates" in *The Prison Journal* 84 (2): 248–64.

Rhodes, Lorna A. 2005. "Pathological Effects of the Supermaximum Prison" in *American Journal of Public Health* 95 (10): 1692–95.

Scarry, Elaine. 1985. *The Body in Pain: The Making and Unmaking of the World*. New York and Oxford: Oxford University Press.

Schmitt, Carl. 2005. *Political Theology: Four Concepts of the Concept of Sovereignty*. Trans. George Schwab. Intro. Tracy B. Strong. Chicago and London: University of Chicago Press.

Sparks, Richard, Anthony Bottoms, and Will Hay. 1996. *Prison and the Problem of Order*. Oxford: Clarendon.

TAYAD Komite Nederland. 2002. *Documentation on the Death Fast in Turkey*. http://prisonsenturquie.free.fr/hungerstrike.pdf/ accessed on 22 March 2010.

TBMM. (Türkiye Büyük Millet Meclisi.) [Grand National Assembly of Turkey]. 2000. *Genel Kurul Tutanağı*. [Proceedings.] 21st Period, 3rd Legislative Year, 18th Convention, 2nd Session, November 21. http://www.tbmm.gov.tr/ accessed on 22 March 2010.

TMK. (Terörle Mücadele Kanunu.) [Law for the Struggle against Terror]. 1991. No: 3713. http://www.mevzuat.adalet.gov.tr/html/809.html and http://www.icj.org/IMG/Turkey1991law.pdf accessed on 22 March 2010.

TIHV. (Türkiye Insan Hakları Vakfı.) [Human Rights Foundation of Turkey.] 1992. *Türkiye Insan Hakları Raporu '91*. [Turkey Human Rights Report '91.] Ankara: TIHV Yayınları.

TIHV. 2001. Türkiye Insan Hakları Raporu. Ankara: TIHV Yayınları. http://www.tihv.org.tr/index.php?TArkiye-AEnsan-HaklarAE-Raporu accessed on 22 March 2010.

TTB. (Türk Tabipleri Birliği.) [Turkish Medical Association.] 2000. *F Tipi Cezaevlerine Ilişkin Türk Tabipleri Birliği Raporu* [Turkish Medical Association's Report on F Type Prisons]. Special Report. http://www.ttb.org.tr/rapor/f_tipi.html accessed on 27 February 2005.

Ward, David A. and Thomas G. Werlich. 2003. "Alcatraz and Marion: Evaluating Super-Maximum Custody" in *Punishment & Society* 5 (1): 53–75.

Virno, Paolo. 1996. "Virtuosity and Revolution: The Political Theory of Exodus" in Paolo Virno and Michael Hardt (eds.) *Radical Thought in Italy: A Potential Politics*. Minneapolis and London: University of Minnesota Press. 189–210.

Way, Bruce, Donald A. Sawyer, Sharen Barboza, and Robin Nash. 2007. "Inmate Suicide and Time Spent in Special Disciplinary Housing in New York State Prison" in *Psychiatric Services* 58 (4): 558–60.

Yetkin, Fevzi, and Mehmet Tanboğa. 1990. *Dörtlerin Gecesi*. [The Night of the Four.] Ankara: Yurt Kitap-Yayın.

13

REFUSING MERCY

CHALLENGES TO THE STATE'S MONOPOLY ON VIOLENCE IN IRAN

Arzoo Osanloo

Introduction

In an interview with philosopher Giovanna Borradori just after the 11 September attacks, Jacques Derrida commented on the unquestioned logic of sovereignty: "On no side is the logic of sovereignty ever put into question (political sovereignty or that of the nation-state—itself of ontotheological origin, though more or less secularized in one place and purely theological and nonsecularized in another): not on the side of the nation-states and the great powers that sit on the Security Council, and not on the other side, or other sides, since there is precisely an indeterminate number of them" (Borradori: 2003). Derrida's comment was important not just because he noted the relative acceptance of the nation-state system, but also because of his suggestion that the theological state and the secular participate in a similar enduring logic, one that needs greater investigation, not for the religious effects of one versus the other, but for the material consequences of the nation-state, which both the theological and secular share.

In this chapter I consider contemporary acts of refusal or defiance to state penal authority in Iran, such as Akbar Ganji's 2005 hunger strike and Hashem Aghajari's 2002 refusal to appeal his death sentence, in the context of a broader constellation of issues involving, on the one hand, theories of sovereign power and legitimate violence, and on the other hand, contemporary Iranian politics. The Iranian example speaks to Derrida's comment in that it is a nation-state that is not solely characterized by theocratic power, as it is often portrayed, but rather by that of sovereign power in the context of the modern nation-state.

The recent struggle for ideas and political pluralism in Iran, while at times violent and unpredictable, characterizes the beginnings of a new period in the country, a time when lay persons are literally forsaking their lives for integration in and reformulation of religio-political arenas as they make claims on these spaces that for a generation now have been monopolized by religious authorities. While the current geopolitical climate has intensified the internal tensions and rendered their sources more visible, similar tensions—eruptions—emerged at the end of the Khatami reformist period, and were perhaps made even more visible due to the political divisions at that time.

"Iran's Salman Rushdie"

One case that stood out was that of Iranian history professor Hashem Aghajari, who in the fall of 2002 was sentenced to death for a speech he gave in June of that same year before a gathering of students in Hamedan, a city in northwestern Iran. Aghajari spoke at a conference commemorating the twenty-fifth anniversary of the death of an Iranian philosopher and sociologist, Ali Shariati, who is credited with revitalizing Islamic teachings for modern society and popular audiences. Using Shariati as his point of reference, Aghajari called on the people themselves to revitalize Islam in Iran. He charged the students with the challenge of reading the Qur'an and forming their own ideas about its meaning. By learning to think for themselves, he said, the students would lead an Islamic reformation, and just as the Christians had rescued their faith from the clergy, so must the Muslims. Aghajari stated, "Just as people at the dawn of Islam conversed with the Prophet, we have the right to do this today. Just as they interpreted what was conveyed at historical junctures, we must do the same...For years, young people were afraid to open a Qur'an. They said, 'We must ask the mullahs what the Qur'an says.' Then came Shariati, who told the people those ideas have become bankrupt" (Aghajari 2002).

Aghajari was accused of apostasy and insulting Islamic values, leading some to refer to him pejoratively as Iran's Salman Rushdie. Conservative members of Iran's complex Islamic republic government saw his message as a challenge to the legitimacy of Shi'ite authority, which is based on a structural hierarchy in which the people follow the wisdom of accomplished clerics, those who have attained the highest ranking as "sources of emulation" (*marajeh-ye taqlid*). The marajeh, whose numbers are very few in Iran, are granted final authority with respect to exegesis among the *'ulama* (religious scholars). But in Iran's blended religio-republican state system, the highest authority in Iran's leadership, the *Vali–e Faqih* (Guardian of the Jurisprudence), is supposed to be the most accomplished of the marajeh.[1] Thus, the once personalized system of exegetical consultation is monopolized by religio-state actors governing through institutions that were created through the republican model of state organization and forged from the example of the French Republic. So when Professor Aghajari discouraged people from blindly following the religious leaders, saying instead that Islam actually forbade it, many hardline religious officials saw it as an affront and a call to contest their religiously inscribed state authority.

In August 2002, Professor Aghajari was arrested and imprisoned. On 6 November 2002, he was tried in a closed hearing and sentenced to death by hanging, for insulting Islam's prophets—charges of blasphemy. The case stemmed from a heated political struggle for power between two factions of government—hardline conservatives and reformists. Professor Aghajari was a member of the Organization of Mujahedin of the Islamic Revolution (OMIR), a reformist party which had pioneered many of the attempted modifications to Iran's government at that time. In fact when the verdict was handed down, Iran's *Majlis* (parliament) was considering a bill submitted by the reformist President Khatami. The bill, intended to curtail the powers of the hardline judiciary, would have suspended rulings by this court that the president deemed to be unconstitutional.

Aghajari had the right to appeal, which would have allowed for the possibility of a compromise charge and a lighter sentence, as had hap-

[1] The Vali–e Faqih is a lifetime appointment. The Vali–e Faqih is selected by a group of eighty-six members of the *'ulama*, the Assembly of Experts. This Assembly is elected by the people once every eight years.

pened in similar cases. But much to everyone's surprise, he refused to appeal the sentence, stating only that, "those who have issued this verdict have to implement it if they think it is right or else the judiciary has to handle it" (cited in Freund 2003). In the face of widespread protests throughout Iran, particularly among students, as well as international outcry, Iran's Vali–e Faqih, also known as *Rahbar* (religious leader) suddenly intervened extra-legally and ordered the sentence to be reconsidered.

The legal process that ensued led to a February 2003 decision by the highest court in the land, *Divan-e Aaliye Keshvar*, quashing Aghajari's death sentence. The high court then sent the case back to the lower court that had issued the execution ruling and ordered a new trial. A judiciary spokesman, Gholamhossein Elham, said that the court of the first instance must "correct procedural failings and issue a new ruling," which, he said, "could be the same as the first" (BBC News 2003). When the case was retried, however, the sentence was reduced to five years, most of which was credited as time-served.[2]

Aghajari referred to his call for peopled-reform as "Islamic humanism," an approach to exegetical governance that rests with the people, not solely the *'ulama*. This people-centered reform lies precisely at the heart of current internal (and some external) challenges to the legitimacy of Iran's sovereign authority. Aghajari's story serves as a preface for a story about Akbar Ganji, whose hunger strike tells a different story to be sure, but one that also challenges sovereign power through acts of defiance—that is, a challenge to state power to which the sovereign is unequipped to respond. And in the face of such defiance, the sovereign accommodates. Both cases help us understand the workings of sovereign power. I also note that these types of challenges are not new nor should they be considered outside of the context of wider debates about the nature of the Iranian government and the legitimacy of its leaders and institutions in what is now a post-reformist period. At a time of continued reckoning with the limitations of Iran's Islamic republicanism, the case of Akhbar Ganji's imprisonment and hunger strike will give us pause to think about the nature of the state and the limits of Islamico-republican governance in Iran.

This chapter explores theoretical issues that emerge from a concern with what Susan Buck-Morss (2000) has called the "wild zone of sov-

[2] The new sentence was three years in jail, two years probation, and the suspension of his social rights for five years.

ereign power," where the people have legitimated a power over their lives only to find that they have no control over it. Such power takes shape through a circular logic of sovereignty in which the state that preserves the law also creates the law, and thus has the greatest stake in seeing it carried out (Benjamin 1978). The state reveals its power when it exercises violence in the name of the law, what is also referred to as the power of exception. One form of exception in which the state reveals its power is in its ability to pardon or to grant mercy. This act of exception situates the sovereign outside of the law, but subjects others to it.

The framework for sovereign power rests and builds on the "docile" subject of Foucauldian biopolitics, the idea that the sovereign's power makes subjects—not only by determining whether they will live or die, but also by inscribing their very subjecthood in relation to the state—as citizens, as immigrants, and as legal or illegal (Foucault 2003). Thus, even as citizens, bodies are always subjects of the governmental strategies; in a modern era they are born of a new kind of sovereign power, where it is the bare life that is at stake—the life stripped of its political inscriptions and therefore any legal recognition it might have (Agamben 1998). But this power is mutually conditioned. That is, the subject must respond accordingly and perform the role assigned to him or her—whether it is in the camp, which Agamben explores, or in these cases, offenders of the Islamic state: Aghajari and Ganji.

But what happens when the subject refuses to partake in the act of receiving and accepting the sovereign's rule, a necessary precondition for sovereign power? Thus this chapter explores how the refusal to accept mercy articulates with sovereign power.

Velayat-e faqih, Sovereign Power, and the Challenge of Hunger Strikes

Most Iranians were aware of the hunger strikes by Akbar Ganji, a reformist journalist who was imprisoned in Iran for six years for crimes against Islam. In the Islamic republic, such offenses are also crimes against the state and thus tantamount to treason. Ganji worked as an investigative journalist at the daily paper *Sobh-e-Emrooz*. He was arrested on 22 April 2000 after appearing before the press court. In July 2001, he was sentenced to six years in prison. He was accused of anti-Islamic activities for his writings. Primary among them were his reports pointing to leading government officials, including former President Hashemi Rafsanjani and former intelligence minister Ali Fallahian, of having been involved in the murder of opponents and intellectuals in late 1998. He was also accused of taking part in a conference in Berlin (about reform in Iran) which the press court found to be "anti–Islamic."

The fact that Ganji's writings challenged the authority of leading figures in the state very openly was, and continues to be, a topic of grave concern, especially for those state actors who are in unelected positions. This is due, in part, to the fact that today many of Iran's religious elite do not ascribe to the rationale for Shi'i Islamic governance, *Velayat-e Faqih* (Guardianship of the Jurist), which just after the revolution was Khomeini's thesis justifying the authority of the 'ulama and their supervisory powers over the population.

The theory of the Velayat-e Faqih posited that in the absence of the Hidden Imam, the last Imam of the Shi'i Imamate, who is in hiding until the Day of Judgment, an authority on Islam needs to be in charge to guide the people to live according to Islamic principles; thus emerged the idea of a guardianship of the jurists. The idea of guardianship is believed to have been first introduced into *fiqh* (Islamic jurisprudence) by tenth century theorists of *ijtihad* (independent juridical interpretation), but the Velayat-e Faqih evolved into a theory of governance alongside the development of the modern nation-state. Later theorists debated the degree of intervention by the ecclesiastical authorities in matters of governance.[3] That is, the question that emerged for scholars concerned the extent of the role of the guardianship of jurists: is it merely a consultative and advisory role, or is it a supervisory role with authority to issue final rulings? The contemporary statist version of *Velayat-e Faqih*, however, is an innovation mapped onto the republican state model and was theorized by Ayatollah Khomeini in the 1960s, while he was in exile in Najaf, Iraq and when he began thinking about an alternative to Iran's monarchy (Algar 1981). In

[3] The more absolute version of *Velayat* was introduced in the Shi'i jurisprudence through the well-known text, *Javaher-al-Kalem*. Later, Ayatollah Molla Mohammad Mahdee Naraqi (1749 CE/1128 AH—1830 CE/1209 AH) encouraged a more modest level of political engagement for the *'ulama*, or a limited version of *Velayat-e-Faqih*. This debate continued during the Iranian Constitutional revolution of 1906–11, in which the ulama was granted an extensive guardianship over state matters.

1970, Khomeini delivered a series of lectures on this theory of state, in which he theorized an overriding authority for the *fuqaha* (Islamic jurists) and published the work in the same year entitled, *Hookoomat-e Islami* (Islamic Government). Scholars have argued, however, that in this work Khomeini appears to have reconsidered the limited guardianship for which he had called in his earlier works, including in 1942's *Kashf-al Asrar* (Secrets Unveiled), revising it to be an absolute theory of state governance (Algar 1981; Abrahamian 1982). In Hookoomat-e Islami, Khomeini clarified the role of the Islamic guardianship to include an overriding power of veto and law-making by the just jurists. The Guardianship of the Jurist requires that the governance and administration of the state conform to the sacred law of Islam. Khomeini's theory of a more absolute guardianship was a novelty in Shi'i Islam because it rejected the separation of political life from the religious, and delegated the authority of leadership of the state solely to qualified Islamic jurists or religious scholars.

While Iranian intellectuals debated the role of *Velayat* in governance in ecclesiastical forums, few lay persons participated in such debates outside of universities and the *hosseiniyeh* (Shi'i congregational halls). In the press, however, Ganji questioned the notion of *velayat* (guardianship) and what it means to have Islamic jurisprudential scholars in supervisory and unelected roles. By doing this in the public sphere, he squarely placed this question as a debate to be considered by lay audiences, thus posing a direct populist challenge to the Guardianship of the Jurist and opening the discussion to non-clerics, just as Aghajari had done in his address to students.[4]

In 2000, Ganji was arrested and tried in the then newly established press court, a court that is outside the reach of the justice ministry but within the branch of supervisory authority of the Vali–e Faqih; it is a court that determines breaches of Islamic principles. Ganji was initially sentenced to ten years in January 2001. In May 2001, the appeals court reduced the sentence to six months. Two months later, however, Iran's highest court, Divan-e Aaliye Keshvar, quashed the May sentence on technical grounds and imposed a six–year sentence. In May 2005, after all legal remedies and appeals had been exhausted,

[4] While this provocation elicited public dialogue about the nature of the supervisory role of the Vali–e Faqih and his offices, it should be noted that the issue was not a new one in ecclesiastical circles.

Ganji went on a hunger strike to protest his imprisonment and the charges against him.

In a statement he said, "I protest against my illegal and unjust imprisonment ...[sic]...I am beginning an unlimited hunger strike this evening. No one should be imprisoned—not even for a second—for expressing an opinion" (RSF 2005). The hunger strike caused a controversy over the summer of 2005, both domestically and internationally, when Ganji refused any food for over sixty days. But his hunger strike was more than just an act of protest. It was also an act of defiance, a challenge to the authority of the sovereign to mete out punishment and to do so with impunity. Ganji thus was challenging the sovereign's monopoly on legitimate violence.

The head of the Judiciary, a hardline official, suggested that Ganji could be pardoned if he asked for the Leader's grace. Ganji refused saying that he would not renounce his views and instead demanded unconditional release. The perplexed *'ulama* argued over his case, even some of those whom he had publicly accused in his written work spoke out in favor of his release.[5] But Ganji refused mercy and continued to be imprisoned. He served out his sentence and was released in March 2006.

Stories of defiance such as these are not uncommon in Iran, nor are they unheard of in the context of Western Judeo-Christian nation-states. These cases, in which the state offers reprieve if the guilty party asks for mercy, reveal important tensions between modern state power, the rule of law, and challenges to authority.

Questions for Analysis

Through these two cases, I am considering two questions: (1) In Iran, is the refusal to ask for mercy akin to a "pure" notion of martyrdom? That is, is requiring subjects to ask for mercy an act of premodern barbarism? (2) What does the concept of mercy mean for the articulation of sovereign power, in the contemporary nation-state system?

In my analysis, I consider these acts of refusal as constitutive acts of modern sovereign power that play out very specifically in the examples

[5] *BBC News*, 5 August 2005. The head of Iran's Judiciary, Ayatollah Shahroudi, as well as former president and 2005 presidential candidate, Hashemi Rafsanjani, took up Ganji's cause, even though Ganji had openly accused Rafsanjani of having played a part in the 1998 murders of Iranian dissidents.

I give of Iran, but also can be seen elsewhere as modern iterations of contemporary sovereign power.

Some analyses have situated cases such as Aghajari's refusal and Ganji's hunger strike in the context of Shi'i Islam's preoccupation with self-sacrifice and martyrdom (Freund 2003). Initially, both men were strong supporters of the Iranian revolution that ousted the Shah, and both supported the rise of Khomeini and Islamic governance. Ganji was a member of Iran's Revolutionary Guard and Aghajari was a soldier who lost a leg in the war with Iraq. Indeed, in a 2002 speech, Aghajari called for a religious renewal. Yet the deliberate reproach to the leaders and to the laws of the state—laws under which the two men were accused, tried and sentenced—makes room for another reading. The refusals by these men, the refusal to accept the authority of the state at its most crucial point of legitimacy—the rule of law—also constitutes a repudiation of sovereign power. When Aghajari declined to appeal his case and when Ganji spurned the offer for clemency, each was denying the legitimacy of the state's power over his life. That legitimacy is expressed through the acceptance or acknowledgement on the part of the accused of the sovereign's monopoly on violence, and thus the right to legitimately use that violence on each of them. In the process of refusing, each also rejected the sovereign's power over their lives.

The first point I want to make is that the act of granting mercy is a constitutive act of sovereignty. And in the case at hand, mercy is comprised of a dialogical exchange (Bakhtin 1981) between the sovereign and the accused. Mercy, or the acting out of mercy, is a speech act and has a performative effect—it is choreographed to constitute and reinforce the legitimacy of sovereign power. Thus, the first movement in the act of mercy is a public command, by the sovereign to the accused, to ask for mercy, something only the sovereign can give. The sovereign constitutes the subject as being in the wrong and as having defied the sovereign's authority, the "rule of law." But the accused must then publicly reiterate the announcement of guilt and ask for forgiveness. Conditioned on this act of repentance, the sovereign grants mercy, thus showing that its own status lies outside of the law—the sovereign is not subject to the law, but may subject others to it. In this dialogical act of mercy and repentance, the sovereign also produces the subject as party to the sovereign's law and finally reveals the legitimacy of its acts and its laws, as conditions of its powers. In this respect, mercy is the exception that is constitutive of the rule of law and the legitimacy of sovereign power.

With the sovereign allowing the accused to ask for mercy, the sovereign also opens up a window for denial, as was the case here. It opens up the possibility of a sort of martyrdom, but not the psychological martyrdom that brings one closer to God. On the contrary, by refusing to ask for mercy the accused destabilizes the rule of law, which is the condition upon which the justness of the sovereign power lies. In Aghajari's case I want to highlight the dialogical workings of his refusal because the case was ultimately heard by Iran's high court and remanded back to the lower court for further adjudication and resentencing. How did this process come to pass, since his refusal to appeal? The Ayatollah Khamenei'ee, the Supreme leader, intervened and ordered the judiciary to rehear the case. Yet this was not just an act to save Aghajari's life, as Khamenei'ee could have simply pardoned him. Rather, Khamenei'ee's intervention was intended to rehabilitate the legal process, the manner through which justice is meted out and determined in Iran.

Similarly in Ganji's case, the act of refusal to submit, to retract the accusations made in his writings, precipitated a response from the state—that he had violated the law and that his release was not imminent. After exhausting legal appeals Ganji began his hunger strike, again an act that required action on the part of state actors. For failing to repent, Ganji was threatened with further governmental action, and told that he would never be freed. Though they did not free Ganji and he served his sentence, state actors were forced to refine their legal doctrines, to attempt, under the scrutiny of international observers, to respond, to re-legitimate, and to rationalize Ganji's ill or inhumane treatment. State actors modified their behavior by allowing Ganji medical treatment, home visits and other small concessions. (In a similar move, the US legal decision that recognizes the actions of soldiers in force-feeding hunger strikers in Guantanamo can be seen as a comparative example of this response of legitimation through legality.)

In both of these cases, we see that laws are in the service of state institutions that are concerned most with protecting their monopoly on making law (Buck-Morss 2000). The bodies of the state reveal this power when exercising violence in the name of the law. As Walter Benjamin observed, state agents reveal not only a monopoly on establishing the law, but indeed, in determining the meaning of justice (1978: 279).

The state's offer to grant mercy, thus, suggests a modern sovereign act aimed as a corrective in defining justice, not, as is sometimes suggested in the case of mercy in Iran, a display of premodern barbarity.[6] What is relevant in this context, however, is that state agents' articulation of mercy or pardon is part-and-parcel of the monopoly over the use of violence, which legitimates the state's power or sovereign authority.

Mercy, thus, is a speech act. Indeed for the sovereign it works as the ultimate speech act at-large: a magnanimous act that forces acknowledgement of the power of the state. By refusing the mercy of the sovereign, Ganji also recognizes the state's power; his refusal is a constitutive act. But refusing is an act that also places the power of the sovereign in relief: making it visible for all to see.

Thus, when one asks for mercy he or she must recognize the state; if one does not ask for mercy (as in Ganji or Aghajari's cases) one can or will be killed as a matter of routine. In Ganji and Aghajari's cases, the state, in a sense, "cracked," that is, it had to act, and thus, Ganji and Aghajari made the state's power visible in that way as well.[7] But ordinarily those who do not ask for mercy do not receive it; they die. Ganji's hunger strike, while requiring further action, does not free him from the logic of sovereign power either.

My second point is to extend this discussion beyond Iran to suggest that this critique of mercy (or the pardon power) exists for all modern states. This is by no means a critique of a premodern Iranian religious state as there are parallels right here in the United States. Many scholars have studied the relationship between modern law and the sovereign pardon in contemporary western societies. And, while it is important to highlight the conflicts surrounding theories of justice and punish-

[6] Indeed the press coverage of the two aforementioned cases discussed the decision on the part of state-agents to grant mercy or not in terms of human rights. In another paper, I argue that a nation-state's relationship to human rights standards is increasingly used by international agencies and the media, as well as some local organizations, to measure whether a state is modern or not (Osanloo 2006).

[7] Of course the articulation of sovereign power may vary, as in these two cases. For Aghajari, the state granted mercy, while in Ganji's case, it appeared to allow only minor concessions. Thus while their acts of refusal reinforce sovereign power, the state also acted in response to those refusals and did not simply reproduce the sovereign's power to take life, but the state's actors had to adjust themselves, showing that sovereign power is all-encompassing, producing life as well.

ment with mercy, most critiques do not highlight what appears to be a more disturbing aspect of the power of pardon within the modern liberal rights framework. In this framework we might say that a tension emerges between rights and mercy when the former is modern, precisely because it emerges from an inherent belief in the sanctity of the human being: simply because a person is human, he or she deserves a reprieve, but in the nation-state system the idea of the sovereign is a requirement of the granting of mercy.[8] In the granting of mercy—even if out of respect for human rights—the sovereign further inscribes its authority over the people.

This command and refusal to ask for pardon reveals how sovereign power, in the expression of rationalized laws, hides the foundation of all modern states' powers, and an important character of modern law—what Benjamin has referred to as "the founding violence of law" (1978). Whereas the accused, in a premodern conception of justice, requires a divinely ordained sovereign to grant mercy, the modern conception of rights requires a subject (of the law) to whom mercy can be granted—a subject who can likewise ask for mercy. Agamben notes that the inclusion of this "bare life" in the political realm constitutes the original, if concealed, nucleus of sovereign power (1998). While mercy requires a sovereign, sovereignty expressed through the rule of law requires a willing, individuated subject—and as we see in these cases, a subject who will validate the state ruling, and thus its legitimacy, by asking for mercy. In the above cases, the refusals by both Aghajari and Ganji signal their unwillingness to validate the sovereign's legitimacy, even if their refusals put sovereign power in relief. Zizek refers to this as the "perverse logic of mercy," where it is the dispensing of mercy that proves to be the most efficient constituent of the exercise of power (2004).

Here, then, we can add a layer of complexity to the seeming dichotomous premodern versus modern modes of penal justice (mapped out by some readings of Foucault's *Discipline and Punish*), where it has

[8] Derrida has also written on this issue, noting that "forgiveness transcends and neutralizes the law…What counts in this absolute exception *from* the law, the exception *to* the law, is situated at the summit or at the foundation of the juridico-political. In the body of the sovereign, it incarnates what founds or supports or establishes, at the top, with the unity of the nation, the guarantee of the constitution, the conditions and exercise of the law" (2001: 46).

been suggested that sovereign power has been replaced by a microphysics of power through discipline and later with governmentality. Rather, these modes of power are coeval, simultaneously existing, and in fact, enabling one another in modern societies.[9]

In the articulation of Islamic modernity, through state institutions that are both republican and Islamic, we see productive expressions of modern sovereign power. In this example, premodern and modern modalities of power co-operate in fields in which justice is simultaneously and continually refashioning itself through precisely these kinds of challenges, like hunger strikes, which lay bare the violence of power and force the sovereign to reshape and reclaim its legitimacy.

Conclusion: The Act of Mercy

By refusing to bargain with the state and standing firm in the face of death, Aghajari and Ganji both disrupted the state's power over life and consequently legitimated their own dissident messages to students, activists, and others to participate in their own subject-making through renewed involvement in civic life which would then institute additional challenges to sovereign power, thus engendering further responses.

In my analysis, I have made two main points about mercy in the rule of law. The notion of mercy and the refusal to ask for mercy (or the impending martyrdom) of Ganji have misleadingly been interpreted as premodern acts of self-sacrifice. Mercy, instead, is constitutive of the power of exception granted only by the sovereign authority in the modern state system—she or he who can kill with impunity. Mercy can only be granted by the sovereign power standing outside of the law. The power to grant mercy thus reinforces the unquestionable power of the sovereign. The cases I have discussed are specific to Iran, but we can also draw generalizations to the constitution of modern power. Even in a "secular" state we will see parallels. In the Iranian case, the state announces itself as religious, whereas in the United States, the Judeo-Christian foundations are hidden in the secular formations of the "rule of law." The request for pardon in the US (secular) context

[9] See also, Merry 2001. Many have written about the modern expression of power in studies of torture today. For instance, see Zizek 2004. Writing on Iran, Rejali (1994) has argued that torture today is integral to the modern disciplined society.

requires a similar consecration of sovereign power. In order to save his/her life, the defendant must recognize the power of the sovereign, either the president or the governor, to act with impunity in carrying out the law—either to grant a pardon or to carry out the sentence. The logic of sovereign power is revealed, in either the secular or theocratic context, when the defendant is resigned to the state of "bare life," and must ask the sovereign for mercy. The Iranian example puts the logic of the nation-state into perspective. Some scholars may point to the theocratic nature of the state, and thus conclude that the Iranian case is distinct. The Iranian example reveals, however, that the power of the sovereign to grant mercy is not exceptional to the theocratic state. On the contrary, by questioning the "perverse logic of mercy," the Iranian example also shows that the pardon is similarly constituent of contemporary sovereign power, and puts into question the foundational logic of the modern, secular nation-state.

Bibliography

Abrahamian, Ervand. 1982. *Iran between Two Revolutions*. Princeton, N.J.: Princeton University Press.

Agamben, Giorgio. 1998. *Homo Sacer: Sovereign Power and Bare Life*. Trans. Daniel Heller-Roazen. Stanford: Stanford University Press.

Aghajari, Hashem. "From Monkey to Man, A Call to Islamic Protestantism" transcript of speech delivered in June 2002 in Hamedan, Iran at http://www.iranian.com/Opinion/2002/December/Aghajari/ accessed on 23 September 2007.

Algar, Hamid. 1981. *Islam and Revolution: Writings and Declarations of Imam Khomeini*. Trans. Hamid Algar. Berkeley, CA: Mizan Press.

Bakhtin, M.M. 1981. *The Dialogical Imagination*. Austin: University of Texas Press.

BBC News. 2003. "Profile: Hashem Aghajari" (9 July 2003) at http://news.bbc.co.uk/2/hi/middle_east/3053075.stm accessed on 23 September 2007.

Benjamin, Walter. 1978. "On the Critique of Violence" in Peter Demetz (ed.) *Reflections*. Trans. Edmund Jephcott. New York: Harcourt, Brace and Jovanovich Press. 277–300.

Borradori, Giovanna. 2003. *Philosophy in a Time of Terror: Dialogues with Jürgen Habermas and Jacques Derrida*. Chicago: University of Chicago Press.

Buck-Morss, Susan. 2000. *Dreamworld and Catastrophe: the Passing of Mass Utopia in East and West*. Cambridge: MIT University Press.

Derrida, Jacques. 2001. "On Forgiveness" in *On Cosmopolitanism and Forgiveness*. London: Routledge; 27–60.

Foucault, Michel. 2003. *Society Must Be Defended: Lectures at the College de France, 1975–1976*. Trans. David Macey. New York: Picador.

Freund, Charles Paul. 2003. "Liberal Martyrdom in Iran: An academic takes on the ayatollahs" at http://www.reason.com/0302/co.cf.liberal.shtml accessed on 30 October 2008.

Osanloo, Arzoo. 2006. "The Measure of Mercy: Islamic Justice, Sovereign Power, and Human Rights in Iran" in *Cultural Anthropology* 21(4): 570–602.

Rejali, Darius. 1994. *Torture and Modernity: Self, Society and State in Modern Iran*. Boulder: Westview Press.

Merry, Sally. 2001. "Spatial Governmentalilty and the New Urban Social Order: Controlling Gender Violence through the Law" in *American Anthropologist* 103(1): 16–29.

Reporters sans frontiers (RSF). 2005. "Iran: Akbar Ganji goes on hunger strike" at http://www.rsf.org/article.php3?id_article=13356 accessed on 23 September 2007.

Zizek, Slavoj. 2004. "On Opera: *La Clemenza di Tito*, or the Ridiculously-Obscene Excess of Mercy" at www.lacan.com accessed on 30 October 2008.

14

LOCATING DISSENT

SPACE, LAW, AND PROTEST IN JORDAN

Jillian Schwedler and Sam Fayyaz[1]

Introduction

In March 2002, Jordan's Queen Rania led a march of several hundred Jordanians as a gesture of solidarity with Palestinians during the Israeli invasion of Jenin, Nablus, and several other Palestinian towns. The widely photographed spectacle garnered significant domestic, regional,

[1] Earlier versions of this chapter were presented in several forums, and the authors would like to thank the participants: Participants in the European University Institute Seventh Mediterranean Research Meeting workshop on Political Participation in March 2006; the Islam and the Public Sphere workshop at the University of California at Santa Barbara, April 2006; Columbia University's Contentious Politics Workshop, April 2006; the Policing and Prisons panels at the Middle East Studies Association annual meeting, November 2006; the Eighth Mediterranean Research Meeting workshop on Policing and Prisons in March 2007; and the seminar on Neoliberalism at the University of Massachusetts Amherst, May 2008. In particular, we are extremely grateful to Paul Amar, Jonathan Argaman, Laryssa Chomiak, Barbara Cruikshank, Mona El-Ghobashy, and Laleh Khalili for providing detailed comments on various drafts. All remaining errors and weaknesses are, of course, our own.

and international attention.[2] Over the course of the previous month, thousands of Jordanians had participated in unsanctioned protests, and despite daily efforts that included tanks and tear gas, the regime proved unable to quell the demonstrations. The spectacle of the elegant Queen leading two hundred upper-class Jordanian citizens through the streets of Amman underlined the symbolic stakes of the manner in which the regime has sought to regulate public space in the ostensibly liberal-democratic monarchy. The Queen's march took place along a route devoid of contentious political symbolism, beginning at an insignificant traffic circle and ending at a UNICEF office a few blocks away. Yet, another Palestinian solidarity march planned by the Professionals Associations Complex (PAC) and the Islamic Action Front (IAF) to have taken place just days earlier was far more provocative: the PAC and IAF planned a march that they dubbed a "Sacred Crawl" (*zahaf al-muqaddas*), which was to start at PAC headquarters in the commercial district of Shmeisani and end at the Israeli Embassy—the local emissary representative of the forces directly responsible for the military invasions of the Palestinian towns and cities. Both demonstrations were intended as expressions of Palestinian solidarity, and both were planned as peaceful marches. But only the Queen's march was legally sanctioned, despite taking place in the midst of weeks of unsanctioned marches; the Sacred Crawl was canceled at the last moment under pressure from security officials. The critical point of contention was not the content of the march—Palestinian solidarity—but space: the Jordanian government ruled that protests in close proximity to the Israeli embassy constituted a threat to public order.

These two protest events demonstrate the salience of the spatial dimensions in political protests, a dynamic of political dissent that has received little systematic attention from scholars. What sorts of protest events are permitted? Where may they be held? Who may organize them? To whom are the events visible? And are there limits to what can be said? In this chapter, we explore dimensions of protest through a critical examination of the specific spaces of contestation and the legal mechanisms used for their regulation. The protest events in Jordan during the Spring 2002 invasion by Israeli troops into the Palestinian cities and towns provide a window into these complex practices of political contestation and control.

[2] For example, see Queen Rania's interview with Larry King: http://www.jordanembassyus.org/speech_hmqr04162002.htm

The Legal Geography of Protests[3]

The Jordanian monarchy has sought to produce consensus among its citizens, or at least the appearance of consensus, supporting its unpopular peace treaty with Israel. Jordan's political opening of the early 1990s, though largely reversed by the time the treaty was signed in late 1994, partially succeeded in producing a new legal regime. The regime sought to use legal reforms to foreclose possibilities for political contestation, primarily through the introduction of a new system for obtaining permits for public gatherings. Interviews with a number of political parties and activists indicate that it is the particular locations of the planned protests—and not only the size, topic, and organizers—that may well have determined whether government officials granted permission for the events to be held.[4]

Although Jordan's monarchy is widely and accurately considered by scholars to be more autocratic than democratic in character, freedom of assembly, and thus freedom to hold political demonstrations, is nonetheless guaranteed in the constitution and affirmed in the National Charter, which was drafted in 1991.[5] Following the extralegal riots of April 1989 in response to economic reforms, the government responded by introducing a series of political liberalizations that provided expanded space for legal protests; along with these reforms, a new set of legal reforms also provided the regime with the juridical tools to control protests and the narratives they advance, as well as political activities and citizen relations to the state more broadly. Until 2001, Jordanians wishing to hold protests were legally required only to submit notification of the event to the office of the governorate in which the event would be held. The regime had no formal mechanism for approving or denying events, but in practice government officials

[3] We borrow this phrase from Don Mitchell and Lynn Staheli (2005).

[4] Schwedler interviews with various activists and party officials in Amman, June 2002 through August 2008.

[5] Political demonstrations were common in Jordan during the 1950s; absent during the suppression of political organizations from 1961 until 1966; and then periodic until the 1967 implementation of martial law halted them almost completely. The economic downturn of the 1980s saw renewed protests, particularly in 1988 with the economic reforms mandating the gradual lifting of certain subsidies on food, fodder, and fuel. These activities were extralegal under martial law, as in the case of the riots of 1989 and the mass demonstrations around the Gulf War of 1990–91.

ensured that would-be protesters well understood which events were unwelcome. These messages were transmitted largely via personal phone calls from ministers (including those holding portfolios whose relations to protest activities were non-existent), governors, police officials, and members of the upper and lower houses of parliament.[6] Personal connections were and continue to be the primary conduits through with such messages are conveyed. The regime officially permits protests as long as the formal legal requirements are satisfied, but in practice the negotiation over protests and their political content may completely circumvent these formal procedures and channels even while those formal procedures and guaranteed freedoms are continuously invoked.

On paper, Jordan would appear to be a fully functioning democracy. The liberty afforded to Jordanians to protest through constitutional guarantees, for example, is likewise celebrated in the National Charter, the non-legally binding document of 1991 that was intended to capture the spirit of Jordan's political liberalization, begun in 1989:

> Guaranteeing the basic freedoms of all citizens in such a manner as to protect the structure of a democratic society, preserve the rights of individuals and ensure full freedom of expression and its declaration with complete liberty within the limits of the Constitution.[7]

This formulation provides a formal and institutionalized referent to which the bounds of legitimate activity are stipulated, thereby:

> Preserving the civilian and democratic character of the state, and regarding any attempt to abolish or undermine this character as *invalid* as it would constitute a violation of the Constitution and the pluralist principle and its perception.[8]

Through this language, Jordan's renewed liberal constitutional order[9] is explicitly framed as a democratic order that must be upheld and defended in order for other free and autonomous Jordanians to remain free. "Freedom" in this context imparts responsibility: Jordanians pos-

[6] Schwedler interviews with various activists and party officials in Amman, June 2002 through August 2008.

[7] National Charter, 'State Governed by Law and Political Pluralism.' http://www.kinghussein.gov.jo/charter-national.html

[8] National Charter, 'State Governed by Law and Political Pluralism.' http://www.kinghussein.gov.jo/charter-national.html, my emphasis.

[9] Renewed because the constitution in place prior to the implementation of martial law in 1967 also provided for the individual rights of citizens.

sess the right to be politically expressive, but they share the responsibility of maintaining social order.

We wish to draw attention to the fact that protests are often legal forms of political expression in non-democratic states, far more than is recognized: even limited political liberalization proscribes appropriate forms of political engagement for citizens, and the freedoms of expression and assembly are at least formally protected. But in non-democratic contexts the struggles over the boundaries of legal protest activities hold even higher stakes than in liberal democracies precisely because protest is not widely recognized as a substantive and essential component of democratic political participation, either by the government or by citizens.

Indeed, many protest activities are portrayed not as organized expressions of political dissent but as outbursts of the "Arab Street," which has come to represent two images of the Arab public, both of them condescending: either it refers to the irrational, uninformed, and reactionary public opinion of the choleric Arab masses, or it reflects a vacuous, apathetic, and docile Arab public castrated by the institutions of patriarchy and religiously devoted prostration (Bayat 2003: 11). Thus invocations of the Arab Street—by the international media, western policymakers and government officials, and the region's own ruling elite—function as a contemporary Orientalist trope and metaphor for philistine backwardness, and the unpreparedness of Arabs for substantive democratic political engagement. The Arab Street is mentioned in the same breath as Islamists, both held up as evidence of the need for maintaining strong security states. Crucially, however, the concept also betrays both the spatial dimensions of its name and the reality of a sophisticated and engaged Arab public comprised of savvy activists who negotiate space and coordinate demonstrations on-the-fly, sometimes with the help of mobile technology (Schwedler 2003: 20). Furthermore, the Arab Street as an allegory of an anti-democratic mentality belies the importance of the street—or more generally, public space—as the site of democratic politics. Public space—taken to mean the places and spaces outside of the private sphere, separate from the state, and visible to other citizens—is where democratic politics happens; the expansiveness (or not) of geographical sites of public deliberation and dissent can be an expression of social justice more generally, and the rights of social groups in particular. By associating violence and disorder with public politics in the Arab world, regimes have validated a wide range of repressive techniques which, effectively, extract the public—to mean both the people and the streets—from politics (For example, see Andoni and Schwedler 1996).

The manner in which particular groups are stripped of their rights to utilize public space under autocratic governments has much in common with "public order management systems" (McPhail et al. 1998: 49)—legal codes and policing practices—in Western liberal democracies. The highly touted political liberalization policies enacted by authoritarian governments such as Jordan do not include the validation of street politics, or a more open legal geography of politics and protest. Indeed, Jordan's liberal constitutional order employs both a rights discourse, e.g., legal codes such as the permit system, and a range of surveillance and policing practices to constrain the use and expansiveness of public space.

Scholars of contentious politics have largely neglected the politics of public space in general and the spatial dimensions of dissent in particular. The "spatial turn" in social science has not even been fully embraced by scholars outside of the fields of geography and urban studies. Nonetheless, recent empirical studies in the geography of protests have focused on the spatial considerations activists make prior to and during political mobilization (e.g., Miller and Martin 2000; Wilton and Cranford 2002). Outside of the discipline of geography, recent essays by political scientist and historian William Sewell (2001) and sociologists Thomas Gieryn (2000) and Javier Auyero (2007) suggest a growing appreciation of space's role in contentious politics. As the Spring 2002 protests in Jordan illustrate, struggles over spatial dynamics are continuously at the center of regime-protester engagements. These demonstrations were the most sustained and widespread protests against Israeli actions since liberalization in 1989, even including the widespread protests at the outbreak of the second Intifada in October 2000. Over the years, the regime seemed to be particularly concerned with the location of proposed events, but it has also preferred stationary—and thus more easily controlled—gatherings to marches. For example, on 22 October 1997 a group of students at the University of Jordan planned a march calling for the establishment of a general union of Jordanian students from the center of campus to the office of the Interior Ministry—not a particularly provocative issue, nor one likely to spur wider protests among other citizens. Anti–riot police were summarily called in and prevented the students from marching to the government building—an extreme response that created quite a visible spectacle around an otherwise small-scale and low-profile event. Similarly, protest events in upscale neighborhoods of west Amman are typically policed by dispersing protesters, preventing their arrival and movement, and by bussing those arrested to distant police stations, where they are detained and then released hours later, often without having been charged. By comparison, protests in the refugee camps and on campuses are policed largely through a process of containment: movement outward is stopped and protesters are surrounded, rather than dispersed. Similar dynamics of containment are common for protests in the towns south of Amman, notably the trucking town of Ma'an and the mountain-top town of Karak (Schwedler 2002). These contained protests are mostly tolerated rather than repressed, as long as they remain invisible to outside populations through their spatial containment. Unsurprisingly, the class dimensions of various neighborhoods—not to mention their spatial organization (e.g., the size, width, and layout of streets) and the location of symbolically significant sites of power (e.g., embassies, mansions, government buildings, etc.)—significantly affects policing practices in the course of actual protest events.

On some level the "Jordanian Street" appears to be disappearing to the degree that public activism is being severely girded by a combination of legal measures, the policing of space, and the reconstruction of west Amman in ways that have eliminated many of the previous sites of protest. Traffic circles have been replaced by high-speed underpasses, and barriers around key buildings (such as parliament and foreign embassies) have been expanded. While Jordanian citizens possess the legal right to protest, diverse juridical practices also constrain the dynamics of dissent in ways that seek to strip them of their public character and visibility, their meaning, and their capacity to affect change. So as public space is ostensibly expanding in Jordan with formally increased civil liberties, in practice public political space as place and movement in space has been increasingly constrained by the very legal/rational order that claims to endow Jordanian citizens with freedom. Nevertheless, Jordanians are constructing new spaces for political expression via new forms of dissident politics, including the boycotts of American and Israeli goods and "art protests": murals and handicrafts expressing Palestinian solidarity (Schwedler 2003: 20). In the next section, we explore how these insights provide an alternative picture of the protests in Jordan during the Israeli invasion of Jenin, Nablus, and other Palestinian towns in the Spring of 2002.

The 2002 Spring Protests

On 11 March 2002, following a meeting with Prime Minister Ali Abu al-Raghib, the PAC (Professionals Associations Complex) postponed a series of strikes and marches it had been planning. The PAC had steadfastly refused to seek permits for its events, in direct violation of the temporary public assembly law.[10] With the regime's virtual suspension of the liberal provisions of its political opening of the past decade, the PAC had become a site for political contestation, in the place of a placid parliament that had been carefully crafted through such legal means as restructuring the electoral system and gerrymandering electoral districts. Abandoning its original plan to march from the Professional Associations' Complex to the Israeli embassy, the PAC announced that it would march to a UN building just a few blocks away. The march retained little of its original symbolic significance, and it was further deflated by being forced to take a route of side streets, well out of view of the highly trafficked commercial thoroughfare just one block to the east. And yet just over a week later, Amman was in a state of continuous protest, with thousands of demonstrators on the streets daily, clogging many major streets but also crossing into spaces previously deemed off limits by the regime.

The Israeli military incursion into several Palestinian towns began on 22 March 2002 and lasted for more than a month. Israeli aggression sparked widespread protest throughout the Arab world, but particularly in Jordan, which has a majority Palestinian population, a peace treaty with Israel, and a history pre-dating its independence of intimate connection with Palestinian and Zionist (later Israeli) politics. By 31 March a wide range of political groups and activists had altogether organized more than a hundred demonstrations, marches, rallies, and strikes. Many other Jordanians spilled into the street, making it virtually impossible to distinguish where organized events ended and spontaneous crowds began. Many prominent political activists called for the dismissal of the Israeli ambassador from Jordan, the closing of

[10] The new public gatherings law was a temporary law because it was introduced by the executive while the parliament was not in session, and thus retained a "temporary" status until the new assembly reconvened, which it did following the June 2003 elections (which were held eighteen months late). The assemblies law was among the first that was formally approved by the new assembly in late 2003.

the Israeli embassy in Amman, and the suspension of diplomatic relations between the countries. King Abdullah II urged Israel to put an immediate end to its military operations, but he stopped short of suspending diplomatic relations. Meanwhile, inside Jordan the regime sought to contain, if not entirely shut down, the protests, which it viewed as both domestically destabilizing and internationally embarrassing. Student groups—which government officials alleged to have received assistance from external political organizations—organized several large-scale anti–Israeli demonstrations on the campuses of the University of Jordan, Philadelphia University, and the University of Applied Sciences. Students gathered to chant slogans denouncing Israel's "brutal massacres of Palestinians" and some even urged Hamas to carry out suicide attacks on Israel.[11] Similar protests took place in the Wihdat and Baqaa Palestinian refugee camps at the city's outskirts, while anti–riot police were stationed to prevent the protesters from moving outside the camps.[12]

On 1 April, thousands of Jordanians demonstrated at the University of Jordan and at the Hussein and Wihdat refugee camps. On this occasion, two thousand students attempted to move the protest off-campus. Anti–riot police responded by firing tear gas and water cannon, forcing the demonstrators back into the university premises. That same day, Interior Minister Qaftan Majali made a public statement in the presence of Public Security Department Director General Tahseen Shurdum, encouraging Jordanians to use their right to free expression in a manner that does not disrupt public order and national unity:

> We all have the duty to protect this right against attempts by some who are inclined to infringe upon security and attack public and private property to disrupt public life. Jordan's security, stability, and national unity underpin a national stand that supports the Palestinian people in the face of Israeli aggression. For Jordan, national unity is sacred, and we cannot tolerate any tampering with it.[13]

Majali served as the public face of the Jordanian regime during much of March and April 2002, always quick to remind the public of the sanctity of national unity, public order, and the rule of law.

On 2 April, the IAF stepped up its pressure on the regime by issuing another public statement demanding that diplomatic ties with Israel be

[11] The Jordan Times, Monday, 1 April 2002.

[12] The Jordan Times, Monday, 1 April 2002.

[13] The Jordan Times, Tuesday, 2 April 2002.

severed. It declared that IAF members and other citizens would stage a march to the Israeli embassy in the event that the government failed to heed these demands. At a press conference, IAF secretary general Hamzeh Mansour emphasized that all "demonstrations that are organized by national and political groups are disciplined and responsible"; he then called on the government to "guarantee people's right to freedom of expression."[14] Majali responded that the government "will not allow unlicenced demonstrations that could destabilize security and harm public and private property." He added, "any attempt to disrupt public life can negatively reflect on the Jordanian people's firm stance with their Palestinian brethren, and divert their attention away from Israeli aggression against the Palestinian people."[15]

Over the next weeks, the Jordanian government and the IAF continued their public relations war, with both parties claiming to represent the interests of the Palestinian people. On 6 April, the Jordan Hashemite Charity Organization, an organization under the directives of King Abdullah, held a one day telethon that raised JD 9.5 million (approx. $1.39 mil) in donations for medical and humanitarian aid for Palestinians. Promotional information of the telethon event—which appeared on a state-run television channel—was sent via SMS (text) messages by mobile-service provider Fastlink. Somewhat ironically, Fastlink sent out another SMS message the same day reminding people to join an unauthorized rally at the Kayluti Mosque in the Rabia area in Amman, scheduled to take place after the next Friday's noon prayers.[16]

Four thousand demonstrators poured out of Kayluti Mosque that Friday and attempted to march on the Israeli embassy less than a kilometer away while chanting, "In the millions we go to Jerusalem!" They were met by anti–riot police who blocked the streets and used tear gas and water cannons to break up the demonstration; protestors responded by throwing rocks at the police. A similar clash between police and demonstrators took place outside the Husseini Mosque in downtown Amman, where some two thousand chanted, "Where are the Arab armies?" Police again prevented the protestors from leaving the immediate premises of the mosque or moving into the streets.[17]

[14] The Jordan Times, Thursday, 4 April 2002.
[15] The Jordan Times, Friday, 5 April 2002.
[16] The Jordan Times, Friday, 5 April 2002.
[17] The Jordan Times, Saturday, 6 April 2002.

The following Tuesday, 9 April, Queen Rania led more than two thousand people in the aforementioned march to the headquarters of UNICEF to present a petition to the acting UN resident calling on the United Nations and other humanitarian organizations to provide aid to Palestinians. Organized by the Jordan River Foundation (JRF) as part of its "Hand-in-Hand with the Palestinian People" campaign, the march started in affluent west Amman at Jubilee Circle (the Fifth Circle) and concluded two kilometers away at the UNICEF headquarters near King Abdullah Gardens. The event, which featured a pre-march rendition of the Palestinian national anthem, was held to raise funds for humanitarian aid, and, more importantly, to create a highly visible public spectacle that would demonstrate the Jordanian regime's commitment to aiding Palestinians living under Israeli occupation. Indeed, in a brilliant public relations maneuver, the regime supplanted the dire Majali with the elegant (and ethnically Palestinian) Queen as the face of Jordan's devotion to Palestine. A few hours before the march, the Queen spoke to a crowd of three hundred, mostly women, at a JRF-sponsored fundraising brunch, stating:

> There is much to be done, and each one of us has a responsible role to play. In Jordan, we spare no effort to save our brethren in Palestine from occupation and violence...we need the support of civil society to end [their suffering] and to extend a helping hand in the Hashemite tradition.[18]

Queen Rania's pleas were heeded by several non-political civic associations including the Jordanian Pharmaceutical Association, the Arab Cultural Society, and the Jordanian Women's Federation, each of which called on Jordanians to donate JD 10 ($14) for medical supplies.

Meanwhile, despite government warnings, the PAC and IAF—in an alliance dubbed the National Coalition Against the Israeli Destruction of Palestine—continued its plans to hold its march to the Israeli embassy following Friday prayers on 12 April. Two days before the event, Prime Minister Ali Abu Ragheb met with coalition representatives in an attempt to dissuade the group from staging the "illegal" event—it had not yet received a permit from the governorate—on the grounds that it would disrupt national unity and public order. In addition to these private talks, Majali publicly stated that the government would stop the event from taking place "through every available means" and warned any group that it was compromising public safety

[18] The Jordan Times, Wednesday, 10 April, 2002.

and showing contempt for the state if it chose not to abide by the Public Gatherings Law. The National Coalition insisted that it would defy the ban, but called for a "peaceful and violence-free protest" that would avoid "disturbances and vandalism."[19]

Although Islamist groups such as the IAF are viewed by western audiences as the primary instigators of political dissent, particularly against the United States and Israel, inside Jordan the IAF has been frequently criticized by independent activists for its timidity in confronting the regime over the peace treaty with Israel. IAF leaders have close relations with prominent government officials, and during these (and other) protests they struggled to balance their symbiotic relationship with the regime and their strong advocacy for the Palestinian people.[20] After suffering criticism for their impotence while other groups defied the government ban on protest events, the IAF joined the PAC in calling for a march on the Israeli embassy. Government officials offered few explanations as to why it opposed this particular march, although all understood that protesting in the immediate vicinity of the Israeli embassy was off limits. The governor argued instead that the state could not guarantee the safety of the protesters or the protection of the property of local residents. The PAC and IAF organizers engaged in discussions with various government agencies up until the day before the event itself, at which point they vowed to hold the event with or without having received a formal permit.[21]

On the day of the planned march, however, the coalition called off the demonstration in light of the heavy security precautions taken by the government. PAC leader and coalition member Muhammad Oran said that "after extensive and responsible study of the reality that the government imposed on us by isolating Amman from the rest of the governorates and deploying such a large number of security officials... we decided to cancel the march to the enemy's embassy in Al Rabia."[22]

[19] The Jordan Times, Friday, 12 April 2002.

[20] Islamist support for the Jordanian regime over Palestinian issues has a long history, despite the Muslim Brotherhood's avowed commitment to the full liberation of Palestine. In 1970, for example, the Islamists overwhelmingly supported the regime against Palestinian militants on the East Bank who were launching attacks against Israeli troops in the West Bank. See Schwedler 2006.

[21] Interview with Muhammad Oran, PAC president at the time of the protest, 13 November 2003, Amman.

[22] Schwelder interview with Muhammad Oran, 10 December 2003, Amman.

Indeed, riot police surrounded the PAC that morning, preventing protesters access to the starting point of the march. Oran reported that he and other PAC leaders had difficultly entering the complex; he was successful only because he knew many of the police officers and talked his way through the barriers.[23] Similarly, the IAF Chair of its Consultative Council, Abd al-Latif Arabiyyat, recalled that he asked several officers that morning, "How can you prevent a former speaker of parliament from walking to his office?"[24] Hundreds of anti–riot police were also deployed in the vicinity of the Israeli embassy in Al Rabia, while road blocks, barbed wire fencing, and armored vehicles were set up within a two kilometer radius of the embassy. Prime Minister Ragheb praised the decision to cancel the march, saying that the coalition's "heeding the voice of reason aborted attempts by some to break the law and compromise security." He differentiated the coalition leaders from other troublemakers, chiding the "anarchists' attempts to damage the image of Jordan and its national positions," and thanking citizens for understanding that the heightened security was to protect them and their property.[25]

Our analysis of the protests of Spring 2002 illustrates the ways in which protesters seek to challenge not only specific government policies and actions, but also its normal geographies: those geographies normalized legally as well as physically (through the construction of roads, licensing of businesses, zoning restrictions, etc.) by state agencies. Physically, legally, and symbolically, the Fifth Circle, the streets surrounding the Israeli embassy, mosques, university campuses, and refugee camps are all very different spaces.[26] Public spaces include recognizable geographies of daily movement (Smith and Low 2006: 3), and protest activities are often aimed explicitly at challenging or disrupting those flows. In this regard, many of the protests in Jordan during March and April 2002 sought to starkly challenge the existing geographies of "normal" politics, for example by marching from one symbolic site to another (mosque to embassy), disrupting routine commercial activities, or embarrassing the regime by demonstrating a level of dissent that the regime has sought to conceal, despite overwhelming evidence of its existence.

[23] Schwedler interview with Muhammad Oran, 10 December 2003, Amman.
[24] Schwedler interview with Abd al-Latif Arabiyyat, 2003, Amman.
[25] The Jordan Times, 14 April 2002.
[26] This section draws on the analysis of Smith and Low (2006), pp. 3–7.

Conclusion

The wrangling between opposition groups and various government agencies about permits, locales, and acceptable issues for protest emphasizes the importance of spatial and legal dimensions that subtly shape protest activities. Two years after the Spring 2002 protests, the new images of Queen Rania again leading a march—this time with 250,000 members of Jordan's "silent majority" in an "anti–terror" protest in Amman in April 2004,[27] a clear encore to her Palestinian solidarity march of 2002—beckon a fundamental re-conceptualization of protests activities in quasi–authoritarian contexts like Jordan.[28] Once considered the terrain in which politically unsophisticated and violently reactionary subjects clashed with brutish security services, the emerging narratives of a new "Jordanian Street" as the site of peaceful protest marches denouncing violence and terrorism, and of dancing—rather than club-wielding—riot police (Schwedler 2005), do not correspond to popular representations of Arab public political space.

By legally and discretionarily codifying the boundaries of acceptable political expression, liberalizing autocracies such as Jordan are able to limit the amount and type of political contestation—which is to say that it falls short of threatening the regime's hold on power. These juridical dimensions of the practice of political domination include defining and revising elections laws, adjusting restrictions on political party activities, redrawing electoral districts, and adopting legislation that broadens the range of activities which are considered to "threaten state security" and thus in need of state regulation. Even more importantly, they entail careful control of public space and, in particular, public expressions of political dissent.

As in Western liberal democracies, dissent in Jordan is being normalized as it is formalized in the law and the attending juridical practices; police officers attend and are part of the proceedings of protest planning, while permits take on the meaning of glorified hall passes for activists with day jobs. As Jordan refashions itself as a neoliberal state in which political freedoms are, in practice, sacrificed to advance the

[27] http://www.queenrania.jo/content/modulePopup.aspx?secID=cmnt&itemID=368&ModuleID=press&ModuleOrigID=news

[28] For works calling for a rethinking of regimes neither fully authoritarian nor fully democratic (if either even exist), see Brumberg 2002 and Carothers 2002. For works examining democratic practices emerging in non-democratic contexts, see Schwedler 2006 and Wedeen 2008.

wildly unpopular (among Jordanians) economic reforms that prioritize foreign investment, free trade, and the abandonment of public subsidies, the spaces for dissent are being strictly managed; they are also being severely reduced in a spatial sense. Many of the formerly popular sites of protest have been entirely eliminated through infrastructural development programs, e.g., the public spaces around prominent intersections that disappeared with the construction of high-speed overpasses. At the same time, the government has floated the idea of creating a space in which political dissent will be permitted, albeit highly surveilled and controlled. In December 2005, Prime Minister Marouf Bakhit announced that his government was planning to establish an area for free speech that would "provide a neutral space for people to express themselves in a civilized manner."[29] The imagined "Freedom Square" has yet to materialize, and at least a few members of parliament greeted the initial announcement with skepticism and called it "a publicity stunt," as did Deputy Mamdouh Abbadi.[30] But the idea of the Freedom Square reflects a goal of free speech reduced to the articulations of individuals presented in a confined space that can be carefully monitored and, despite being public, largely invisible. The proposed site—the Hashemite Yards in downtown Amman—is hardly an area well-traversed by most Jordanians. Indeed, with the expansion of Amman westward through the rapid development of new housing, high-end commercial spaces, and a thick network of elite restaurants, night clubs, and lounges, the traditional "downtown" has become literally invisible to the movement and commerce that dominate Amman's economy. The ability to contain political dissent in such a manner must be a fantasy for authoritarian and democratic governments alike; at the very least, however, it underlines how crucial a critical examination and understanding of space will be for our understanding of political dissent everywhere.

Bibliography

Andoni, Lamis, and Jillian Schwedler. 1996. "Bread Riots in Jordan", *Middle East Report*, no. 201 (Fall): 40–2.

Auyero, Javier. 2007. "Spaces and Places as Sites and Objects of Politics", in *The Oxford Handbook of Contextual Political Studies*, edited by Robert Goodin and Charles Tilly.

[29] The Jordan Times, 15 December 2005.

[30] The Jordan Times, 15 December 2005.

Bayat, Asef. 2003. "The 'Street' and the Politics of Dissent in the Arab World", *Middle East Report*, no. 226 (Spring): 10–17.

Brumberg, Daniel. 2002. "The Trap of Liberalized Autocracy", in Larry Diamond, Marc F. Plattner, and Daniel Brumberg, eds., *Islam and Democracy in the Middle East*. Baltimore: The John Hopkins University Press; originally published in *Journal of Democracy* 13 (4) (October): 56–68.

Carothers, Thomas. 2002. "The End of the Transition Paradigm", *Journal of Democracy* 13(2) (January): 5–21.

Gieryn, Thomas. 2000. "A Space for Place in Sociology", *Annual Review of Sociology*, 2000: 26: 463–496.

McPhail, Clark. 1971. "Civil Disorder Participation: A Critical Examination of Recent Research", *American Sociological Review* 36: 1058–1073.

Miller, Byron, and Deborah Martin. 2000. "Missing Geography: Social Movements on the Head of a Pin?" in Byron Miller, ed., *Geography and Social Movements: Comparing Antinuclear Activism in the Boston Area*. Minneapolis, MN: Minnesota University Press.

Mitchell, Don, and Lynn A. Staeheli. 2005. "Permitting Protest: Parsing the Fine Geography of Dissent in America" *International Journal of Urban and Regional Research* 29 (4) (December): 796–813.

Schwedler, Jillian. 2006. *Faith in Moderation: Islamist Parties in Jordan and Yemen*. New York, NY: Cambridge University Press.

Schwedler, Jillian. 2005. "Cop Rock: Protest, Identity, and Dancing Riot Police in Jordan", *Social Movement Studies* 4 (2) (September): 155–75.

Schwedler, Jillian. 2003. "More than a Mob: The Dynamics of Political Demonstrations in Jordan", *Middle East Report* 226 (Spring): 18–23.

Schwedler, Jillian. 2002. "Occupied Maan: Jordan's Closed Military Zone", Middle East Report Online, December 3.

Smith, Neil, and Setha Low. 2006. "Introduction: The Imperative of Public Space", in Setha Low and Neil Smith, eds., *The Politics of Public Space*. New York: Routledge: 1–16.

Wedeen, Lisa. 2008. *Peripheral Visions*. Chicago: University of Chicago Press.

Wilton, Robert D., and Cynthia Cranford. 2002. "Toward an Understanding of the Spatiality of Social Movements: Labor Organizing at a Private University in Los Angeles", *Social Problems* 49 (3): 374–394.

INDEX

INDEX